Recent Reviews of other Odyssey Guides...

"...for coverage of Chongqing and the Gorges, and of the more placid and
historically notable sites below Yichang and downriver to Shanghai, it is unrivalled..."
—*Simon Winchester*—

"It is one of those rare travel guides that is a joy
to read whether or not you are planning a trip..."
—*The New York Times*—

"...Essential traveling equipment for anyone planning a journey of this kind..."
—*Asian Wall Street Journal*—

"If travel books came with warnings, the one for AFGHANISTAN: A COMPANION
AND GUIDE would read, 'Caution: may inspire actual voyage.' But then, this lavishly
produced guide couldn't help do otherwise—especially if you're partial to adventure."
—*TIME*, August 22nd 2005—

"Above all, it is authoritative and as well-informed as only extensive
travels inside the country can make it. It is strong on the history.
In particular the synopsis at the beginning is a masterly piece of compression."
—*The Spectator* (UK)—

"A gem of a book"
—*The Literary Review* (UK)—

"...Quite excellent. No one should visit Samarkand,
Bukhara or Khiva without this meticulously researched guide..."
—*Peter Hopkirk, author of* The Great Game—

"The Yangzi guide is terrific"
—*Longitude Books*—

"...The bible of Bhutan guidebooks..."
—*Travel & Leisure*—

"...Odyssey fans tend to be adventurous travelers with a literary bent.
If you're lucky enough to find an Odyssey Guide to where you're going, grab it..."
—*National Geographic Traveler*—

"...It's a superb book, superbly produced, that makes me long to go back to China..."
—*John Julius Norwich*—

YUNNAN

CHINA SOUTH OF THE CLOUDS

BY

JIM GOODMAN

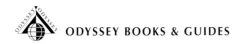

ODYSSEY BOOKS & GUIDES

Odyssey Books & Guides is a division of Airphoto International Ltd.
1401 Chung Ying Building, 20–20A Connaught Road West, Sheung Wan, Hong Kong
Tel: (852) 2856-3896; Fax: (852) 3012-1825
E-mail: magnus@odysseypublications.com; www.odysseypublications.com

Distribution in the USA by W.W. Norton & Company, Inc., 500 Fifth Avenue, New York, NY 10110,
USA Tel: 800-233-4830; Fax: 800-458-6515; www.wwnorton.com

Distribution in the UK and Europe by Cordee Ltd., 11 Jacknell Road, Dodwells Bridge Industrial Estate,
Hinckley, Leicestershire LE10 3BS, UK Tel: 01455-611185; Fax: 01455-635687; www.cordee.co.uk

Distribution in Australia by Tower Books, Unit 2/17 Rodborough Road, Frenchs Forest, NSW 2086,
Australia Tel: 02-9975-5566; Fax: 02-9975-5599; www.towerbooks.com.au

Yunnan: China South of the Clouds
ISBN: 978-962-217-775-8

Grateful acknowledgement is made to the following authors and publishers for permission granted:
Hai Feng Publishing Co. for 'Heaven creates scenic wonders' © 1995; Passport Books for 'Geology of
Southwest China' © 1988; Serindia Publications Inc. for 'Land of the Blue Poppy' © 1990; The University
of Washington Press for 'A Tale of Yunnan' © 1994.

Managing Editor: Helen Northey
Consultant Editor: Patrick Booz
Design: Christopher C Burt, Julia Dillon
Cover Design: Au Yeung Chui-kwai
Maps: On the Road Cartography & Mark Stroud, Moon Street Cartography
Practical Information by Peter Holmshaw
Index: Don Brech, Records Management International, Hong Kong

Additional photography/illustrations courtesy of Chu Tunan 266; Magnus Bartlett 245, 248–249;
Malcolm Rosholt 33; National Geographic 161; Jeremy Tredinnick 16, 19. Chinese woodcuts appear
courtesy of China Books and Periodicals.

Production and printing by Twin Age Ltd, Hong Kong
E-mail: twinage@netvigator.com
Manufactured in Hong Kong

Reading the safety information on these websites is advisable before travelling overseas:
US Department of State: www.travel.state.gov/travel warnings.html
UK Foreign and Commonwealth Office: www.fco.gov.uk/travel
Canadian Department of Foreign Affairs & International Trade: www.voyage.gc.ca/dest/sos/warnings-en.asp
Australian Department of Foreign Affairs & Trade: www.dfat.gov.au/travel/

Jim Goodman thanks Lu Feng above all for his support
and guidance in Yunnan over the years;
also to Zhao Dingding and Zhang Yaobing
of Yunnan People's Publishing House for their help
on his first book on Yunnan.

CONTENTS

The Nu River near Fugong.

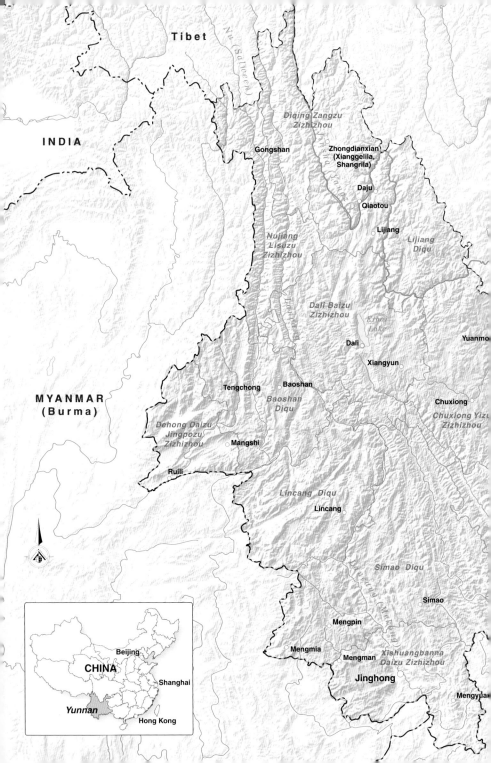

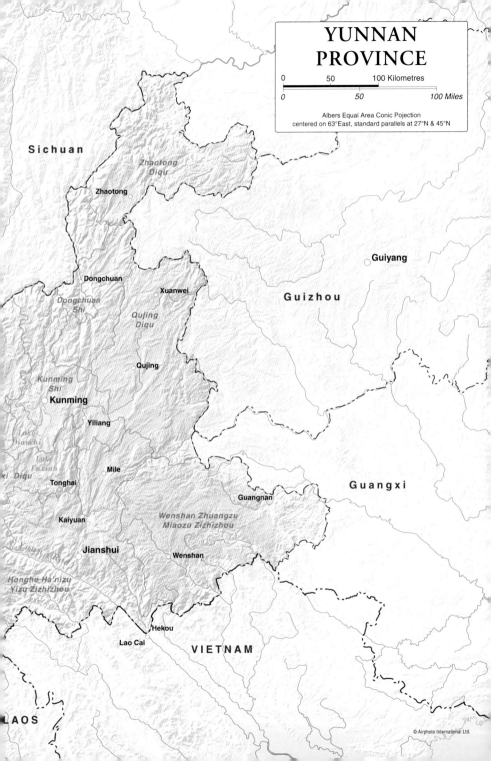

YUNNAN PROVINCE

0   50   100 Kilometres

0   50   100 Miles

Albers Equal Area Conic Pojection
centered on 63°East, standard parallels at 27°N & 45°N

Sichuan

*Zhaotong
Diqu*

Zhaotong

Guizhou

Guiyang

Dongchuan

Xuanwei

*Dongchuan
Shi*

*Qujing
Diqu*

Qujing

*Kunming
Shi*

Kunming

Yiliang

*Lake
Dianchi*

*Lake
Fuxian*

Mile

xi Diqu

Tonghai

Kaiyuan

Guangnan

Guangxi

*Wenshan Zhuangzu
Miaozu Zizhizhou*

Jianshui

Wenshan

*Honghe Ha'nizu
Yizu Zizhizhou*

Hekou

Lao Cai

VIETNAM

LAOS

© Airphoto International Ltd.

PART I ✦ PROVINCE OF WONDERS

Special Place, Special History

SOUTH OF THE CLOUDS

The two ideographs for the word China (*zhong guo*) literally mean 'Middle Kingdom'. The notion of China was that territory bounded on one side by an apparently limitless ocean and on the other sides by inhospitable terrain—steppes, deserts, high plateaux and mountains—inhabited by people who were, in Han Chinese eyes, of inferior cultural achievements. For centuries, the Chinese saw their homeland as the centre of the world. And as they expanded out of their Yellow River heartland, moving mostly south, they occupied similar alluvial plains until they ran into mountains formidable enough to contain their mass migration. As a result, although the Han reside in every corner within the boundaries of contemporary China, they still mostly occupy a middle position—between the sea and the mountains.

In a sense there are two Chinas. One is the Middle Kingdom, the central and eastern provinces, the population almost wholly Han, heirs to thousands of years of history and tradition, the purveyors of a rich and refined culture. Its chief characteristics are recognizable from one end of this Middle Kingdom to another.

The other China is the Periphery, the borderlands where civilizations blend, peoples of different origins mix and Chinese influence is attenuated, modified to varying degrees by the indigenous differences. Among China's 55 recognized nationalities, the Han comprise 92 per cent of the population. But the other 8 per cent reside upon 60 per cent of the land. For those seeking the attractions of multiple cultural exposure, the mingling of Han and non-Han, the survival (or revival) of customs and practices strange and fascinating, the Periphery is the part of China to explore.

Of all the borderland provinces, indeed, one could even say of all the provinces of China, none can boast of as much diversity and as many attractions—physical, cultural, ethnic—as the southwestern province of Yunnan. With 394,000 sq km, comparable to Sweden or California in surface area, it is the nation's sixth largest. For 4,061 km, its western and southern boundaries create international borders with Myanmar (Burma), Laos and Vietnam. To the southeast lies the Guangxi Zhuang Autonomous Region, to the northeast Guizhou Province. The extreme northwest touches Tibet, but the rest of the northern boundary is with Sichuan. In the latter province rain and clouds

The waters of Yuxian Lake overflow a bridge near the shore.

dominate the weather; a legend says that when a Nanzhao prince of Dali visited the Tang-dynasty court (618–907) he told the emperor his land was south of the rainy weather. The Chinese emperor then dubbed that territory *Yunnan*—South of the Clouds.

Yunnan does, in fact, enjoy better weather than its neighbours. Its position astride the Tropic of Cancer, along with its elevation and mountain chains, give it a temperate climate, free from extremes of heat or cold. Much of the province lies on hill-studded high plateaux averaging 2,000 metres in altitude. The snow peaks rise in the west and northwest, while two major ranges, the Ailao and Wuliang Mountains, run northwest to southeast through the heart of the province. South of these ranges the land becomes tropical. Culturally and physically it forms the northern rim of Southeast Asia. Yunnan is subject to annual monsoons from May through October. In other seasons days are often sunny, temperatures mild, with winters cold only in the highlands of the northwest, where most of the snow mountains stand. The highest is Meili Snow Mountain (*Kawa Karpo*), near Deqing, at 6,740 metres. The lowest point is the southeastern town of Hekou, on the Vietnam border, at 76 metres.

Mountain ranges of various sizes dominate nearly every prefecture and are home to a great variety of plants and animals. On their slopes, and in the valleys among them, live 24 different ethnic minorities, with their own languages, customs, lifestyles and religions. One-third of Yunnan's 40 million+ inhabitants are ethnic minorities, living on two-thirds of the land. Despite modernization, most still maintain their traditional way of life; the fondness minority women show for their ethnic clothing and ornaments makes Yunnan China's most colourful province.

PRE-HISTORY

In another epoch, long before man existed as a species, Yunnan was home to dinosaurs. In 1938 the Chinese palaeontologist Yan Zhoujian unearthed a fossilized skeleton in Lufeng County, 104 km west of Kunming. This was China's earliest dinosaur find. In 1981 a team from the county's Cultural Bureau dug up another, nearly intact, six-metre-long, two-metre high fossil. These and pterodactyl fossils are on display at the county's museum. The walking dinosaur specimens, all of the plant-eating, long-necked type, stand in a room with paintings on the walls of these dinosaurs in busy Triassic jungles (c. 250–200 million years ago). No big-jawed, ferocious carnivorous types here, nor among the dinosaur finds elsewhere in the province, mainly in Chuxiong Prefecture. But who knows how many fossils were ground up by ancient quack apothecaries and sold as dragon bone medicine?

(previous pages) Skeleton Python Pagoda (also known as the Fotu Pagoda) takes its name from a Nanzhao legend (see p. 308). It is near Xiaguan and rises 39 metres tall.

In a later epoch, long after the demise of the dinosaurs, Yunnan hosted a number of strange (now extinct) mammals. Among these was an important hominid on the human evolutionary chain, a creature called *Ramapithecus*, which had as many human characteristics as simian. Discoveries, also in Lufeng County, began in 1975 and culminated in the excavation of a nearly complete skull in 1980. Its age was determined to be eight million years old.

North of Lufeng, 200 km from Kunming, sits Yuanmou County, the other major palaeontological digging area. The earliest find here, in 1965, was a pair of teeth similar to, but larger and nearly three times as ancient as the teeth of Bejing Man, long considered China's oldest human ancestor. Hand-made stoneware and evidence of the use of fire discovered along with the teeth pushed proto-man's history back to 1.7 million years ago. The new sub-species of *Homo erectus* was named Yuanmou Man. Then discoveries in the late 1980s revealed an earlier model, dating back 2.5 million years. This set of teeth was similar enough to Yuanmou Man's to be obviously in the same line of evolution, yet sufficiently different to earn a new species name—Orient Man. Almost incidentally, excavators also found the fossils of a small, three-toed horse.

Yuanmou County has also yielded many relics from the Stone Age, including an entire Neolithic (c. 6000–2000 BC) village at Dadunzi, near the county seat. Near Chuxiong city, the prefectural capital, bronze drums have been excavated, dated to 690 BC. The find supposedly confirms Yunnan as the birthplace of the Bronze Drum Cult, associated with the Zhuang, Yao and other peoples in southern China and Southeast Asia.

DIAN

Bronze was introduced to China during the Shang Dynasty, about 1800 BC. The strongest alloy is eight parts copper to one part tin. Yunnan, known also as the Kingdom of Non-ferrous Metals, has abundant supplies of both tin and copper. Dongchuan has long been famous for its copper, while Gejiu is called the Tin Capital of China. The Bronze Age was in full flourish in Yunnan by 1260 BC Proof of that came in 1955 when archaeologists found 48 tombs at Shizhaishan, near Dian Lake (Dian Chi), 40 km south of Kunming. Among the thousands of bronze objects excavated the most spectacular were the lids of cowry-shell containers. The cowries were used as currency and the lids featured figures and props engaged in sundry activities of their daily life: marketing, farming, selling slaves, executing criminals, performing religious rites, fighting wars, spinning and weaving, getting drunk, playing music and lining up to offer obeisance to the King of Dian.

Within the Bronze Civilization Room of the Yunnan Provincial Museum a bronze Dian-period cowrie-shell container sports four long-horned oxen and a horse with gilt rider.

THE BRONZES OF YUNNAN

Bronze art seems to arise almost spontaneously in China. As more discoveries are made and the location of sites increases, the possibility of independent development increases as well.

The discovery in Yunnan of magnificent bronze artwork from the dawn of history excited archaeologists around the world. Farmers ploughing near Lake Dianchi unearthed some mystifying bronze vessels in the early 1950s and notified the provincial museum in Kunming. In 1955, archaeologists struck a treasure trove of 48 Bronze-Age tombs at Stone Village Hill (Shizhaishan), 40 kilometres (25 miles) south of Kunming.

Bronze is an alloy of copper and tin which is stronger than iron if made in correct proportions—eight parts copper to one part tin. Bronze was the first metal ever used by humans. It first came into use in northern China during the Shang Dynasty, around 1800 BC. Yunnan's bronze culture dates from about 1200 BC, near the end of the Shang Dynasty, though most of the bronze artefacts from the 48 tombs date from the Warring States Period (475–221 BC) and the Western Han Dynasty (206 BC–AD 24).

The Dian people in Yunnan mastered many advanced techniques in creating their bronzes, including gold plating and silver inlay decorations. Skill and sophistication of workmanship equalled and surpassed that of the Han. And whereas Han bronze culture seemed to undergo a change in favour or porcelain, the Dian bronzes took on new confidence and variety. Free from the constraints of orthodoxy, the Dian artists could create more freely and respond to the calling of their aesthetic choice. One can even say that 'art for art's sake' was being created in southwest China at that time.

The tombs at Shizhaishan yielded thousands of bronze objects— sewing boxes, figurines, headrests, mirrors, weapons, farm implements, belt buckles and more. Animals, hunting and fighting, took a predominant place among the statuettes and decorations. Archaeologists found 34 recognizable species along with many mythological beasts. Subsequent digs in western Yunnan produced a little bronze house with six kinds of domesticated animals—cow, goat, chicken, dog, pig, horse—pointing to an advanced agricultural society.

Even more revealing were elaborate, three-dimensional scenes cast on the lids of huge cowrie containers and on drums, showing the daily life of a vigorous, productive, slave-owning people. To archaeologists, this was a unique moment in the history of bronzeware. Only in Yunnan did Bronze-Age artisans realistically record the intimate and unmistakable details of their social activity. There were ferocious miniature battles and lively domestic scenes showing the work of women. The rhythms and rituals of agriculture and religion came to life, along with grisly depictions of head-hunting and human sacrifice. The bronze figurines laughed, wept, got drunk. One scene showed pompously dressed chieftains, surrounded by slaves, offering tribute to the King of Dian. Who were these people?

The first historical reference to the Kingdom of Dian appears in the second century BC. Sima Qian (145–85 BC), China's greatest classical historian, mentions that the King of Dian, in the savage southern border region beyond China, allied himself with the emperor of the Han Dynasty in order to subdue neighbouring tribes. In recognition of Dian's new tributary status, a seal was presented to the King of Dian. Other references to Dian appeared here and there in ancient Chinese literature but there was no hard evidence to confirm the kingdom's existence until 1956. That year, tomb Number 6 at Shizhaishan yielded up the seal itself. Four clear characters on its bronze face—Dian Wang Zhi Yin (Seal of the King of Dian)—bound this remote, remarkable tribe to the vast empire of China.

Dian originally referred only to the mysterious, non-Chinese tribe. Later the name came to mean the territorial kingdom as well. The Lake of Dian (Dianchi) outside Kunming has kept its ancestral name for three millennia and the word Dian remains synonymous with Yunnan.

On the basis of available material, archaeologists divide Yunnanese Bronze Age culture into four categories, according to geography. Dianchi culture, Erhai culture (in the area around Dali and Erhai Lake), Northwest Yunnan culture and Yuanjiang culture (or Red River culture, in southern Yunnan). The most important Dianchi culture is concentrated around Lake Dianchi outside Kunming, but extends to Qujing in the northeast, to the Red River in the south, Luling County in the east and Lufung County in the west.

A major element in the bronze culture of Yunnan is the bull, symbol of property and wealth. The depictions of the beast are powerful and realistic, where even the veins on the head and neck stand out. The tiger, too, appears again and again as a creature of strength and awe, holding forth the aspiration of invincibility.

Ancestor worship is clearly presented in the bronze work of Dian. In some cases there is presented a beautiful house-shrine with a snake-stair-case that leads to a roof. It is designed to reach ever upward and to lead the eye that way. A figure with hair braided upward mirrors the stairway. The visual story seems to say: The Dian people can reach to Heaven to communicate with their ancestors by means of the snake ladder; the spirit of the snake stands as an intermediary between the world of men and the celestial world.

(top) A bronze buckle shows two men dancing on a writhing snake. (middle) A cowrie shell container's lid displays a battle scene from the Western Han period. (bottom) A wild boar fights off two tigers—symbolically strong buckles were popular among the Dian.

Knowledge of Dian had hitherto been confined to the writings of Sima Qian, the 2nd century BC Han Dynasty historian. He reported an alliance between the Han Emperor Wu Di and the leader of Dian to subdue neighbouring tribes. The emperor presented the king with a seal commemorating Dian's new official status as a tribute state—in 1956 archaeologists found the seal, which added to the growing knowledge about the vigorous, sophisticated, slave-holding, religious-minded society of central Yunnan. Yet the Kingdom of Dian had no historians or even a system of writing, so its rise and fall, as well as much about daily life, remains a mystery.

Yunnan also enters the works of classical Chinese chroniclers in connection with a later Kingdom of Dian, during the Warring States Period (475–221 BC). The reigning Zhou Dynasty held sway over only a small fief around its capital Loyang, in Henan Province. The rest of the old Zhou state was split up into several competing kingdoms, including Jin, the largest of them all.

With the break-up of Jin in 403 BC, the most powerful contenders were Qin in the northwest (which ultimately unified China in 221 BC) and Chu in the south, mostly between the Huai and Yangzi Rivers. The state of Chu—largely non-Han in population, probably of Dai or Zhuang stock, with Yao and Miao comprising sizable percentages—looked south to expand its holdings when Qin began gobbling up the smaller northern kingdoms.

At the accession of King Wei in 339 BC, Chu dispatched an army under the command of General Zhuang Qiao, a relative of the king, to conquer southern lands. Zhuang swung into Yunnan from the northeast and eventually occupied the plain around Kunming. Annexing the territory to Chu, he called it Dian and stayed on as governor. Meanwhile, Qin continued to strengthen its position by invading and conquering its Sichuan neighbours, Ba and Shu, in 316 BC. This immediately put pressure on Chu and cut off Dian from its home country. Zhuang Qiao tried to reach Chu via Guizhou but ran into too much resistance from tribal peoples there. He then proclaimed Dian an independent kingdom, which he and his descendants ruled over for the next two centuries. The ruling caste from Chu intermarried with local people and adopted local culture, which itself was non-Han and probably somewhat related to that back in Chu.

When Qin Shi Huangdi unified China he did not seek to extend his domain southward, nor did the succeeding Han emperors for their first century of rule. But Han Wu Di (140–86 BC) was expansionist by nature. Campaigns to subdue Nanyue (present-day Guangdong Province) and Tonkin (northern Vietnam) so impressed the King of Dian, he volunteered to become Wu Di's vassal. This suited the emperor fine. He let the King of Dian retain de facto rule over the newly created Commandery of Yichou, and was thereby free to pursue his real interest, which was to secure a trade route to Burma and India.

CHRONOLOGY OF PERIODS IN CHINESE HISTORY

Neolithic	7000–2600 BCE
Five Legendary Rulers	2600–2070 BCE
Xia	2070–1600 BCE
Shang	1600–1027 BCE
Western Zhou	1027–771 BCE
Eastern Zhou	770–256 BCE
Spring and Autumn	770–476 BCE
Warring States	475–221 BCE
Qin	221–206 BCE
Western (Xi) Han	206 BCE–25 CE
Eastern (Dong) Han	25–220
Three Kingdoms	220–280
Western Jin	265–316
Eastern Jin (Including Sixteen Kingdoms)	317–439
Northern and Southern Dynasties	420–589
Sui	581–618
Tang	618–907
Five Dynasties	907–960
Liao (Khitan)	916–1125
Northern Song	960–1127
Southern Song	1127–1279
Jin (Jurchen)	1115–1234
Xixia (Tangut)	1038–1227
Yuan (Mongol)	1279–1368
Ming	1368–1644
Qing (Manchu)	1644–1911
Republic of China	1911–1949
People's Republic of China	1949–

This ambition remained unfulfilled in Wu Di's lifetime, but emperors in the Later Han Dynasty (25–220 AD) took up the task. In 69 AD the empire established the Yongchang Commandery on the broad plain between the Mekong and Salween Rivers (Chinese: Lancangjiang and Nujiang) at modern Baoshan, and later the Commandery of Tengyueh, modern Tengchong, near the border west of the Salween. These became the most distant Chinese outposts on the Southern Silk Route. When the Han court was strong it could maintain these posts, but when weak the route and its posts were taken over by local tribal chieftains. The Han made no attempt to colonize the province or even to extend the empire's authority beyond the trade routes. More mountains and malaria-ridden plains lay beyond them, effective barriers to further Han penetration of the province.

By the beginning of the 3rd century, the Han empire began to disintegrate. Its final collapse in 220 was followed by the Three Kingdoms era: Wei in the north, Wu in the south, Shu in the west. Of these, Shu was the weakest, but gifted with the long, three-sided war's greatest statesman and military strategist—Zhuge Liang. Unable to expand east or north because of Shu's strong rivals, Zhuge Liang first campaigned south against rebellious native vassals in Yunnan. He reduced Yichou to direct rule from Shu, marched east to Qujing and Zhaotong and west to Chuxiong, relieving pressure on Baoshan in the southwest, the only area that had remained loyal to Shu. In seven campaigns he subdued the indigenous tribes, winning their allegiance by leaving their customs intact and their chieftains in power to rule as Shu's governors. This policy foreshadowed tactics to be pursued by the Yuan, Ming and Qing dynasties when they took over control of Yunnan and extended their authority into remote areas.

NANZHAO

In 264, thirty years after the death of Zhuge Liang (234), Wei conquered Shu. The annexed parts of Yunnan broke up into mini-states while the western tribes threw off suzerainty and regained their full independence. When Wei reunited the empire by defeating Wu in 280, it did not seek to regain control of Shu's Yunnan territory. This new Jin Dynasty fell in 316 and until Sui reunification in 581, China was split into several short-lived northern and southern realms. None were strong enough to assert claims over any part of Yunnan. By the time the Tang Dynasty succeeded the Sui in 618, Yunnan had undergone important changes and was ready to resist any attempts at subjugation.

The centre of power in Yunnan had shifted from Kunming to Dali, 400 km west. The Tang emperors sought to pacify their frontiers by encouraging the

The Nanzhao Culture City in Dali has a recreation of the original royal palace (top) and wax figures representing the king, queen and ministers of the old court (bottom).

political consolidation of border states, having them acknowledge Chinese suzerainty and then protecting the areas themselves. By this time six small states, or *zhao*, had established themselves in the west. These zhao acknowledged Tang suzerainty in 647. The most important one, Nanzhao, was in the south, centred around modern Weishan.

In 718, at the peak of Tang power, Nanzhao's King Piluoge unified the six *zhao*. Twenty years later he marched north and subdued Tibetan and Yi tribes that had given Tang China trouble in southwest Sichuan. The court was pleased at its vassal's success.

But relations soon deteriorated. Piluoge's successor, Geluofeng, was insulted on a state visit to a Tang prince, failed to have his grievance addressed by a court distracted by the Yang Guifei affair (the emperor's mistress), and broke off Nanzhao's fealty to the Tang court. The Tang reacted by dispatching a huge punitive expedition against the Nanzhao capital of Dali. But Nanzhao defenders annihilated this army at Xiaguan in 751, putting 60,000 Tang soldiers to death. Three years later an avenging army set out from Chang'an and met the same fate.

Then China suffered the throes of the An Lushan Rebellion (755–63), leaving the empire a shadow of its former self. Nanzhao took advantage by seizing portions of Sichuan and for the next 100 years periodically waged war, sometimes in alliance with Tibet, against Tang China. Nanzhao in this period also occupied northern Burma and pushed east and south to Guangxi and Vietnam.

But by 879 the kingdom was too weak to carry out expansion. Its invasion of Sichuan was easily repulsed and it suffered a disastrous defeat in Vietnam the following year. Though the Tang Dynasty was in accelerated decline, Nanzhao was in no position to gain from the empire's demise. The very different climate of Burma made Nanzhao's stay there short-lived, and their conquest of Han-populated territory created new problems for the non-Han ruling class, who could not successfully assimilate their new subjects into the national polity.

Nanzhao's territory, which extended into Guizhou and Hunan, began to contract just as the Tang Dynasty began crumbling. In 902, five years prior to the end of the dynasty, a satrap assassinated the Nanzhao ruling family and usurped the throne. Internecine fighting continued until ended by coup in 937, carried out by an official of the Bai ethnic group. The new Kingdom of Dali lasted more than three centuries. It was smaller than Nanzhao, for it allowed the further-flung provinces to secede, and in reality had direct control only over the area that today comprises Dali Prefecture, with Erhai Lake at its centre.

Nevertheless, the Dali kingdom enjoyed a peaceful existence. The first Song emperor, mindful of Tang difficulties in the southwest, declined an invasion.

Instead, the Song policy was to do nothing to interfere with trade, for Yunnan was a source of horses for the Song armies in their endless battles with mounted invaders from the north. After the withdrawal of Nanzhao from the Upper Irrawaddy plains, the new state of Burma did not try to expand east into Yunnan. Nor did Tibet ever revert to its aggressive policies of the early Tang centuries. So the Kingdom of Dali had no external enemies and no motive to keep a strong standing army of its own. When faced with the sudden need for one, in 1253, Dali was unprepared.

THE COMING OF KHUBILAI KHAN

In the 13th century the Mongol Empire began advancing on China. Mongols destroyed the Jin state north of Song territory in 1234. But Song forces held off Mongol assaults on the Yangzi River provinces. So the Mongols decided to capture Sichuan and then outflank the empire from the southwest. Without waiting for the full conquest of Sichuan, in 1253 Khubilai Khan marched a huge army out of its camps in Gansu, south through the mountains of western Sichuan, and crossed the Dadu River, traditional boundary between Dali and China. He then swept into Yunnan at Yongning, near Lugu Lake, easily crushing the feeble resistance put up by local Mosuo and Pumi.

Before moving on, Khubilai formally annexed the territory and left behind Mongol officers to run it for him. These men married Mosuo women and their descendants became the ruling clan in the district, the only patrilineal clan in an otherwise strongly matrilineal people. The Khan did not interfere with their customs or lifestyle, nor make exorbitant demands for taxes or manpower.

Moving south, the Mongol army reached the Yangzi River, in Yunnan called the Jinshajiang (River of Golden Sand), east of present-day Lijiang. The local Naxi, rather than resist, helped Khubilai's forces cross the river on goatskin rafts. Then they guided the Mongols to the Lijiang Plain, where the army camped at what is now the Old Stone Bridge in the old town of Dayan. Khubilai invested the Mu chieftain of Lijiang's Naxi with the authority to run the county in his name. To express his gratitude for Naxi assistance and cooperation, the Khan also established a Naxi classical music orchestra and left them scores of Tang and Song-dynasty court music. Boasting the oldest continuous classical music tradition in China, the Naxi orchestra survives to this day, still playing the music the Khan left them.

Khubilai's next stop, in fact his main objective, was Dali. After a single skirmish outside the northern gate, the Dali king surrendered. As at Lijiang, the Khan left him with all practical power, but the Kingdom of Dali lost its independence. Kubilai marched east, formally annexed Yunnan and appointed General Saidanchi Zhansiding its Governor. The general was a Central Asian

Muslim, under whose rule large numbers of Hui soldiers (Muslim Chinese) came to settle in the province. Today, the Hui in Dali honour Yunnan's first governor in an annual commemorative rite, on the 16th day of the 4th lunar month.

Vulnerable now on all frontiers, the Song government steadily weakened and in 1279 it fell. The new Yuan Dynasty ruled a bigger-than-ever China, which incorporated Yunnan for the first time in its history. But life did not improve much in Yunnan now that it was part of the Celestial Empire. Tribes in the remote areas resisted authority and the Dai principalities in the south were largely unaffected by the conquest. The following century, when Mongol authority crumbled elsewhere in China and the new Ming Dynasty reestablished Han political control of the Middle Kingdom in 1368, Yunnan still hosted a large Mongol presence.

Fearing the Mongols might regroup and use Yunnan as a base to attack China, Ming Emperor Hong Wu in 1381 decided to drive them out of Yunnan once and for all. Had there been no Mongols remaining in Yunnan, Hong Wu might possibly have left it alone, like his Song predecessors. But there were. Ming troops confronted them at the Baishi River near Qujing, completely crushed them, then chased down fugitive Mongols all over central Yunnan. One group only managed to escape, live in disguise, change their way of life and wait until the political climate improved enough for them to admit they were Mongols. This community survives today in Tonghai County, at the foot of Peacock Hill in Hexi township.

MING AND QING RULE

Under the Ming, the sinicization of Yunnan accelerated. Waves of immigrants, mostly from the Lower Yangzi region, followed Ming armies to Yunnan, occupying the plateau lands and highland valleys. The walled cities that sprang up were built on the Ming model of north China. Many of the outstanding religious monuments and temples of the province date their construction to Ming times. So does the road network and the iron suspension bridges that spanned the Lancang and Nu rivers for the first time.

Administratively, the Ming governed the Han-inhabited areas directly. But in the minority areas they established the office of *tusi*—local chieftain—who was usually a member of the majority ethnic group in that area. The first Ming emperors were vigorous rulers and in the early 15th century Emperor Yong Le launched naval expeditions as far as Indonesia, Arabia and East Africa. These were commanded by one of Yunnan's most famous sons—Admiral Zheng He of Jinning, on Dian Lake south of Kunming.

The Southern Silk Road to Burma and India passed through Yangbi and in the Ming Dynasty, the Yulong Bridge was constructed to cross the river.

The Ming Dynasty, like the Song, faced its gravest threat from the north. Manchus began encroaching in the 17th century and by 1644 established their own dynasty—the Qing. The last Ming prince eventually ended up in Yunnan, in the western outpost of Tengchong. Wu Sangui, the disaffected Ming general who invited the Manchus to Beijing, was dispatched to deal with him. Wu's army invaded Yunnan in 1657 and defeated the last Ming army in the Gaoligong Mountains. The prince fled to Burma. But there his royal host, to avert an invasion and to effect the withdrawal of the Chinese army, handed over the prince and his retinue to Wu Sangui. He took them back to Kunming and executed them. The Qing court rewarded Wu with the office of governor of Yunnan.

Wu soon felt improperly compensated for his services, even though his power extended to neighbouring provinces, and in 1673 he declared independence. Five years later, still locked in struggles in Sichuan and Hunan, he proclaimed himself emperor, but died five months later. His grandson succeeded him but could not keep the new state together. In 1681 Qing troops took Kunming and wiped out Wu's entire family.

Though Yunnan was the locus of Wu's rebellion, events did not involve the non-Han peoples. After the last Ming prince's arrest, tribal chieftains made haste to declare their allegiance to the Qing. When the Manchus conquered Yunnan they left the tusi system intact for four more decades. Then, having consolidated their authority everywhere in China, the Qing began dismissing the chieftains and appointing their own magistrates to rule directly. Only in the most remote areas did the tusi system persist.

THE MUSLIM REVOLT

The Qing Dynasty began to decline after its mid-18th century apogee. Corruption and maladministration became rampant. Discontent spread to all classes. In addition, imperialist powers greedily awaited the opportunity to stake out territorial claims. In 1851 the Taiping Rebellion broke out and in two years the rebels had captured Nanjing and proclaimed their Kingdom of Heavenly Peace. In 1855–56 Britain humiliated China in the Second Opium War. Meanwhile in Yunnan, avaricious officials were plundering the province's commerce in the form of exorbitant taxes and transport levies. This fell heaviest on the Hui community, who ran most caravans.

As descendants of Mongol army soldiers, the Hui in Yunnan were never trusted by the Qing government. They suffered the harshest exactions and repressive measures of any community. In 1855, following several atrocities and retaliations, the Hui raised the banner of revolt. The spiritual leader of this long and bloody attempt to turn Yunnan into an independent Muslim sultanate was a Dali-born Kunming mullah named Ma Dexin. The revolt's military chief, who came from a village near Dali, was Du Wenxiu, who renamed himself Sultan Suleiman of the newly born Peaceful Southern Kingdom (Ping Nan Guo). Du's forces conquered most of western Yunnan, all the way to the Burmese border, and besieged Kunming several times, capturing it briefly in 1863 before being driven back.

The two sides waged war back and forth across central Yunnan, taking turns laying siege to the walled cities. It was the last major conflict in the world where wars were fought in this manner. Armies slaughtered the inhabitants of captured cities and exterminated entire village populations if they lay in their path. The conflict basically affected the area between Tengchong and Qujing, and as far south as Mojiang and Jianshui. The Hui themselves were far from united. An important faction in the Kunming area fought on the government side, while jealousies and quarrels squandered temporary advantages won by the rebels.

Du's high point came when he besieged Kunming in 1868. But the capital held out, forcing Du to abandon the siege the following year. From then on a series of defeats led to the attack on Dali itself in 1872. The following year the city fell and the victorious Qing beheaded the erstwhile Sultan. It still took another year to pacify the area and annihilate the last recalcitrant resisters. The government troops then took a terrible revenge on the Hui, massacring them in the thousands. Hui were forbidden to live within Dali again. In Tengchong, Qing troops rounded up Muslims and hurled them over the waterfall to their deaths. The disruptions of the Revolt and its aftermath, followed by a famine and a total breakdown in commerce (it was years before the caravans recovered) reduced the population from eight million in 1855 to three million 20 years later.

THE WARLORD ERA

In Yunnan, some remote areas such as Lijiang were run by court-appointed Chinese administrators, though most were governed almost as private fiefs by the tusi chieftains. Many of these were Han or else belonged to minorities other than the leading one in the district. These local heads, especially the hereditary ones (some were lifetime appointments, though not hereditary), usually saw themselves as nobility vis-a-vis the tribes in their charge. The latter suffered as much oppression from them as they did from the Han. In many areas, where the tusi was of a different ethnic group than most of the district's people, the people largely ignored him. In Ninglang County, for example, the Mosuo tusi

An Account of the Muslim Rebellion (1855–1873)

*T*he Mohammedans of Yunnan are precisely the same race as their Confucian or Buddhist countrymen; and it is even doubtful if they were Mohammedans except as far as they profess an abhorrence for pork. They did not practise circumcision, though I am not sure if that rite is indispensable; and they did not observe the Sabbath, were unacquainted with the language of Islam, did not turn to Mecca in prayer, and professed none of the fire and sword spirit of propogandism.

That they were intelligent, courageous, honest and liberal to strangers, is as certain as their ignorance of the law and the prophets. All honour to their good qualities, but let us cease to cite their short-lived rule as an instance of the 'Great Mohammedan Revival.'

The rebellion was at first a question of pork and of nothing else, beginning with jealousies and bickering between pig butchers and the fleshers of Islam in the market place. The officials who were appealed to invariably decided against the Mussulmans. Great discontent ensued and soon burst into flame.

The first outbreak seemed to have originated among the miners, always a dangerous class in China, who were largely composed of Mohammedans. The usual measures of exterminative repression were adopted by the officials; their Confucian hostility against any faith or society which possessed an organization novel to or discountenanced by the Government, was aroused; a general persecution ensued; the Mohammedans made common cause, excited, it is very possible, by their travelled hadjis; and so began the period of disorder and disaster with which we are acquainted.

The commander of our Chinese escort—whose name, by the way, ... is not inappropriate to his profession, 'Hill-echoing Thunder'—narrated to us how he conveyed with exceeding difficulty four foreign guns over the rugged route from Yunnan Fu (Kunming), and how the capture of the city was to be attributed solely to his own exertions. One gun was irreparably damaged en route, but the surviving three laid and pointed by himself, according to his account, terminated the rebellion. There seems no doubt that these guns, cast by French workmen in Kunming, were really the main cause of the Mohammedan surrender.

General Thunder told us, what was subsequently confirmed, that when the Mohammedans had surrendered and given up their arms, Tu Wen-hsiu, the so-called 'sultan', came into the camp of the beseigers, borne in a sedan chair, and inquired for Ma, the Imperialist commander. Being introduced to his presence, he begged for a cup of water, which being given him, he said, 'I have nothing to ask but this—spare the people.' He then drank the water, and almost immediately expired. It appears that he had taken poison, which was suddenly brought into action by the water. His head was immediately cut off and exposed, and, heedless of his prayer— probably the most impressive and pathetic ever uttered by a dying patriot— the victors proceeded to massacre the helpless garrison and townsfolk.

The greater part of the able-bodied men, no doubt retaining some of their arms, succeeded in escaping; but a number of unresisting people, principally old men, women and children, fled from the city into the rice fields that border the lake. Hemmed in by the Imperialist pursuers, they entered the water, into which they retreated further and further; and being still pressed, were either forced out of their depth by the crush, or sought a refuge from worse ills in a voluntary death. The number of those who perished in that way has probably been greatly exaggerated. The foreign press puts it at from 3,000 to 9,000. General Thunder, undoubtedly an eye-witness, and probably a participator, told me, as we sat in the sunny verandah of a temple overlooking the scene of these horrors, that he did not think there could have been more than 500 corpses, or 'the water would have stunk more.' The gallant general was of the opinion that Tu Wen-hsiu was a good and conscientious ruler, and respected even by his Imperialist foes; but for the Muslims generally, he professed much contempt.

Grosvenor, *Parliamentary Report: Mission Through Western Yunnan, China*, No. 3 (1878) had no control at all over the Yi in the mountains, who indulged in clan feuds according to their own laws, and periodically raided the valleys with impunity. On the other hand, the tusis of Gengma, Mengding, Luxi and Zhefang were Dai princes backed by large Dai populations, with standing armies and enough local prestige to resist sinicization and get away with paying lip-service obeisance.

Yunnan's distance from an imperial court in the final throes of terminal illness enabled not only isolated trans-montane tribal potentates to ignore Beijing's writ. The province's Chinese saw themselves as somewhat separate from the rest of China. Even before the Qing dynasty fell in 1911, Yunnan was already in the Warlord Era. Native governors ran the province as they pleased, accountable neither to the Manchu court nor to the Republic that succeeded it. As a result, much of Yunnan's farmland was given over to opium production. Yet the warlords did keep order of a sort in the province, if only to protect their illicit trade.

During the Civil War years, Yunnan, under its warlord-governor Long Yun, mostly steered clear of both sides. Two Red Army contingents passed through on the Long March, 1934–36. The first, under Mao Zedong and Zhu De, made a feint on Kunming, then swerved through the northeast, crossing into Daliangshan in Sichuan. The second, under He Long and Xiao Ke, marched west across the central plateau, turned up to Lijiang and crossed the Jinshajiang at Shigu. The army camped for the winter in Zhongdian (now officially called Shangri-La) before heading north to join the other Red forces at Yan'an. While landlords and other Communist targets hid in the cities, the Communists won friends among the common people, Han and non-Han, by paying fair prices for goods and services, a practice so unlike that of any other armed force passing through, in particular the rival Nationalists. Long Yun did his diplomatic best to keep both armies out of Yunnan.

WORLD WAR II

In 1937 Japan launched a many-pronged invasion of China. Losing control of the entire eastern half of the country, the Nationalist government relocated in Chongqing (Chungking), Sichuan, with some ministries and industries moving to Yunnan. To keep supplies coming into western China, the Nationalists had a road constructed from Kunming to Dehong, the famous Burma Road, using mostly corvée labour conscripted from tribes along the route. The road followed the old Southeast Silk Route as far as Baoshan and continued to Wanding, Dehong. Goods and war material continued to come from British Burma over the bridge at Wanding until the Japanese overran Burma in 1942 and closed the route.

This group of WWII fighter pilots intercepted a flight of 21 Japanese medium bombers and 20 fighters over one of our fields on April 28, 1943, and shot down 11 and eight probables. Seated on fuselage is Edmund Goss. Seated on the wing are John Alison (left) and Roger Pryor. Standing, left, Joe Griffin, Mack Mitchell, John Hampshire, and Hollis Blackstone. Hampshire, from Grants Pass, Oregon, was on the way to becoming the leading ace of the China Theatre. In a few weeks of flying he had brought down 14 planes confirmed and several probables, a record which exceeded Robert Scott's in less time. And then one day the winds of fate changed and Hampshire was himself shot down and killed.

By that time the Americans were involved in the Pacific War as much as the British. New supply routes were organized out of British India. One was by land from the eastern Himalayan town of Kalimpong, near Darjeeling. From here pony and mule caravans travelled up through Eastern Tibet, then into Yunnan at Deqing, thence down to Zhongdian, Lijiang and Xiaguan. From there fresh caravans carried the goods to Kunming and from the capital to Sichuan or other parts of Yunnan. The trade enriched many Khampa Tibetans as well as Naxi and Bai along the way.

The other route was by air, over that section of mountainous Burma and Yunnan called the Hump, and famous as one of the most hazardous air routes in the entire world. Much of this operation was carried out by the civilian volunteer pilots of Claire Chennault's Flying Tigers, who had a base in Kunming and whose boss was a strategic advisor to General Chiang Kai-shek. Chennault kept telling Chiang that his air unit could defend western China against any Japanese advance. The implication was that Chiang needn't deploy his own forces in defence, which was music to Chiang's ears, since he preferred to keep his forces intact for the post-war showdown with the Communists. This attitude infuriated General Joseph Stillwell, the American responsible for the Sino-Allied defence against the Japanese.

Yet no one could deny that Chennault's Flying Tigers were men of great courage. An uncomfortably large number of transport planes crashed when buffeted by the unpredictable winds and storms of the Hump. Even in recent years Yunnanese farmers have discovered the remains of planes in various mountain locations in the west of the province. And the older folks still remember the sacrifices made by American and British pilots in the war, reflected in the very friendly and favourable attitude they have nowadays towards tourists from these two countries.

UNDER THE RED FLAG

World War II marked the end of Yunnan's de facto isolation from the rest of China. The industries and institutions (universities, for example) set up as wartime expedients continued after the Japanese surrender. China's Civil War resumed but did not affect Yunnan until the end, when those Guomindang remnants too distant to escape to Taiwan retreated to Yunnan, making a last stand in the west, like the last of the Ming princes. Local people felt no fondness for the Nationalists and aided the Red Army's campaign to drive them across the frontier into Burma. From there they made occasional forays into Yunnan, but as the Communists extended their administrative control, these soon ceased. The Nationalists turned to the opium business in northern Burma and henceforth became part of Southeast Asia's history and not China's.

*Mao Zedong and Patrick J. Hurley at the start
of the 1945 Chongqing coalition talks. (John Colling)*

Now firmly in control of Yunnan, the Communists set about reorganizing and reforming the province. But in the beginning, mindful of the social and economic differences between the Han areas and the minority areas, they moved gingerly. They kept Long Yun as governor until 1956, and in the minority areas worked together with tribal leaders to effect change. The tusi office was abolished. Dai princes' authority was curbed. The affected personnel, however, were given new positions in the reorganized governments. By the mid-1950s, most minority-dominated areas were set up as autonomous prefectures, counties and even townships.

Autonomy did not mean a hands-off policy. It meant that in a Yi Autonomous County, for example, the personnel of the leading political positions had to be Yi. Han cadres were also encouraged to learn the minority languages and become familiar with the customs and beliefs of the people they worked with. In theory, any proposed regulation that grossly conflicted with local custom could not be introduced. Gradually the Party trained its own minority cadres, setting up the Minority Nationalities Institute in Kunming for this purpose. By the time this group was ready for administrative duties back in their native lands, the Party was ready to inaugurate serious reform campaigns, such as the abolition of slavery. Some mistakes in carrying out policies were made, but adequately corrected, and in general the reforms were successfully implemented and accepted by the peoples concerned.

Not quite the same claim could be made for the reforms of the Great Leap Forward or the Cultural Revolution. One can only say the Han suffered as much as the non-Han, perhaps moreso, for the remotest mountain minority areas were scarcely touched. However, since 1979, when China changed direction under Deng Xiaoping, progress in Yunnan has bounded forth. Economic liberalization has fostered rapid commercial growth, while agricultural produce has risen manyfold. Fancy new high-rise office buildings and department stores have replaced the old, brick-and-tile, two-storey shop house neighbourhoods, not only in Kunming but also in prefecture and county capitals throughout the province.

When the government finally opened Yunnan to foreign tourists in the mid-1980s modernization had already taken hold. Prosperity reigned as shopping malls were thronged and more and more hotels and bank buildings rose from the rubble of the old neighbourhoods. This prosperity has continued, and now Kunming and other big cities have traffic problems. Communications improve every year, with ever more minibuses going to ever more destinations. And they are usually full, as the rural folk take advantage of the transport system to get more involved in marketing their surpluses. Yunnan is becoming a perpetual motion province.

Yet modernization has by no means wiped out tradition. In addition to launching the economic reforms, the Deng government also reversed Party policy on minorities. Ethnic costume was no longer forbidden. Minority customs and festivals were not only permitted again, they were even encouraged and subsidized through grants to the autonomous county governments. To varying degrees, the minorities in the province responded with an enthusiasm that inaugurated a new, revivalist phase in their history. Ethnic pride has returned to Yunnan, augmented by tourist interest in many places, but plainly evident in counties where tourists rarely tread.

For centuries Chinese policy towards the non-Han people was to gradually assimilate them within the Han body politic through the powerful influence of Chinese culture. They would be fully accepted when they identified themselves as Han. Even the Communists pursued this goal, however they might have voiced equality between nationalities. The ultimate aim, climaxing in the Cultural Revolution, was to turn everyone into Han-style communist citizens.

Now that aim has been officially abandoned. It is not sinicization that is the antagonist to tribal tradition, but modernization. At this moment in their history, Yunnan's minorities are flaunting their ethnic identity, very visibly, across wide parts of the province. That, and the varied and often beautiful places in which they carry on their traditions, make Yunnan a most interesting, even exciting place to explore.

A group from the Yi minority in Dayao County in traditional finery and Mao hats.

The Yunnanese

EARLY SETTLEMENT

The first movement of people from China proper south into Yunnan took place in the 4th century BC, at the height of the Warring States Period. King Wei of Chu inflicted a crushing defeat on his eastern neighbour Yue, whose largely Dai population fled southwestward to western Guizhou, northern Guangxi and eastern Yunnan. Flush with this victory, King Wei sent Zhuang Qiao to conquer central Yunnan. Meanwhile, Qin destroyed the Sinicized Dai states of Ba and Shu in Sichuan. Refugees from these states also fled to Yunnan. Most of the immigrants settled in the relatively flat plateaux of eastern and central Yunnan. They became the majority inhabitants of the new Kingdom of Dian, which Zhuang Qiao set up when cut off from his homeland by the Qin conquest of Sichuan.

Not until Emperor Wu Di of the Western Han Dynasty did any Chinese ruler show interest in Yunnan. Then Dian became the Yizhou Commandery of the Han Empire. When the Han Dynasty weakened in the 3rd century AD, Yizhou shook off its allegiance. To reestablish Han suzerainty, Zhuge Liang in the Three Kingdoms Period campaigned against Yunnan. Half his forces had the easier task of taking control of the eastern and southern areas, while the Shu Prime Minister himself led the other half of his army into the tribal strongholds of the west.

Upon the victorious conclusion of both campaigns, Zhuge Liang reorganized the province's administration. The eastern part of Yunnan became the Prefecture of Jianning, with the capital at Qujing. The central parts became the Prefecture of Yunnan (here the name was used for the first time), capital at Kunming, ex-Yizhou. The western portions were left in the control of native chieftains, who recognized Shu suzerainty and ruled on Shu's behalf. In Yunnan and Jianning, Han officials ruled directly, for the population was already Sinicized. In time these people dropped their earlier identities and considered themselves every bit as Han as the immigrants of the Ming era (1368–1644).

During the Nanzhao ascendancy (after 732 AD), the cities of Yunnan and Jianning Prefectures were initially part of the Tang-administered territory. But in the subsequent wars between Nanzhao and Tang China, these Han-dominated areas were lost to Nanzhao's expansion. Kunming became the second city of the Kingdom of Nanzhao and whatever Han immigration there was

Zhuge Liang led an expedition from Shu, one of the contenders in the Three Kingdoms Era, to subdue and win over the tribes in Yunnan in 225 AD.

in the time before the conflict now halted. Not until after the end of the Yuan Dynasty (1279–1368), when Yunnan had already been a Chinese province for a century, did the immigration resume.

MING MIGRATIONS

Because the Mongols they had just overthrown still retained a significant presence in Yunnan, the new Ming emperor campaigned in the province to clear it of Mongols. He wanted to incorporated the province into the Chinese Empire and thus decided to develop the region and sinicize it once and for all. Yunnan was once again reorganized: in the remote areas, *tusis* were established after the Mongol tradition and the Han areas administered directly.

Above all, the Ming rulers encouraged immigration, especially from the overpopulated provinces along the Yangzi River. Besides the pioneers who headed for vacant farmland, many took up occupations in the growing towns. The larger and more important urban centres erected walls and gates on the Ming model of northern China. Ming rulers also lavished patronage on Daoist and Buddhist monuments and monasteries, partly motivated by a desire to fix up its new province with a permanent Chinese cultural identity.

(above) Buddhist stone sculptures from the Nanzhao era at the ruins of Shibaoshan.
(right) Door gods at the entrance to temples and homes was a Han custom that spread across the province.

Immigration from the Yangzi areas proceeded in waves, each time from a different place. Each group chose a different place to settle, the newcomers bringing with them their own peculiar customs or dialects from their former residences. In the early 15th century, for example, a large contingent from Nanjing settled on the plain of Yongsheng County, Lijiang Prefecture. Virtually no one else settled there and Nanjing migrants in later centuries went to Baoshan and other places. But Yongsheng residents even today still speak a 15th-century version of the Nanjing dialect. Tourists from modern Nanjing can recognize this.

Kunming, on the other hand, has a strong northern element both in its dialect, which is close to Mandarin, and its people. This was the place where the Ming court dispatched its political exiles and troublesome intellectuals. The Qing government did the same.

THE SPREAD OF HAN CULTURE

The Middle Kingdom's enormous prestige, especially in times of strong dynastic empires, ensured a major cultural influence throughout the Periphery. Until Islam reached the far west of China, there was no real competition. Dai, Zhuang, Qiang-dominated states in the Zhou Dynasty, and the non-Han competitors of the Warring States Period and the border kingdoms after China's unification, aped the institutions and symbolism of the Celestial Empire even when, as with Nanzhao, they stubbornly maintained their independence.

Though Nanzhao's religion was heavily influenced from India, no major cultural rival existed yet in the lands south of Nanzhao. The multi-ethnic state never developed a distinct cultural identity of its own, and the only way it could become a powerful state was to expand into the rich, productive lands of its rival—China. Nanzhao did periodically march into Sichuan and Guizhou, and even transferred great numbers of the conquered territory's native population back to Nanzhao. But this only furthered the advance of sinicization.

The conquest of Dali and the incorporation of Yunnan into the empire in 1253 (and later under the Ming) only affected those parts of the population long sinicized or, in the west, those having long interaction with the Chinese state. Ming-era migration into those parts of the province was heavy. But the Ailao and Wuliang Mountains still acted as a barrier to Han expansion. South of these mountains lay the tropics, with malaria-infested plains. And in the northwest the only Han were soldiers charged with keeping the frontier safe from bandits, mostly Khampa Tibetans.

In the remote counties, where the imperial government had installed its tusis, the Han believed that once the tribal chiefs were won over to the Han way of doing things, they would promote their own people's assimilation. Besides patronizing tribal leaders, the government tried to install Han-style education into the areas. Viewing this as a cultural assault, however, many a tusi resisted. Opposition to assimilation was especially adamant in the northern Yi areas and among the Dai of the southwest, with their very different, equally sophisticated, Southeast Asian heritage.

Elsewhere Han influence spread with the development of commerce. Han migrants opened businesses in every major town. Unused to business per se themselves, many tribal peoples feared not the wrath of the Chinese military expedition so much as the craftiness of the Chinese trader. As time passed and the Han presence became familiar in most frontier areas, this suspicion eased. The eventual spread of education and administrative control, and nowadays of television and cinema, caused greater absorption. Only the most remote areas are still relatively free of the Chinese cultural impact.

MODERN TIMES

Han immigrants continued coming to Yunnan in the Qing Dynasty (1644–1911), but at a reduced rate. After the suppression of the Muslim Revolt, the province was slow to recover and in no condition to welcome, for example, refugees from the collapse of the Taiping Rebellion. The declining power of the Qing Dynasty meant the court was in no position to sponsor Yunnan's recovery. The province did not really attract outsiders again until World War II. Many of those who fled to Yunnan from the eastern provinces stayed on after the war, increasing the proportion of Han in the population.

With the end of the Civil War and the post-1949 development of Yunnan, more outsiders moved in. Now the Han settled in some of the remoter areas, too, staffing the administrative, education and security organizations. Immigrant farmers from Guizhou and Sichuan also set up new rural settlements. When the central government launched Deng's reforms in 1979, more Han, especially from Sichuan, moved to Yunnan for business reasons or to look for jobs in the expanding economy. But the proportion of Han to non-Han in Yunnan has been constant for decades.

PROVINCIAL PRIDE

Today the majority of Yunnan's Han are descendants of the Ming-era immigrants, who were hardy pioneers in their day, settling a distant land that only recently had become part of China. A measure of this frontier spirit persists today in the special attachment the Yunnanese have towards their homeland. It was the last Han-majority province to enter the Chinese body politic. With its unique geographical variety and large ethnic diversity, it differs from other Chinese provinces and its people have so imbibed these aspects of Yunnan that they refer to the rest of China as *wai sheng*—the outer provinces.

Ever since the 1980s and the economic reforms, Chinese in the 'outer provinces' have been on the move, migrating from village to town, from northern provinces to southern ones, from western areas to eastern areas, and also in the opposite directions, in the belief that the grass is always greener on the other side of the boundary.

Yunnanese mostly stay put. Of all the provinces in China, including the rich southeastern ones, Yunnanese would rather live in Yunnan than anywhere else. In chance encounters in the restaurants, a traveller finds that the more familiar he or she is with the sights of the province, the happier the local companion becomes, as if flattered personally by the attention the traveller has given to his beloved homeland.

CHARACTER TRAITS

Beyond provincial pride, the average Yunnanese is contented with life, be it as a farmer or as someone involved in business, industry or administration. This gives them a sense of self-confidence, which has a beneficial effect on their view of foreign visitors. They do not shy away from them (although they may ignore them) and the typical quick encounter is polite and often friendly.

Enjoying a continuous prosperity, the Yunnanese have, at least in the cities, adopted all the trappings of modern life. Dance halls, cinemas and karaoke bars provide options for entertainment, yet nearly every town has a park of some sort where men bring their caged songbirds, and hang them on the branches to provide a natural serenade while they play board games, chat with one another or just sit and smoke, lost in contemplation.

In the mornings those parks, and perhaps the temple compound as well, become venues for mass tai chi exercises and other fitness routines. In Kunming this includes ballroom dancing, with mostly middle-aged partners, to the sound of portable cassette players. This will take place adjacent to groups doing slow-motion kung fu or sword-wielding. Besides exercise, the other,

A Dai woman's intricate silver hair ornament is representative of the handicraft skills common to Yunnan's many ethnic minorities.

perhaps more important motive is to meet fellow singles of the opposite sex, for most dancers are divorced or widowed. The collective dances thus are key social events for the lonely hearts, places where one can meet prospective lovers on one's own, for free.

Yunnanese are very health-conscious by nature. At big meals various dishes are included because they are good for the health, as are certain beverages. Blind masseurs provide services for the stiff and the sore in city streets in the evenings. Others offer passers-by a thorough cleansing of the ears, holding aloft the long swabs they use. Local television stations air health shows often and every Yunnanese is aware of the province's reputation as a pharmacological treasurehouse. Shops selling 'Yunnan Rare Drugs' abound. And on market days in the hills and remote areas merchants selling herbal medicine always turn up.

In personal relations the Yunnanese consider themselves liberal, tolerant, straightforward, polite and honest. At least these are the traits they consider most worth having. In their treatment of guests they are almost ceremonious in their attention to the guest's comfort. With those people they find most enjoyable, Han or minority people, even foreign, they will form a strong friendship. Yunnanese take their friendships seriously and a new friend finds the way open to more new friends as a result. Unlike neighbouring countries, where close friendships are mainly limited to parties of long acquaintance, Yunnanese friendships cross the boundaries of class, age, sex, race and nation.

The general broad-mindedness of the Yunnanese also means a respectful attitude towards the minorities. They have interacted with them for many centuries and for 50 years the government has drummed into the people the concept of the equality of nationalities. Besides, the minority presence is a big part of what makes Yunnan special to the Yunnanese. They are less likely to look down on the minorities, and in the age of tourism have come to appreciate them more.

Towards the foreigner the Yunnanese attitude is generally favourable. The province did not suffer humiliations from foreigners as did other parts of China in the last decades of the Qing Dynasty. Apart from individual explorers, some missionaries and a handful of scientists, Yunnan's first experience with foreigners came with World War II. And those foreigners were there to help Yunnan, not plunder it. Contemporary travellers are all beneficiaries of their legacy.

The Ethnic Mosaic

THE VARIETY

Variety is the principal component in any description of Yunnan's ethnic minorities. Inhabiting the highest mountains to the lowest valleys, and every kind of location in between, in all sorts of ecological and climatic conditions, ethnic minorities engage in many different lifestyles throughout the province. They are all heirs to old and independently developed cultures that have ordered their lives for many centuries. Customs and traditions have forged their identities as separate peoples, distinct from one another even in those areas occupied by more than one of them.

Migrations from all directions into Yunnan, combined with the geographical diversity, account for this variety. Yunnan has 24 officially recognized minority nationalities (*shaoshu minzu*). Some are minor spillover populations from neighbouring provinces. Others are small and confined to particular localities. But others are large, spread over several prefectures, and comprise many sub-groups. Until recently most minorities have lived relatively isolated from the mainstream of historical events. Levels of economic development, as well as cultural achievements, vary enormously from remote area denizens, who supplement simple farming with hunting and gathering, to sophisticated plains dwellers with cities and traditions of art and literature.

Most ethnic minorities have evolved their own particular religious systems, animist with ancestral veneration. The unseen forces in nature, from the benevolent to the dangerous, are all classified as spirits, sometimes with given names. Customs, taboos and rituals are devised as the people's means to deal with these spirits, to keep them placated, or to propitiate them, so that they do not upset the harmony of life; these spirits can cause epidemics, make people ill or weak, start fires, send down storms, arrange for droughts or blights and make other mischief. Societies have their own specialists who conduct rituals and communicate with the spirit world to insure that life proceeds without problems, either by preventive measures or by remedial action for anything disharmonious in their environment, from illness to crop failure.

Most of the traditional cultures are animist, but some follow the large, organized religions. Here and there are Christian communities, the fruits of successful missionary work during the last decades of Western colonial empires. The Hui are Muslim Chinese, but they are not the only Islamic community, for there are Dai Muslims in Xishuangbanna and Tibetan Muslims

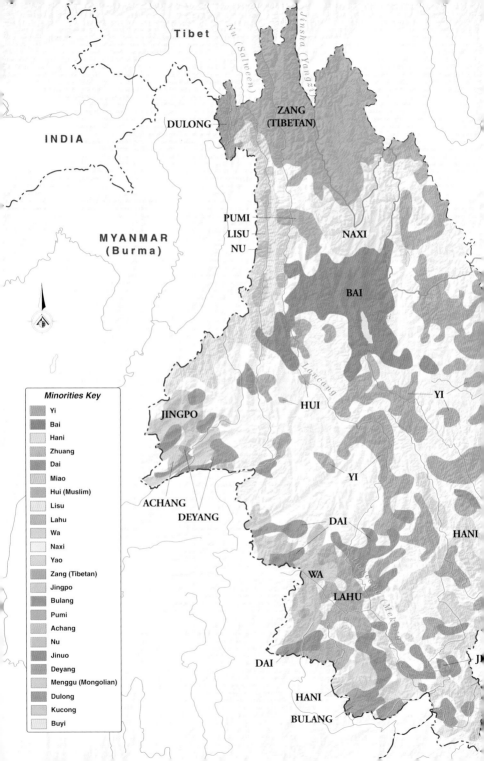

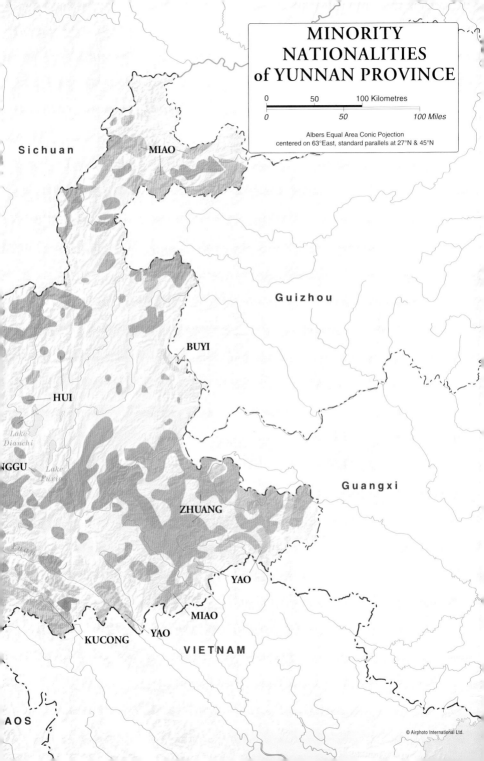

MINORITY
NATIONALITIES
of YUNNAN PROVINCE

0	50	100 Kilometres

0	50	100 Miles

Albers Equal Area Conic Pojection
centered on 63°East, standard parallels at 27°N & 45°N

Sichuan

MIAO

Guizhou

BUYI

HUI

Lake
Dianchi

NGGU

Lake
Fuxia

Guangxi

ZHUANG

YAO

MIAO

KUCONG   YAO

VIETNAM

AOS

© Airphoto International Ltd.

in Diqing. Several minorities are Buddhist, but of three kinds—Theravada, Mahayana and Tantric—the practices of all three are laced with Daoist or ancient animist aspects.

With a population of over 4.7 million the Yi are Yunnan's largest minority, with over 25 sub-groups scattered over all sections of the province except the southwest. Large numbers live in Sichuan, too, and small groups in Guizhou and Guangxi, making them China's fourth biggest nationality. The Bai, with over 1.5 million, are the second largest, living mostly in the west. The Hani, at 1.4 million, inhabit the Ailao Mountains and the hills in the south to the borders of Southeast Asia. The Zhuang, the nation's most numerous minority group, number over 1.1 million in Yunnan. Most of them live in Wenshan, but small communities live quite far from there, such as Ninglang County in the northwest and Pu'er in the south. The Dai, nearly as numerous, rank next, inhabiting the southwest and south-central areas. Those in Ailaoshan and Honghe Prefecture are mostly animist, the other Dai primarily Buddhist. The Miao, with just over one million, reside mainly in the eastern half of the province but, like the Zhuang, have migrated in small groups to more distant places like Jingdong and Lijiang. The Hui, at 640,000, also live largely in the eastern and central prefectures, but have large communities in Dali and Baoshan Prefectures and small numbers in every major town.

Other minorities are less dispersed. The 600,000 Lisu live mainly in the far west. The 450,000 Lahu are in the southwest, from western Xishuangbanna to southern Lincang Prefectures. The 380,000 Wa are in the mountains of the southwest border with Myanmar. The nearly 300,000 Naxi dominate Lijiang County and spill over into the adjacent counties of the northwest. The 190,000 Yao are in the south and southeast. The 130,000 Tibetans are almost all in Diqing Prefecture. The 90,000 Bulang live in western Xishuangbanna and southern Lincang. The 55,000 Buyi all live in Qujing Prefecture, near the eastern provincial border.

Even smaller groups exist as distinct nationalities, confined to even smaller areas, or living in groups of villages among larger nationalities. The Achang, with 33,500, live only in two Dehong counties. The Pumi, with 33,000, are split between Ninglang and Lanping Counties. Most of the 28,000 Mongolians live in Tonghai County. The 27,000 Nu only live in the upper Nujiang area. The 20,000 Jinuo inhabit two counties in Xishuangbanna. The 18,000 De'ang are clustered in a few southwestern counties. The 12,500 Shui are near the junction of Yunnan, Guizhou and Guangxi. The 6,000 Dulong inhabit the valley of the same name in the remote northwest, west of the Nujiang.

CLASSIFICATION

All ethnic minorities have their own name for themselves, which may not be the name they are known by today. Early Chinese writers tended to lump Yunnan's tribes into three groups: the Qiang, the Wu-man and the Bai-man. The Qiang today are a recognized separate nationality, but in ancient times the term covered a number of western mountain tribes who were neither Han nor Tibetan. The Wu-man were the darker ethnic groups, today identified with Yi groups, Hani, Lisu or Lahu, while the lighter-skinned Bai-man were the Dai and Zhuang, and perhaps the Bai. As Chinese writers became more familiar with the non-Han peoples of the southwest, these broader classifications broke down into specific, separate names. As time went on and more isolated peoples were discovered, the list of names grew longer and more complicated.

After the establishment of the People's Republic in 1949, the government undertook the task of reclassifying the minorities. Peoples were grouped together as members of an individual minority nationality on the basis of origin and history, language, culture and religion. The Hui, who are Chinese Muslims, are the only minority classified strictly on the basis of religion. Common origins, linguistic affinities and culture have been the main factors in determining whether ethnic groups were a separate nationality or a branch of one. Thus, for example, the people of Xiaoliangshan who call themselves Nosu, a semi-pastoral group who also raise potatoes and buckwheat as staples, were grouped together with the terrace-builders of Ailaoshan, who call themselves Nisu, Alu or Blan. All are branches of the Yi because of roughly the same origin myths, basic cultural similarities like the role of *bimaw*, or ritual specialists, and languages that were recognized as dialects of the same tongue.

Sometimes one factor outweighed the others in the reckoning process. The Mosuo of Lugu Lake and Ninglang County, for example, are officially a branch of the Naxi, although they are matrilineal and tantrists, unlike the Naxi, and their dialect differs not only in nearly all the vocabulary, but also in grammatical elements, such as the interrogative form. Yet because they are both descended from a people to the northwest who divided into two streams, one to Yongning, one to Lijiang, they are both classified as Naxi. To complicate matters, the Mosuo who live just across the border in Sichuan province are officially considered Mongols (Menggu).

A few of the smaller ethnic groups were not immediately recognized as separate nationalities. The Pumi achieved official recognition only in 1962, the Mongolians and Jinuo in 1979. Some never got it, like the Kami of Mengla County, who look and live like the Dai. Others were classified as a sub-group

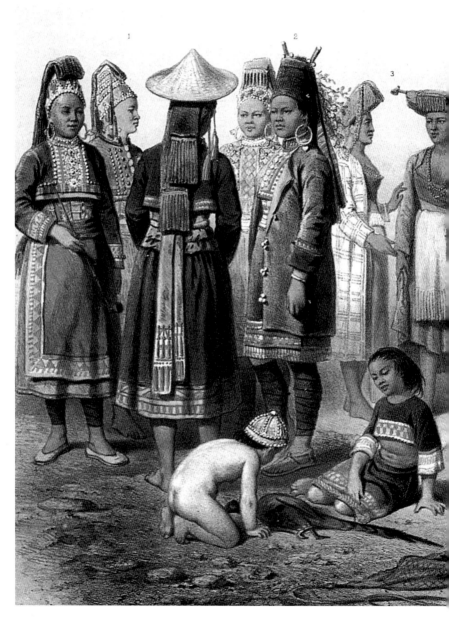

Mixed populations of Southern Yunnan drawn in the mid-19th century for the Mekong Exploration Commission Report of Louis Delaporte and Francis Garnier.

Delaporte wrote this, "On the right side, there is a family of fishermen from Che-pin Lake.
Then a native of Talan and his wife. The last group shows women of the Pa-y race."

of a recognised minority, like the Kucong of Jinping and southeastern Mengla, who are officially a branch of the Lahu, though the nearest Lahu are a few hundred kilometres away.

For two generations now the classification and official naming of the ethnic minorities has held without change, other than additions of late recognition. It has been accepted by the minorities themselves, who use the names, especially when talking to outsiders. The Xishuangbanna Hani branch call themselves Akha. Their language is *Akha do*. Their traditional rules of behaviour are called *Akhazang*. But Chinese classifiers gave them the name Aini because Akha sounded too similar to a derogatory word in local Dai. With each other they use the word Akha, but with outsiders refer to themselves as Aini.

The De'ang used to be known as Benglong, but contemporary De'ang don't use that name anymore. Nor do any but the elderly Mosuo refer to themselves as Hlikhî, as they all did a generation ago. For centuries people knew the Yi of the northwest as the Lolo. But that term also has derogatory connotations, so the name Yi was bestowed. The Yi in northwest Chuxiong Prefecture, however, still call themselves Lolopo. The Pumi were known as Hsi-fan, and are still called that by some of their neighbours, but not by the Pumi themselves.

LANGUAGES

Most Yunnan languages belong to the Sino-Tibetan linguistic family, in four different groups: Zhuang-Dong (or Tai-Kedai), Tibeto-Burman, Miao-Yao and Chinese (Sinitic). In the first group, the Zhuang, Dai and Buyi tongues are in the Zhuang-Dai branch and Shui is in the Dong-Shui branch. Within the Tibeto-Burman group, Tibetan is in one branch, Jingpo and Dulong are in the Jingpo branch, Pumi is in the Qiang branch and Nu and Achang belong to no particular branch. The Yi branch comprises Yi, Lisu, Naxi, Hani, Lahu and Jinuo. Within the Miao-Yao group, all the Miao dialects are in one branch, all the Yao dialects in the other. The Chinese group includes the Chinese spoken by the Hui—and of course the Han—and Manchu is spoken by a few city dwellers.

The Bai language has not been definitively placed. About one-third of its vocabulary is taken from Chinese and its word order is, like Chinese, subject-verb-object. All Tibeto-Burman languages, with which it was once classified, run subject-object-verb. One language outside the Sino-Tibetan family is the Mongolian dialect in Tonghai, a member of the Ural-Altaic family. The Mon-Khmer linguistic family includes Wa, Bulang and De'ang.

Among the larger minority nationalities, each language has dialects. Yi has six, for example, and even within one dialect the variation in vocabulary, thanks to centuries of isolation, can be great. Local peculiarities affect all dialects of all the major Yunnan languages. Sometimes people speaking the same official dialect have trouble understanding others of the same dialect from a hundred kilometres away. Loan words, especially, tend to vary, depending on the identity of the nearest neighbour. Some Hani loan words are taken from the Dai, others from Chinese, others from Yi. Loan words in Jingpo or Wa tend to be taken from Dai. Lisu, Miao and Yao tend to take new words from Chinese.

Until recent decades and the spread of Chinese-style education, most minority societies were illiterate in their own languages. The better educated were taught in Chinese, not in their own tongues. Few languages developed alphabets and only the Dai alphabets, one in Xishuangbanna and a different one in Dehong, were for general, secular use. Other alphabets were only intelligible to religious specialists.

Tibetan has an alphabet, but for the Lhasa dialect, which is almost unintelligible to the Diqing Tibetans, and so the alphabet is only useful to monks and lamas who have studied in Lhasa. Government office signs are bilingual, but the average Diqing Tibetan can more likely read Chinese than Tibetan.

The Yi alphabet, an ancient syllabic script whose letters resemble the simplest Chinese ideographs, was intelligible only to the *bimaw*, the ritual specialist who was custodian of the Yi books. In recent decades, though, Yi scholars in Sichuan standardized the script, compiled a gargantuan Yi-Chinese dictionary and soon Yi-run publishing houses began putting out books in Yi. Some of these were textbooks used in experimental bilingual schools, wherein the Yi language and script are also taught. One such successful school is in Bainiuchang, in Ninglang County.

The Naxi religious specialist, the *dongba*, used books written in an archaic pictographic script, supplemented by marks that indicated pronunciation or grammatical elements. The pictographs did not work the same as Egyptian hieroglyphics, however. They summarised the content, serving as much as mnemonic devices as narrative.

Shamans among the Shui used a text for divination that employed a script of about 100 characters, as well as a set of pictographs. Some of the characters were Chinese ideographs, some were adapted, or rendered upside down, or were altogether new inventions.

Missionaries in the 19th and early 20th centuries devised scripts for their converts' languages, based on Latin letters, with tones indicated sometimes by letters at the end of each syllable, sometimes by diacritical marks. Reversed and upside-down letters indicated vowel sounds that were unlike the standard Latin ones. The main purpose was to translate and print Christian literature in

Mixed populations of Northern Yunnan drawn in the mid-19th century for the Mekong Exploration Commission Report of Louis Delaporte and Francis Garnier.

Delaporte wrote, "The family of natives on the left of the plate are from the village of Nga-
da-ti on the road to Dali. The two women in the middle are Lisu women from Ma-chang.
The other figure is a Man-tse with a pointed turban. The seated women are Sifans and on
the right is an Y-kia and his wife, both from Ma-chang."

the native language. After 1949 the government employed linguists to devise scripts, again using Latin letters, for all minority languages lacking a writing system.

Types of Housing

Most ethnic minority people live in the rural parts of Yunnan, in villages or hamlets. The family house or compound is the norm, rather than the apartment buildings that dominate the towns and cities. On the high plains and secluded valleys of the northern half of the province, minority people's houses usually resemble those of their Han neighbours. The typical rural Yunnanese compound is made of mud brick, with wooden posts, doors, beams and floors, with moderately sloping roofs of fired clay tiles. Among the Han and those people with Han-style ancestral veneration traditions, inside the front door the family ancestral altar stands against the back wall of the front room. This also serves as a receiving room for guests and sometimes as the family dining room. Besides the kitchen, the other rooms, including some rooms upstairs, are bedrooms. Other second floor rooms are used for storage.

A mud brick wall, 1.5–2 metres high, topped by tiles or pine boughs to protect it from the rain, encloses a yard adjacent to the house. Here the farmer keeps his animals, so a cattle shed, pigpen or chicken coop may stand within. In the front part of the wall is the entry gate, usually roofed and sometimes sporting decorative carvings on the struts and brackets. Houses are close to one another in most villages, separated by narrow stone paths (paved in richer villages), but the enclosed yard affords a measure of privacy.

Variations exist in this pattern. The bricks are not always baked and sometimes they are made of clay. Usually houses stand on stone foundations, but in recent years new houses have begun using cement for the foundation (and sometimes the whole building). In the northwest the walls are constructed of rammed earth. The building crew places two long parallel boards on the ground spaced as far apart as the desired width of the wall. Then men and women bring baskets full of dirt and empty them into the trench between the boards. Other men stand above the filled trench and pound the dirt with poles to pack it tight. When it reaches the level of the top of the boards they remove the boards and remount them one width higher. The new trough is filled, rammed tight and so on until the wall is finished. The last task is to tamp down the sides to give them a smooth finish.

Northwest Yunnan has more architectural diversity concentrated in the two prefectures of Lijiang and Diqing than anywhere else in the province. Every major ethnic group has its own house type. On the Tibetan Plateau two basic house types are in use. On the plains of Zhongdian County (now Shangri-La), the Tibetans build broad, two-storey houses with big wooden posts, thick walls, fairly flat roofs of wood tiles, within a yard enclosed by a compound wall. People ascend to the second floor to a capacious receiving room with a fairly high ceiling, fireplace, wooden cabinets and low tables, with wooden water buckets and butter churns in the corners. Yaks and cattle live underneath, ponies, pigs, chickens and dogs in the yard. The outer walls are whitewashed and windows are small, but often covered with carved and painted screens. Tibetans in the more mountainous Diqing County use the same materials and also whitewash the outer walls. But their houses are bigger, quadrangular, often three stories high and with two or more cubicles standing at the corners of the flat roof. Homes here look more like fortresses.

Off the plateau, the Yi and Mosuo traditionally favour the log cabin. First they cut the logs to size and mark them with numbers to indicate their order. When constructing the house they lay the logs at right angles, notched into each other, not nailed. The slightly angled roofs are of wooden tiles and held down with stones. Among the Yi a rail fence encloses a large compound yard, part of which is allotted to vegetable patches, and houses stand far apart. Mosuo cabins are larger but compounds smaller and usually close to each other. The biggest building is the single-storey main house, while the auxiliary buildings are two stories.

In Lijiang, the old town of Dayan is an exhibit of classic Chinese urban architecture—wood and stone, tile roofs, sliding doors, small walled compounds with ornate gates and interior gardens. At each apex of the roof a carved, often painted, symbolic pair of fish hangs down. Some are stylized shapes. Some are quite detailed. The fish represents water and is supposed to magically protect the house from the fire of the lightning demon. Occasionally these are yin-yang symbols instead. If they are staunch Party supporters, house owners hang up red stars, just as they replaced portraits of the traditional door gods on the front gate with posters of Red Army soldiers.

Bai architecture is distinguished from Naxi by its preponderant use of stone. Around Dali it could even be marble, for the area was long ago famous for its marble. In fact, the Chinese word for it literally means 'Dali stone'. Consequently, though the Bai use wood on the front walls and compound gates, the prevailing colour is light grey, in contrast to the dark red of Dayan's homes. For their houses, the Bai roof the compound wall with grey tiles and paint arabesques below the house roof apex. The front gate is often elaborately carved and painted and sometimes, especially in the Dali area, so are the posts and doors of the front wall of the house itself.

In the mountains of central Yunnan, particularly in Yi villages, the mud-brick houses are quadrangular, with the interior central part open to the sky.

The main receiving room is behind this open, usually sunken courtyard and the kitchen is to the side. Sleeping rooms are upstairs and the flat roofs are used for drying crops. It's possible to reach the end of the block by stepping from roof to roof, as Yi houses are packed against each other and have no adjacent yards.

Ailaoshan dwellings, Dai in the valleys, Yi, Hani and others in the hills, are mud-brick houses on stone foundations. Roofs are flat, also used for drying crops, but part of each roof is surmounted by an extra room, with a sharply sloped thatched roof. The hearth and brick oven of the kitchen is just inside the doorway. The first room is the receiving room. Behind it lies the parents' bedroom. Other rooms are for sleeping or storage.

South and southwest, the proportion of wood increases and bamboo is also employed. The Dai houses of Dehong and Lincang are clay-brick and rest on the ground. But their hill neighbours use wood and bamboo and raise the house on stilts, with thatched or wooden tiles for the roof. Lincang Wa houses have tall, steeply sloped, thatched roofs that overhang nearly to the ground. A tablet-shaped section is cut away in front of the steps to the front door. But in Simao the Wa roofs are less angled, the houses stand slightly higher off the ground, and they have an attached balcony of split bamboo. This is the same model for the Aini houses of Xishuangbanna, which, however, often have wood tile roofs in the manner of the Dai houses in the plains.

Dai in Banna lived in wooden houses on stilts with rail fences around the compound. This is still the style in remoter villages, but in the past decade the Dai have replaced wood with brick and installed high brick walls around their yards. The new houses are raised on brick piles, but the general shape and the sloping, wood-tiled roofs remain. The classic, broad wooden house, raised on stilts, is still popular among some of the Zhuang of Wenshan, who also have those on the ground, as well as brick ones in the eastern townships, but smaller and different in appearance from the Han brick houses.

ETHNIC COSTUMES

Distinctive costumes, often colourful, are the most immediately appreciated aspect of minority nationality cultures. Each of the 24 nationalities has its own traditional clothing and within each minority the various sub-groups all have separate styles, in many cases a totally different look than that of their ethnic cousins. Furthermore, each sub-group prescribes the clothing components by sex as well as age, and sometimes by rank, role or status. The diversity of ethnic costumes in Yunnan surpasses even that of languages.

Ethnic styles have changed over the centuries, for they have always depended upon the type and availability of materials as much as their use. With

Yi villages in Honghe, as well as Dai villages along the Red River, feature flat roofs which are used for drying crops and laundry.

A Mosuo log cabin along the shores of Lugu Lake.

modern communications in place throughout the province, more and different materials can be purchased in markets now, and the end of isolation means exposure to new influences and the almost inevitable change in aesthetic taste. The most obvious example of new influences has been the increased use of colour. Aniline dyes have produced a greater range of colours for both cloth and thread than the limited natural dyes procurable in any one minority-inhabited area. Textile mills produce cotton and woollen cloth cheaply and women who would have had to weave it at home a generation or two ago can now buy it at the store.

The markets also stock huge amounts of inexpensive, modern-style clothing and many minority people have come to prefer this to their own traditional costumes. Or they mix the new with the old. In general, men have abandoned their traditional costumes and dress like the Han men in towns, or they wear surplus military clothing. Around the world, men are the first to give up their ethnic costumes. They are outside the village more, more likely to know the majority community's language and understand the comments about them in the towns, more apt to conceal their ethnic identity in social or commercial encounters so as to become part of the anonymous mainstream. In Yunnan, the only minority men who may still dress in their ethnic style are the Tibetans, the Dulong, the Lisu, some northern Yi groups and the Yao. But among the rest, many men will carry their ethnic group's shoulder bag or keep a set of traditional garments for special occasions like the biggest annual festival, weddings or funerals.

Some ethnic groups are more fashion-conservative than others. In Zhaotong Prefecture, on the walls of a 3rd century Han prince's tomb, is a mural that depicts the sundry peoples of the vicinity who attended the funeral. The Yi are easy to recognize, for the male figures wear wide-legged trousers and big turbans. The women wear ankle-length skirts and wide-brimmed hats, and both sexes wear long capes. This is essentially the same costume worn by the Yi today in the same prefecture, plus across the border in Daliangshan, Sichuan, and in Xiaoliangshan, Ninglang County. Not quite so ancient evidence in the form of illustrations, made by the official artist Louis Delaporte on the French Mekong Expedition in the 1860s, show that the basic components of Miao, Aini and Red Lahu have not changed since then.

In other cases the changes are within the cultural aesthetic milieu. The availability of so many colours of thread has led to an explosion in colour. Among those groups where tradition has remained strong—various Yi, Hani and Miao in particular—the younger generation of female embroiderers do more outstanding work than their mothers. Occasionally the youth add to the costume. The Huayao Yi girls, when fully dressed in heavily embroidered vest, hat and belt with big wide ends that drape over the buttocks, add one item their mothers never wore—a narrow tasseled sash, also fully embroidered, which is tucked into the belt at the sides.

Not all cloth production has been left to the mills. For reasons of economics or just personal preference, women in various parts of the province still weave their own cloth. Some spin the thread and dye it, too. Thread can be cotton, wool or hemp, the latter the most laborious to produce, requiring a long series of washings in various solutions before the hemp stalks are finally transformed into something which can be spun.

Wool thread comes from sheep and is used by the northern Yi to weave the more expensive types of capes. The cheaper variety uses felt wool. Tibetans also use wool thread for knitted mufflers and sweaters, like all people in the colder parts of Yunnan, but also for weaving wide woollen belts and for carpets.

Two basic loom types exist in the province: the simple backstrap loom and the wooden-framed, larger loom with bench. The first type consists of a set of bamboo sticks, the backstrap and a wooden beating sword. Fully portable, it can be set up anywhere. Those used in Yunnan produce cloth up to 50 cm wide and make anything from belts to sarongs. The woman winds the thread around the end stick, then around the stick nearest her. Thinner sticks go at spots in between the weaver and the end stick, which is mounted on a post, wall or tree up to two metres away. One stick is employed as a continuous string heddle, which separates every other thread and enables the weaver to open a shed in the warp, through which she slips the weft thread on a shuttle. The beating sword is used to bunch the weft threads firmly against each other. Tension is maintained by the weaver herself, as she leans against the strap that connects to the warp stick nearest her. The Wa, Nu, Jingpo, Jinuo and some Yi use this type of loom.

Other weavers of the Dai, Yi, Miao, Buyi, Hani and Zhuang use a larger, wooden-frame loom that usually sits on the front porch or just inside the house, beside a window. A much longer bolt of cloth is possible on one of these looms, 50 metres or more, for the warp threads are wrapped around a cylinder at the far end. They are first passed through a reed to keep them separate and in order. Then they are inserted through two or four sets of loop heddles, one by one, which are connected to foot-operated treadles. By depressing one or one pair of treadles, the weaver opens the shed, shoots the weft shuttle through and pulls the reed towards her to knock it into place. The use of four shafts, which can create more complex textures, is less widespread.

Besides embroidered patterns and pictures, minorities embellish their

*Hongtou Yao women in Jinping elaborately
embroider their shoulder bags in bright, flashy colours.*

Lahu girls in Menglian adorned in their traditional attire.

*Huayao Yi means 'Flowery Waist', after the lush and colourful
embroidery on costume components around the midriff.*

costumes with silver studs, coins, badges and ornaments, cowry shells, Job's tear seeds, beads, animal fur, feathers and shiny green beetle wings. Silver is the preferred metal of ornamentation for most minorities. Gold is popular among the Dai. Most minority women wear fancy headdresses. Sometimes the style indicates marital status. With some of the most assimilated groups, this is the last component of the traditional costume retained, as a kind of ethnic badge for those women unwilling to sinicize or modernize completely. In other places it's the shoulder bag. But in a surprisingly large percentage of communities, the traditional costume, among the women anyway, is still the norm for everyday wear. In such areas ethnic pride is at its strongest.

ARTS AND CRAFTS

In terms of hand-crafted arts, many of the minority women's costumes are themselves works of art. While closely resembling other costumes of the same sub-group, the artistic tradition still allows room for individualist touches in making choices among embroidery patterns or decorative embellishments. Military-style uniformity is not the tribal way. The general style sets the limits. The details are left to the individual.

Many of the minority women's costumes are definitely attractive, but do not require much work or activity to create them. The truly artistic minority women are from those groups in which a proper costume takes a long time to make, such as the full year required for a Huayao Yi girl's costume, and she only embroiders the cloth and doesn't have to make it. Most Miao, some of the Zhuang, the non-Buddhist Dai, the central and southern Yi, some Yao groups, the Aini in Xishuangbanna and Simao, certain Honghe Hani and the Bai around Dali all emphasize embroidery. The beauty of women's clothes is locally judged by the artistry of the embroidery.

In a few cases it's the beauty of the batik. This is also a long and involved process, in which the intended design is laid onto the cloth in wax. When the cloth is dyed the wax prevents the dye from touching the design, which then comes out white when the cloth is rinsed and the wax removed. The Miao have been the leading specialists of this art, using the finished cloth for their skirts. Nowadays, though, factories are producing the same designs by printing. Rolls of this cloth are sold in the markets in Miao areas. The original technique is also practised by Yi groups in the south and southeast.

Another method of putting designs or pictures on cloth is the tie-dye technique. This means tying knots in the white cloth, immersing it in the dye, usually indigo, then after rinsing untying the knots. Where the ties bind the cloth the dye doesn't reach, so when untied the cloth shows the pattern in white. The Bai around Dali are especially good at this, though except for headscarves and the occasional vest cloth they don't use it much themselves. But they turn out piles of cloth pictures and rolls of material for making clothes, both products aimed at the tourist market. Another group employing the technique is a Hani sub-group in Yuanyang County, who attach a tie-dyed strip of cloth to the front of their jackets.

Besides personal adornment, ethnic minority handicrafts include articles of mundane domestic use and the plastic arts employed in spiritual works. A good sense of design and ingenuity are evident in the use of local materials like bamboo, wood and clay to make the utensils and containers of everyday use. Mountain people cut sections of bamboo to make cups and drinking mugs, outfitting some with handles. The Jingpo beer mug may also sport designs painted on it in black, like a sunrise or a pair of crossed machetes. The ubiquitous bamboo also serves as building material for houses and bridges in the south, as well as spoons, dippers and chopsticks. Split into thin strips bamboo can be woven into baskets, fish traps, rice dishes, small round and oval containers, dinner tables and sitting mats. The Dai and the hill dwellers of the south and southwest are particularly adept at bamboo work. The Dai also make the best clay water containers, with incised or painted surface designs.

Further north, wood is the main material for cups, bowls, ladles, trays, buckets and butter churns. The Naxi chisel and carve simple bowls, plates and thick cups from blocks of wood. The Tibetans and Yi use lathes to shape the wood. The former also inlay the cups and bowls with silver and adorn the outside with bands of silver with repoussé designs. The Yi lacquer their wooden vessels and utensils in red, yellow and black colours. Bands of wavy, intersecting lines and spirals decorate the exteriors. One type of wine cup uses an eagle's claw for the base stand, and in the past it could only be used by the Black Yi nobility.

Wood is also a prime building material and posts, doors, gates and windows in some areas are delicately carved. Bai and Tibetan woodcarvers are the best in the province, though Tibetan skills were for the most part confined to religious architecture. Not so with the Bai, who were employed throughout the west for house construction, adorning the homes of the wealthy with wonderfully carved plants and flowers, gibbons and dragons, other animals real and mythical, religious figures and symbols. Even in recent years, Naxi homeowners have hired Bai construction workers from Heqing to make their homes and also to carve the gates, door panels, brackets and windows.

Besides house exteriors, Bai craftsmen also have a reputation for fine furniture, using carved wood in conjunction with marble to make elegant

Baishuitai Naxi dancers at the Zhongdian Horse Races. Minorities are often called upon to provide traditional entertainment at big festivals like this.

(above) Nisu Yi in Yuanyang use pile technique to embroider the broad belt ends that hang over the buttocks. (right) A Huayao Dai weaver at work on a traditional loom.

tables, chairs and benches. Working with marble alone, workers turn out vases, ashtrays, decanters and lamp stands. Dali shops also sell small slabs of marble, often mounted on wooden stands. What makes these slabs attractive is the natural pattern formed by the veins of the stone when it is cut and polished. These often resemble misty mountain ranges, much like a Chinese ink-brushed landscape painting.

One other way in which wood is a medium of art is in block printing. Craftsmen carve low-relief designs and figures on blocks. Smeared with ink, these blocks stamp the design on paper. The resulting print is then mounted on a wall. During Lunar New Year people tack up the block prints over the doorways. The best prints come from the west, particularly Dali and Weishan.

In other places designs are cut from the paper itself. The Dai in Dehong are skilled at this. Using black, gold or white paper they scissor out sections to create silhouetted Buddhist temples, votive objects and peacocks. In the southern counties of Honghe Prefecture, Yi women cut intricate floral, geometric and other designs on strips of paper which they then pin to cloth. Taking a needle and thread, they embroider the cloth according to the designs cut on the paper, removing it afterwards.

The last major Yunnanese arts worth considering are sculpture and painting, both of which have, until recent decades, generally been employed in the service of religion and ritual. Each has a long tradition in the province. The stone sculptures at Shibaoshan, dating from the Nanzhao era (8th and 9th centuries), are the most celebrated works of their kind in Yunnan. Other Nanzhao specimens are on display in other cities, such as the stone pillar at the Kunming City Museum. Later sculptors worked in bronze and samples of their work are on view in Lufeng and Dali museums. In the Ming era, Chinese artisans cast the huge bronze Confucius in Shiyang, Chuxiong, while Dai casters produced Buddha images of various sizes for the temples of the south and southwest.

Dai artists also painted murals on temple walls, depicting the bliss of Heaven and the tortures of Hell, but the work is cruder than that of their ethnic cousins in Laos and Thailand. The best religious murals, however, are in a few old temples in Lijiang. These are large, spectacular works, full of details, which contain elements from the Chinese and Tibetan painting traditions. The Naxi also used to illustrate the covers of their pictographic manuscripts and paint religious figures and symbols on wooden swords, called *khobya*, which were inserted in the burial grounds at funerals.

In contemporary painting, the ethnic influence on the province's art is reflected in the founding and development of the Yunnan School of Painting in the early 1980s. After 1979 painters were freed from the strictures of government policy on art, wherein they were restricted to Han-style landscapes, realistic portraiture or propaganda work. The Yunnan School featured non-realistic portraits, with angular faces and elongated limbs, bold colour contrasts and subject matter and themes drawn from the life and beliefs of the ethnic minorities.

Many such painters came from the south, with a heavy accent in their works on exotic hill folks and slim Dai peasant girls in scenes of lush vegetation. Naxi painters incorporated the style of the dongba pictographs and painted mythical and mystical scenes inspired by tales in the old books. The Yunnan School style has stopped evolving and much of the work now is derivative. But it was a breakthrough in its time and is still eye-catching to those who see samples of it for the first time.

FESTIVALS

Every traditional society has its festivals, which are like public cultural statements. The less assimilated a people, the more festivals and open ceremonies they are likely to have. Even modernized societies stage annual collective events. And the more sinicized ethnic groups in Yunnan retain at least one major traditional festival, providing at least one opportunity every year for people to publicly proclaim their ethnic identity and give vent to the lingering lure of their traditions. For some participants this may be the only occasion they will dress in the ethnic style and sing in their own language, or participate in rituals that they would ordinarily feign not to believe in.

The big festivals stir the ethnic soul because they are such visible reminders of the people's heritage. Collective celebrations reaffirm the solidarity and relationships of family, clan and tribe. They allow the individual to bond with a larger group. They are a venue for the declamation of shared values and ethnic pride. And so they are eagerly anticipated every year, for traditionally only good things happen during festivals. The particular reason for having the festival is almost incidental.

These reasons vary considerably. Some festivals mark seasonal events, like New Year, rice-planting time, harvest, and so on. Others honour particular deities or cultural-historical heroes. Some resemble nature-worship rites, while others feature rituals for ancestral and guardian spirits. Some are for children, or to mark the end of puberty or to honour the elderly. While every big festival by its public nature provides the chance for young love to blossom, some peoples have festivals specifically designed to provoke that.

Except for a few more widely observed festivals like New Year, the Torch Festival of the Yi, Bai and Naxi, the Sanduo Festival of all the Naxi, the Jingpo Munao and the Water-Sprinkling Festival of the De'ang and all Dai groups, most large festivals in the province take place in the restricted areas inhabited by the smaller nationalities. Or else they are celebrated by a single sub-group of a major ethnic community and observed only in one county, maybe even just one particular township.

In many of the autonomous counties and prefectures the biggest annual festival is government subsidized, which usually means the county or prefecture capital sponsors public events like parades and music and dance shows. City authorities arrange accommodation for village performers whom they bus in from distant parts of the county. Shows may also include local primary and middle school troupes, speeches and other non-traditional intrusions, yet the music and dance is authentic, and the ethnic spirit is as evident here as it is in the totally ethnic mountain villages.

Most minority nationality dances are of the line or ring type. Usually the males dance in one group, the females in another. Occasionally the choreography includes arm and body movements in addition to steps. Dances in the north, and those involving both sexes together in the south, are usually vigorous. Slower, more decorative gestures and movements are the feature of Dai women performers. These dances will be accompanied by a small orchestra with flutes, drums, xylophones, bells, etc. The up-tempo group numbers usually have a drummer and one or more on flute, gourd-pipe or three-string guitar.

Tibetan monks and Naxi dongbas stage religious dances. The movements are often slow and deliberate, with exaggerated steps and sword-wielding motions. They are always costumed affairs and in the Tibetan case include dancers wearing large, sometimes grotesque or comical masks.

(previous pages) Yi villagers in Wudi, Chuxiong, dressed as tigers to honour their mythical ancestor, mime farming activities in their annual ritual dance.

THE ETHNIC IMAGE

Music and dance are an integral part of the ethnic image in Yunnan. Not only are they a strong element in minority cultures, they are the easiest things, besides costumes, to identify as ethnic. Hence they are exotic, especially in the eyes of government people and private individuals involved in promoting Yunnan as a tourist destination. Yunnan has been a Chinese province for over seven centuries and has been under Han cultural influence even longer. It is not without its Han cultural achievements—monuments, temples, Ming-era city gates and towers, sculptures and murals. But tourists don't target Yunnan to see the Han legacy, for it is more spectacular elsewhere. Yunnan's scenic attractions are a factor, but many other provinces have such, too. The variety offered in Yunnan may be greater, but that is always viewed in conjunction with the province's principal feature—the variety of its ethnic minorities.

The ethnic image pervades Kunming and the major tourist destinations of Jinghong, Luxi, Dali, Lijiang and Zhongdian. Billboards showcase costumed minorities. Hotels dress their staff in the ethnic style. Big restaurants stage floor shows twice a day wherein most acts are minority dances. Tour company brochures and advertising posters emphasize the colour and entertainment of ethnic costumes and dances. Everywhere the ethnic minorities are presented as a feast for the eyes and ears.

But is this exploitation? The minorities themselves don't think so. The women don't wear their costumes because tourists like them, but because they themselves like them. In general, they view tourist interest in them as flattering, rather than annoying. The proliferation of ethnic entertainment shows they consider a growing recognition of the value of minority music and dance. In addition, the recruitment of ethnic minority entertainers means more people will be involved in the preservation of their culture.

It just so happened that, historically speaking, Yunnan opened its doors to tourism and exposed its minorities to the non-Chinese outsiders at the moment when the minorities had recovered from the assaults on tradition waged by the Cultural Revolution and other past political campaigns. Economically better off than ever before, with their ethnic pride restored and an attitude towards their own traditions that ranges from respectful to revivalist, Yunnan's minorities were quite ready for the Tourist Era.

Snow Peaks to Steamy Jungles

ECOLOGICAL ZONES

Once upon a very distant epoch the great southern continent of Gondwanaland broke apart, dispatching the Indian subcontinent north towards the Asian landmass. Eventually, inching its way across the oceans, riding the restless tectonic plate, the subcontinent crashed into Asia. At the point of direct impact the invading subcontinent punched against the plate on which Asia rested and forced up the land at its edge, creating the Himalaya Mountains. The land behind the mountains rose to become the Tibet-Qinghai Plateau. The land over a thousand kilometres to the east was also jolted. As a result of the crinkling of the land, mountains rose throughout the area. Rivers that existed before the collision subsequently wore down trenches in these mountains, and formed valleys that separated the mountains into ranges, creating the isolated venues for human settlement many millennia later.

Yunnan is still a seismically active area. The entire northern half of the province particularly suffers the ravages of periodic earthquakes. In recent

(above) The roots from the epiphytes in the branches of these banyan trees in Dehong seem to support their trunks.
(left) Meili Snow Mountain is Yunnan's tallest peak at 6,740 metres high.

times alone a devastating quake struck the west, especially Dali, in 1924. Tonghai was nearly leveled in 1970. A major quake rocked Lijiang in 1996, while in 1998 earthquakes struck Ninglang in the northwest and Xuanwei in the northeast. The south is not exempt from this kind of disaster, for a quake killed scores in Lancang in 1992, and 2007 saw severe damage in the Pu'er region. It does seem, too, that most earthquakes occur in winter, forcing people into the open cold, just as nature takes away their protective shelter.

Yunnan's elevation is highest in the northwest, lowest in the southeast. The land between consists of successively lower plateaux, interspersed with mountain ranges. In the west these run north to south, but the province's two major ranges, Ailaoshan and Wuliangshan, run northwest to southeast. The valleys and plains, too, lie at progressively lower altitudes the further south they are.

The Tropic of Cancer runs right through Mojiang, which is practically in the centre of the province. Thus the province lies in the geographical borderlands of the temperate and tropical zones. Consequently it has an enormous range of ecological niches, from the Arctic zone of the snow mountains' highest slopes to the fully tropical environment of most of Xishuangbanna.

The southeastern corner of the Tibetan Plateau is actually within the boundaries of Yunnan's Diqing Prefecture. At an average altitude of 3,500 metres, the elevated plain of Zhongdian County and the settlements of Diqing County are the highest inhabited zones in the province. The air is thinner, the sky clearer, the climate colder. Up on the mountain slopes, where herders take their yaks, winters are arctic.

Yaks themselves are high-altitude animals, built to live in the thinner air; they cannot survive long in the low-altitude plains and are rarely seen below 2,000 metres. On the Zhongdian County plateau, the alveolar pressure, which measures the amount of oxygen that can reach the bloodstream, is about 60 per cent. People and animals born at sea level have to adjust. Mountain dwellers, on the other hand, have a 20–60 per cent higher concentration of haemoglo-bin-catching red corpuscles in their circulatory systems, enabling them to breathe normally in thinner air.

High mountain plants are stubbier, with thick leaves and long roots. Animals are bigger, with long hair or thick fur. Birds for the most part migrate out of the area with the coming of frost in the autumn.

Just off the plateau the vegetation changes. Forests consist of the tree and animal species associated with the northern temperate zone. Deciduous trees compete with evergreens for space. These become mixed with tropical plants,

THE GEOLOGY OF SOUTHWEST CHINA

The geologic history of Southwest China is certainly one of the most fascinating, complex and scientifically important of any region in the world. By far the most significant event in shaping the major landforms of the area was the collision of the Indian subcontinent with Asia, some 40 to 50 million years ago. Driven by internal forces that are not yet fully understood, a dozen crustal fragments moved slowly across the surface of the Earth. The Indian plate travelled steadily northward at the rate of 15 to 20 centimetres per year, eventually closing the eastern arm of the ancient Sea of Tethys that once lay south of Tibet. It finally rammed into the Asian continent and caused 2,000 kilometres of crustal shortening and compression. India continues its relentless penetration into Asia, but at the slower rate of five centimetres per year.

This titanic collision created tight folds and overlapping crustal slices in the basement rocks of the Asian plate, thus forming the thickest crust (70–80 kilometres) and the highest mountains (the Himalaya) in the world. Mountain-building was not limited to the Himalaya, however, as the highlands of eastern Tibet, western Sichuan and northern Yunnan were all significantly affected. Today, signs of the rapid uplift in these areas can be seen in exceptionally deep gorges, with deposits of alluvial gravel perched several hundred metres above rivers that predated the collision. The rivers eroded downward as quickly as the mountains rose. A marvellous example of this is Tiger Leaping Gorge, where the Upper Yangzi River (*Jinsha Jiang*) has etched a spectacular gorge through 370-million-year-old Devonian marble, 4,000 metres beneath the ice and snow of Yulong Xue Shan, one of Yunnan's highest and most beautiful peaks.

The deformation of Asia as a result of the collision with India does not end here, however. To compensate for the continuing indentation, large blocks of China are slowly being driven outward on its unbounded sides into the basins of the South China Sea and the Pacific Ocean. The resulting horizontal movement has formed structural planes such as the Red River Fault in western Yunnan, along which the Red River now runs. This movement has caused the crust in Yunnan to pull apart and form grabens, extensive down-dropped areas. Some of these have filled with water to create large lakes, such as Dianchi near Kunming and Erhai near Dali.

Movement along the Red River and related faults has caused numerous high-magnitude earthquakes in Southwest China, some greater than 7.0 on the Richter scale. In addition, these faults allowed abnormally high heat flow to reach the surface of the Earth, creating the numerous hot springs in the region, and acted as conduits for the mineral-rich waters that helped deposit the well-known gold reserves of Yunnan and western Sichuan. They appear, however, to have had little or no influence on the important deposits of iron, copper, lead, zinc and tin in Yunnan, antimony in Guangxi and mercury in Guizhou.

The results of the collision with India have been superimposed on much older basement rocks that form the continental craton of Asia, the stable relatively immobile area of the Earth's crust. These deep basement rocks, as most others on the globe, do not comprise a homogeneous mass, but rather form a mixed collage of material that has increased in size over the past three billion years. Micro-continental fragments were welded together by global tectonic forces perhaps similar to those that are now driving the Indian plate. In fact, the cratonic basement of China consists of three large and several smaller blocks of Precambrian rock (older than 600 million years), fused together along suture zones. The large Precambrian block that underlies most of southern China is known as the Yangzi Craton. Surface exposures of these rocks are rare in southwest China and are usually limited to peripheral zones. In northern Guangxi, 2.86 billion-year-old granites can be observed along the southern cratonic border.

In contrast, the basement rocks that border the Yangzi Craton on the north and west, and which underlie Sichuan and western Yunnan, consist of folded rocks and micro-continental fragments that attached to the cratonic block, probably between 600 and 200 million years ago. An example of this, known as an accretionary fold belt, is the Sichuan Basin, formed by subsidence in an oceanic trench between 200 and 160 million years ago (Triassic-Jurassic). The basin first filled with a mixture of marine marl (clay and small organisms) and fine clastic sediments (fragments of pre-existing rocks) known as flysch. Later (140 to 100 million years ago), the basin was filled with non-marine sandstone and conglomerate. These units now contain major deposits of coal and gas. The subsidence that generated these rocks in eastern Sichuan occurred long before the continental collision with India. The area was preserved as a structural basin throughout the subsequent periods of deformation because of its great distance from the point of initial collision.

A vast, shallow sea covered a major portion of the Yangzi Craton from early Cambrian through Triassic times (600 to 200 million years ago), depositing fossiliferous limestone throughout Guangxi, Guizhou and eastern Yunnan. Subsequent continental uplift and withdrawal of this sea left large areas of limestone exposed to the atmosphere. Where fractures in the limestone were numerous and rainfall abundant, acidic groundwater percolated downward and dissolved the limestone, forming caves, caverns and sinkholes. Formations such as these are common throughout southwest China. At certain localities where the limestone was particularly well fractured and soluble, the continuous dissolution by acidic groundwater caused underground holes to widen, ceilings of caverns to collapse, and numerous sinkholes to form in adjoining patterns. In time, the surface of the limestone terrain in such areas formed a network of numerous short gullies and ravines that terminated abruptly where they discharged their waters into subterranean channels. Erosion by wind and water continually reshaped the more resistant hills, leaving a spectacular collection of elongate and odd-shaped remnants of honey-combed chambers, passageways, caves and tunnels. Known as karst topography, this type of geomorphology gets its name from the Karst Mountains of Yugoslavia where it is particularly well developed.

Karst topography was formed in this manner at Yunnan's well-known Stone Forest, 126 kilometres southeast of Kunming. Here, elongate water channels, caves and passageways have been etched into 270 million-year-old Permian limestone. Even more spectacular, perhaps, are the exotically shaped karst formations naturally sculpted from 300 million-year-old Devonian limestone along the Lijiang River between Guilin and Yangshuo in Guangxi, truly a place where art and geology are one.

— From *Southwest China Off the Beaten Track,*
by K. Mark Stevens and George E. Wehrfritz,
Collins, London, 1988.

trees and animals further south, until crowded out by the lianas, bamboos, vines and lush jungles of the southern lowlands.

The river valleys of central Yunnan already contain many tropical species, which flourish especially in the lands south of the Ailao Mountains. Broad stretches of central Yunnan, though, are virtually treeless, but blessed with rich coal deposits, enabling human settlement. Yunnan's mountains also impede the smooth progress of the annual monsoons, trapping and twisting the weather currents, so that some parts of the province are wetter than others. The northeast also gets the winter rains that spill over from Guizhou and Sichuan.

Sometimes the river valleys are broad enough to provide land for extensive cultivation, sometimes too dry, rocky and narrow for human habitation. The province's central lakes allow people to make a living by fishing and are thus part of a different ecology. Besides certain river valleys, scattered parts of Yunnan somehow miss most of the monsoon rains and are largely arid zones with sparse vegetation, nearly deserts. The ecological variety of Yunnan includes just about everything except a seaside.

An alpine stream meanders through a valley in Baimanangshan, Deqin County.

Dadieshui Falls, the tallest such in Yunnan, spills over the rocks near its base in Lunan County.

RIVERS, LAKES AND WATERFALLS

Some of the best-known rivers of East Asia flow through Yunnan. In the northwest three of them carve nearly parallel routes through the mountains less than a hundred kilometres apart—the **Yangzi**, the **Mekong** and the **Salween**. The Yangzi, known in Yunnan as the Jinshajiang, or River of Golden Sand, makes two great hairpin bends in Lijiang County, then turns sharply east south of Yongsheng. The Jinshajiang then runs along the prefecture border with Chuxiong for a while, briefly enters Sichuan, turns south back into Yunnan near Yongren, then east again, becoming the boundary between Sichuan and Yunnan until the northeast corner of Zhaotong Prefecture.

The other major river flowing into eastern China out of Yunnan is the **Pearl**, or West River. It begins just north of Qujing and empties into the sea just west of Hong Kong. It's not much more than a wide stream for much of its course in Yunnan, though. From above Qujing the river flows more or less south, as the Nanpanjiang, until just above Kaiyuan. Then it turns northeast and exits Yunnan in southeast Luoping County.

Several important rivers flow into Southeast Asia. Of these the greatest are the Nujiang (the name of the Salween in Chinese) and the Lancangjiang (Mekong). The Nujiang tumbles out of eastern Tibet to flow directly south through the prefecture named after it. Then it runs between the ranges of the Gaoligong Mountains through Baoshan and enters Burma just east of Dehong.

The Lancangjiang runs down the western side of Diqing Prefecture, separated from the Nujiang by a long, high mountain range. Then it bends slightly southeast, forming the prefecture boundary between Lincang and Simao for part of its course, runs through Simao to enter Xishuangbanna and exits where China meets Laos and Burma. From there it continues through the Southeast Asian countries of Laos, Thailand, Cambodia and Vietnam. Though bridged at many points, neither the Nujiang nor the Lancangjiang is navigable very far in Yunnan.

Other rivers flowing into Southeast Asia are the Daying and Ruili Rivers in Dehong, the Nandinghe in Lincang, which all go into Burma, and the Babianjiang and Yuanjiang, which go to Vietnam. The latter is better known by its English name—the Red River—and in Vietnam flows through Hanoi and empties into the sea near Haiphong. While running in a dry, narrow trench for much of its route in Yunnan, it has stretches of great beauty, where the terraces of Ailaoshan rise near its banks. Most of the rivers in Yunnan first flow through high, relatively dry mountains and then descend to verdant tropical plains, with points of great scenic beauty in between.

Equally pleasing to the eye, with more readily accessible viewpoints, are the big lakes in central and western Yunnan. Sizable bodies of water, not big enough to be marked on small provincial maps, mountain tarns and picturesque reservoirs pop up all over Yunnan, often playing a role in local legend and custom. The largest lake is **Dianchi**, near Kunming. At 360 sq km it ranks as China's sixth largest. It is 40 km long and 14 km at its maximum width. Passenger boats carry people from one shore to another, transport boats haul loads of rock from the quarries near the shores, while pleasure boats cruise, primarily in the northern part, and fishing boats meander all over. Off shore from the villages huge round traps float on the surface and a small fleet of skiffs awaits the proper hour, which varies according to the season, to be launched onto the lake to drag nets in the water.

The deepest body of water in Yunnan, and the second deepest in the country, is **Fuxianhu**. In Chinese it means 'fairies standing arm in arm', after a local legend. Its average depth is 87 metres, at its deepest measuring 155 metres. Such a depth gives Fuxianhu 12 times the storage capacity of Dianchi, in addition to a deep blue-green colour. Lakeside dwellers use large traps of split bamboo to catch fish here and in the smaller lake, **Xingyunhu**, just to the south, which flows into Fuxianhu.

On the western shore of Xingyunhu fishermen use rod and line at the water's edge, or float just offshore in rubber inner tubes. At an average depth of just six metres, Xingyunhu is the most shallow of Yunnan's large lakes. A little further south, just north of Tonghai, lies the slightly bigger lake called **Qiluhu**. Local legend claims it was once a much bigger lake, until the immortal monk Li Panfu used his staff to make a sinkhole on the eastern shore. This siphoned off much of the water and created a new expanse of farmland. Roughly the same size, 14 km long, backed by mountains to its north and beside a broad plain to its south, is **Yilonghu**, next to Shiping in northern Honghe Prefecture, the last of central Yunnan's chain of lakes.

The other significant lakes lie in the west. Yunnan's second largest, **Erhai**, 41 km long and 3-9 km wide, lies beside the Dali Plain. Low, barren, red earth hills rise on its eastern shore. The western side is flanked by a narrow, heavily populated plain backed by the towering, forested Azure Mountains (*Cangshan*), with peaks over 4,000 metres. Fleets of single-sail fishing boats frequently ply the lake waters. Smaller, less active lakes lie near Eryuan and Jianchuan, both north of Dali. Over the prefectural border with Lijiang, north-northeast in Yongsheng County, sits the quiet lake called **Chenghai**. Almost due north of this, on the Sichuan-Yunnan border in Ninglang County's Lesser Cool Mountains (*Xiaoliangshan*), lies **Lugu Lake**, probably the most beautiful body of water in the entire province.

None of the big rivers drop significantly on their courses through Yunnan to create decent waterfalls. But many of the smaller rivers and tributaries do. All along the canyon carved by the upper Nujiang, small feeder streams drop over cliffs before they reach the river, punctuating the route with long, thin, pretty waterfalls every several kilometres.

The biggest waterfall in Yunnan, 30 metres wide and dropping 96 metres, is **Daduishui**, the cataract formed by the Bajiang River in southwest Lunan County. The **Jiulong Falls**, northeast of Luoping, is nearly as impressive. Other attractive falls include the one near Babao, eastern Wenshan, where the cataract splits into several falls as it tumbles over the last boulders, the several cataracts at Huanglianhe, above Daguan in Zhaotong Prefecture, and the series of falls, big and small, on the Duoyi River south of Luoping, near the border with Guangxi.

(following pages) The peaks of Jade Dragon Snow Mountain tower over the southern end of Tiger Leaping Gorge.

FAMOUS MOUNTAINS

According to local mythology, the father of all mountains in the province is **Laojunshan**, southwest of Shigu in western Lijiang. At 4,247 metres it is far from being the tallest, but it is certainly one of the prettiest. It stands near the prefecture's junction with Nujiang and Dali, with scarcely a hamlet within a day's walk in any direction. More bears and wild cats live in the vicinity than people. Stepping down its slopes are dozens of clear, clean ponds, ringed by dense fir and pine forests and, in springtime, blooming azaleas. Known as **99 Dragon Pools**, it is the least visited of Lijiang's natural beauties.

Easier to see and explore is the great massif that dominates the Lijiang Plain—**Jade Dragon Snow Range** (*Yulong Xue Shan*). Its name stems from the imagination of the ancient Chinese who, when looking at its 13 peaks from the east, pictured dragons lying in the clouds. The permanently snow-capped mountain figures heavily in the folklore of the local Naxi, who have bestowed names on all its glens, creeks, crags and groves, and it is sacred to Tibetans as well. The range was accorded official status as a sacred mountain during the Nanzhao era and the oldest temple at its base dates to that time.

Jade Dragon's tallest peak measures 5,596 metres, exactly 200 metres more than **Habashan**, its neighbour just north across the Jinshajiang in Zhongdian County. From its confluence at Qiaotou with the Chongjiang coming down from Zhongdian, north to the riverside Naxi town of Daju, the Jinshajiang runs right between the two snow mountains in a trench called **Tiger Leaping Gorge**. It got its name because a hunter was chasing a tiger through here once upon a time, and when his prey came to the narrowest part of the gorge it escaped with a mighty leap across the river.

The other famous mountain in the northwest is **Meili Snow Mountain**, near the town of Deqing. Rising to 6,740 metres, it is far and away the highest in the province. Local Tibetans know it as *Kawa Kharpo*, invest it with great sacred power and make pilgrimages to it in the winter months. A sizable glacier slides down its southern face and can be reached on foot in a day's journey from the starting point on the road, a few kilometres north of the viewpoint above Deqing.

Tibetans and Naxi are not alone in viewing certain mountains as sacred. The Mosuo look upon **Lion Mountain** on the shore of Lugu Lake as the manifestation of their most important deity—the Goddess Ganmo. Several mountains in western and central Yunnan are sites of religious veneration, home to Daoist and Buddhist temples and monasteries. Among these are **Shibaoshan** in Jianchuan County, **Jizushan** in Binchuan County, **Weibaoshan** near Weishan, **Xiushan** in Tonghai and Lion Mountain in Wuding. Even animists revere certain mountains because of myths or culturally important legends associated with them. Examples of these include **Tanhuashan**, north of Dayao, where the Yi heroine Miyilu played out her tragic role, remembered today in the Festival of Putting Up Flowers, and **Luofengshan** in Heqing, where the Bai carry out rituals to mark the vernal equinox.

THE BEAUTY OF EROSION

Mountain ranges were the most spectacular result of the tectonic shifts that caused the formation of Yunnan. But they were only the grandest, most visible evidence of the general reshaping of rock and earth that took place. Tucked away in scattered sites throughout the province are innumerable hillocks, boulders, pillars, cliffsides and rocks in interesting patterns, shapes and formations that make them stand out sharply in their environments. The wind and rain of many eons has worked on all rocks everywhere, while the tremors of a still seismically active Earth rearrange what's exposed to the creative forces of the elements. Every now and then nature produces masterpieces of sculpture, rocks of all sizes, each a unique work that seems to be another of the Earth's inexhaustible supply of aesthetic statements.

Most of this strange natural rock sculpture is in limestone, but some is located in areas that miss the rain during monsoon seasons. It's as if they were directly underneath holes in the monsoon clouds that otherwise blanket the province. Or perhaps the clouds swirl all around the hole, rarely sliding over it. So while rain has been a partner with the wind in creating the limestone beauties wrought by erosion, in a few notable places, dry as a desert, the wind has worked alone.

Erosion is usually a negative image, the consequences of bad farming, bad use of the environment, bad weather, bad planning, bad luck. But given that the Earth will have its spots of no material, agricultural or pastoral use, it's a compensation when such spots are eroded in a way that appeals to man's sense of beauty and imagination.

The best examples in Yunnan of the beauty that erosion can create, besides the limestone Stone Forest, are the Earth Forest of Yuanmou County, Chuxiong, and the Painted Sand Forest in Luliang County, Qujing. The **Earth Forest** (*Tulin*) lies just south of the main road connecting Yuanmou with Yongren, about a third of the way to the latter. A dirt road turns up alongside a creek and the valley for several kilometres is quite verdant and fertile. Suddenly the road veers away from the creek, the green disappears and the dirt road has come to the entrance to the park.

The seldom visited Earth Forest stretches out 50 sq km and is the part of Yunnan that most looks like the desert hills of Morocco or the Valley of the Moon in Jordan. Entire cliffsides resemble the facades of Gothic cathedrals, columned Greek temples, or European castles with turreted towers. Other pinnacles rise from a round base and taper at the top almost to a point, looking like some of the pagodas in Southeast Asian temple compounds. Still others suggest various animals or even humans.

The rocks and pillars of the **Painted Sand Forest** (*Caise Shalin*) in Luliang County are almost as evocative and, like the outstanding formations in the Earth Forest, have been given names by the imaginative Chinese. Unfortunately, at the end of the 1990s, construction of a road through the park and several theme park-style buildings took place. And in parts of the park now it is difficult to tell what is natural and what is the result of the blasts of dynamite. Even more intrusive was the introduction into what was supposed to be a nature preserve, of gigantic new stone sculptures of corpulent Buddhas, Chinese historical figures, etc, made by artists invited in for the effort from northern China and foreign countries.

Limestone Attractions

In the Permian Age 270 million years ago much of modern Yunnan was covered by sea. With major shifts in the Earth's crust the sea receded while its limestone bed rose up and broke through to make a new tableland. As the sea-water seeped away it nibbled at this limestone, while acidic rain pounded it from above. Most of the limestone eroded, leaving weirdly shaped pillars behind. Lunan County's **Stone Forest** (*Shilin*) is an 80-hectare concentration of these pillars, but the phenomenon exists over much of the county. Little 'stone groves' are often the backdrop to Sani villages and pop up on hillocks all along the main connecting roads.

Limestone is also a primary component of many of the small hills in the plains of Honghe and Wenshan Prefectures. At Babao in eastern Wenshan such hills are clustered close together over several square kilometres. A small river winds its way among them and Zhuang villages lie at their bases, their farms filling the flat land between them. At Qiubei in northwest Wenshan the cluster of hills is perhaps even more dramatic. Boats ply the river at Puzhehei and a cruise here compares well with the better known Li River trip out of Guilin.

The hills of such landscapes rarely rise more than a few hundred metres from the plain. In other parts of the area limestone hills seldom merit attraction for their shapes or eroded slopes. But many contain karst caves where the water has gradually seeped through the rock and, dripping from the cave's ceiling, left deposits in the form of strange stalactites. Rock walls with

Swallow Cave, 40 kilometres east of Jianshui, is part of Yunnan's largest cave complex.

fluted sides, stalagmites resembling mushrooms or lions, caves within caves, slender, icicle-like petrifactions and subterranean streams are all illuminated by banks of coloured lights that augment the mysterious spectacles of the Earth's womb.

Quite a number of these splendid karst caves lie in groups near Kunming at Jiuxiang, Yiliang County, and near the Stone Forest in Lunan County. Bigger grottoes, each with its own unique feature, are further on. Besides having two capacious caverns full of stalactites dripping from the ceilings and stalagmites studding the floors, Qujing's **Heaven-made Grotto** (*Tianshangdong*) has a small, upper-level chamber called the Musical Cave because the stalactites, when gently struck, make musical sounds.

In northern Honghe, Luxi's Ancient **Alu Caves** (*Alu Gudong*) are named after an indigenous people a thousand years ago who inhabited the cave group. Perhaps it was the Alu imagination that supplied the names for the natural sculptures, identified as flying dragons playing in the waterfall, elephants racing, crocodiles leaping and Axi girls dancing. Unique to this cave group is a species of transparent fish, which swims in the limpid, 800-metre-long, underground Yusan Stream. Visitors ride boats to view the stone patterns of the ceiling reflected in the water and interesting little stalagmites jutting up to pierce the surface.

The biggest cavern in the province, several kilometres long and up to 33 metres high inside, is **Swallow Grotto** (*Yanzidong*), 40 km east of Jianshui. Besides the usual marvellous pillars, stone curtains and petrified animals, what gives the cave its fame is its use by myriad swifts to make their nests. These nests, made simply with the bird's saliva, are edible, the primary ingredient of bird's nest soup. Annually the local people gather and market them.

Tropical Plains

The plains of the south and southwest resemble those across the border in Myanmar, Laos and Vietnam. Rather than the elevated plateaux common to the rest of Yunnan, the land consists of broad alluvial plains broken by small hill ranges. Bamboo and palm are the dominant indigenous trees, though rubber tree plantations cover large swaths of the highlands. Extensive virgin rainforests are still preserved here, such as the 35 km stretch between Jinuoshan and Menglun in central Xishuangbanna. Most of the trees are tropical evergreens, as well as deciduous hardwoods whose leaves drop in spring, the dry season. Thus the tropical forests, except for the woods near the peaks of the highest mountains, do not display the red, yellow, orange, maroon and purple colours that run riot in so many northern forests every autumn.

Yunnan's lush tropical forests are home to a great variety of jungle flowers, plants and epiphytes. Strangler figs begin as epiphytes—plants that grow in a trough created by a big tree's twisting branches. Seeds are left there in birds' droppings. Eventually the plant starts living off its host, spreading its own growth across the branches and trunk and sending its own roots down to the ground below. Finally the parasite tree takes over completely and outgrows the original tree.

Banyans are another species which look as if their lower branches are being supported by subsidiary trunks. These are roots, though, not trunks. A few banyans standing together can look like a dense grove. One such group is a major tourist attraction on the Wanding-Ruili road in Dehong. Occasionally the twisted trunk and branches appear to assume a new and recognizable shape, like Mengyang's Elephant Tree. Or it has so many thick aboveground roots the single tree resembles a forest, like the one at Daluo, near the Myanmar border in Xishuangbanna.

The south and southwest are blessed with an abundance of water. Not only is the land watered by several rivers and innumerable creeks and streams that begin as gushes from springs high in the surrounding mountains. The area also receives more rain than the rest of the province, being the first part of Yunnan to get the monsoon and the last part to see it leave. Irrigation is widespread and most farms are in steady use, producing more than one crop per year. Throughout the year rich green is the dominant colour of the plains, interspersed with harvest yellow.

WEATHER AND THE WORK CYCLE

With its mountains, high plateaux and northern counties all part of the temperate zone and its low-lying valleys and southern hills part of the tropics, Yunnan's climate varies from one end of the province to another. Yet one factor is common to all sections: Yunnan is on the monsoon route, which means summer rains everywhere, from the tropical rainforests of Xishuangbanna to the Tibetan Plateau in Diqing Prefecture. The eastern part of Tibet is also within the monsoon's reach.

Some parts of Yunnan, however, are wetter than others, just as some parts are colder. But with so much variation in the province's ecological environments the weather patterns mean different things to different people. In general, though, the rural work cycle is determined by the passage of seasons, requiring different work when the weather changes. During the dry season, November to April, a range of activities take place, which do not during the rainy season from May through October.

After the harvest of the crop raised during the monsoon, farmers then plant those crops that are not so dependent on water—wheat, sugar cane, certain vegetables. General field work is intermittent, freeing men for construction jobs and women for weaving or embroidery. Crafts in general attract more labour in the winter than in the summer. Trade is brisker, too, including long-distance trade. Winter is the season Tibetans, for example, journey from Diqing to all corners of Yunnan to sell forest products like plant and animal parts used in medicine.

For most in the province the main crop, the one they spend the most time upon, is rice. And as rice cultivation requires a lot of water, farmers raise it in the rainy season, which is therefore the busiest time of year. Some of the plains farms are irrigated and can produce a second and even a third crop per year. But for sure, one crop will be rice raised in the rainy season. And even those who don't grow rice plant their own staple in the monsoon months, be it the barley of the Tibetans, the corn of some Lisu, or the potato of the northern Yi.

Before the rains come, the plains and terrace farmers prepare seedbeds of rice plants. When the rain floods the paddies, the farmers transplant these seedlings, often working in large groups. Men mostly do the digging, women the planting. After the planting the fields must be weeded at least twice, and smaller vegetable plots attended to throughout the season. Outdoor work is muddy the first part of the season, but after mid-monsoon the rains gradually diminish. It rarely rains non-stop all day or for several days in a row, even at the monsoon's peak, but even less so in the latter half of the season. Sunshine returns ever more often, ripening the crops.

By September in the plains and lower-altitude valleys like Nujiang and the terraces along the Red River, the rice is ready for harvest. So is most of Zhongdian's barley. During this month and next farmers are busy cutting, threshing and winnowing the grain. On the dry-rice farms of the hills, the crop takes another month to fully ripen, but by the end of October hill farmers are at their harvest.

In mid-autumn the fields have all been cropped and farmers, mostly the men, now plough the fields, either preparing for a winter crop or just giving the earth a post-harvest turnover before letting it lie fallow until spring. Collecting fodder and firewood is the women's job at this time—a year-round chore, in any case.

Farms with irrigation may follow a different work cycle, including those where only one crop can be raised per year. The terrace-builders of Ailaoshan, for example, whose fields are permanently flooded with water, plant rice as early as March. That's partly because the water that rice plants require at the

The sandstone pinnacles of the Earth Forest in Yuanmou County are one of the many geological attractions in Yunnan.

beginning of their growth is already there and partly because the type of rice grown takes a month or more longer than that grown in the plains.

Not all the non-urbanites are farmers, of course, for in the mountains of the north many of the inhabitants are at least semi-pastoralist. For individual Tibetan, Lisu, Naxi, Yi and Miao families, herding is the main occupation. Such people follow the seasonal cycles as set by the needs of their animals. In Diqing yak herders take their animals to pastures on the higher slopes of the mountains every summer, then bring them down to the valleys and plains when it's too cold to graze, the snow line is lower and not many plants are left in the high-altitude pastures. Yi herders do the same with their goats and sheep in the northwest and northeast, and shear them twice yearly. In contrast to herders, those who fish for a living depend less on seasonal changes than on the day-to-day weather.

FLORA AND FAUNA

The life of plants and animals is totally regulated by seasons and weather. Every spring a motley assortment of flowers bloom in the forest of the mountains, especially camellias, rhododendrons, azaleas, osmanthus and, in the south, orchids and magnolias. Deciduous and fruit-bearing trees in the north bud and blossom in spring. Leaves and fruit grow through the summer, and in the autumn the apples, pears, persimmons and pomegranates ripen and fall, while their leaves and those of other trees turn crimson, gold, maroon and fiery orange before they dry up and flutter to the ground.

The northern forests are full of evergreen species like fir, larch, cypress, spruce and pine, though some portions of the pine and larch forests in the northwest turn yellow in autumn. Among the other deciduous trees are oaks, walnut, mulberry, gingko, camphor, willow, juniper and in the south palm, tung-oil, teak, acacia, banyan and bamboo. The greatest species and sub-species diversity is in the northwest forests of Lijiang, Zhongdian and Deqing Counties, and in Xishuangbanna.

This extends to birds, too, of which Yunnan has a great range of species, concomitant with its many ecological micro-zones. In addition, it is on one of the major migration routes from Southeast Asia to Central Asia and back. Among the most beloved of birds are the peacock, conscripted as a Dai symbol in the south and southwest, the black eagle, the ancestral animal of the northern Yi, the black-necked crane, which flies to Napahai in Zhongdian County every year, the red pheasant and the silver pheasant, the hawks that Naxi men keep as pets in the old town in Lijiang, and the swifts of Jianshui whose nests make a soup.

A Naxi harvesting wheat in Dadong. Most farms in Yunnan still rely on hand labour at harvest time.

A lotus blossom floats serenely in a pond. The lotus is the flower most closely associated with the Buddhist religion.

A yellow azalea is common to the Lijiang area.

Pink azalea. The azalea is one of the most common flowers in Yunnan, especially in the northwest region.

Camelias have been cultivated in Yunnan since the 6th century.

The many environments of Yunnan's hills and valleys provide niches for a range of animals big and small. While admittedly they live in a habitat much reduced, wild animals do thrive in the many protected areas in the province. Anti-hunting propaganda is posted all over those places where hunting was a tradition. Travellers can still find animal parts used as medicine in the remote towns and rural markets, like bear paws, antlers, bear bile, dried Big Gecko and various horns, hooves, bones and internal body organs. But rarely are live animals for sale, except snakes, lizards, squirrels and maybe a baby civet cat.

Big animals live in Yunnan still. The largest are the wild elephants of central Xishuangbanna, which can be viewed quite easily from the towers in the park sited at the edge of their preserve. More difficult to catch sight of is the tiger, partly because it's mainly a nocturnal animal, partly because it's disappearing. Other cats have been more successful surviving, such as the leopard and the smaller marbled cat and golden cat. The commonest is the jungle cat, yellow-brown and the size of a small dog. Martens, otters, pangolins and river deer are the other major resident mammals of the southern and southwestern jungles.

Further north, civets, weasels, hedgehogs, barking deer (*muntjacs*), foxes and wolves prowl the forests. The higher slopes and the mountains of the northwest are home to blue sheep, musk deer, leopard, red (or lesser) panda, wild goat and black bear. Sometimes hunters shoot foxes, otters and red pandas to make winter caps from the pelts. But this practice seems to be disappearing nowadays and the only animals still liable to be lined up in the sights of a rifle are small birds and occasional squirrels, to supplement the hunter's diet.

(*above*) A leopard cat captured in Wenshan. (*right*) A pet slow loris in Xishuangbanna. Hill people often make pets of captured small jungle animals.

The Provincial Palate

MEALS IN YUNNAN

For the Yunnanese dining is a serious matter. Meals are considered an important aspect of daily life and cooks often lavish much attention on their preparation. The province is blessed with an abundance of vegetables and a variety of meat and fish, and has long enjoyed a nationwide reputation for its cuisine. European travellers writing a hundred years ago called the Yunnanese 'born cooks'. Besides the ordinary ingredients common to Chinese food in the southwest, Yunnan also uses condiments, spices, jungle food, river and lake food and other items that are specific to this province and not part of meals beyond its borders.

Meals are social occasions also, for people in Yunnan rarely dine alone. That would limit the number of dishes, so the advantage of dining with others is having a wider selection of tastes, enhancing the eating experience. Dinners often number several participants for social reasons as well. Banquets become business meetings, family reunions, celebrations of a local team's victory in a sporting event, the nearly ritual welcome to a special guest and venues for a collective date. Yunnanese like banquets and keep a ready stock of excuses on hand to hold one.

Travellers who wander into a restaurant with a banquet in process, or even just a table with several diners, will probably be invited to join. It's a chance for the Yunnanese to show their hospitality to strangers. And as the servings of a meal's components are always more than what can be consumed, the addition of another participant is easily accommodated. The guest is advised to eat slowly, for at banquets, or any collective meal, no one hurries. Drinking, smoking and conversation continuously interrupt the consumption of the food. A good meal is a leisurely affair and with some people the social aspect is as important as the culinary.

When several people eat together in a restaurant, they usually sit at a round table with a circular rotating section in the centre. The different dishes are served in bowls and on plates, chopsticks and individual bowls distributed and the wine cups filled or bottles of beer opened and poured. Whenever diners order liquor with the meal, the custom is to serve the rice and soup after the liquor has been finished. This can certainly extend the time spent at the dinner table whenever a large quantity of liquor is involved: the more alcohol the more toasting, the more conversation, the slower the progress of the meal. Dinner among a group of Hani men, for example, can last two hours or more.

Local Bai run most of the restaurants in Heqing city.

LIQUOR AND TEA

For most men in Yunnan dinner is incomplete without *jiu*—the Chinese word for distilled spirits. If not one of the fiery liquors or medicinal wines, then beer (*pijiu*) will do. But some kind of alcohol is essential. It aids digestion, too. And when meals are taken in groups, liquor is even more in demand for its value as a social instrument, stimulating the spirit of conviviality which prevails at the event.

When the first round is poured the men raise their cups in a toast and take the first sip. Occasionally the meal may begin with a *ganbei* toast, which requires everyone to quaff the entire contents of the cup. In any case, while refills are immediate and even though people may take only sips at a time, once the meal has started one of the diners periodically takes the bottle and tops up the cups until all the liquor has been poured. In some places it's the custom to toast each time one wants to have a swallow.

Several breweries operate in different parts of the province. Their brands each dominate the beer market in their own and neighbouring prefectures. Dali Beer has probably the best distribution in the western and central prefectures, with Lancangjiang Beer in second place. Others are more restricted, like Longjing in the south and Yulong in the northwest. The only beers available in practically every county seat are national brands, like Qingdao. Some restaurants do not keep beer in their refrigerators and serve it at room temperature. But customers can request the staff put a bottle or two in the freezer compartment to chill it somewhat while the food is being prepared.

The range of hard liquor at any given restaurant is greater. Among the commercial spirits, the most popular are those distilled from maize. In the northwest the ones made from barley and from buckwheat outsell the maize liquor. Strong wines are made from plums and can be as potent as the liquors. Home-made and medicinal liquors are among the beverage selections in the restaurants. Usually these are in big glass jugs, like the fruit wines, with various ingredients supposed to be of health-enhancing value. These may be chips of wood, shavings of animal bones, entire snakes, etc.

Certain medicinal jiu is peculiar to a given area because the ingredients are only found in that area. The Mosuo of Lugu Lake and Yongning celebrate Duanwujie on the fifth day of the fifth month. The main festival activity is to gather herbs from the forests of Lion Mountain. Back home they make and consume a broth from a portion of the herbs and insert the remainder into jugs of jiu.

The Mosuo are also famous for their *sulima*—barley beer—which they frequently serve at meals, especially if they have guests. Though it tastes different from the rice beer produced by the Wa and Jingpo, it is made in the same way. First the brewer steams the rice or barley, spreads the cooked grain out on a table, sprinkles some yeast on it, then puts the grain into a large jar, sprinkles a cup or two of water to moisten it and covers the jar, perhaps even wraps blankets around it. After three days—four or five in cold weather—the fermented grain smells like beer. The brewer adds water, the amount varying according to the amount of grain, and lets it sit overnight. The next day the beer is strained from the mash and ready to serve. Almost as strong as the weaker commercial beers, it has a slight sweetness in the taste, not from sugar but from the dextrose released by the fermentation process.

If the goal is spirits, then the fermentation goes on several more days until the original grain has turned to liquid. Then the mash is boiled and distilled. Tibetans in Diqing do not make beer from their barley mash but instead distill it all. Every household consigns a portion of the annual barley harvest to the production of *qingkejiu*—barley liquor. The Naxi of Lijiang use barley in conjunction with sorghum, wheat, yeast and spring water to make a deep amber, sherry-like wine called *yinjiu*. Unique to Lijiang the wine is often sold in special brown or white ceramic jars.

Most of those who drink alcoholic beverages only do so at meals. But karaoke bars have opened in even the remote towns, so the venues for social drinking have increased. Yunnanese hold their liquor well, so the sight of a drunkard staggering around bothering everyone he meets is extremely rare. Nor does liquor provoke aggression or lead to fights. Yunnanese can get quite intoxicated at times, but maintain control of themselves. The northern Yi are heavy drinkers, but are more likely to wax poetic in their conversations the more liquor they imbibe.

While not everybody drinks alcohol in Yunnan, everyone drinks tea. It is the first beverage poured out in a restaurant, served even before the diner has made an order, and the refreshment immediately offered a guest by a host. Tea contains several natural chemicals with anti-inflammatory and germicidal properties, and others which stimulate the nervous system and aid the metabolism. Thus drinking tea promotes the digestion of meat and fat, two elements common to the diet of just about everyone in the province, and helps discharge nicotine out of the system for smokers. Taken regularly in doses of moderate strength, tea acts like a medicine to maintain physical health. In addition, it has a pleasant flavour.

Yunnan's annual tea output is the sixth largest in China. The gardens lie mainly in the southern hills, with large parts of Xishuangbanna, Simao and Honghe given over to tea cultivation. Menghai County, according to some, is the oldest tea-producing place in China. The 'King of Tea Trees', estimated to

Markets and Wineshops

S tarting in distant villages early in the morning, the streams of farmers began to emerge on Likiang soon after ten o'clock, along five main roads. The streets were jammed with horses loaded with firewood; people bringing charcoal in baskets on their backs and others carrying vegetables, eggs and poultry. Pigs were either carried, tied up, on poles by two men, or led by women, who held the leash in one hand and gently prodded the the animal with a switch in the other. Many other kinds of merchandise were carried either on the backs of the people themselves or on their animals. There was the noise of hooves on hard stone, loud talk, shouting and much laughter. In the market itself there was great tumult with all these crowds trying to pass each other and jockeying for the best positions on the square. On the previous night sturdy stalls had already been pulled out of the common pile, or dragged from surrounding shops and set in rows in the centre. Women and girls brought heavy bales of textiles and spread bolts of cloth on the stalls. Haberdashery, spices and vegetables were displayed in separate rows. Shortly after noon the market was in full swing and was a boiling cauldron of humanity and animals. At about three o'clock the market session reached its climax and then began to decline.

Main street was lined with dozens of 'exclusive bars' and thither thirsty villagers, men and women, turned their steps. After a tiring day in the market the numerous tea-shops in Chinese towns and villages are crowded with congenial parties of men and women relaxing over pots of tea. In this respect, the customs of Likiang were quite distinct. There were no tea-shops, and if anyone drank tea at all during the day it was brewed in miniature earthen jugs on the brazier concealed somewhere in the back room. Everyone, men, women and children, drank wine, white or sweet yintsieu. No self-respecting child above two years would go to sleep without a cup of yintsieu.

The 'exclusive bars' were neither bars nor were they exclusive. They were general stores where, in addition to salt, sugar, salted vegetables and haberdashery, wine was kept for sale, both to be taken away in customer's own jars or to be consumed on the premises. The shops were uniformly small in Likiang and, in addition to the counter facing the street, there was a longer counter at a right angle to it, leaving a narrow passage from the door ro the inner rooms of the shop. A couple of narrow benches were put before this counter and there the people sat drinking wine.

Anyone could have a drink at any shop, but some villagers acquired preferences for particular shops. These regular and faithful customers grew intimate with the lady owner, and always gave her the first option on whatever they were bringing to the market for sale. Similarly the lady favoured them with special discounts on whatever they wanted to buy from her. Actually such relations between the established clients and the shop owner were not so simple. The lady also acted as their broker, banker, postmaster and confidante. Baskets with purchases were left in her keeping whilst the customers went out for more shopping. Small loans were negotiated with her on the security of the next deliveries of whatever they usually brought to the market or against growing chickens or pigs. When clients could not pay for their drinks or purchase, credit transactions were permitted by the lady, who got her husband or son to record them in simple Chinese. Wallets with cash were sometimes deposited at the shop for safe-keeping by the farmers whose villages were not safe from robbers. As there was no postal service to remote villages, the wine-shop was a favourite accommodation address. Letters were duly forwarded to the recipients by safe hands. Confidential advice was sought by the clients from the lady on the problems of engagement and marriage, childbirth and funerals. And, of course, every lady wine-shop owner was a Bureau of Information par excellence. She knew the curricula vitae of everybody within a radius of a hundred miles, and I doubt whether there ever existed a secret in Likiang that was not known to her.

Madame Lee was an old woman, very erect, stately and handsome, with aquiline features and large lustrous eyes. She belonged to the cream of Likiang society and was much respected both in the town and in the villages. Everybody knew her and she knew everybody.

It was not easy to get a seat at Madame Lee's shop in the late afternoon. In an emergency she permitted me to sit behind the counter on a small stool, facing the other customers. Men and women came to have a drink or two before starting on their trek back to the village: but in accordance with nakhi customs, no woman sat down in company with a man. Women usually took their drinks standing in front of the shop and chatting meanwhile with Madame Lee. It was quite common for women to treat men to drinks; nobody tried to prevent her from paying the bill. As soon as his drink was finished, a man would go and somebody else would drop into his place. It was wonderful to sit at the back of the shop in comparative gloom, and watch through the wide window the movement in the narrow street, as though seeing on a screen a colour film of surpassing beauty. Sooner or later everybody who had attended the market session had to pass through Main Street at least once or twice. Old friends could be seen and invited for a drink or new acquaintances made. Any stranger could be waved to and asked to share a pot of wine, without any ceremony or introduction, and I was sometimes stopped in the street by total strangers and offered a cigarette or a drink. No such liberties were allowed for women, but now and then one of them, who knew me well, would slap me on the shoulder and say, 'Come and let us have a drink!' and she would have to take her drink standing up so as to avoid a local scandal.

With the deep blue sky and brilliant sunshine, the street was a blaze of colour, and as we sat and sipped our wine from Madame Lee's porcelain cups, mountain youths, in the sheer joy of life, would dance through the streets playing flutes like the pipes of Pan. They looked like wild woodland creatures in their sleeveless jerkins and short skin pants.

Occasionally something would happen to shock or amuse the town. Once, I remember, a stark-naked man appeared in the market and proceeded leisurely up Main Street. I was sitting at Madame Lee's. He went from shop to shop, asking for a drink or a cigarette. Women spat and turned away their faces but nothing was done to stop him. The truth was that the brazen Likiang women could hardly be shocked by anything, but they had to put on some show of modesty and embarrassment in order to avoid acid and biting gibes from the men. A policeman was never to be seen in the streets, and it was only at the end of the day, when somebody bothered to rout one out from the police station, that the demented man was led away. He was not jailed, for there were no laws or statutes in Likiang about indecency in public. Such matters were largely decided by public opinion. One could always go a few hundred yards towards the park and see dozens of naked Tibetans and Nakhi swimming in the river or lying on the grass in the sun in full view of the passers-by and in front of the houses. There was a lot of giggling and whispering amongst the passing women and girls, but there were no complaints. A line, however, had to be drawn against nakedness in the public market.

Peter Goullart, *Forgotten Kingdom*,
John Murray, London, 1955

be over 800 years old, stands at Nannuoshan, in the centre of the prefecture, while another tea tree in Bada township, 1,700 years old, is dubbed the 'King of Wild Tea Trees'.

Varieties of tea include green, black and compressed tea. Black tea is actually called red tea in Chinese (*hongcha*), while the compressed tea is black tea compressed and hardened into bricks, and so also known as brick tea. This is the easiest to transport and that favoured by people in rural and remote areas, particularly among Naxi, Yi and Tibetans. Dianhong black tea and Pu'er tea are the most famous types.

Pu'er tea originated in Pu'er County and the plants that produce it grow all the way to the Myanmar and Laos borders. It has a long trade history and was exported to Tibet via Dali and Lijiang, then up the **Tea and Horses Road** (*Chama Gudao*) through Deqing Prefecture to Tibet. The small compressed 'bricks' of tea, actually in the shape of a small bell, known as *tuocha*, travelled in caravans organized by Muslims and Tibetans. The latter exchanged horses for the tea and a few Tibetans converted to Islam. Today a small mosque stands in Diqing city, used not by Hui but by Muslim descendants of Ming and Qing Dynasty Tibetan tea traders. Tibetans in Diqing today still prefer the traditional brick tea, adding yak butter to the brew to make the buttered tea that is the staple beverage of the Tibetan Plateau.

SMOKERS' HAVEN

Tobacco is a major cash crop in Yunnan. The province ranks second nationally in the production of cigarettes and cured tobacco, and near the top in consumption. Non-smoking visitors can't help but notice the proliferation of smoking in Yunnan: people smoke everywhere. The first thing men do when meeting a friend, or being introduced to someone new, is to offer a cigarette. Owners of small restaurants pass out cigarettes to their customers at the start or finish of the meal. Some people smoke while eating, or take cigarette breaks every 20 minutes during a leisurely dinner.

The Yunnanese see smoking as a true pleasure and the offering of a cigarette as a gesture of friendship. Yunnan has a broad range of cigarette brands, from expensive to cheap. The most costly, over 40 yuan per packet, are not often sold. The leading quality brand is 'Hongtashan', slightly more expensive than imported '555s'. 'Yunyan' and 'Ashima' cost less, and middle-quality brands like 'Honghe' and 'Hongmei' are popular in the rural areas. The most popular cheap brand is 'Chuncheng', while the unfiltered 'Xiangyun' sells for only one yuan per packet. At big parties, weddings, funerals, etc, the host will distribute the best cigarettes he can afford, preferably Hongtashan, for its status value.

A Dali area Bai gentleman uses a very long bamboo pipe to enjoy his smoke.

In the rural and minority areas, instead of a cigarette, the host may offer a large, bamboo smoking bong. Water is kept in the lower part of the tube, so that the smoker, when holding a cigarette over the pipe attached to the tube, or taking a puff on a pinch of blonde tobacco burning in the pipe, filters the smoke through the water before inhaling it into his lungs.

Smoking is also part of minority nationality lifestyles, some more than others. Hani funeral customs require the placing of a few objects, symbolic of the life of the deceased, on top of the grave after burial. Among the Aini branch of the Hani this means a smoking pipe, a knife, and other objects for men, or a spindle, loom reed, etc for women. But the Hani in Ailaoshan place a smoking bong on the graves of both male and female. The first thing a Hani host does when receiving a male guest is to empty the smoking bong, put fresh water inside, and hand it with a pinch of tobacco to the guest. After that the host makes tea, whereas in other societies the tea precedes the tobacco.

Ailaoshan Hani women generally don't smoke, but their ethnic cousins in Xishuangbanna and southwest Simao do, smoking sun-cured, hill-grown tobacco in bamboo pipes with medium-length stems. Yi women in Lijiang and Zhaotong Prefectures also smoke, but in pipes with brass bowls. The champion lady smokers, though, are the Wa, who use long-stemmed silver pipes with ornate designs, slightly curved at the bowl. When not using them they tuck the pipes into their belts or, in Menglian County, in the silver bands that hold their caps in place.

LOCAL SPECIALITIES

Basic southwestern Chinese dishes are available throughout the province, but minority cuisine and tasty local specialities enhance the Yunnan eating experience. Some restaurants exist primarily to serve these dishes, such as the many in Kunming that offer the capital's own special food (*mingcai*)—over-the-bridge rice noodles (*guoqiao mixian*). This consists of a big bowl of steaming chicken-and-herb broth, served with rice noodles and a plate of thin strips of meat (mostly pork) and items like chopped scallions, tofu skin, pigeon egg, etc. The diner empties the plate into the soup, which cooks the meat, adding salt, chilli, soy sauce and vinegar to taste. The meal is said to be the invention of a Mengzi scholar's wife, who delivered it daily to her husband while he studied at an island pavilion in the city's South Lake, reached by crossing the bridge from the land. To keep the soup hot enough to cook the thinly sliced meat, she added vegetable oil to create an insulating layer on top.

Another dish peculiar to Kunming is rose rutabaga, fried with slices of pork tenderloin. A popular local snack is a rice flour cake (*dajiujia*) fried with ham, eggs and vegetables. In Yiliang County, east of Kunming, the speciality is roast duck (*kaoya*). Several restaurants offering this lie bunched together at the edge of town, on the Lunan road, while girls stand outside them trying to flag down customers coming back from the Stone Forest. In Lunan County itself, the *mingcai* is fried slices of goat cheese (*rubin*), lightly browned and served with black pepper. Further east, Luxi has the province's best red peppers, Xuanwei the finest ham, while Qujing's specialty is cold pea jell (*jidou liangfen*). This is made from soaked, crushed white peas, which are filtered, cooked and cooled. The jelly slices are then flavoured with ginger, soy sauce, prickly ash oil, sesame oil, chili oil, *Amomum tsaoko* and aniseed oil.

South of Kunming, Yuxi is known for its unique sweets. These include the delicate pastry *saqima*, sweets rolled in baked soybean flour (*huangdou mian*) and the candied wax gourd. The latter is supposed to cool the body's innards, relieve coughs and moisten the lungs, besides being tasty. The lotus root dishes (*lianou*) in Chongjiang are reputedly Yunnan's most delicious. Lying near the tip of Fuxian Lake, Chongjiang's other specialty is the lake fish called *kanglan* ('braving the waters'). The best fish served in Jiangchuan are the 'anti-current fish' from Fuxian and the 'big-head fish' (*datou yu*) from the shallow waters of Xingyun Lake.

Farther south, around Qilu Lake in Tonghai County, fish is not the *mingcai*, but eel (*manyu*), which comes not from the lake itself but from the feeder streams, notably around Peacock Hill, where the Mongolian villages lie.

Deep-fried bamboo grubs are a favourite 'drinking' snack in the southern counties of Yunnan as they are throughout the Dai regions of Asia.

Restaurants on the main road in front of Xingmeng specialize in preparing eel. A few serve Beijing-style roast duck (*beijing kaoya*), and Kunming residents as well as Chinese tourists from the north drive four to five hours down here to patronize these restaurants and marvel at how much the taste resembles that in Beijing.

Continuing south, Shiping is famous for its bean curd (*tofu*). In the evenings groups of people hover over charcoal grills and dine on grilled tofu cubes, dipping them in soy sauce and chilli powder. In Jianshui, the mingcai is chicken cooked in an earthen pot (*qiguoji*). A small steam tube, or chimney, rises from the middle of the pot. The meat is lightly flavoured with pseudo-ginseng or ginger. The county is also known for its unique grass sprout (*caoyao*), a candle-sized plant shaped like a miniature elephant tusk, with a consistency like bamboo shoots.

In the tropical south bamboo shoots are a regular part of the diet. The Dai in Xishuangbanna pickle some, which they lightly fry and then boil with fish in a soup. Glutinous rice (*nuomi*) is a local favourite, too, often coloured brown and sometimes cooked in a pineapple. The Dai also cook rice inside bamboo tubes, turning them over an open fire until done. Another Dai way of grilling chicken or fish is by wrapping it in lemon grass (*xiangmao cao*).

A Dai woman sells tofu in the market at Gengma. The area is famous for its tofu specialities.

Most Yunnanese restaurants display the available food,
making it easy for customers to choose dishes.

Dai sauces are pungent and the favourite combination of flavours is hot and sour. Dai food in Dehong, Simao and Lincang is similar and restaurants in the towns serve from big pots containing the various, already prepared selections. Dehong can boast of perhaps the province's best rice, from Zhefang township, for it was a specified item of tribute demanded by the Qing court.

The cuisine of the south is much influenced by the tastes of Southeast Asia, while that of the central and northern plateaux is the creation of Ming-era Han immigrants. The *mingcai* of the west are mostly the special dishes of the minority nationalities. Mushrooms and other edible fungi are popular and, in the Yi areas, different preparations of mutton. The Yi of Chuxiong occasionally hold a grand banquet in which they cook an entire ram. The first set of dishes comprises up to 30 assorted cold selections, prepared from the hooves and parts of the face and head of the ram, dipped in soybeans with mint. These are taken with jiu. The next set consists of 30 types of mutton, including meat fried, steamed, dried, boiled, wrapped in egg rolls, in rice wafers, and roasted in a bamboo tube which is set aflame and waved around the table before being broken open and the contents served.

The mountains behind Dali provide some wild vegetables for the local cuisine. Among these are *gaohe* greens, boiled and dipped in sesame oil, *shutoucai* leaves, minced with ham, *mailancai* stems and roots, which are pickled, and the tops of wild pepper trees, fried in oil. Erhai Lake supplies people with various kinds of fish. The small species, known as 'oily fish' for its glossy scales and high fat content, smells like chicken when cooked. Larger fish go into casseroles with bean curd, bamboo shoots, egg rolls, mushrooms and cubes of meat cooked along with the fish. Dali also has goat cheese, but cut in strips and deep-fried, as well as a delicious, large, crispy snack (*rushan*) made from fried cream.

In Lijiang the Naxi sometimes indulge in the Eight Bowls Dinner (*tubawan*). This comprises three kinds of pork, chicken with fungus, fish, ham, cheese wafers and salted eggs. Among the snacks consumed at the night stalls, or served as a separate dish during meals, is *mabu*, a Naxi word for a sausage of glutinous rice cooked in pig's blood. Among the Yi in the mountains, the common snack and often main filler of the meal is a buckwheat bread (*baba*), shaped like a thick pancake and cooked in a wok. The Naxi also eat many kinds of wheat *baba*, sweet and salty. In Yongning the Mosuo specialty is 'three-year-old dried pig (*zhu biaorou*)'. Removing the bones and intestinal parts after slaughtering , and then salting the pig, the Mosuo use the carcass as a pillow or mattress in the meantime. Symbolically the dried pig represents wealth. Girls stand on it at their puberty rites and in the past it was part of the tribute paid to the tusi and the monastery. The real function of the 'boneless pig' was a kind of insurance for times of shortage or famine.

On the Tibetan Plateau in Diqing Prefecture barley is the staple crop. A portion of it each year is converted into *qingkejiu*, but most is ground into flour and consumed as *tsampa*. Stored in lidded bowls, it is taken with a spoon and tossed into the mouth, or mixed with butter tea to create edible, doughy balls. Tsampa eaten this way is especially common and useful in monasteries.

While Tibetans like pork, goat and chicken, the meat speciality is dried yak. Sometimes they have it freshly butchered, but as the yak is a big animal, much of the meat is dried and as jerky it lasts for months. Yak milk is made into both butter and cheese, with each area's cheese slightly different. Zhongdian's is a bit sour, Benzilan's sweet and Deqing's a touch salty and served with melted butter.

FRUITS AND SNACKS

Even on the Tibetan Plateau fruit stalls are full, stocked with the produce of the river valleys. Here and in the highlands of the north and west, bananas, oranges, pears, apples, peaches, plums and persimmons fill their trees. Mountain people carry pack-baskets full of these fruits to towns on market days. The Yi in Dayao County, and others in the northwest, bring walnuts from their hill plantations. Chestnuts are popular in central Yunnan, heated in woks at street stalls.

The further south one goes the more tropical fruits appear in the markets. Pomegranates are common in Jianshui and southern Honghe. And in the tropical areas of the south and southwest, fruit stalls offer mangoes, jackfruit, pomelos, watermelons, strawberries, lychees and pineapples. For snacks to accompany their drinks, people have dishes of shredded dried beef and perhaps a bowl of pickled radish. Deep-fried bamboo grubs and bee larvae are also popular.

When not having noodles for breakfast, especially rice noodles (*mixian*), Yunnanese may have steamed dumplings (*jiaozi*) or small meat-filled steamed bread (*baozi*). Or they may have a small rice meal with fried vegetables and maybe an egg.

HOT POT

Some restaurants specialize in hot-pot meals. Originally a Mongolian method of cooking several ingredients at once, the hot pot (*huoguo*) now forms part of Yunnan's food experience. A circular, trench-like container, with a steam chimney rising from the centre, sits over hot coals. The cooks pour water or broth into the container and add a potpourri of meats and vegetables, which are all boiled together to create a soup. Diners remove pieces of meat—usually beef, pork, mutton and sometimes dog—and dip them in soy sauce or something more piquant before eating. Generally, at least three people dine at hot-pot meals, but the very nature of the preparation means that numbers can easily increase.

Hot-pot ingredients vary according to the tastes of the customers, how much they are willing to spend, and local availability of produce. Usually a single animal dominates the meat items. If it's to be pig, for example, then portions of the liver, heart, brain, and stomach will go into the broth, in addition to hunks of pork. The same goes for sheep or dog. Fish and chicken and a little beef or yak are also added, along with sausage. Non-meat ingredients generally include egg roll, bean curd, bean curd skin, mushrooms, lotus root, cabbage, potatoes, scallions, various greens and noodles.

PART II ◆ HISTORICAL EXPLORATION

Han Chroniclers and Marco Polo

EARLY MENTION

When those early Ming-dynasty migrants made ready to trade in their familiar environs in East China for the mysterious frontier lands of the southwest, one might wonder what their expectations were. The concept of a guidebook hadn't been invented yet. Travel literature was still a couple of centuries down the line. Middle Kingdom poets had not visited Yunnan and no literary-minded Han even thought about touring there and keeping a journal, until Xu Xiake—a geographer-traveller—visited in the mid-17th century. Painters hadn't been there, either. So no matter how thoroughly a prospective migrant might research the topic, no image of Yunnan could be found.

He would find some mention in the chronicles, histories and diplomatic records of former dynasties if he could gain such access, but if he were looking for information on what Yunnan was like physically and culturally he was bound for disappointment. Classical chroniclers paid scant attention to such things. Trained in the Sino-centric atmosphere of Confucian scholarship, Han writers took little interest in the cultural aspects of the barbarians. Only when they had dropped their tribal ways and adopted Chinese culture were they considered worthy of study.

Thus the great historian Sima Qian recorded Dian's voluntary vassalage to Emperor Wu Di, because it was an historic, diplomatic event, but he had nothing to say about the nature of the state of Dian.

The court certainly wanted to know about Yunnan, but for reasons of state. The scholars it employed drew up reports concerning tribute items, trade routes and potential trade goods, military disposition and arms, estimated revenues and other such things in order to make policy decisions. The only real cultural information might be a report on the holidays or important customs and habits of the ruling personalities so that the court's diplomats could avoid committing *faux pas*.

Precisely because it adopted so much of Chinese culture, despite periodic political enmity, the Kingdom of Nanzhao attracted more attention from the chroniclers than any other border state in pre-Kubilai Khan China (before the mid-12th century). The Tang Dynasty's southwestern nemesis was

A 19th century lithograph depicts a convoy of merchandise making its way through the forests of Yunnan.

occasionally on good terms with Chang'an and even when they squabbled, Nanzhao maintained respect. When a Tang envoy went to Dali on a reconciliation mission in 794, his royal host proudly showed him the gifts a Tang emperor had bestowed over 50 years previously. Nanzhao's court had carefully preserved them throughout the intervening decades of war. These were people the Chinese found worth remembering.

When the two states were on good terms, the Chinese couldn't help but notice how much Nanzhao aped the Celestial Empire's administration, court trappings and state symbolism. Nanzhao sent students to study in Chinese academies. Envoys resided in each other's capitals, and at times a temporary alliance was sealed with a dynastic marriage, which meant more Chinese going to Dali for periods of time, bringing back more reports. Much less interaction transpired between the two dynasties' successors, the Kingdom of Dali and the Song Dynasty.

EVOLVING IMAGE

Migrants in the Ming era probably knew that Yunnan was mountainous and the weather good. After all, it was South of the Clouds. They had probably heard it was full of barbarians, too, but perhaps knew little else. Like any newly opened frontier, it was rumoured to be dangerous. Migrants from Sichuan might have been more familiar with Yunnan—it being next door—but their own long interaction with Nanzhao centuries earlier also left a negative image in the collective memory. Nanzhao's 829 invasion caused widespread death and destruction in Sichuan. The invaders cruelly tortured captured soldiers before killing them. They also kidnapped thousands of Han civilians, particularly craftsmen, and took them back to Nanzhao to work as slaves in their skilled occupations.

By the time the Ming Court appointed its first Governor of Yunnan, China had enjoyed some four centuries of peace with the people of what was once the Kingdom of Nanzhao. After the final accord with Nanzhao in the declining decades of both dynasties, the only conflict the Chinese had in Yunnan was with Mongols. Yet knowledge of the province was still restricted to Tang-era documents on Nanzhao.

Besides the administrative and diplomatic details, the chronicles described peculiar trade items, often part of the tribute sent to Chang'an or Chengdu in those periods when a less truculent Nanzhao agreed to do so. These included elephants, carved ivory, gold, silver, amber, jewels and tin, plus textiles unlike the ordinary cloth woven in China. Later chroniclers drew attention to the religious architecture, such as the Three Pagodas near Dali.

Mainly concerned with assessing Nanzhao's strength as a state, chroniclers made special note of organizational details, particularly when such differed from their Chinese counterparts. They recorded the Tibetan influence in court, such as the sumptuary laws regarding which tiger skin robes had to be worn by which officials on state occasions, and who could wear what specific badge. A home-grown innovation, however, was the use of red cane staffs and golden belts, utterly unlike anything seen at the Tang court.

Chinese observers were naturally curious about Nanzhao's military aspects. The kingdom had a high reputation for its swords and in periods of peace this was one of the most sought-after trade items. From somewhere in the wilderness of Nanzhao came a herb that the troops used to poison the tips of their spears and arrows. They wore armour of elephant or rhinoceros hide. Some warriors tattooed their bodies with magic prescriptions against wounds. Discipline was strict. Bravery was rewarded, cowardice severely punished. Its exact ethnic composition is still not clear and maybe never will be, but this is all the world knows so far about the army of Nanzhao, the country Tang China never tamed and Song China never dared take.

MARCO POLO

In between the end of Nanzhao and the first Ming-era Han immigration, Yunnan was conquered by Kubilai Khan, in 1253. Several years after the formal founding of the Yuan dynasty (1279), the Great Khan dispatched the Italian merchant Marco Polo, whom he had already come to employ, to the southwest part of the empire, including Yunnan, on state business. The Italian traveller was the first Westerner to ever see this province. Polo did not have the time or the opportunity to see the whole of it, nor did he assign much space to it in the narrative he dictated years after the visit.

Moreover, the entire *Travels of Marco Polo* is coloured by the chronicler Rustichello of Pisa, who aimed to give the book a dose of pot-boiler sensationalism here and there to make it a good seller. Anyone hoping for insight on medieval Yunnan won't be satiated by what can be gleaned from the observations of Marco Polo.

Nevertheless, this report does describe aspects that are familiar to anyone who knows the province. Polo journeyed to the Khampa Tibetan areas in the western Sichuan mountains and to Yunnan's Deqing Prefecture, but in his writing he does not differentiate one place from another. He describes it as desolate mountain country, sparsely inhabited outside the main towns. An abundance of musk deer were on the route and he could smell the musk in the air. It was a chief trade item of the Khampas.

THE EUNUCH ADMIRAL

In the year 1381, a ten-year-old Muslim boy named Ma He played among the fishing boats of his village, Kunyang, and dreamt that Lake Dianchi was a boundless ocean. His father and grandfather had made the pilgrimage to Mecca, at Asia's farthest limit, and had told rousing tales of the seas beyond China. The distinguished family, descended from an early Mongol governor of Yunnan, still remained loyal to the dynasty of Kubilai Khan, and helped Yunnan put up resistance to the new Ming Dynasty that had seized power in China.

That year, a Ming army stormed into Yunnanfu, as Kunming was then called, and encircled Lake Dianchi, sweeping up captives. Ma Ho was seized, along with other boys, castrated, and sent into the army as an orderly. By the age of 20, the bright lad had become a junior officer, skilled at war and diplomacy. His abilities won him influential friends who helped him move to Nanjing, China's capital, during a turbulent period of wars and revolts. There he gained power and prestige as a court eunuch and the emperor gave him a new name—Cheng Ho or, as now spelled, Zheng He.

For 300 years, China had been extending its seaborne power, building up widespread commerce, importing spices, aromatics and raw materials from different parts of Asia. The arts of shipbuilding and navigation reached their height during the early Ming Dynasty. In 1405, the emperor appointed Zheng He as 'Commander-in-Chief of All Missions to the Western Seas', whereupon the eunuch admiral set sail on a mission of exploration and trade. He took 62 ships carrying 27,800 men—the largest naval fleet in the world at that time. It was the first of seven far-flung voyages that took him to the Indian Ocean, Persia, Arabia and the east coast of Africa.

On his fourth trip, Zheng He visited every major port of South and Southeast Asia and brought back envoys from more than 30 states to forge diplomatic relations and pay homage to the emperor of China. After the ambassadors had resided for six years in the new capital of Beijing, Zheng He made another voyage and took them all home again.

Thanks to Zheng He's genius, China held power over much of maritime Asia for half a century. However, China never established a trading empire, in contrast to the European nations who soon began exploring the Earth's oceans, too. Instead, Zheng He's discoveries encouraged Chinese emigrants to settle in foreign countries, where their communities have flourished ever since.

Zheng He's atlases, logs and charts bequeathed a priceless record to the world and made maritime history. On his seventh and last voyage, between 1431 and 1433, Zheng He revisited all the distant places he had discovered 25 years earlier. He died in 1435, honoured throughout China but best beloved by the people of the southwest in the land of his birth, Yunnan.

Zheng He, the 'eunuch admiral': immortalized by this statue in the Memorial Park of Jinning (Kunyang).

The rough route was infested with wild beasts and bandits. Vigilance and arms were necessary to counter the latter, but Polo's party apparently met no highwaymen. To fend off the big cats and bears they built campfires of bamboo, which made frequent explosions, frightening off the predators. In this they followed local custom. Perhaps they also had to conduct trade in the currency Polo describes, made from salt bricks, with a worth fixed at so many measures of gold.

In Yunnan Polo visited Kunming, Dali and a place five days west on the way to Burma, probably Baoshan. Such places are identified by their Mongol names—Yachi, Kara-jang and Zar-dandan. Almost the first thing he noticed was the fine horses. He also tried the fish caught in Dian Lake and stayed a while in Kunming, 'a large and splendid city'. At that time, besides the 'idolaters' (Buddhists and Daoists), the city was home to Muslims and Nestorian Christians. He ate rice-based meals and sampled the jiu distilled from fermented rice. And in the well-ordered markets he found that cowry shells were the medium of exchange.

Moving west, Marco Polo came to the former Kingdom of Dali. The first thing this merchant noticed here was the plenitude of gold, found in the mountains and streams in the north, where it was both mined and panned. The local name of the Upper Yangzi—Jinshajiang, River of Golden Sand—derives from this geological fact. Cowries were used as money in Dali markets as well, and the horses were even sturdier then the ones he witnessed previously; Dali exported colts to India. A local practice was 'to remove two or three joints of the tailbone, so that the horse cannot flick the rider with its tail or swish it when galloping; for it is reckoned unseemly'.

In each place he stayed Polo picked out only a few things to talk about at length. But then this was a European who was used to seeing totally strange things everywhere he went, ever since coming to China. He was a merchant by nature, a political envoy by current occupation, and so covered little in the way of cultural observations in his narrative. He selected the oddest customs he saw or heard about and narrated only these, and the reader must remember that Rustichello embellished now and then.

Nevertheless, the narrative on Yunnan does describe a shaman going into trance to cure a patient. Polo records the shaman's contact with the offended spirit blamed for the illness, the shaman begging the spirit's forgiveness of the patient, asking what would appease the spirit, conveying the message back to the patient and so on. In its broad outline and much of its detail, this could be an account of contemporary shaman healing sessions in many of the remote areas of Yunnan.

Other sections are of dubious veracity. He told of the great crocodiles that lived in the lake near Dali. He reported that one tribe in Yunnan killed guests who were kind, gracious, good-hearted people, not for their money, but so that such qualities would live on in their own household. He claimed Khampa households offered their comely, unwed daughters to their guests. After enjoying her favours, the guest was to leave her a scarf or other token that she could publicly display, adding it to her collection, as evidence of how desirable she was. For the more affairs she had while single, the more valuable she would be as a wife. Polo concluded: 'Obviously the country is a fine one to visit for a lad from sixteen to twenty-four.' Perhaps this was one of the narrative sections Rustichello embellished. The Khampas certainly don't do that nowadays.

YUNNAN IN LITERATURE

Poetry in the Tang dynasty explored a broad range of human emotions. Most poets were scholars who at one time or another in their careers served as government employees. As such they were shifted around, never tarrying too many years in a single post. Friendship, often expressed as the sorrow of parting from a close comrade, became a leading theme in their work. Schooled in the dynastic chronicles, poets also dealt with historical matters, including those of the contemporary era, imparting to their themes proper, Confucianist morality.

It is in this context that Yunnan imagery makes its first appearance in Chinese literature. The wars with Nanzhao, especially the disastrous campaigns against it in the mid-8th century, and Nanzhao's invasion of Sichuan in 829, inspired poets with anti-militarist themes. None of these poets had been to Nanzhao, though, so the use of descriptive imagery is sparse. All the striking details are of the armour and weaponry of the Nanzhao warriors. A Tang poet didn't need to see such things himself, for they were recorded by court chroniclers and were probably common knowledge in the government bureaucracy. The few poems dealing directly with events in Nanzhao concentrate on the woes of ordinary Han soldiers and lament the waste and slaughter of war.

This early Yunnan also developed a reputation as a pestilential place. In 'Lamenting the Nanzhao Capture of the People of Sichuan', Yong Tao describes Yunnan as a land where 'poisonous gasses are ever green, miasmic shades hang low'. In Bai Juyi's 'The Old Man with the Broken Arm', the old man relates how he crippled himself as a young conscript to avoid being sent to dangerous Yunnan, for 'as the flowers fall from the pepper trees, poisonous vapours rise'.

Certainly malaria was a problem in Yunnan then. Its prevalence in the southern plains precluded Han settlement, for they were even more susceptible than the Dai. As long-time dwellers of the tropics, the Dai had at least built up some innate resistance. Nevertheless, when the People's Republic assumed control of Xishuangbanna, a 1950 health survey discovered

42 per cent of the population had been or still were affected by the 'miasmic shades' of malaria. Mass campaigns against the mosquito and its breeding grounds quickly reduced the percentage to a negligible number. Ming-dynasty migrants, however, must have conceived of the place as malaria-ridden, and heat in summer was also part of Yunnan's image. At any rate, the perceived dangers of tropical disease long confined immigration to the cooler, elevated plateaux of the northern prefectures.

While few prospective migrants would have been familiar with Tang-dynasty poetic images of Yunnan, a good proportion would have heard of Yunnan in the context of *The Three Kingdoms*, a long historical novel of 120 chapters detailing the break-up of the Han Empire and the ensuing struggles for supremacy between the states of Wei, Wu and Shu. The story, attributed to Luo Guanzhong in the late 14th century, already had portions made into popular dramas during the explosion of theatre activity in the Yuan Dynasty. With its strong characterizations, detailed descriptions of the combatants, their pedigrees, armour, weapons, horses and trappings, and the contests between opposing mounted heroes, it is like the *Iliad* as written by Froissart. Yet in its emphasis on strategy and morality, it is very much in the classical mould. It has remained down through the ages the most popular Chinese novel ever.

Six chapters (85–91) narrate the conquest of Yunnan by Zhuge Liang in 225. At that time, local rulers in Kunming and other places revolted and joined the general tribal uprising led by Meng Huo. Seven times Zhuge Liang captures Meng Huo and sets him free. Six times the recalcitrant Meng Huo claims he was captured only because of trickery or betrayal and refuses to submit. Zhuge Liang, anxious to win him over in the end, allows the tribal chief to go and organize his troops and have another round. At last, overcome by his adversary's magnanimity, Meng Huo on his seventh release voluntarily submits.

Not much physical description of Yunnan is given, beyond the stock images of 'rampant pestilence' and 'the morning miasma', except for a picture of the mountain forests. They are full of 'giant pines and cypresses, luxuriant bamboo and rare flowers'. The soldiers of Meng Huo are either naked and painted or wear armour of rhino hide or rattan, like the warriors of Nanzhao, and use the same kind of poison-tipped weapons.

The Yunnanese heroes (one is a woman—Meng Huo's sister) play cameo roles in the story. Brave and boastful, one by one they either submit or, in a few instances, die in defeat. Meng Huo has a bigger role, almost as the archetype of the Yunnanese tribal leader. As such, he is more fully drawn. On the plus side he has dauntless courage, perseverance, the pride of independence and an

Zhuge Liang defeated Meng Huo for the seventh and final time near Qujing, after which the Yunnan rebel offered his submission.

ingrained sense of forthrightness and honesty. On the debit side he is not a practised thinker; although able to plan an attack, he has no contingencies in case the attack fails, and he relies on traditional kinship ties for allies, having no skill at creative diplomacy. In short, Meng Huo lacks the qualities that usually can only be developed by personalities formed in the context of an advanced civilization, like the Han.

Yunnan is the venue for one last scene in the novel when Zhuge Liang's forces are about to cross the Jinshajiang and return to Sichuan. An angry river god has stirred up the waters to such a turbulent state that the army dares not cross. Seeking native advice, Zhuge Liang is informed that to calm the waters he has to follow local custom and sacrifice to the river god the heads of the captured tribals, called Man (barbarian) by the Han. He agrees to the ceremony, dons Daoist vestments for the rite and conducts it himself.

But using a play on words, Zhuge Liang substitutes the heads of meat-filled dough (man) for heads of the barbarians (Man). The waters become calm, demonstrating that the wily minister can outwit the gods as easily as he can the generals of Wei and Wu. The *mantou*—steamed bun—has been popular ever since.

Surveyers From The Colonies

19th Century Travellers

T he 19th century was the heyday of European imperialism. It was also the century when most of the last blank spaces on Asia's map were filled in by intrepid explorers. These individuals were not exactly proto-tourists, but men driven by a desire to make their mark by contributing something additional to the sum of Western knowledge about the lands and peoples of the East. The colonial era provided a range of opportunities for those seeking a career abroad. But it took a special breed to disdain the easy job of administration and prefer the adventure of plunging into the unknown.

Starting from the south and gradually annexing their way up to the border with China, the British and French took over most of Southeast Asia. The Dutch took Indonesia, and of China's southern neighbours only Thailand remained independent. The ever-ambitious British and French cast covetous eyes on Yunnan, believing it to be the gateway to China's riches, and as such it was bound to enter the imagination of many adventurers in Burma and Indo-China.

Those who chose the course of exploring Yunnan were well educated, generally from the privileged classes, sometimes attached to the military missions in the colonies, sometimes trained civilian specialists. Brought up in the atmosphere of imperialism, they were intensely nationalistic, convinced of Western cultural superiority, but also intellectually stimulated by the general acceleration of knowledge in all fields that accompanied the Industrial Revolution.

Explorers who kept accounts of their journeys did so with the aim of informing an audience of people very much like themselves, who might wish to undertake similar adventures. This attitude, however, caused passages to be written where the author declined to describe a certain city or valley because one of his predecessors had already published a recent description. Nevertheless, as every explorer set out to make an original contribution to topographic knowledge, their books contain a wealth of information about life and travel in Yunnan in the last decades of the Qing dynasty.

Unlike modern travellers, they did not have the advantage of guidebooks to help plan their itineraries, so they sought information in advance. Often they encountered more uncertainties than facts, and after setting out, they found that they were frequently misinformed along the route, by accident but also by design.

Documents could be troublesome. Even before the British took over Upper Burma and the French occupied northern Laos and Vietnam, colonial officials were able to secure authorization from the indigenous princes for the explorers to proceed through their territory. But sometimes the exact route was specified and local magistrates refused to permit alterations. At major urban centres the explorers had to deal with jealousies and conflicts between advisors to the local prince. Officials could be obstructionist, especially if insufficiently plied with gifts from the Europeans. Travellers had to obtain separate passports to enter China, only to find border officials reluctant to honour them.

In those days, nobody travelled lightly. Explorers usually didn't know how long their journey might take, nor what might be available along the way. So they tended to overdo it in the beginning. The French Mekong Expedition started out with 150 cases, of which 15 were trade goods, one case contained scientific instruments, while the rest comprised 500 kg of hard rations, biscuits, twice-baked bread, 300 kg of flour, 700 litres of wine and 300 litres of brandy. The Irrawaddi Expedition a generation later was much less encumbered, but remembered to bring implements for shoeing horses, plus leads, pack saddles, halters and other tack. Looking for possible railway routes at the turn of the century, Major Davies took 10 baggage mules with three muleteers and packed an array of scientific instruments: a prismatic compass, two aneroids, a boiling-point thermometer, six-inch sextant and artificial horizon for taking latitudes on clear nights and a plane-table for determining longitudes.

Transportation was more often than not on foot, though there were exceptions. McLeod's party on their 1827 trek through northeast Burma to Jinghong rode on six elephants. Light boats were possible for parts of the Mekong journey. Bullock carts carried men and baggage over paths in the plains. But most forward progress was on foot or pony, across unpaved or badly cobbled roads. And in the high mountains landslides sometimes obliterated trails and the explorers and their local porters had to spend hours each day chiselling new paths up the slopes.

In most places the explorers visited they were the first foreigners the local population had ever seen. The reception could be anything from a grand, official welcome to an intensely intrusive curiosity. The French Mekong Expedition had to resort to firearms to disperse crowds, and barricade themselves in their quarters to keep impetuous locals from disturbing them.

Most such incidents occurred in the larger, Han-inhabited towns. In the mountains, among the minorities, their reception was generally more hospitable. The Irrawaddi Expedition found the Hani in Ailaoshan almost obsequious as they dropped to their knees to kowtow to the foreigners. Francis

A cliffside inn along the road between Tong-tchouen and Mong-kou as drawn by a member of the Garnier-Delaporte expedition to Yunnan in the 1860s.

Garnier of the Mekong Expedition reported huddling over campfires with the friendly goatskin-clad Yi in the mountains northeast of Dali.

Hotels didn't exist in those days. When in the Buddhist Dai areas, the explorers, in accord with local custom, lodged in temple compounds. In the cities of central Yunnan they were put up in government quarters, such as the examinations hall in Kunming. But in the mountains they often had to pitch camp, and in the northwest were sometimes forced to find an overhanging ledge for the night—only limited protection against cold and wind.

Paper money was not in circulation and the explorers had to exchange their silver for the Chinese zinc coins common at the time. These were intrinsically less valuable, and therefore a much bulkier load than the silver rupees or silver piastres.

Bandits were a constant threat, especially in the west and northwest. Rapacious officials wanting bribes for permission to continue, or to provide escorts through dangerous areas, plagued many an expedition. Theft of supplies or equipment was another problem. If the article stolen was of importance, such as an irreplaceable scientific instrument, the explorers would halt the journey and hunt down the thief, usually successfully.

The major expeditions took along medics, who made it a habit to treat the ailments of the local population, thus ingratiating the Europeans. But these same medics were not so successful handling the diseases picked up by the explorers themselves. Medical knowledge of tropical diseases like malaria, dengue and dysentery, their prevention as well as the treatment of those afflicted, was still in its infancy. The leader of the Mekong Expedition, wracked by dysentery, expired in Huizi, north of Kunming and a few of the Dulong on the Irrawaddi Expedition died during the crossing of northern Burma.

While originally motivated to further the glory of France or Britain, or to make a signal discovery that would assure their fame, the explorers undertook long, hard journeys that also broadened their minds and left them with what Louis de Carné, the youngest member of the Mekong Expedition, called 'one of the best fruits of travel... a respect for humanity'. Their intellectual curiosity was aroused by the strangeness of all they saw and in some cases they did their best to understand the odd customs they observed. Davies even compiled vocabulary lists every time he ran into a people he hadn't met before. And in writing accounts of their journeys, while including professional information on topography and trade, they recorded the lifestyles and customs of the minorities, which today prove to be of great value in tracing their historical development.

COLONIAL ADVANCES

French involvement in Indo-China commenced in the Napoleonic Era. In 1802 Pigneau de Behaine recruited 300 Frenchmen to fight on the side of the Nguyen family in Vietnam's civil war. After Waterloo (1815), its expansion within Europe put to an end, France turned its attention overseas, joining the carve-up of Africa and Southeast Asia. By mid-century Cambodia and southern Vietnam were under French control and Tonkin (northern Vietnam) was under pressure. Yet by 1860 it was obvious that France's possessions in Indo-China were a financial liability. It was this assessment that led to the Mekong River Expedition later that decade.

The objective was to determine whether, as was fervently hoped, the Mekong could serve as a commercial waterway to the presumed riches of Yunnan. When it became apparent early on that the river was unnavigable all the way, the expedition proceeded anyway, looking for alternative trade routes. Garnier, second in command, placed new hopes on the Red River and in the 1870s a French-led convoy made one shipment of arms to Yunnan using the Red River. The government of Tonkin opposed and blocked further attempts, but within a decade Tonkin was under French control and French commercial ambitions revived.

Yunnan's western frontier was with Burma, a country devoured in stages by the British. When the Burmese overran and occupied Assam in Northeast India in the 1820s, they ran up against the British, already entrenched in Bengal. This culminated in the first Anglo-Burmese War in 1825, ending with the British annexation of Arakan and Tennaserim. A generation later, friction between the old regime and the new colonial power sparked the Second Anglo-Burmese War in 1852, in which the British acquired Lower Burma. The court retreated north to Ava, but weak kings proved unable to slow the colonial juggernaut. In 1886 the British took over the last lands of the Burmese king, whom they deposed.

Thus in the last decades of the tottering Qing dynasty, China faced new, vigourous, expansionist neighbours on its Yunnan borders. Moreover, the exact line of those borders had never been demarcated. In the south and southwest the status of the various Dai states and Wa areas was unclear. Jinghong, for example, paid land revenue and other taxes to China, but had a Burmese Resident at court and sent regular tribute to Ava as well. The French members of the Mekong Expedition didn't consider themselves really in China until they moved into Simao County. And their maps of Yunnan designated the entire lower Ailao Mountains, between the Red River and the current border with Vietnam, as unadministered tribal territory.

After France annexed Tonkin, it arranged for a bilateral commission to demarcate Tonkin's border with Guangxi and Yunnan. The Chinese were forced to renounce dubious claims to parts of Lai Chau Province within Vietnam, while Chinese Black Flag bandits made trouble for the French on the Guangxi side. On the frontier with colonial Burma, the British in 1899 renounced any claim to Xishuangbanna, though the French grabbed two of the districts for northern Laos. The Wa-inhabited border areas were only roughly divided and official demarcation did not occur until the 1950s, after the British had left.

The French Mekong Expedition

On 5 June 1866, the French Mekong River Expedition departed Saigon with the aim of finding out how close to the Chinese border the river could be navigated. Before the year was over they had discovered the Khone Falls in southern Laos, an effective barrier to long-distance navigation. Nevertheless, the party continued upriver along its banks, traversing ever-rougher country in ever-hotter weather until they reached Luang Prabang on 29 April. There they took a four-week rest.

Exhausted by the effort to get that far, the party jettisoned most of its baggage, sent its collections of jungle specimens on to Bangkok, and reduced loads to one bag per person. Setting out again on 25 May, they soon faced the onset of the rainy season, further complicated by political troubles when trying to pass through the petty states of northern Burma. They reached Jinghong at the end of September, which was as far as the Briton McLeod had reached in 1827. The local Dai officials were inclined to refuse the party permission to proceed, until the expedition leader, Doudart de Lagrée, showed them a letter from Prince Gong, a brother of the recently deceased emperor.

The explorers departed Jinghong on 2 October 1867, and in two weeks reached Simao. A fortified city 300 years old, lying in a plain surrounded by low mountains, Simao was the first genuinely Chinese city the explorers had encountered. They were overjoyed to at last be in China, with the petty intrigues of the Dai and Burmese now behind them. But they were aware that they had walked into a province wracked by the Muslim Revolt. Jinghong itself had been briefly occupied by the rebels, and as they travelled further north they would come across evidence of the devastation wrought by the war.

The Chinese mandarins in Simao extended their best hospitality, in spite of the explorers' decrepit appearance. One of them, though, tried to remove Lagrée's hat to see the back of his head. Rumour had it that Europeans were so powerful because they had a third eye in the back of the head, with which they sought out riches while appearing to be looking at something else. This act of curiosity was still within the explorers' concept of levity, so it did not cause offence. The mandarins were anyway cooperative, both here at Simao and at the next stops of Pu'er and Mojiang.

The next major stop, on 17 November, was at Yuanjiang. Here they had their grandest reception, greeted by a party of mandarins bringing the explorers an escort of 200 soldiers and porters. Posters bearing the guests' names were hoisted aloft, cannons boomed and music played. The chief magistrate demonstrated that even in so remote a place as Yuanjiang he was not without his own small collection of modern gadgets. These included a watch, a telescope and a stereoscopic viewer, which he used to look at erotic pictures.

Of greater significance to the French was Yuanjiang's proximity to the Red River. That this waterway, which empties into the sea below Haiphong in Vietnam, might be the river road to China, rather than the Mekong, ignited flames in Garnier's imagination. He tried taking local boats as far as they would go, but soon came to dangerous rapids banked by high, perpendicular cliffs. No amount of cajoling or threatening could induce the boatmen to take him any further.

Disappointed for now, but still harbouring hopes of navigation downstream somewhere, to be explored at a future date, Garnier made his way to Jianshui to join the rest of the party. Arriving ahead of them, he aroused the immediate and overbearing curiosity of the local residents. When a crowd took to hurling stones at him to see how he would react, Garnier fired off a few quick shots with his revolver. The crowd, amazed that a firearm could shoot successive rounds without having to reload, quickly scattered.

The rest of the party arrived soon and the entire group was then insulated from the unruly populace by the mandarin Li Daren. This powerful magistrate had been responsible for clearing Muslim rebels out of the area and under his protection the explorers were safe from unwanted scrutiny. They experienced similar conditions in Tonghai and were obliged to barricade themselves there. (In Tonghai they also experienced a freak early snowstorm, which for the Vietnamese in the party was their first ever look at snow.) But nothing untoward happened in Jiangchuan and from here on their reception was normal and civil.

Leaving Jiangchuan and skirting Xingyun Lake, the party came to its first grisly evidence of Yunnan's civil war. There on a plain beside the lake stood hundreds of unburied coffins, containing victims of a cholera epidemic that followed recent fighting in the area. Continuing towards Kunming, they passed by many villages that had been burnt to the ground. They arrived at Kunming on 23 December for a two-week rest and a discussion of what to do next.

Since leaving Jinghong for Simao, the Mekong Expedition had veered further and further away from the river they were supposed to be surveying. Now Garnier let his scientific interests take hold of his thoughts and, always eager to be the first Frenchman to discover anything, he proposed that he take part of the group west to Dali to once again explore the course of the Mekong. Lagrée, by now extremely ill, acquiesced, his own interest being simply to stay put and try to recuperate.

The Muslim Revolt was still raging, though Kunming had fully recovered from its brief occupation by the rebels several years earlier. Du Wenxiu's forces

*During the Mekong Expedition of Garnier and Delaporte in 1866–1868
they visited the city of 'Siu-tcheou' while it was hosting entry exams for officer-cadets in
the provincial army.*

They wrote of this scene, "A trench had been dug and each rider showed his riding skills in the most difficult positions from one side of the feild to the other. There were many onlookers. On the right you can see three locals (Miao-tse). The middle one is holding an Amherst pheasant, a magnificent game bird from the nearby mountains."

were at the moment mostly quartered around Dali, but one never knew when they might move east. As insurance for the road, as well as to serve as an introduction to the self-styled Sultan of Dali, Garnier secured a letter from the most respected mullah in Kunming. This document requested all good Muslims to aid the explorers on their purely scientific mission. Garnier hoped this would be sufficient to persuade the Sultan to allow the party to continue to the Mekong.

However, keeping in mind that central Yunnan was the most frequent battleground in the war, the French decided to take a longer, but safer, route to Dali. They proceeded north to Huizi, in Qujing Prefecture, where Lagrée stayed to convalesce. Garnier's group then turned west to the Upper Yangzi, becoming the first Westerners since Marco Polo to see the river this far into the interior of China. They then re-entered Yunnan and swung southwest through present-day Dayao County en route to Binchuan.

From there the party continued towards Dali, seeing Erhai Lake for the first time on 1 March. But they never did get to meet Du Wenxiu, for he and his advisors would not believe they were French explorers on a scientific survey. Rather, the court at Dali considered them English spies and made it clear the party would be killed if they tried to enter Dali.

Garnier's group then had to retreat, over much the same route, to Huizi, which they reached on 3 April and learned that Lagrée had died of amoebic dysentery on 12 March. The Expedition was over. Garnier gathered the survivors and took them to Shanghai, where they embarked for Saigon. Though they had failed to find a viable trade route into China after all, they had accumulated a wealth of information about Yunnan, hitherto a practically unknown province. Two members of the expedition, Garnier himself and Louis de Carné, published their findings, to guide and excite all who would follow in their wake.

ARMS ON THE RED RIVER

Of the Red River, Garnier actually explored only a short stretch downstream from Yuanjiang. This is some of the most desolate territory in Yunnan, full of bald, desiccated hills, even today sparsely inhabited. The river is so shallow during the first part of the year that people wade across it easily. Though blocked by rapids between steep, sheer cliffs, Garnier believed that downstream the Red River was probably navigable, all the way to Hanoi. Perhaps anticipating that one day Hanoi would fly the French flag, Garnier fantasized that this would be the long sought river road to China's riches.

A drawing from life by Delaporte of the Garnier expedition perhaps made somewhere along the Red River.

Within five years of this optimistic prediction an adventurous French businessman put it to the test. His name was Jean Dupuis. He had heard of the Red River trade possibility in Shanghai, when the Mekong Expedition members were there at the end of their long journey, and thus began pursuing the connection almost at once. For his first cargo he chose a commodity greatly in demand by the Chinese government: arms and ammunition. In the spring of 1871 Dupuis obtained a commission from Kunming to bring a shipment into Yunnan.

Next, instead of trying to secure permission from the Tonkin government, Dupuis went to France to talk up his project. When he departed in spring 1872, he had what he thought was semi-official backing. This implied the French government hoped he would succeed, but couldn't openly support the attempt. That gave this impetuous adventurer all the sanction he needed. After the rains concluded that autumn, Dupuis loaded his arms in shallow-draught vessels and sailed into Yunnan, brandishing his commission from Kunming as his excuse to ignore Vietnamese objections.

Brazenly passing the border town of Lao Cai, Dupuis entered Yunnan at Hekou (then called Songping) and sailed over another 100 km to Manhao. Today Manhao is a small, riverside town on the Gejiu-Jinping route, near a picturesque view of the river. There Dupuis unloaded his cargo and transferred it to a pony caravan north to Mengzi, where the government buyers waited. Flushed with success, Dupuis claimed credit for both proving and discovering the commercial potential of the Red River, ignoring Garnier.

The following year (1873) Dupuis was ready for another run, only this time he chose salt for his cargo. Salt was a government monopoly in Tonkin, exacerbating the attitude of the Vietnamese, already outraged by Dupuis' first shipment. This time they blocked his passage. Dupuis promptly hoisted the French flag, as if to display official French government backing. At this point both Dupuis and the Vietnamese contacted Admiral Dupré of the French mission in Saigon. Dupré saw the situation as an opportunity to advance French interests in Tonkin. He dispatched Garnier with a small force to help Dupuis.

Together, Dupuis and Garnier had but 400 armed men with them, not all of them soldiers. Some were Vietnamese supporters of the Le family and the Trinh lords of the north, who had been displaced after the civil wars by the Nguyen of Hue. But Garnier, convinced of Western superiority and styling himself 'the Great Mandarin of France', demanded that the Vietnamese give up the citadel in Hanoi, which they of course refused. On 20 November Garnier's forces made a surprise attack and captured it.

Next day the Vietnamese, allied with Chinese Black Flag bandits, counter-attacked. After repulsing the first assault, Garnier decided to make a sortie. But in pursuing the enemy he split up his small band and then ran into an ambush set by the Black Flag forces. They captured and beheaded him. Dupuis escaped. Dupré disavowed Garnier's actions and the French had to sign a treaty with Tonkin, which expressly prohibited commercial use of the Red River by foreigners.

Yet in 1882 the French took over Tonkin anyway. Theoretically, the Red River route to China was open again, but the border first had to be demarcated; this work began in 1884. The Black Flag bandits were still a force in the region and harassed the border commission constantly. Based in Hekou, they sailed downriver to attack the French commission, killing a few. Eventually the work was completed and commerce with Yunnan commenced. Hopes were high for trade in tin and other minerals and a French Trade Mission was set up in Mengzi. The volume of trade, however, never amounted to much. The river was just too shallow.

UP THE WESTERN CANYONS

Scientific interest replaced commerce and politics as the motive for the next major French journey up the Red River. This was the Irrawaddi Expedition of 1895, led by the Prince Henri d'Orléans, which set out from Hanoi with the objective of finding the sources of the river that ran through the heartland of Burma. After crossing into Yunnan at Hekou, the two junks took three days to get to Manhao, at which point the party disembarked and trekked up to Mengzi to organize their convoy across Yunnan. They were guests of the French Trade Mission in Mengzi, a pleasant city then and now, dominated by the scenic South Lake. They also exchanged their silver piastres for Chinese zinc coins, which required the addition of an extra mule for each sack of 1,400 coins.

On 27 February 1895 the expedition left Mengzi for the Red River, trekked west along its valley, then, near Honghe, struck southwest into the mountains. At Dayangjie they learned of a route to Simao, via present-day Jiangcheng (then called Menglei), and arrived there 6 April. Simao was then a bustling town of 10,000 inhabitants and by that time, like Mengzi, a port of entry for foreign goods. Large warehouses stored tea and cotton. The explorers rested here four days and then, adequately reprovisioned, headed in a west-northwest direction to see the Mekong before going on to Dali.

Émile Roux, the expedition's scientist, measured the river's current at 2 mph (3.2 km per hour). With its many rapids, too, the river appeared to snuff out any leftover dreams of making any part of it a trade route. Roux judged it 'not a commercial artery but, on the contrary, a great obstacle to trade'.

The group arrived in Dali on 26 May for a 12-day stay. The city was finally recovering from a 20-year plague that followed the final suppression of the Muslim Revolt. The local missionary, Fr. Guilcher, received them and treated the group to some *yinjiu* (special wine) from Lijiang. Roux was complimentary about the city's inhabitants, noting the use of marble in their sturdily built homes and the delicate Bai silver jewellery, since then rarely found, with tiny blue kingfisher feathers glued to the surface.

The expedition then moved to the Lancangjiang (Mekong) over the old Jihong Bridge, then headed west to present-day Liuku and began trekking up

A 19th century engraving of a gorge formed by a tributary of the Lancangjiang.

the Nujiang canyon. About a third of the way to Fugong they turned back east, crossed the Gaoligongshan and proceeded north up the Lancangjiang canyon, passing Weixi and finally stopping just inside Deqing County at the Lazarist Catholic Mission at Cikou. Roux and the Prince were, needless to add, delighted to meet a fellow Frenchman so far from home. While in the area they witnessed the local version of the Torch Festival and were introduced to the Naxi *dongba* script.

Rather than continue up the Lancangjiang, the Expedition opted to cross the mountains to the west via the hillside village of Londrjé (Londré). Pilgrims on the way to Meili Snow Mountain (Kawa Karpo) were sometimes caught in avalanches at the pass above this village. A locally recognized custom gave Londrjé residents the right to collect jewels and clothes off the corpses of avalanche victims, in return for giving them a funeral. While crossing this range, they espied a magnificent mountain whose steep sides sweep upwards from the plain. They named it Francis Garnier Peak 'because it regally dominates the valley of the Mekong to which the great traveller has forever attached his name'.

Back in the Nujiang valley again, their main encounters were with the Lisu, the same Lisu sub-group they had met before in lower Fugong County. The women dressed in long hemp skirts of white, grey or black and wore caps of beads and discs cut from shells, much as they do today. They and their neighbours, the Nu, believed the Frenchmen to be government agents sent on an inspection tour to learn the people's justified grievances. And so they frequently entertained them with songs and dances.

Getting as far as modern Gongshan, the Expedition struck west again for the Dulong River, to assess its connection with the Irrawaddi (also spelled Irrawaddy). This is still one of the least accessible areas in Yunnan, full of forests, mountains, wild animals and only scattered small settlements of the Dulong ethnic minority. There are no roads. A hundred years ago few trails existed, either. The French managed to hire Tibetan and Dulong guides and porters, but everybody wound up cutting steps into the cliffs, for avalanches had covered most routes going to the west.

This was the wildest stretch of the entire journey. Progress was slow and laborious and they often had to camp out in the open, while nearby fresh tiger and rhinoceros tracks augmented the discomforts and worries about getting through the night, as well as the next day. Nevertheless, after reaching the valley around Fort Hertz (*Putao*) in northern Burma, they still had to cross the Paktai Mountains to reach the valley of the Brahmaputra and the Indian state of Assam.

Speak of the Devil

In the morning we had another beautiful walk round the snow-clad mountains to the village of Yangpi, at the back of Tali. There was a long delay here. News of my arrival spread, and the people hurried along to see me. No sooner was I seated at an inn than two messengers from the yamen called for my passport. They were officious young fellows, sadly wanting in respect, and they asked for my passport in a noisy way that I did not like, so I would not understand them. I only smiled at them in the most friendly manner possible. I kept them for some time in a fever of irritation at their inability to make me understand; I listened with imperturbable calmness to their excited phrases till they were nearly dancing. Then I leisurely produced my passport, as if to satisfy a curiosity of my own, and began scanning it. Seeing this, they rudely thrust forth their hands to seize it; but I had my eye on them. "Not so quick, my friends," I said, soothingly. "Be calm, nervous irritability is a fruitful source of trouble. See, here is my passport; here is the official seal, and here the name of your unworthy servant. Now I fold it up carefully—put it back in my pocket. But here is a copy, which is at your service. If you wish to show the original to the magistrate, I will take it to his honour myself, but out of my hands it does not pass." They looked puzzled, as they did not understand English; they debated a minute or two, and then went away with the copy, which in due time they politely returned to me.

If you wish to travel quickly in China, never be in a hurry. Appear unconscious of all that is passing; never be irritated by any delay, and assume complete indifference, even when you are really anxious to push on. Emulate, too, that leading trait in the Chinese character, and never understand anything which you do not wish to understand. No man on earth can be denser than a Chinaman, when he chooses. Let me give an instance. It was not so long ago, in a police court in Melbourne, that a

Chinaman was summoned for being in possession of a tenement unfit for human habitation. The case was clearly proved, and he was fined £1. But in no way could John be made to understand that a fine had been inflicted. He sat there with unmoved stolidity, and all that the court could extract from him was: "My no savvy, no savvy." After saying this in a voice devoid of all hope, he sank again into silence. Here rose a well-known lawyer. "With your worship's permission, I think I can make the Chinaman understand," he said. He was permitted to try. Striding fiercely up to the poor Celestial, he said to him, in a loud voice, "John, you are fined two pounds." "No damn fear! Only one!"

Rarely during my journey to Burma was I offended by hearing myself called "Yang kweitze" (foreign devil), although this is the universal appellation of the foreigner wherever Mandarin is spoken in China. To-day, however, (May 6th), I was seated at the inn in the town of Chutung when I heard the offensive term. I was seated at a table in the midst of the accustomed crowd of Chinese. I was on the highest seat, of course, because I was the most important person present, when a bystander, seeing that I spoke no Chinese, coolly said the words "Yang kweitze' (foreign devil). I rose in my wrath, and seized my whip. "You Chinese devil"(Chung kweitze), I said in Chinese, and then I assailed him in English. He seemed surprised at my warmth, but said nothing, and, turning on his heel, walked uncomfortably away.

I often regretted afterwards that I did not teach the man a lesson, and cut him across the face with my whip; yet, had I done so, it would have been unjust. He called me, as I thought, "Yang kweitze," but I have no doubt, having told the story to Mr. Warry, the Chinese adviser to the Government of Burma, that he did not use these words at all, but others so closely resembling them that they sounded identically the same to my untrained ear, and yet signified not "foreign devil," but "honoured guest." He had paid me a compliment; he had not insulted me. The Yunnanese, Mr. Warry tells me, do not readily speak of the devil for fear he should appear.

G.E. Morrison, *An Australian in China*,
H. Cox, London, 1895

The northerly route passed through the homeland of the fierce Mishmis, who were said to be more likely to murder strangers than to help them get to the plains. The southerly route had already been taken by English travellers. So, in the spirit of true explorers, the Expedition elected to go directly westwards, which no European had done yet.

It was a fatal decision. The mountains were sparsely populated and the group began to run out of food. Fever struck some, especially Roux, and the possibility loomed that the entire party might starve to death before they reached a supply depot. When Roux became too sick to walk, he insisted on staying where he was, with a couple of attendants, so as not to slow the others' progress. The Prince and the rest pressed on.

Unencumbered by the sick and injured, the remainder of the party moved quickly to the first settlement, dispatched relief to Roux and waited for them in the village. Roux arrived safely and the Expedition, minus a few Tibetans and Dulong who did not survive the rigours of the crossing, made a near-triumphal entry into Sadiya, in Upper Assam. There they boarded a boat for Calcutta. Having made accurate investigations of the Irrawaddi's tributaries, they could claim a successful journey, more so than their Mekong Expedition predecessors.

SCOTT'S EXPEDITIONS

While the French entered Yunnan by following the rivers of the province that ran into Indo-China, the British got in initially through those that flowed into Burma. The first European to penetrate Yunnan as far as Jinghong was the British Captain McLeod. He journeyed up the Salween in northeastern Burma on elephant back, stopped in Kengtung and then struck north-northeast into Xishuangbanna. His journal of the trip contains little physical or ethnic information, unfortunately. Jinghong was a town of but 300 households then and its ruling house was in the throes of a succession struggle.

This, plus the unprecedented nature of McLeod's unauthorized visit, made further progress into China impossible. At that time Western merchants were only permitted access into China via Canton (modern-day Guangzhou). With no reference from the Chinese government and no permit, McLeod was politely but firmly told he had to return to Burma. To assuage his feelings, the officials treated him to a banquet and several rounds of drinks, after which everyone loosened up and became friendly. But they didn't change their minds. McLeod had to return by the same route.

Even in Burma, McLeod had to go back the same way he came, always a frustration to a true explorer. This was partly because very few roads existed in the Shan States. When the British finally took over Upper Burma in 1886 they dispatched officials to survey the Shan States, right up to, and sometimes over, the border with Yunnan. Lieutenant Daly, during his time as Superintendent of the Northern Shan States, led an expedition out of Lashio that passed through Menglian on its way to Kengtung. Soon afterwards Daly's position was assigned to George Scott, who would become the most indefatigable surveyor of them all.

These surveying expeditions had several objectives. The first was to define boundaries, both between the various petty Shan states and the international borders with China and Thailand. Within these boundaries the British intended to maintain the peace, to facilitate trade. Actual administration was left to the Shan princes themselves. Scott added motives of his own: to learn as much as he could of the cultures of the peoples he met as he passed through, and to make a collection of Southeast Asian artefacts and Shan manuscripts.

Of a robust nature, endlessly curious about what lay beyond, an astute and careful observer of indigenous cultures, Scott made his leisurely expeditions in the cool, dry winter months. Yet Scott wasn't a tourist. He was on government business, which was to bring some semblance of law and order to a region that was largely ignorant of the concept. This was especially true in the Wa Hills, for the Shan princes had never attempted to subjugate them.

Scott made his first tour of the Wa areas in 1891–92. The Wa, whose fearsome reputation as head-hunting warriors Scott had already heard about, lived in fortified hilltop villages, hedged with thorn bushes. No hostilities ensued on this trip, but the seeds of mutual suspicion were sown. On this trip he also moved into Yunnan and went to Ximeng. But rather than go further into Yunnan he turned west into the Wild Wa area, as the Shan called it. His guides refused to take him to the higher, more remote villages, returned their wages and left.

Five years later Scott traversed much the same route, better armed and equipped, and met with much resistance. Burning down villages as a reprisal for tribal resistance was Scott's way of dealing with the Wild Wa. But some figures in the British government in Burma were upset over this and an order was issued banning British subjects from entering the Wild Wa areas.

There was still the matter of the border. Scott next travelled through the Shan States into Yunnan and went to Kunming to open border negotiations. He proposed to delimit the frontier according to the 'effective limit of Chinese administration'. The Chinese rejected this, for that would mean the unadministered Wa areas would eventually go to the British. And then the Chinese could not pursue nor retaliate against Wa warriors who raided the Wa areas administered by China. Scott returned without a deal and the border in the Wa Hills remained undemarcated until Burma regained its independence in 1948.

THE SEARCH FOR A RAILROAD LINK

The next wave of explorers into Yunnan out of Burma was once again trade-oriented. No river routes anymore, for enough was known by the end of the century that none of the rivers were suitable. Now it was a railroad link. The British had extended the line to Mandalay, and eventually to Myitkyina, and hoped to outflank the French by constructing a railroad that would begin in Upper Burma, cross Yunnan, and terminate at a Yangzi River port. The title of the best memoir of the period, Major Davies' *Yunnan: the Link between India and the Yangtze*, reflects the obsession that motivated these explorers.

Several surveyors undertook the task, beginning in the last few years of the 19th century, and continuing for a decade before the British finally abandoned the idea. Most set out from Myitkyina and entered Yunnan via the road to Tengchong—then called Tengyueh—the old Southwest Silk Route. Every surveyor searched out a different part of Yunnan, covering nearly all but the southeast, which was pretty well conceded to the French. Davies, the most adventurous of them all, never returned to home base the same way he came. Even when the landscape forbade the idea of a railroad, Davies still found something of cartographic or commercial interest.

He was also fascinated by the various ethnic groups he met. Even though he had a timetable to follow, he always gathered as much rudimentary knowledge as he could about their way of life and compiled word lists for the purpose of comparing dialects. In general, and this was a century ago, he noted that the women dressed in their ethnic costumes, but, except for the Wa, Tibetans and some of the Yi and Lisu, the men dressed Han style.

For the most part he was well received in Yunnan, in contrast to Sichuan and Guizhou, where he was often called 'foreign devil'. That occurred rarely in Yunnan, though he did encounter rudeness here and there, such as at Jianshui, where the city folk's manners hadn't improved since the Mekong Expedition passed through. At Mengzi he enjoyed the company of a small European community and in most minority areas he got along very well with the locals.

Only in Deqing was it different. Davies reported that he usually had to force his way into a Tibetan house to get accommodation for the night. Then he would show his reluctant host some money and state his willingness to pay for the food and bed. Once that was understood, the Tibetans became the most gracious hosts. How different it was a century later, when Zhongdian (Tibetan: Gyeltang; now renamed Shangri-La) was first opened to foreign tourists, and in no time it was Hello City.

Drawings from the Delaporte-Garnier Mekong Expedition to Yunnan in the 1860s.
They wrote, "Tribesfolk from Yunnan: No. 27 is a Muslim from Dali city, said to display a
mixture with Chinese traits, but chosen for his 'Arab' characteristics, more pronounced
than usually found."

The Botanists

THE DIVERSITY OF YUNNAN'S FLOWERS

Gardening has always been a favoured pastime of the leisured classes in the West, particularly in Britain. As the British acquired an empire in all parts of the world, aristocrats and wealthy merchants who cultivated gardens sought to include new ornamental flowers from the exotic corners of the Earth. To seek new species and bring them back, they sponsored and supported expeditions by individual botanists or botanical and horticultural societies. Using the pretext of funding a scientific endeavour, what the patrons really hoped for was the discovery of a beautiful new species of flower that they could introduce to their gardens and show to their friends.

Certainly the contracted botanists hoped for such a result, too, but it didn't necessarily top the list of their objectives. As their work involved the study of nature, and only part of it was undertaken in the controlled conditions of an indoor laboratory, they were people who enjoyed the outdoor life and possessed an innate yen for travel, especially to faraway places where new plants and flowers could surprise and delight them. The possibility also loomed that the botanist might discover a previously unknown species, thereby winning the right to name it. In the field of botany that was a more plausible ambition than the cartographer's hope of finding a new cape, river or bay that could bear his name.

When Europeans began exploring Yunnan in the 19th century and publishing their accounts, botanists were among the most avid readers. They perused all the books on Yunnan and began targeting the parts of the province they themselves wished to explore. With such great physical diversity, the province could not fail to be rewarding for any expedition seeking rare plants.

Yunnan has over 2,500 kinds of flowers. The province is famous for eight of these, the camellia, azalea, magnolia, primrose, lily, orchid, rough gentian and *Meconopis integrefolia* (yellow poppy). The latter two are found mainly in the northwest. The other six grow all over the province.

Of these eight flowers the camellia is the provincial favourite. Its discovery and cultivation date back to the Sui Dynasty in the 6th century. In Yunnan the camellia originated in Tengchong County, where the temperate climate, regular rainfall, high humidity and acidic soil provided the most favourable conditions. In Zhaoyun village, Yunhua township, 20 km north of the county seat, an 800-year-old camellia stands over 16 metres tall, with a crown of 50 square metres. (The same county is home to a rhododendron tree over 25 metres tall, with a crown of 60 square metres.) Venerable camellia trees are often found in old temple courtyards, too, such as the 600-year-old one at Lijiang's Yufeng Temple. Its flowers are red, but other camellias give forth blossoms of white, silver, red, pink, mauve and purple. The camellia has been designated Kunming's official city flower.

Even greater in variety of colour is the azalea. This flower also comes in several shapes. Over 200 species grow in Yunnan and it is especially common in the Azure Mountains (*Cangshan*) behind Dali and the slopes of the Jade Dragon (*Yulong Xueshan*) and Haba snow mountains in the northwest.

The orchid, native to South China and most abundant in Sichuan, Guizhou and Yunnan, has been cultivated for 2,000 years. Yunnan has more species and varieties of orchid than anywhere else in the world. Chinese have always rated it as the most graceful and elegant of flowers, primarily because of its fragrance. Different varieties bloom at different times of the year and one kind or another will be in bloom during each of the four seasons.

The first of the famous flowers to blossom at the end of winter, heralding spring, is the primrose. Also originating from southwest China, the 158 types in Yunnan grow all over the province. In Chinese it is called *yingcao*—cherry grass—although it bears no fruit, just a riot of colour for New Year.

The Chinese call the magnolia *yulan*—the jade orchid—because its colour is like jade and its delicate fragrance resembles the orchid's. Similarly, when the flowers have fallen off and little green leaves begin to grow in their place, their colour is the same as jadeite or jasper. The magnolia flower buds are used as a remedy against the common cold and its fresh, crisp petals are edible. Yunnanese fry cakes of wheat flour, magnolia petals and sugar as a dessert treat. The bulbs of the lily are also edible and have medicinal value. Traditionally, because its densely packed petals were seen as a symbol of unity and cooperation, it was presented as a gift to newlyweds. Its graceful form made it a favourite ornamental flower. Around 20 types exist in Yunnan.

Distribution of the last two famous Yunnan flowers is restricted to the high mountains of the northwest. The rough gentian is the more common, with ten species in the province. The bell-shaped flower is normally blue and has a short stalk; from a distance it appears to grow right out of the ground. The *Meconopis*, a member of the poppy family, grows on the high, steep mountains at 3,000–3,500 metres. The moraines and cliffsides that harbour this flower, which looks like a wild poppy, are fairly inaccessible, so this flower is rarely seen in its natural environment.

Flower enthusiasts from all over China visit Yunnan just to view the famous eight flower varieties. But in the same areas, or along the way, hundreds of other species grace the fields and forests. A list of just some of the common ones is enough to excite the imagination of any botanist: roses of all hues,

Orchids from the jungles of southern Yunnan, Burma, and Laos:
(from top to bottom) Vanda trees, Dendrobium farmeris,
Dendrobium pierardii (left) and Thunbergia grandiflora (right).

white and yellow clematis, peony, dwarf blue iris, primula, barberry, yellow violet, cream-coloured potentilla, saxifrage, bougainvillea and purple columbine.

A natural garden like Yunnan was an easy choice when the Chinese government decided on a venue for the last major exposition of the century. Kunming, whose gardeners already cultivate 2,500 kinds of flowers, native and imported, became the site of Expo 99, an International Horticultural Exposition that drew over a million visitors.

TREASURES OF THE JADE DRAGON

Of all the areas in Yunnan, the northwest boasts the greatest botanical diversity. The three great parallel rivers—Nujiang, Lancangjiang and Jinshajiang (Salween, Mekong and Yangzi)—plunge into the province in Deqing and Nujiang Prefectures, carving deep canyons between Yunnan's highest mountains. Thus the climatic and ecological zones range from subtropical to arctic, producing an abundance of plant and flower types, with something in bloom at any time of year.

Of all the innumerable locations in the northwest for botanical surveys, the most rewarding is Yulong Xueshan, Jade Dragon Snow Mountain, the 5,596-metre-high massif that dominates the Lijiang Plain. The entire province has some 13,000 kinds of plants and specimens and more than half of these can be found on this single mountain. As a protected nature reserve it is spared the axes of loggers and its 20 separate primeval forest communities contain more than 400 types of tree. The snub-nosed monkey, the mascot of Expo 99, makes its home here. So does the clouded leopard, the red panda (also known as the cat-bear, or lesser panda), musk deer, black bear, civet, wild ass, blood pheasant and silver pheasant.

Ten months of the year the mountain is decorated by blooming flowers. Its five kinds of camellia and 50 varieties of azalea bloom in spring, creating great swaths of pink, white and red on the slopes. Rhododendrons, white and red, stay in bloom till early summer and at that season's end, the 50 kinds of rough gentian begin blooming at the mountain's base. Small artemisia flowers of red, yellow, pink or white blossom in the marshes and in the glens by the forest edge. Among other flowers, Jade Dragon Snow Mountain has 60 kinds of primula, eight of *meconopsis*, six flowering crabapple types, four species of peony and 20 types of lily.

The mountain is also home to a great number of medicinal plants. The first thorough survey was carried out in the early Qing Dynasty and 386 were identified. Now that number has passed 800, with a few, like the ginseng from Jilin Province, of recent introduction. Research is still being carried out today, while local use by the Naxi of herbs and medicinal plants from Jade Dragon is on the increase. Herbal tea is a popular commercial product sold in the markets and restaurants and the yeast for making *yinjiu* also comes from the mountain.

The first Western description of the Jade Dragon range came in Bacier's 1837 *Univers*. The first botanists arrived in the late 1880s: Horace from Britain, sponsored by the Royal Botanical Gardens to collect azaleas, and the Frenchman Père Delavay, who spent several years making the first extensive botanical collection. In Simao, Augustine Henry, the British Customs Service officer during the last two decades of the 19th century, compiled a Yi language dictionary (never published) and collected dried plants from the area. These he sent to the Royal Botanical Gardens at Kew, arousing new interest in western China among European botanists. In 1900 the Royal Exotic Nursery hired Ernest Wilson to make expeditions there. The success he had on the first of his four trips to the area demonstrated the richness of the region's floral treasures.

FRANK KINGDON WARD

While Wilson was still in the field during the first decade of the new century, George Forrest began his well-organized, business-like expeditions. Financed by a British gardening consortium, Forrest was already a veteran collector in the Jade Dragon area when Frank Kingdon Ward made his first major field trip, further north in western China. Returning to Shanghai in September 1910, he was hired four months later by the Liverpool botanical firm of Bees, Ltd to collect plants in northwest Yunnan and eastern Tibet.

In February 1911, Ward entered Yunnan via the Bhamo-Tengchong road. The resident British consul in Tengchong recommended Deqing (then called Atuntse) in the far northwest. Within a few days Ward was on his way. It was perfect hiking weather.

For a professional botanist like Kingdon Ward, setting out from Tengchong in February must have been glorious. Scarlet rhododendrons and pink camellias bloom in profusion then. Purple orchids, white dip-roses and pink peach blossoms enhance the scenery on the way to Dali. From Dali he travelled straight north on the main pack road to Shigu, at the first bend of the Jinshajiang. He followed the right bank slightly northeast to Judian, then turned sharply west over the Hengduan Mountains to Weixi. He got a bit disoriented close to Weixi, followed the wrong river briefly, wound up being lodged by kind-hearted Lisu, who put their humble house at his disposal and steered him in the right direction.

The town of Weixi stands in a narrow valley on a tributary of the Lancangjiang, which flows into the great river 38 km to the northwest. It was then 'a small unwalled city with cobbled streets, patches of cultivated ground being freely interspersed with tiled houses of wood or mud bricks; but the pear trees now in full blossom gave a brighter appearance to the shabby temples and monasteries'. So wrote Ward in his account of the journey, *Land of the Blue Poppy*, published in 1913. Most of the area's inhabitants were, and still are, Naxi, who settled in frontier garrisons set up by the Mu rulers of Lijiang during the Ming Dynasty. As a major commercial centre, and today capital of the Weixi Lisu Autonomous County, Weixi was home to Chinese, Tibetans and Lisu, the latter mostly residing in the valleys along the Lancangjiang, halfway up to Deqing.

Upon reaching the Lancangjiang, Ward noted his entry into an arid part of the province, concluding that this valley marked the northern limit of the monsoon. The terrain was much rougher, too, and steep cliffs on one side of the river necessitated crossing to the other side on rope-bridges. At least these were sturdier than the 11-metre-long bridge of twisted lianas, which sagged horribly when he stepped on its not-very-secure planks, crossing a torrential stream in Yangbi on the way to Dali. At that time the rope-bridge was common in the Lancangjiang and Nujiang valleys, as well as those of their tributaries, whenever the cliffs on both banks were steep and the river narrow. The average rope-bridge was about 15 metres long, though some in Nujiang spanned wider gorges.

The 2-cm-thick rope was made of twisted strands of bamboo. It was strung between platforms on either bank, twisted several times around an upright post. A half-cylinder wooden slider ran on top, liberally greased before use, to which was attached leather thongs. The rider passed one pair under the thighs and one pair under the armpits. When released from the platform the rider moved about 15 km per hour over the river, keeping hands free of the rope, which got very hot from friction with the slider. The rider sagged before reaching the other side and had to hoist himself up the last few metres.

Accidents were rare on such ingeniously simple devices. Baggage and pack animals were ferried across the rivers the same way, pulled up the last little bit by people on the receiving platform. But they could certainly daunt those seeing them for the first time. Ward's escorts from Weixi balked at crossing the river on the rope-bridge. One of the soldiers, after being properly bundled up for the trip by Tibetans, panicked and begged to be untied. So Ward stepped forward and became the first of the party to go across. When he made it without mishap the others found the courage to follow. As for Ward, 'After that first experience there was nothing I enjoyed so much as a trip across a rope-bridge.'

Going north up the Lancangjiang valley, Ward's party arrived a few days later at Cikou, a small village that was the original site of the Catholic Mission, established by French Lazarist priests a few generations earlier. In the 1905 Tibetan revolt the church was destroyed and a new one built at Cizhong, a few kilometres north. A couple of the priests who had met Prince d'Orléans and his party on the Irrawaddi Expedition of 1895 were still at the mission. They provided lodgings for Ward, his escorts and guides. From Cikou it was a three-day march to Deqing.

Deqing was at that time a big village of 250 houses. It changed hands five times in the 1905 rebellion and since then had a resident garrison of 100 Chinese soldiers. Many Han merchants had established themselves by 1911, the year Ward first saw it, and while the monastery had been rebuilt, none of the local lamas were left, having been killed in the rebellion, or having fled after its suppression. Deqing was peaceful in 1911 and Ward made it his base for the next six months, first taking a two-week excursion in the immediate area to see Khawa Karpo (*Meili Xueshan*) and collect plants.

Having by the end of May accomplished all he could in the vicinity until the next set of flowers began blossoming in September, Ward took a break to observe a local Tibetan festival. He didn't join them on their processions to the summits of the nearest hill to the east, to the north and to the west to pray, prostrate and burn incense. But he paid attention to the children's activities on the first day. They gathered flowers in the hills, made swings to ride, and picnicked on the cakes they had been preparing all week. In the evening they returned to the main square in Deqing to dance and play games. The girls dressed in their finest Tibetan clothing, loaded with jewellery, formed opposing ranks of four per side and, with arms linked, danced and sang, each side singing a verse in response to that sung by the other. The boys organized various games, usually with one in the middle trying to tag one of the others in the circle around him. Unfortunately, Deqing Tibetans no longer observe this festival.

In June, Ward made an excursion to the Nujiang (Salween River) from Cikou, camping on the mountainside as he crossed the range dividing the Lancangjiang from the Nujiang. Once he camped beside an *Asclepias* tree in full flower, perfuming the night air. Another night he would wake up in the morning and spot a beautiful nearby orchid in the first light. As he descended in the direction of the Nu River, the naturalist side of his character was superseded by the humanist, for he now met members of the Nu ethnic minority, a people he had never before encountered.

"...there was nothing I enjoyed so much as a trip across a rope-bridge."
—Frank Kingdon Ward.

Ward was now in what is today the northeast corner of Gongshan County. He found the Nu lifestyle completely different from that of the Tibetans. Unlike the latter, the Nu did not engage in any kind of trade, 'being in the enviable position of having everything they require', as Ward put it. They raised hemp for their clothing and grew maize, buckwheat, tobacco, wheat and fruits, used bamboo and gourds for vessels and containers and crossbows for hunting. They carried loads with a head strap attached to the basket, crossed the gorges on rope-bridges and in stature were shorter than the Tibetans. All this suggested to Ward an origin to the west, in the jungles of northern Burma.

Ward continued to the Nu River, turned upriver and soon passed out of Nu country by crossing the border into Tsarong District of southeastern Tibet. He proceeded as far as Mangong, turned around and trekked back to the Lancangjiang, this time on a northern route via Londrjé. Back in Deqing for a while, in midsummer he struck north for Batang, a Khampa Tibetan town in western Sichuan on the Upper Yangzi. In September he was back in Deqing, heading east to Dongzhulin and Benzilan, at the time the late summer flowers were blooming in profusion..

Frank Kingdon Ward's last excursion within Yunnan was in November, with a return to the Nu country. This time he descended to the river via Londrjé, striking southwest. At the Nu River he turned east back to Cikou and from there downriver to Weixi, from where he retraced his steps back to Tengchong and into Burma. Appended to his memoir of the expedition was 'a preliminary and incomplete list of plants collected', which identified 200, of which 22 were new species. He had also collected seeds for 76 of the plants, which he turned over to Bees, Ltd nurseries.

Following this success Ward set up a base in Lijiang and began collecting there. George Forrest still turned up occasionally, but the two didn't get along; Ward never credited Forrest with having preceded him. However, Ward steered clear of the Gaoligongshan area in lower Nujiang Prefecture in later years, where Forrest, with a Naxi team of 20 assistants, had made several collecting excursions. Unlike Ward, Forrest never kept a record of his trips.

But their rivalry paled when compared to the professional competition that arrived in Lijiang in 1922. This was Joseph Rock, who would end up staying in the China-Tibet border area for some 27 years. The personality clash was now three-sided and Rock's was the prickliest of them all. Forrest soon retreated to Burma and Ward henceforth returned to the Nujiang, thence up into eastern Tibet and west into northern Burma.

JOSEPH ROCK

When Joseph Rock arrived in Lijiang he was 38 years old and had a solid reputation as the world's leading authority on the flora of the Hawaiian Islands. Born in Vienna, he emigrated to America in 1905, gradually made his way west and landed in Honolulu two years later. In 1908 he was appointed the first Botanical Collector of seeds and specimens for the Division of Forestry of the Territory of Hawaii. The aspiring young botanist soon proved to be a thorough and meticulous investigator. In 1913, the year he became an American citizen, he published *The Indigenous Trees of the Hawaiian Islands* and in 1917 *The Ornamental Trees of Hawaii.*

For all his dedication to work in Hawaii, Rock's secret passion was China. As a boy of 13 in Europe he began studying the Chinese language and in his free time in Hawaii devoured every book he could find on the Middle Kingdom. Offered a job with the U.S. Department of Agriculture to collect plants in southwest China, Rock leaped at the chance. The job was temporary, but Rock's skills as a cartographer and photographer landed him assignments with the National Geographic Society. Its magazine published many of Rock's articles in the 1920s and early '30s.

Rock fell in love with the mountains and landscapes of Lijiang, but he didn't care at all for Dayan, the main town. Instead, he made his headquarters in the village of **Nguluko**, just beyond Jade Pond, the last village north on the plain, about 20 km from Dayan. He lived in an ordinary, two-storey stone and wood Naxi house, much the same as others in the village. The house is still there, and now houses a small museum with photographs by Rock.

Nguluko lies right at the foot of Yulongshan and Rock was ideally placed for his botanical studies. In exploring the nooks and crannies of the vicinity he discovered the local Naxi had names and stories for every site. Gradually Rock shifted the focus of his research from plants to people. He became fascinated by the religion and history of the Naxi, particularly the role of the village ritual specialist—the *dongba.*

Rock observed as many of the rituals as possible, taking photographs and recording the procedures with scrupulous attention to detail. He learned the Naxi language, and eventually even the pictographic script, and when he heard of a ritual he hadn't yet seen, if it was not scheduled soon he simply paid the dongbas to dress up and perform it for him personally. His zest for scientific thoroughness made him want to observe everything. It also meant writing up the findings in sometimes exasperating detail, which led to quarrels with his sponsors over the editing of his articles for publication.

Rock did not restrict his exploration and research to the Jade Dragon vicinity. Though he returned again and again to Nguluko to continue his studies of the Naxi, he was a restless soul, never able to stay put for long. Nor did he completely adjust to the life of a reclusive, expatriate scholar in China. He would soon tire of his surroundings, return to America for professional reasons, like identifying plants for a botanical museum, find that he didn't fit in there, either, and look for a way back to China. He got the Arnold Arboretum to back an expedition to Gansu Province in northwest China and the National Geographic Society to sponsor expeditions to various places in southwest China.

Rock was not gregarious by nature. The Chinese, whose culture he admired intellectually, he came to despise personally. His view of the ethnic minorities was completely paternalistic, seeing them as child-like and naive. He hired many, treated them kindly, but the relationship remained one of master and servant. Consequently he never socialized with them and was scandalized when people he knew, like Peter Goullart and Edgar Snow, made it a point to do so.

(above) Joseph Rock's former house in Nguluko, which now belongs to a local.
(right) Portrait of Joseph Rock (Dr. Joseph F. Rock/National Geographic Image Collection).

In the early years of tourism in Lijiang, in the 1980s, a few elderly Naxi men liked to introduce themselves to Western backpackers at the restaurants by the Mao statue, claiming they learned English as one of Joseph Rock's students. In actuality the only lessons Rock ever gave were to his assistants on how to press and preserve plants and to his cook on how to prepare European-style cuisine. Rock wouldn't have had the patience to teach English.

Though he lived and worked among the Naxi villagers, Rock did so in a grand, patrician style designed to set him above and apart from the plebeians around him. He believed it guaranteed respect and cooperation from the natives, an opinion apparently confirmed whenever he was in the company of other Westerners (the Roosevelt party on their way to shoot pandas in Sichuan, for example), whose shabby appearance and attempts to live native-style did not win the respect of the local people. No matter who the company, if any, Rock always dressed up for dinner, as well as for any engagement or appointment.

When on a long expedition, Rock's baggage included his bulky photographic equipment, cartographic and surveying instruments, boards for pressing plants, lots of food and beverages (he never tried to live off the land), camping and cooking gear and a folding bathtub. Supplies included those for the armed escorts. With such a mule train as Rock's it was advisable to have them along, and perhaps their noticeable presence helped insure that Rock never fell victim to the bandit gangs that roamed the border regions during the Republican era.

Despite the leisurely pace and relative comfort of his journeys, Rock was often beset with illness, which made him an irritable man. On the other hand, even when well, any delays, ostensibly for security reasons, also irritated him. His imperious manner of dealing with people did not lay the grounds for friendship and in all of Rock's years in Yunnan, the only true friend he made was the Mosuo magistrate of Yongning.

In writing up his reports on the region, Rock had little good to say about most local magistrates and governors. The tusi of Yongning was a notable exception and Rock wrote approvingly of his temperate and just governance, the lack of jails in the district, and his diplomatic endeavour to keep the Mosuo homeland free from the encroachments of Han immigrants and opium growers. The tusi's aristocratic bearing and chivalrous personality also appealed to Rock, who affected such manners himself.

The *tusi's* clan was descended from Mongol officers, whereas the other Mosuo clans still practised their original matrilineal way of life. Rock cast aspersion on the moral standards of such a system, and declined to investigate it very far. But he remained good friends with the tusi, who gave Rock the use of his villa on Nyorophu Island in Lugu Lake. Rock spent many weeks here in this heavenly location, translating Naxi manuscripts. Today no building remains on this island, for Red Guards in the 1960s tore away every last trace.

By the mid-1930s the great political conflicts engulfing eastern and central China began to affect Rock's career, particularly his finances. Funding from abroad began drying up and he was forced to cancel expensive expeditions to faraway mountains and spend more time in collation of manuscripts in Nguluko. Great changes were coming, foreshadowed by the passage of the Red Army in 1936 and the increasing conflict with Japan. Rock happened to be in Kunming in September 1938 when the Japanese bombed the city. He quickly left for Lijiang.

But even Lijiang was no longer the same. The Nationalist government retreated to Chongqing and with the Japanese blockade of shipments to western China, new supply routes were opened beyond China's western frontiers. Lijiang suddenly became an important commercial city. Caravans constantly came through from eastern Tibet to Dali, having originated in British India. The Nationalist government was also getting involved in the area's affairs. To run one of its local development programmes, it hired Peter Goullart, who, like Rock and a few missionaries, stayed throughout the war years.

PETER GOULLART

Though not a botanist, Peter Goullart's name is linked with Rock's in the annals of Lijiang because they both lived there in the 1940s and flew out together on the same aeroplane in August 1949. Goullart, some years younger, was born in White Russia to an aristocratic family with connections in the country's leading scientific and philosophical circles. Fatherless at two, he was raised by his mother and educated by a succession of private tutors. He developed an early interest in China and Mongolia, augmented by his grandmother's tales of travels there with her husband.

After the Russian Revolution of 1917, the family fled all the way to Vladivostok. They holed up there for a year before finally securing passage to Shanghai. After his mother died in 1924, Goullart befriended a Daoist monk near Hangzhou, stayed some time in his monastery and in future years often returned for solace and study. In the 1930s he worked as a tour guide out of Shanghai until war with Japan curtailed business. In 1939 he joined the Chinese Industrial Co-operatives.

His first assignment was in Xikang (*Hsi K'ang*), the mountainous prefectures of western Sichuan, but back then a newly created, all-but-autonomous province of its own. Its powerful and totally corrupt officials obstructed Goullart at every turn, eventually putting him under house arrest. The Finance Minister, who was also President of the Chinese Industrial Co-operatives, got him freed. At his own insistence Goullart was eventually sent to Kunming and from there dispatched to Baoshan and Tengchong to survey those towns as potential sites for setting up cooperatives.

Goullart first detoured to Lijiang, of which he had heard much already, liked what he saw and found it a more appropriate site than Baoshan and Tengchong, which were basically trans-shipment centres and military outposts. Goullart's request was at first refused but eventually agreed upon. He was dispatched alone, though, for no Chinese would take up a post in Lijiang, considered 'barbarian land', where the food was unpalatable and the streets unsafe for Chinese. No other foreigner was available for the post because all of the group that had volunteered for executive service in the cooperative movement, except Goullart, had been manoeuvred into quitting or had resigned in despair over the malfeasance and obstructionism of their Nationalist government colleagues.

Unlike the naturalists Frank Kingdon Ward and Joseph Rock, Goullart quite liked Dayan. Ward called it 'a sorry place indeed', only conceding that it was 'yet picturesque, with the snow peaks to the north looming over it'. Rock's supercilious impression was of 'a conglomeration of mud huts and a market place, which is to [the natives] a metropolis of marvelous splendour'. Neither man liked the crowds of cities anyway and Dayan had 50,000 residents. Goullart, perhaps less critical of urban life after so many years in Shanghai, found it 'scrupulously clean' and moved into a Naxi house on the hill just above Sifang Square.

In contrast to Rock, aloof and isolated in Nguluko, Goullart plunged into native life, enjoyed drinking yinjiu in the wine shops run by the women along the stream, attended festivals, weddings and funerals and took an interest in local history, culture and the ethno-diversity of the region. His main work was in the villages and he was astute enough to realize that he had to demonstrate his own sincerity, as well as the practicality of his programmes, to win the hearts and minds of the locals. Otherwise they might not be even willing to try.

An iron-making cooperative in Mingyin township and the introduction of modern medicine were his proudest achievements. Other ventures included cooperatives for copper-mining, leather-tanning, shoemaking and wool-spinning. He paid attention to the workers' welfare and his account of the period, *Forgotten Kingdom*, reveals his humanism, with its personal anecdotes. One story tells of being forced to give the Naxi patients bitterly unpleasant placebos along with the medicine because the Naxi didn't believe any medicine could be effective unless it made the patient feel bad in the beginning.

Forgotten Kingdom also describes the activities of traders, caravan leaders, brigands, soldiers and individual peasant families in the heyday of Lijiang's wartime economic boom. People of the other ethnic groups in the area—the Bai, Yi, Tibetans, Mosuo and Lisu—he also describes, both in general terms and in individual portraits of those he encountered.

About the only thing Goullart did not keep up on in Lijiang was politics. When the war ended, the caravans ceased, inflation soared out of control, brigands had to be repulsed and civil war resumed in China. Lijiang's prosperity evaporated and as Nationalist strength ebbed, financing for the cooperatives began drying up. Still, Goullart, like Rock, hung on in Lijiang, believing he was just going to have to ride out a short period of readjustment.

By 1948 it was clear even in Lijiang that the Communists would soon win the war. Suddenly old resentments of peasants and labourers began exploding and government magistrates began disappearing. Yet in the spring of 1949 Goullart was surprised to find that so many of his own cooperative members turned out to be Communist cadres, now installed as new government officials. Anti-foreign sentiment reached ugly new levels and both Rock and Goullart resigned themselves to the inevitable and made plans to leave.

Hoping for a future change of mind by the new government, and not wanting to give the impression that he was fleeing for good, Goullart pretended that the plane arranged by Claire Chennault was merely for him to go pick up some more medical supplies. And so he packed only essentials and left much behind. Rock was under no such illusion and brought all his manuscripts, artefacts, plant specimens, equipment and so forth on board.

Rock spent the next few years in Kalimpong, India, hoping for permission to return to Lijiang. It never came and China's increasing estrangement from the West in the 1950s made the prospects bleaker. He published his seminal works on the Naxi as well as the Naxi dictionary and even returned to botanical work in Hawaii. But neither he nor Peter Goullart were ever able to see Lijiang again, the home in China they had been so reluctant to leave.

Going Remote for God

MISSIONS IN 19TH CENTURY YUNNAN

T he surveyors sought to tap into the riches of Yunnan, the botanists its trove of exotic plants and flowers. The third type of European adventurer in 19th century Yunnan went after a different kind of treasure—the harvest of human souls. This was the missionary, whose entry into the province coincided with Western political and commercial penetration of China's interior. As a result, the missions were always part of a foreign presence imposed on an unwilling but weakened China. In Yunnan no missions existed until gunboat diplomacy cleared the way.

Between 1842 and 1860 Britain and France forced China to sign treaties which, among other things, established conditions that made Christian proselytizing possible. These were mainly in the form of special privileges accorded to foreigners. The 1842 treaty, following the First Opium War, granted Europeans extraterritoriality, meaning Chinese authorities could not arrest them. Subsequent treaties conferred more rights on foreigners and the 1860 agreement granted missionaries the same status as government mandarins. They were permitted to wear the same clothes, to be addressed with the same deference and have the same claim on government services.

Moreover, the implication was always clear that the Western powers would enforce full Chinese compliance as violently as they deemed necessary. The missions themselves were as aware of this as the Chinese. Confident of their countries' backing, they claimed the right of protection over their Chinese converts, exacerbating the resentments of local officials. Though the missions and their home states failed to support the Taiping rebels (in the former's case largely because of doctrinal differences), the Chinese bureaucracy was well aware it was the foreign religion that inspired the revolt. The mandarins never ceased to view the missionaries as subversive and made as much trouble for them as they could get away with.

Back in Europe, the missionary enjoyed a high degree of prestige. This was the last century in which a career in the Church appealed to a respectable percentage of Europe's best and brightest. The missionary was the equivalent of the government official who volunteered for an overseas assignment or the military officer who enlisted for service in the colonial army. Society pictured the missionary as a man of patience and courage, labouring diligently in the wilderness to bring God and civilization to the Chinese. And both the missionary and the society sponsoring him believed the Chinese were singularly lacking, and in dire need of, both concepts.

Missionaries, like the surveyors and botanists and everyone else undergoing a Western education, were schooled in the imperialist attitude towards the world at large. They saw themselves as not just God's representatives in the East, but also as Western civilization's. To them the West was powerful, modern and expansive because it had the true religion. The only way the rest of the world could catch up to the West was by first adopting its religion. Then progress and modernization would automatically follow.

When musing on the advantages to be gained by opening Yunnan to foreign trade, the surveyors limited their speculations to the possible profits that would accrue to their own countries. Nary a thought was given to how the proposed commercial links might improve the life of the Chinese. The botanists never expected their own work to in any way rebound to China's benefit. But the missionaries, by the conceit that Christianity was equated with social progress, easily convinced themselves that China's conversion could only be for its own good.

The Social Darwinism of the imperialist era affected the missionary's training as much as it did the soldier's or the politician's. It also had its beneficial aspect, for to demonstrate the validity of their equation the missions introduced schools and hospitals in places that hitherto had none. Some of these schools achieved such a high scholastic reputation that, despite their opposition to the missionaries' presence, Chinese mandarins sent their sons to them.

Certainly the missionaries had a strong conviction in the righteousness of what they were doing. In most cases they needed it to sustain their spirits in lonely, isolated outposts, where they were subjected to official harassment and generally failed to make many converts. Belief in the rewards of eternity helped them to carry on.

Like any profession, the missionary one had its adepts and its non-entities, a few stars and a larger pack of mediocre time-servers. The goal of the missions was to saturate the country with priests and ministers, but they tended to concentrate on the more populous and easily accessible cities, mainly in the east. These were considered the plum assignments with the greatest possibilities. Missions preferred to send their best men there. Aside from some who volunteered, who proved to be the most successful, the hinterland assignments went to the less qualified, less experienced, and certainly less talented of the lot.

Two main organizations dispatched missionaries to Yunnan in the latter half of the 19th century (and continued to do so until 1949). The first, already established in Sichuan in 1756, was the Société des Missions Étrangères de Paris, which concentrated on remote areas and ethnic minorities. The

The Catholic College of the Yunnan missions in Long-ki as drawn by Delaporte in 1868. He wrote, "The Catholic settlement is perfectly situated for both security and communications. Built on a hill and surrounded with strong palisades, it has been spared by all freebooters who had looted the country so far. The spirit of those that lived there and the European arms they deployed were the most reliable defences it possessed. Mountain bear and leopard were numerous in this part of Yunnan. A little way to the east-north-east on a hillside overlooking the Houang Kiang River stood the seminary and mission school."

Protestant China Inland Mission (CIM), founded in 1877, tended to stay in the cities. The French were far better at their trade. In 1894 they had 33 French priests and eight native priests in Yunnan, with 15,000 converts. China Inland Mission had 23 missionaries but only 11 converts.

The difference can be explained by their work styles. The British followed the CIM policy of non-intervention in disputes between the people and the government. The French defended their flock against the officials. The British missionaries lived aloof, mandarin-style, while the French priests involved themselves personally with their parishioners, became their doctor, lawyer and counselor as well as their priest.

Judging from the encounters reported by surveyors and botanists, the French were more gregarious and imaginative by nature. Only a French missionary could have produced the ethnography and dictionary that Paul Vial did for the Sani of Lunan County. And only Frenchmen would have introduced viniculture and wine-making to their converts, as the Lazarists did in their Tibetan parishes on the upper Lancangjiang.

After the turn of the century, Protestants began coming in to Yunnan from British Burma and had some success among the minorities of the border areas. The French success was steady, but not without its price in martyrs, particularly in the northwest. Both Catholic and Protestant missions were in constant danger throughout central Yunnan during the Muslim Revolt, subject to threats and restrictions by the rebels. Sensing there would be no future for proselytizing if the rebels won the war, the Yunnan Deputy Apostolic Vicar, Père Fenouil, manufactured gunpowder for the government forces.

Still, missions were subject to the political repercussions of actions their governments took, for the Chinese never stopped seeing them as agents of those governments. Their resentment could take many forms, such as refusing to allow the mission in Weixi to buy land. The priest had to make do with four square metres on the ground floor of a convert's home, to serve as living quarters and church. Other forms were more lethal. Père Vial barely escaped assassination in 1891, while Fr. Terras in Dali was not so lucky and was killed in 1883.

Missions survived frontier rebellions at the end of the Qing dynasty and the turmoil of the early Republican period. In 1915, the China Inland Mission counted 1,063 missions throughout the country and they had Protestant rivals in the growing number of German Lutherans and American Pentecostals and the United Methodist Mission. The Société des Missions Étrangères de Paris posted 319 missionaries and 208 native priests in 1915. Those numbers continued to grow during the Nationalist era, as did their official tolerance, for Chiang Kai-shek was a Christian and allied with the Christian powers of the

West. Thus it was inevitable that, given the missions' close and historic connection with the imperialist era, when Chiang Kai-shek fled to Taiwan the new government closed down the churches and evicted the missionaries.

TIBETAN CATHOLICS

One of the most remarkable conversion campaigns ever waged by 19th century Western missionaries in Yunnan was also one of its earliest successes, among, of all people, the Tibetans. To anyone familiar with the absolute frustration the missions experienced in Tibet the previous century, when French Capuchin missionaries spent the best years of their careers there without making a single native convert, the term 'Tibetan Catholics' must seem like an oxymoron. Like 'Jewish Muslims', one half of the term seems to contradict the other half. Yet Tibetan Catholics do exist, not anywhere near Lhasa, where previous attempts to evangelise met with miserable failure, but in Kham—the eastern marches of Tibet, the mountains of Sichuan and especially in northwest Yunnan. Here a Catholic community has survived for well over a century in two villages on the upper Lancangjiang, about 80 km south of Deqing.

In 1852, right before the Muslim Revolt restricted the missionaries' freedom of movement, an intrepid young Lazarist missionary named Père Renou arrived in the province. He immediately set out for its northwest corner, not stopping until he reached the Khampa monastery at Dondrubling (*Dongzhulin*), 104 km northwest of Zhongdian. Disguised as a Chinese merchant, Renou befriended the head lama and stayed several months to learn the local dialect of Tibetan. After his departure, Renou continued to Deqing, then turned south along the Lancangjiang, eventually settling at Cikou village, on the right bank several km south of Yanmen township.

More Lazarists reached the area in the following years. After their first success in establishing a church at Cikou in 1867—in Chinese-style architecture—the French priests went on to construct more, further north, in Deqing, Yanjing (then called Ya-ko-lo) and Batang. Their success partly depended on their distance from Lhasa and its ecclesiastical hierarchy, helped by the Khampa habit of selective obedience to the dictates of Lhasa, but was mainly due to the character and work style of the hardy missionaries themselves.

The missionaries lived at the same level as the villagers, growing their own food and drawing their own water, quite in contrast to the sedentary lamas whose novices did all the work. They kept an open house and were always

(following pages) Cizhong Catholic Church in Deqing. Tibetans on the Lancangjiang (Mekong River) were Yunnan's first Catholic community.

available for advice or help, whether or not the petitioner was a Christian. They were straightforward and honest, in contrast to the crafty, devious lamas, who taxed the people heavily and who lived a sumptuous, worldly life too much at variance with the traditional Tibetan image of saintly men. The French drew in converts by the example of their own lives, as easily as netting fish in a well-stocked lake.

However loyal their local congregations might be, life beyond the mission was still risky. These were not adherents of a new Buddhist sect the lamas could debate with, but advocates of a wholly different religion, one with no place for lamas. In many cases, especially from monasteries in isolated, remote districts outside Tibet itself, where the lamas were accustomed to being a law unto themselves, the lamas felt threatened by the foreign priests. In 1881 Père Brueux in Yanjing was murdered in a case never solved. In 1887 the lamas instigated an uprising that led to the burning down of churches in Batang, Yanjing and Deqing and the desecration of Père Brueux's grave. In 1905 the Khampas rose in a wider revolt, laid waste to Chinese buildings and other signs of non-Tibetan influence, such as Cikou's church, where they also murdered the two French priests.

In a few years their replacements returned to Cikou, took one look at the charred shell that was once their mission and decided to move to Cizhong, a few km north. In 1909 their faithful Tibetan converts commenced construction of a new church, in stone this time, which was completed in 1921 and protected by a garrison of 30 Chinese soldiers. The priests introduced grape cultivation to Cizhong, which lies on a long, narrow plain on a spur above the river, and the village still has its wine production, kept in a cellar of the church. The priests also wrote diaries all those years (now stored in Zhongdian) and, for such a faraway place, had a fair-sized library covering a wide range of subjects.

Government protection lapsed long before the last priests left in 1949. In fact, in that year, one more martyr—Père Maurice Tornay—joined the list of murdered fathers. Tearful parishioners, who included a few Naxi and Han settlers in Cizhong, promised to hang on to their faith, but no foreigner got back in to Cizhong until the early 1990s. Now they can see for themselves that Tibetan Catholics are not an oxymoron but a genuine living community that did indeed keep its promise.

At 2,000 metres, **Cizhong** is the last settlement on the upper Lancangjiang where rice can be cultivated and, with its neighbour Cikou, is the southern-most Tibetan settlements in the valley. The church stands at the northern end of Cizhong village, in grey stone, with arched windows and entrance, a tall bell tower rising in front, topped by a Chinese-style tiled roof, the only Oriental element given to its exterior architecture. It was renovated in recent years and is in good shape today. Besides its spiritual role it is also host to an orphanage and school in the same compound.

The interior architecture is European and the decorations Tibetan. Great archways stand at either side of the pews of the central altar to Jesus, while above this is a panelled ceiling. Yet the figures filling the spaces between the arches and the ceiling, as well as on the ceiling itself, are the images one sees in the big monasteries—butterflies, lotus flowers, yin-yang symbols and celestial dragons. The interior also houses two subsidiary altars, on the left to Mary and Child, on the right to Joseph and Child.

The missionaries left without ordaining a local priest, so the church today is in the charge of a rector. Sunday services are thus reduced to lighting candles and incense and reciting Christian texts translated into Tibetan. Sometimes the congregation chants like lamas, at other times they sing in groups, with occasional melodious passages, one chorus in high pitch, one chorus in low.

After so many decades they have memorized the texts, such as 'De Profundis' and 'Cantique au Saint Coeur', printed generations ago and rescued from the fire at Cikou in 1905. The texts include the notation of medieval Gregorian chant. The services last about two hours and attract mostly the older folks, who proudly wear their medals and rosaries all day. They are friendly and gracious to Western tourists, seeing them as fellow Christians. And they are especially curious about the French, hoping the missionaries will return, for they have not had a proper Mass in Cizhong since 1949.

SOUTH OF SICHUAN, WEST OF GUIZHOU

Shortly after establishing themselves in Cikou and Deqing, the French set up missions in some of the large cities of central and eastern Yunnan, where they were relatively safe from attack during the Muslim Revolt. By 1870, as the revolt was drawing to a close, they had made 8,000 converts to Catholicism, to add to the 80,000 converts they could count in Sichuan. Their eventual rival in the field, the Protestant China Inland Mission, didn't get started until 1877. The CIM mainly confined itself to the cities and its missionaries rarely made converts among the urban Chinese.

Nor was the Société des Missions Étrangères successful in all of its ventures, especially in the urban areas. When the French Mekong Expedition met French priests on their way through Yunnan, the more religious members of the expedition, the leader Lagrée and the young Carné, were favourably impressed by their piety and perseverance. They saw the missionaries as dedicated, selfless workers for a cause that would bring glory and honour to God as well as to their own homeland, which most were destined never to see again. Garnier, less pious himself, was not so complimentary, contrasting the missionaries' inflated claims of success with the obvious paucity of their congregations.

In the hinterland the French did better. When working among minorities the French missionaries combined conversion efforts with an active role defending the interests of the minorities in any conflict with Han officials. In rural Han areas they sided with the poor against the magistrates and the rich and powerful. In this way the weak and oppressed identified the new religion with improvements in their lives. The number of Catholics in Yunnan continued to rise, while the Protestant missionaries, who had targeted the Han elite, believing their conversion would induce the masses to follow, got scanty returns for their toil.

Following their own lead in the northwest, the French struck out from Deqing to cross the Biluo Mountains into Gongshan, the northernmost county in Nujiang Prefecture. The first priest arrived in 1888, settled among the Nu people, made converts and in 1904 established the first Catholic church in Nujiang in the village of Baihanluo. Altogether seven missionaries came to work in the county in the early decades of the 20th century; churches were

(above) A Tibetan hymnal, 'The Canticle of the Sacred Heart', rescued from the burning of the Cikou Church in 1905. (right) Worshippers leaving the Cizhong church.

erected in Chongding, Cikai, Chala, Pengdang, Dimaluo and Qiumatong, the last being a Tibetan village in the far north.

In the same year of their entry into Gongshan, the Société transferred Père Paul Vial from Dali to a new mission among the Sani in Lunan County. It was a fortuitous move. Vial had not been making progress in Dali, but in Lunan he was not only moderately successful as an evangelist, he launched a side career as ethnologist and linguist. Besides reports on his activities for the Société's newsletter, Vial wrote scholarly volumes on the history, culture and customs of the Sani and compiled a Sani-French dictionary.

Vial mistrusted individual conversions, believing them only partial and not likely to endure in isolation. He preferred the more time-consuming but surer policy of converting whole families and entire villages. His indefatigable defence of Sani interests, whether Christian or not, endeared him to all of them. He only managed to convert a handful of villages during his tenure, but these villages have remained Catholic to this day, the churches renovated and active, a testimonial to his career in Lunan.

The 20th century witnessed new entries in Yunnan's evangelical field. German Lutherans set up the Marburger Mission in Kunming and 15 other cities. Most were within 200 km of the capital, Jingdong and Yao'an being the furthest away. Like the China Inland Mission in generally the same cities, they had only limited success.

Quite the opposite must be said for the United Methodist Mission, which expanded into northeast and north-central Yunnan via bases in Guizhou. Samuel Pollard achieved a mass conversion of the Flowery Miao (*Hua Miao*) of Zhaotong Prefecture in 1904. But this phenomenal success was due to the circumstances of a critical moment in local Miao history. Pollard was a talented man with a fresh approach, but his greatest advantage was accidental: he happened to be in the right place at the right time.

The Miao in northeast Yunnan and northwest Guizhou at that time were at the bottom level of a three-tiered sociopolitical order, below the Han and the Yi. The Han at the top had held political power since direct rule was instituted in Guizhou in 1644 and Yunnan in 1728. The Han population was concentrated in the towns and cities, plus the market centres and villages on the main transportation routes. At the middle level of this order stood the Yi, ensconced in the strongholds of their rural estates. Yi landlords enjoyed practical autonomy within their own domains, ran their estates as they pleased and carried on their blood feuds with impunity.

When the Yi lords needed troops to fight their internecine battles they could induct their Miao tenants. Besides military service, the Yi subjected the Miao to a wide range of taxes and levies, corvée labour and even annual rites of obeisance. The Han government also extracted taxes from the Miao. In recent years they had imposed still more, needing new revenue to cover the expenses of subduing rebellions and paying indemnities to the Western powers.

Historically, the Yi treatment matched that of the Han officials towards the Miao further east, in Guizhou, Hunan and in areas adjacent that had long been abandoned by the Miao. Emigration was one Miao solution to their oppression. Revolt was another option.

Miao revolts were always presaged by popular millenarianism and the projected appearance of the Miao King, who would drive out the Han and make the Miao masters of the land. Shamans or other charismatic individuals would then claim to be the Miao King and trigger the bloodshed. Initially successful, the uprisings ultimately failed, ending in savage repression and expulsion.

When Pollard and his colleague James R. Adam arrived in Zhaotong and began preaching, the Miao were on the verge of another hopeless revolt. Already in the millenarian mood, the Miao took special interest in the story of Christ, identifying emotionally with the tortures of the crucifixion, which reminded them of tortures inflicted on them by the landlords and bureaucrats. Attendance at the sermons mushroomed. Mass conversions soon followed as whole villages enlisted in the new religion.

At the same time they awaited the Miao King, so obviously predicted in the missionaries' story of the Second Coming. Some even conjectured that Pollard himself was the Miao King. Meanwhile the Miao coming into town in such massive numbers, when usually their visits were rare, aroused the suspicions of both Yi and Han. Yi landlords inaugurated a campaign of repression against the Christian Miao, burning villages, seizing property, beating, torturing and imprisoning them. Yet the more severe the persecution the more the Christian movement spread. It was not long before virtually all the Miao of Zhaotong Prefecture had embraced Christianity. The movement even spread to the Miao in Wuding and Luquan Counties, north of Kunming, under the stewardship of Arthur Nichols of China Inland Mission.

Just as the situation reached boiling point in late 1904, Pollard intervened. He persuaded the magistrates to issue proclamations protecting the Christians. Things simmered down for a while but the landlords launched a fresh campaign in 1906-7. Again the missionaries obtained proclamations from the magistrates, this time sent directly to the Yi lords. Pollard and Adam themselves visited the lords to urge their compliance.

Han officials resented the foreigners' interference and talked openly of expelling them. When Pollard found out he threatened them with reports to their superiors. The local officials at once backed down and even promised to take no action against the Christians. The threat implied the officials' dismissal, for it was in the end backed by Western military power, thanks to the privileges granted the foreigners by treaty.

Hostilities continued off-and-on for the next several years. Gradually, however, some of the Yi also became Christians, rendering obsolete the conflict between the two races over religion. The millenarian aspects of Miao Christianity faded, as did expectations of the Miao King's imminence. Yet the missionaries' prestige was so high the Miao remained faithful adherents of the new religion. Samuel Pollard's other great achievement was to devise a written form for their language. That made the Miao literate, raising their status in their own eyes to an equal level with the literate Yi and Han.

East of Burma

After World War I, with the British in control of relatively pacific northern Burma for well over a generation and both British and American missions in the Shan States and in Chiang Mai, Thailand, Protestant missionaries continued to extend their work into Yunnan. The American missionary J. Russel Morse arrived in Gongshan in 1925, where a thriving Catholic community already existed. Undeterred by this, and encouraged by the prevalence of unconverted villages, Morse set up the first church in Gongshan in 1933, then journeyed to the Dulong Valley and set up churches in four separate villages.

Christian Wa singing in the church in Ankang.

Having put Protestantism on a firm foundation in Gongshan County and trained native ministers, Morse left for northern Burma to proselytize west of Gongshan and up into southern Tibet. His converts in Gongshan stayed firm and spread the faith. Their rivals, the French, were equally active in the inter-war years and the two branches of Christianity often competed simultaneously for the allegiance of the same village. Today the Catholic Nu of Shuangla worship in their church on the east bank of the river, while the Protestant Nu of Shuangla hold services in their church on the west bank.

In northern Burma's Kachin State, missionaries had been very active among the Jingpo and Lisu and in the 1920s began

Climbing the sword ladder.

evangelizing among the same two communities across the border in Yunnan. Besides Morse and his wife Gertrude, the Frasers also worked among the Lisu of Nujiang. Fraser originally started with the Hua Lisu of Tengchong County. The memoir of his visit there, written by his wife, narrates how they arrived in a Hua Lisu village in time for the Sword Ladder Festival, when the men climb barefoot up a tall ladder with machetes as rungs, sharp side up. They witnessed the fire-walking event held the night before and the next day observed the climbing. The author doubted the swords were all really sharp, but had no way of explaining how the men climbed up and down without cutting their feet. She attributed the feat to the strong power of the devil. And because the devil obviously had a hold on the Hua Lisu, they decided to work among the Black Lisu further north instead.

Presumably the devil's power was weaker in Nujiang, for the Frasers found no local custom that could put a brake on their confidence, the way the sword-climbing had done. Both the Frasers and the Morses scored many successes in

Nu and Lisu villages. Here, too, the missionaries devised a way to write the Nu and Lisu languages, mainly so their converts could read the Bible and the hymn books in their own tongues. But while no millenarian tradition haunted local tribal history, the new Christians saw conversion, augmented by the new literacy, as raising their status vis-a-vis the Han, Tibetan and Dai.

No Zhaotong-like social conditions prevailed in Nujiang, for the Han, Tibetan and Dai were relatively few and mostly far away. Christianity had no local opposition here, unlike the Lancangjiang missions, and expanded at a normal pace. Elsewhere in the west, its introduction depended on the safety of the area. And as lawlessness spread during the warlord era, mission activity in the west and southwest was largely confined to tribal pockets here and there, fairly close to the Burmese border. In general, missions targeted those people on the Yunnan side of the border whose relatives on the Burma side had already been converted.

Throughout the 1920s and 30s competition in mission work multiplied, with smaller sects like the Assemblies of God and the Church of Christ joining the field. American Baptists worked among the Wa and the Lahu and French Catholics proselytized among the Jingpo of Dehong, entering via Burma. In 1910 the American Baptist Rev. Marcus Young set up in Nuofu, a Lahu township in southern Lancang County, southeast of Menglian city. His son and successor, Vincent Young, built the church which still stands on a hill above the village, a large, one-storey, yellow wooden building on stilts, with a plain interior.

Lahu in the township, and most Lahu in Lancang County, are Christian. Baptist missionaries also worked in Ximeng, Shuangjiang, Gengma and Cangyuan, but were less successful. The Nuofu church serves as headquarters for all five counties.

In the south, Christian penetration began even before the end of the 19th century. In 1893 Reverend Daniel McGilvary arrived in Jinghong on elephant-back. To the astonishment of the crowd, the moment he dismounted he began to preach. In 1897 he was joined by W. Clifton Dodd and W.A. Briggs. In 1917 Jinghong had its first mission, with a congregation of about 100.

Meanwhile Dodd and his wife began exploring other Dai and Zhuang areas to see how ripe they were for conversion, especially the animist Dai, like those on the Red River. Dodd predicted they would all become Christians within a generation. On his journeys Dodd carried along a nickelodeon show on the life of Christ to use as a preaching aid. Attendance was good, for the villagers had never seen such a contraption before. But Dodd and his wife, who completed his memoirs after his death, attributed interest to the inspiration of God, never to the novelty of the nickelodeon, and so exaggerated the impact of the

Christian message. In fact, the Red River Dai did not convert and to this day remain animist.

CHRIST AND CIVILIZATION

The missionaries did not consider their work complete with the introduction of Christ into the converts' consciousness. At the same time they saw it as their duty to bring Western civilization as well. Brought up in the imperialist age, they took a paternalistic attitude towards the people of Yunnan, be they Han or ethnic minority. Missionaries believed in the superiority of Western civilization as firmly as they believed in God and the afterlife. Conversion was not to be limited to religion. It must encompass the whole Western idea of civilization as progress, as the extension of social services and the broadening of opportunities for personal advancement. Allegiance to Christ was the first step to adopting the Western world view, to be rewarded with material improvements in the new Christians' lives.

Thus the missionaries opened clinics and schools wherever they set up bases. Medical services provided instant tangible benefits, while schools imparted the concept that by diligence and study one could raise one's station in life. Some of the schools acquired such a reputation that the mandarins sent their children to them. They did not convert, except in a few cases, but the missionaries welcomed their attendance, for at least they would get a proper dose of Western ideas—and that was half the battle.

Invoking their prestige as privileged foreigners, and anyway perceived locally as agents of the imperial powers, the missionaries supported their congregations in disputes with outsiders, such as landlords and government officials. This was not always the case, for the China Inland Mission policy at first was to refrain from intervening in such disputes. The success of the French, who employed the opposite approach, persuaded CIM to change its mind by the turn of the century. Missionary defence of their converts' material interests was a key factor in the acceptance and growth of the foreigners' religion.

Aware of the earlier history of Christianity in China, when the Rites Controversy at the end of the 17th century ruined a possibility of converting the imperial Manchu court, missionaries were instructed not to interfere unnecessarily in local customs, unless they were completely contrary to the Christian way of life. The Wa, for example, could not become Christian unless they gave up head-hunting. But aside from such obviously unacceptable customs, traditional tribal life was not to be eradicated, only improved.

Besides the improvements in material life, which accrued with the coming of the missionaries, another important factor aided the conversion campaign.

Missionaries made little headway among the Han, Dai and, except for the upper Lancangjiang, Tibetans. These people had older and more sophisticated cultures, spread more or less uniformly over wider areas, than the simpler societies of the isolated valleys and mountains. There, traditions and customs could vary from one county to the next, even within the same ethnic group. Much of the unity apparent in Han, Dai and Tibetan cultures can be attributed to the standardization brought about by literacy. This standardization, in which the guiding concepts are the same among a widely spread and numerous population, gives such cultures strength and prestige when viewed by outsiders like the hill folks.

The minorities, with the arrival of the missionaries, thus had three cultural options open to them. They could try to retain their tradition in its entirety and live like their ancestors. They could alter their lifestyle along the lines of their Han, Dai or Tibetan neighbours. Or they could change their ways according to the guidelines of the Western missionaries. In places where no serious conflicts ever developed between the minorities and the Han, Dai or Tibetans, Christianity made little headway. But where discrimination and prejudice were rife, the missionaries found a better reception.

The key element in giving the tribal community a new sense of ethnic identity and pride was to make them literate in their own language. Missionaries in the northeast experimented with various writing systems for the Hua Miao dialect before settling on one of phonetic signs based on the Latin alphabet, which was later called the Pollard script. In the far west they devised scripts for Lisu and Nu, like the Pollard script using Latin letters for equivalent sounds and reversed letters for sounds with no Latin or English equivalent. In Lunan, Vial based his transcription of Sani on French orthography, and different churches working in the south and southwest introduced alphabets for Jingpo, Lahu and Wa.

The Han, and even the Dai, laid claim to cultural superiority by virtue of having writing and literacy. Now the tribal converts were literate as well, a significant boost to their self-esteem. Granted the output at the beginning was strictly religious, such as translations of the Bible, the new literacy would eventually be put to use in other ways, such as recording folk literature and keeping records. The Lisu and Nu previously used notched boards for their records.

In some cases the missionaries went too far in trying to impose Western moral codes, such as their insistence in Lijiang that Naxi adopt temperance as part of the Christian way of life. Naxi men like to drink, but they have never had a reputation for alcoholic excess. They saw no reason to give up their glass of jiu at dinnertime or their social cups of yinjiu. So they rejected the new religion. In Lijiang the missionaries never made a single Naxi convert. The Lisu, on the other hand, did have a reputation for excessive drinking, but no missionary demanded they give it up; hence, many Christian Lisu.

In general, the missionaries encouraged their ethnic congregations to retain those things that distinguished them from the Han. Christianity would enable them to redefine themselves. It would be the element in their identity to link the past with the future. Père Paul Vial epitomized this approach. He sought to preserve the Sani's innate religiosity by linking traditional religious symbols with Christian ones. Thus he placed crosses on Sani sacred stones, held prayer sessions on traditional ritual days, and replaced the charms on baby caps with Christian medals. He took a keen interest in Sani history and mythology and promoted a new, Christian Sani image, modern but distinctly non-Han. And like so many missionaries working among the minorities, he thought *mes enfants,* as he called them, were more occidental by nature than oriental.

CONTEMPORARY CHRISTIANITY

After Japan's surrender in August 1945, the uneasy alliance between the Nationalists and the Communists had no reason to continue. Civil war soon resumed, but the Nationalists were on the defensive from the outset. By the beginning of 1949 the Communists' ultimate triumph was already apparent, though it was not until 1 October that Mao proclaimed it publicly. Missionaries knew their time was up as well and many left even before the expulsion orders came. Paranoia about what the atheist Communists might do to Christians, especially those long protected against government officials by the foreign missionaries, caused some to panic. When the Morses left upper Nujiang for Burma, for example, thousands of fearful Lisu joined them on the exodus. By 1951 no resident missionary was left in Yunnan.

Yet the government by no means intended to stamp out the foreigners' religion now that the missionaries were gone. For several years there was no interference as the Communists went through the process of reorganisation and the complex business of autonomous areas. In 1957 the government began its own 'civilizing mission', as the French used to call theirs, with a mass campaign against 'superstition', directed against Christian, Buddhist and animist tribal societies. Yet some churches stayed open.

True repression of Christian practice came only with the Cultural Revolution. Then churches were closed, some damaged as well, and services forbidden. People with past links to the foreign missionaries were dragged out for punishment or summarily imprisoned. The xenophobic mania of the Red

Guards categorized all Christians as foreign agents, but the Red Guards found excuses just as fast to attack Buddhist priests and monks, too. All religions in Yunnan suffered during those years when the Red Guards tried to force their ideology on the people (1966–76).

With the Reform era, Christianity in Yunnan, like Buddhism and Islam, could be openly preached and practised again. The government repaired and restored old churches, like Nuofu's, Cizhong's and Kunming's, or disbursed funds to construct new ones, like Guishan's in eastern Lunan County. But 20 years of official opposition, sometimes outright repression, did leave scars. Many congregations have revived and churches are active, but the younger generation, brought up in the heyday of militant secularism, is less involved.

At the end of the 20th century about 300,000 Yunnanese were Christian, mostly from the minority communities. In a few areas, like Nuofu, foreign missionaries are in touch again and make annual visits. But no foreign priest or minister resides in the Christian communities. Foreigners cannot obtain residence visas for missionary work. So the missionaries have been coming in as tourists or teachers or international aid workers. And they preach, but privately, almost by appointment, never overstaying their visas, nor arousing any public interest in their activities.

The development of Christianity now is almost strictly local. And it varies. Churches in Yunnan, like elsewhere in China, are both 'aboveground' and 'underground'. The former are registered with the government and hold their services openly. The latter meet in secret and consist not only of Catholics who retain allegiance to the Pope but also those Christians who believe in the separation of Church and State, that no church should have anything to do with any government, and vice versa.

Practice, or rather the intensity of it, also varies in Yunnan's Christian world. The Hua Miao in the northeast, having long enjoyed legal and political equality with the Han and Yi, are less fervent believers than in Pollard's day. They even successfully lobbied the government in the 1980s to have scholars devise a new alphabet to replace the one the missionaries gave them. On the other hand, the relaxed atmosphere of the Reform era has led to expansion in other areas, such as Yingjiang County in Dehong, among the Jingpo villages. And in the cities live the largest percentage of recently converted Christians—young Han Chinese.

Closing the Frontier

THE LAST STAND OF THE GUOMINDANG

Soon after the end of World War II, China's Civil War resumed. Well entrenched in the north, the Communists commenced their inexorable drive into central and southern China. The great military campaigns and titanic battles of this ultimate phase took place well outside Yunnan. But the province was certainly not isolated from the political currents of the struggle. The Red Army had made a generally favourable impression on its passage through Yunnan during the Long March and the Communists had established clandestine cells in most large cities by the late 1940s.

The Nationalists, in the final stage of their retreat by the beginning of 1949, hoped to use Yunnan as a base to regroup and continue the fight. They did not reckon with their rival's success in already infiltrating much of the province. Communist cadres started coming out in the open and in April, for example, led an armed uprising that took over Jianchuan in Dali Prefecture. Soon the entire northwest came under Communist control. Governor Long Yun declared himself in favour of the Communists even before the Red Army marched into Yunnan in October.

The 93d Division of the Guomindang's 8th Army, soon to be known as the Lone Army, retreated to the west. Red Army forces caught up with and defeated them, pushing them over the border into Burma's Shan States. There the 15,000-strong remnants of the Lone Army, under General Li Mi, set up bases in the remote hills. They constructed airstrips to receive supplies from Taiwan via night flights out of Thailand. In July 1951, Li Mi led an invasion of southwest Yunnan, but a month later the People's Liberation Army (PLA) drove his troops out once and for all.

At this point Li Mi opted for retirement. As per a United Nation's resolution, he and part of his army were repatriated to Taiwan. But several thousand troops stayed behind in Burma, setting up new bases in the Wa areas. To counter any new invasion in China's portion of Awashan, the PLA entered Ximeng in 1951. The following winter the PLA marched north into the Lancang County section of Awashan and drove leftover Nationalist troops across the frontier. The Lone Army was reduced to hit-and-run guerrilla raids, which continued for the rest of the decade.

Meanwhile, the Communists consolidated their control over the border areas. In Xishuangbanna the PLA undertook several land reclamation projects and enticed defectors from the Lone Army by offering pieces of land to those

who deserted the Nationalist cause. Negotiations began with newly independent Burma to demarcate the frontier, a task that took several years. Lone Army guerrillas continued to harass the border areas, so in the dry season of 1960-61 a joint PLA-Burmese Army campaign cleared them out of the Shan States altogether.

REORGANIZATION

Every new regime in Chinese history faced the pressing task of rebuilding a war-torn nation. The smashed or decayed administrative apparatus of its predecessor required immediate reorganization. With the foundation of the People's Republic, the Communists followed this pattern of response throughout the country, but in Yunnan the process took longer. The Han portion of the population was no problem, for the Nationalists had won few adherents to their cause and the overwhelming majority of the Han welcomed the Communists. But two-thirds of the province was inhabited by ethnic minorities, especially in the border areas, which were still a security problem. Their attitude towards the Han, and therefore any Han-administered government, was mostly a question mark.

Beyond re-establishing administrative control in the Han-dominated areas and making new arrangements in the minority-dominated areas, the new government faced other daunting problems. Good roads in Yunnan were few. It took a month to get from Kunming to the southwest border and nearly that

A mural commemorates the welcome given to Zhou Enlai and Burmese president U Nu during their visit to Wanding in 1961.

long to reach Jinghong. Malaria was rife in the southern half of the province, while epidemics raged unchecked. The population of Simao, for example, a victim of both scourges, had fallen to 1,000.

One of the first measures taken in Yunnan was a mass campaign against malaria, which the PLA launched in 1950. Improvements in sanitation and drainage attacked the mosquito breeding grounds. By 1956 the infection rate had been dramatically reduced to 1 percent of the population. The campaign's success had two other consequences. Much of the population had been using opium as its main defence against the effects of malaria, which only suppressed the symptoms. Now people had no such excuse to raise or use the drug and the government eliminated its cultivation in the same period. The conquest of malaria also opened the way for Han immigration to the south. Xishuangbanna's population, which had a negligible Han percentage before 1949, is now one-third Han.

The most complex issue involved the administration of the minority areas, especially along the international borders, where the same ethnic groups lived on both sides of the frontier. Proclaiming the new government dictum on the equality of all 'minority nationalities', yet aware that the different groups were likely to be initially suspicious, the PLA indoctrinated its troops on ethnic sensibilities before dispatching them to a new area. The policy was to create autonomous areas in whatever prefecture, county or district the minorities dominated.

For the first several years the government set up autonomous zones in the frontier areas. (Eshan Yi Autonomous County, in 1951, was the sole exception.) Before organizing administration, the PLA distributed gifts of grain, seeds and tools to the minorities. The state now controlled commerce and manipulated it to the ethnic groups' benefit. After gaining their confidence, the PLA set up local militias to help deal with border security. Then they established autonomous governments, beginning with upper Nujiang in 1951. Upon formation these all vowed 'to improve production and safeguard national defence'. By 1956 all the border counties except Ximeng had been organized; then it was the turn of the interior counties. Ximeng remained under PLA administration until 1965.

Ostensibly the autonomous areas were supposed to be run by the minorities themselves. Obviously, they would have to be trained to administer them in a fashion compatible with the broad outlines of government policy. The state founded the Minority Nationalities Institute (*Minzu Xueyuan*) in Kunming for this purpose in August 1951. The following April, 400 minority cadres graduated, generally from the interior counties. But gradually more cadres from the frontier areas were enrolled. By 1956 the Institute had trained 17,000 minority cadres, who now made up 15 per cent of the province's total.

The priority given to the border areas over the interior counties reflected a dichotomy that continued throughout the decade. When it was time to launch reforms, the government moved more cautiously in the frontier areas, preferring to work with traditional leaders. The Dai-dominated areas of Dehong and Xishuangbanna became autonomous prefectures in 1953 and six months later the Dai *sawbas* were invited to a ceremony in Kunming. There, government officials gave them seals of office in a rite straight out of the feudal era.

Because Lone Army guerrillas continued to annoy the border areas, where historical interaction with the Han was less extensive and more recent than in the interior counties, the government first concentrated on winning over all 'anti-imperialist and patriotic forces'. Political consolidation preceded social reforms. That proved difficult, however, because many of the ethnic minorities had an instinctive distrust of Han governance. Despite PLA indoctrination, some cadres and soldiers did indeed look down on the minorities as backward and troublesome, who ought to be grateful for the improvements in their lives the Han were introducing.

For some Han cadres and soldiers, a condescending attitude might have come easily. Inspired by the revolutionary zeal that characterized the first years of the People's Republic, they had an almost missionary attitude about spreading the tenets and benefits of the new socialist order. Physically and socially, Yunnan was a hard tour of duty for those from far beyond the province, unused to the tropical heat of the southern lowlands or the ruggedness of the mountains. Party literature of the period emphasized the 'high, cold, desolate mountain regions' of Yunnan, and its poverty and backwardness.

Everywhere the goal was to improve production. One aspect was to dispense tools, seeds and fertilizer. Some minorities had never used fertilizer before, it being taboo in their cultures. Cadres found they had to spend much time persuading the locals to abandon that taboo. Many other tribal customs, mostly involving the division of labour and customary allocation of land and other resources, stood in the way of the goal, leading some cadres to adopt an ever dimmer view of minority cultures the more they learned about them. At a Chinese Communist Party (CCP) meeting in Kunming in 1956, Party leaders attacked 'Great Han chauvinism' as the main cause of the slowness or failure of most newly organized cooperative movements.

ENDING SLAVERY AND OTHER REFORMS

The last thing the Party wanted in Yunnan was to alienate from the outset any of the minority nationalities, especially in the border areas. Though the Party was committed to making great changes in social and economic life throughout the country, in Yunnan's border areas the communists moved gingerly, sometimes spending years ingratiating themselves before introducing any radical measures. Cadres cultivated relationships with traditional leaders, hoping to win their cooperation when it came time to inaugurate reforms.

Certainly reforms were due in many ethnic societies. The status of women in most was generally low, their restrictions many, their marriages arranged. Abuse of power and crude exploitation did exist, some of it of recent origin and exacerbated during the chaos of the Nationalist era. A few Dai princes had been collecting tribute from the poor hill people of their states and conscripting them for 'dirty' tasks, such as husking grain and preparing manure. Yi landlords in the north were exacting exorbitant rents from their hapless tenants.

For cadres aiming to increase production, the greatest obstacles were the practices of usury and slavery. Usury not only kept rich tribal personalities powerful—for among those practising it, indebtedness, with interest, was passed on to the debtor's heirs—it spoiled any initiative to work more than the

WHEN SALT WAS KING

Among the economic changes experienced by Yunnan after the founding of the People's Republic was the reorganization of the salt trade. After 1949, salt came to Yunnan from the east coast, with a steep fall in its price. Prior to that most of the province obtained its salt from three sources within Yunnan itself, and its distribution and sale was a jealously guarded government monopoly. Wells sited between Pu'er and Jingdong supplied the southern and southeastern parts of the province; those beside the thousand-year-old Bai village of Nuodeng, near Yunlong, serviced the western parts. Although its people no longer work in the wells, Nuodeng has made a successful shift to farming and its 200 sturdy, attractive, traditional-style houses reflect its continuing prosperity.

The most productive wells, however, were at Heijing, in the centre of Chuxiong Prefecture, which provided salt for central and northern Yunnan. (Zhaotong and Qujing got their salt from Sichuan.) Lying in a pleasant valley astride the Longchuan River, with its red sandstone bed and banks, this small town was once full of fancy houses, some of which still stand as testimony to its former wealth. A century ago more such houses stood beyond the present limits of the town, when Heijing was far bigger—so prosperous its per capita income was greater than Chuxiong's, its value to the provincial government in Kunming at least as important.

These surviving traditional houses were home to the wealthy salt traders—a species of businessmen that became extinct with the founding of New China and the reorganization of the nation's commerce. Those black holes in the riverbank are abandoned salt wells. Heijing once had eight functioning wells, though today only one remains open.

The town's name is a contraction of Heiniujing–Black Buffalo Well. It was named after the black buffalo that discovered the well 2,000 years ago when taken for grazing in the area by a local Yi girl. Later the buffalo fell into this well and, according to legend, metamorphosed into a huge boulder still there at the bottom.

This was the first salt well in the vicinity. Serious production only began in the Tang Dynasty (618–907). It peaked during the Ming (1368–1644) and Qing (1644–1911) Dynasties, when the government organized and supervised the salt trade and regulated its distribution, partly to insure supplies to all parts of the province, partly to guarantee the collection of revenue. By controlling the salt business, the Yunnan government secured its most dependable source of revenue. By the end of the Qing Dynasty salt tax collection constituted 47 per cent of provincial revenue. Salt was equally important to the revenue of other provinces. Yuan Shikai used it as collateral to obtain foreign loans to finance his bid to found a new dynasty during 1915–16. Provinces opposed to him, like Yunnan, announced their secession and spent their salt revenue on quickly raising defense forces.

Heijing produced its salt from wells that were up to 80 m deep. Seven or eight men turned a huge wheel, to which was attached a wide pail two metres long to scoop up the brine. The work crew then boiled the brine in large cauldrons until only a residue remained. This they pounded and cleaned, then laid out on the flattened area of the riverbank to dry and be shaped into blocks. These blocks they then cut into cakes for transport, with saws like that used by loggers. On one side the cakes were stamped with a tax receipt and a brand name.

Caravans conveyed the salt from Heijing to various destinations in central Yunnan, sometimes using pack mules, sometimes porters. Six sentry stations were erected in the vicinity of Heijing to watch for smuggling which, given the nature and importance of the commodity, was always rampant. Porters themselves chipped off bits of the salt cakes they were carrying and sold them later. Arrested smugglers had their salt confiscated, but were jailed for only two nights, then released, a policy that had little impact as a deterrent.

To acquire the right to participate in this lucrative trade an aspiring Heijing salt producer first had to purchase a licence from the provincial government. Government agents established quotas for the registered producers, allocated the brine and collected the tax on the spot. But producers devised various schemes to obtain more brine, exceed their quota and sell the surplus on the black market. Even without cheating, though, licensed producers could grow wealthy just meeting the government demands. By the end of the Qing Dynasty, 84 families possessed salt licences. They were the richest folk in town.

That anyone at all got fabulously wealthy dealing salt may seem extraordinary at first. Nowadays salt is easily available, sells for 1.5 yuan per kg and as a preservative has largely been replaced by refrigeration.

(following pages) Nuodeng, a 1000-year-old Bai village near the salt mines of Yunlong County.

Rice costs an average 1.8 yuan per kg. But before 1949 salt was worth four times as much as rice. The standard of currency in the old days was the *liang*, known to Westerners as the Chinese silver dollar. One such dollar bought 1.8 kg of salt or 7–8 kg of rice.

With no competition and a constant heavy demand, Heijing's salt trade generated wealth for everybody in town, not just the 84 licence holders. Porters only had to work 3–4 hours per day and received one silver dollar in return. That was quite a good living back then, especially for unskilled manual labor. Heijing's porters handed down their easy jobs from generation to generation, while immigrants to the town were employed at the production sites.

Within the town wealthy families employed large household staffs of cooks, servants, gardeners and so forth, commissioned tailors to make their clothes and artisans to decorate and furnish their homes. Itinerant merchants made frequent stops and the town hummed with prosperity. Even the vegetable vendors wore ornaments of gold and jade.

To enjoy their wealth and leisure, the salt traders built fine, multi-storey mansions for themselves. They hired skilled craftsmen, many from the Dali area, to embellish their homes with intricately carved wooden chairs, tables and cabinets, plus decorative plaques and panels on the doors. They installed screen windows, arched roof supports, painted tiles under the courtyard eaves, dragon-headed water basins and sculpted lion heads on the bases of the house posts.

Some of these old houses remain occupied, their courtyards still imbued with traditional elegance. A fine example is the modest but well-maintained Bao family house in the lower town just past the memorial gate. Others, like the five-storey, 99-room Wu family mansion, the biggest in Heijing, have been empty for years, their furnishings long ago removed, staircases rickety, floorboards occasionally missing. But it's still a very atmospheric building to explore.

Religion also attracted the patronage of the rich. Before 1949 the town and its environs boasted 50 temples and mosques, plus one Christian church. Contemporary Heijing has but four: Zhetian Buddhist Temple in the lower town, Zhenjuechan Buddhist Temple high up on the west bank hill, Feilaisi just above the upper town and the Wenchan Confucian Temple in the upper town. Wenchan was the most important, featuring its own ceremonial gate, a pond, elephant-headed roof struts and dormitories for students.

Here the salt traders sent their sons to study. For a small town, Heijing had a high number of accomplished scholars, several of whom passed the final round of imperial examinations. Their descendants today proudly keep the commemorative boards issued to them by the court in Beijing.

The salt traders cultivated Confucianism in all its aspects. Virtuous wives, defined as those who embodied Confucian principles when they became widows, were also honoured by the Qing court, especially in the years of the Dowager Empress Cixi (d. 1908). The Memorial Gateway for the Chaste and Dutiful Women at the head of the lower town was erected to honour several such Heijing ladies. Even today the Confucian tradition remains influential, for Heijing people, especially the older generation, are known for their conservatism.

That may explain the subdued contemporary nightlife. There's little to do after dark but enjoy a long meal with friends, washed down with cups of the local Lolo brand of jiu (wine, spirit). But in its heyday nightlife in Heijing sparkled with parties and public spectacles hosted by the rich. The main street was lined with opium dens and mahjong parlours, where the porters tended to spend the greater part of their time and wages. Food vendors worked the residential lanes where the salt traders lived. From the upper stories of their high-walled houses the customers lowered a tray by rope, the vendors filled it with various dishes, the householders hoisted it up and then lowered down the money.

Aside from the opium addicts, most Heijing residents spent the evening watching one of the public opera performances sponsored by a rich family. For ten months of the year at least one opera, often more, performed nearly every night. Heijing had its own opera troupe, but most shows used professional Beijing and Yunnan Opera troupes, whom the salt traders paid to come to Heijing.

Life in old Heijing was easy and good. The salt traders devoted much of their wealth and leisure to the pursuit of culture. In doing so they enriched not only their own lives but also those of all the town's residents. When they disappeared as a class no one took their place. Heijing shrank and took on the character of an ordinary small town in Yunnan. Evocative relics remain, from the memorial gates and vacant mansions to the carvings on the posts and doors, and even the ancient salt wells. With a little imagination the visitor can conjure a vision of Heijing in its prime, when houses were works of art, scholars were venerated, high culture was glorified and salt was king.

minimum necessary to pay off the next installment. Slaves, of course, had the same lack of incentive towards production. And as an institution, slavery was anathema to the revolutionaries.

Yet even in this instance the Party moved cautiously, relying for the time being on persuading influential slave owners to voluntarily free their slaves in return for positions of importance in the new local governments. Slavery was not widespread in Yunnan, mainly confined, in its most complex form, to the Yi of the northwest, while less sophisticated systems prevailed among the Wa, Jingpo and some Lisu. Rich Han in Kunming had house slaves, but these were freed by decree after the Red Army came. Meanwhile the Party had manifold other concerns to attend to which would affect a greater proportion of the population.

Land reform, already in effect in most of the country, began in Yunnan in the spring of 1951. First steps were the reduction of rent and taxes, followed by the break-up of large estates and the encouragement of cooperatives. Most minority areas were initially exempt, partly because groups like the Wa, Hani, Bulang and Lahu had no wealthy land-owning class anyway. With these peoples the cadres concentrated on improving agricultural output. Mobile dispensaries, the near-eradication of the malaria scourge and other such improvements in health meant an increase in population. Moreover, a survey undertaken in 1956 discovered that previous population estimates of the hill people were incorrect. These new explorers found there were actually far more of them. And so the land must be made to yield more.

Not until 1956 did the Party begin dealing with the slavery issue. Some Wa and Jingpo owned slaves, rarely very many, who could conceivably work their way out of bondage and could marry non-slaves. Apparently a relatively recent custom in both societies, it was not overly common and the cadres had only minimal trouble persuading the Wa and Jingpo to give up slavery.

Ninglang County, where the institution had been entrenched for centuries, proved to be much more difficult. The Yi, who constituted the majority of this mountainous county's population, had two classes of slaves, as well as two classes of the free. At the top, comprising 15 per cent of the Yi, were the Black Yi aristocrats, who owned most of the land and slaves, organized the raids that augmented the supply of the latter, carried on feuds and ruled their domains without regard to Chinese law.

Below them were the White Yi, about 50 per cent of the total. They could not be sold nor killed with impunity, but they were basically serfs of the Black Yi, subject to tithes, services, and periodic conscription as soldiers in their lord's feuds. The remaining 35 per cent were the two kinds of slaves—those of the field and those of the house. The field slaves were better off, for as long as they turned over to the lord his share of the crops, they were rarely bothered. They could even raise cash crops, usually opium, on their own and use the income to buy their freedom.

They might instead opt to buy their own slaves, and those slaves might in turn grow opium, sell it and buy their own slaves, too. These latter unfortunates would thus belong to the slaves of other slaves—the lowest status possible.

As for the house slaves, they hardly ever had a chance to make money and thereby alter their status. Their treatment depended on the personalities of their owners. Some were kind, others brutal. Owners could free their slaves on their own initiative if they wished. Once in a while, a slave conscripted for the latest of the lord's feuds performed some singularly valorous deed in battle, perhaps saving his master's life, and was granted freedom as reward.

However seldom such voluntary setting free took place in Ninglang Yi society, it was part of the system as much as slaves owning slaves who owned slaves. When the Party in 1956 decided to eliminate the entire system, cadres counted on the precedents of voluntary emancipation to persuade Black Yi lords to go along with the reform. By then most of them were ready anyway, for they were aware of what had been happening in China during the past several years. They surrendered most of their land as well. In return the Party gave them the promised positions in the new local government so that they retained a measure of social prestige.

Not all Black Yi agreed to reform, however. A small number of lords on the high and remote hills resisted, drafting their tenants and slaves into guerrilla forces who attacked and harried PLA troops and their new Yi allies. The revolt took two years to subdue entirely and the large PLA cemetery in Ninglang attests to the ferocity with which recalcitrant slave owners waged their armed struggle.

Besides the military campaign, the PLA and Party cadres had to resettle slaves who fled the hostilities, establish new villages and allocate land. They also had to educate the newly emancipated on a whole new attitude towards life. With persistence and persuasion as watchwords, cadres carried out the most thoroughgoing reform of any minority society in Yunnan. It proved to be one of the most successful revolutionary measures in the province, for today no Yi—Black, White or ex-slave—yearns for a return to the old days of feuding, raiding and slaving.

POLITICS IN COMMAND

Until the end of 1956, Party policy towards Yunnan's minorities still emphasized the gradualist approach, with persuasion and good example the primary means of effecting change. In the interior counties marked out for agricultural reorganization, 'peaceful, consultative land reform' was the means, rather than the mass meetings to denounce and try landlords that had transpired in other parts of the country. Cadres were constantly instructed to be aware of 'minority sensitivities', as the Party categorized a broad range of cultural differences. It encouraged its cadres to learn minority languages and live in the style of the people with whom they worked.

In general, the Party interfered little in the matter of local customs, proscribing only those which threatened lives or physically abused people. Thus the grosser forms of punishment some groups had, like the heavy wooden collar worn by Tibetan convicts or the chains and fetters some Yi lords used to punish slaves or tenants, were outlawed. The Aini practice of destroying newborn twins or deformed babies was also forbidden and cadres were dispatched to the remotest villages to announce and explain the new law. Head-hunting was proscribed in Wa areas whenever the government established its control. The few cases that occurred as the practice was being suppressed were due to blood feuds rather than raiding for the spring's fresh skulls. They were settled according to the Wa custom of compensation.

Those customs the cadres considered an affront or threat to human life and dignity could be eliminated simply by banning their practice and persuading the tribal people themselves to enforce the ban. More difficult was the task of dealing with taboos and customs of non-action, like the Lisu taboos on fertilizer and the many instances of certain people traditionally not doing certain kinds of work.

This required time and patience. To demonstrate the harm of a taboo on manure, for example, the cadres had to make an experimental field with manure use, reap a predictably better harvest and thus convince at least some of the skeptics to try breaking the taboo the next time they planted. The cooperative movement also started small, with cadres persuading a few of the poorest families to pool their efforts, then using the improved results as the main argument inviting others to join.

In 1957, however, the political climate in the country changed. The Anti-Rightist Campaign swept China and in Yunnan toppled Long Yun and the old guard, the Dai sawbas, the ex-tusis and traditional minority leaders. As the nation prepared for greater radicalization, the new line on minorities was that their 'special characteristics' should not delay their socialist development.

Otherwise, social disequilibrium would develop as the Han majority became socialist. As for Yunnan and its different ethnic minorities, a Party conference in Kunming in December of 1957 decided that all nationalities must travel the socialist road together.

As the Great Leap Forward commenced, cadres organized mass campaigns to build irrigation works, aqueducts and reservoirs. No longer constrained by 'minority sensitivities', they speeded up the cooperative movement by ordering minority people to join. Increased regimentation was seen as the way to stimulate production. The Party announced a policy of 'Three Transformations': physical, social and mental. In practice, this meant changing from swidden (so-called slash and burn) fields to terraces in the hills, and implementing the use of fertiliser on the plains; the introduction of new production relationships appropriate to socialism; and a determined campaign against 'superstition'.

The new policy was a failure. Inflated reports of gains in output, so ruinously typical of the period nationally, led to even greater regimentation and ever more fanciful, triumphal claims. Taxes in Xishuangbanna, for example, actually increased the more control the state took over the land, for revenue had to be seen to equal the dramatic rise in production. Thus the Dai farmers had to work much harder than before, in fact harder than ever in their history. Traditionally, Dai farmers from Banna to Dehong never laboured more than was absolutely necessary to maintain a relatively comfortable, self-sufficient existence.

At the end of 1957 the Dai chairman of Dehong Prefecture, along with nine ex-sawbas, fled to Burma's Shan States. Though the chairman returned himself the following year, the others did not. And what had been a trickle of clandestine migration out of the prefecture became a steady, swelling stream. The same exodus affected other Dai areas, with Banna Dai slipping into northeast Burma, Thailand and Laos. In the mountains along the southern boundaries entire villages relocated a few kilometres over the border, safe from the intrusions of the cadres.

By February of 1959 the retreat in policy commenced. Far from achieving new record harvests, agricultural output had actually declined. Exhortation was dropped as a governing principle and all-out attacks on customs suspended. The reorganization of agricultural landuse continued, but the gradualist approach again prevailed. This milder policy lasted several years, until the launching of the Cultural Revolution in 1966 and a decade of coercion and chaos.

The new target in the minority areas was 'little nation chauvinism', which was interpreted to mean anything that made ethnic cultures different.

Churches, mosques and temples were all closed and damaged, while monks, priests and imams were put to work or imprisoned. The government either banned the ethnic festivals or transformed them into political rallies. The Bai Raoshanling, for instance, with its three days each honouring a specific deity, became the Festival of the Three Constantly Read Articles, with each day devoted to mass recitations of one of Chairman Mao's three famous short pieces. Red Guards also banned traditional ethnic costumes and fined anyone caught wearing one.

Nevertheless, geography somewhat modified the Cultural Revolution's ravages. Those places easy to get to, like the plains, river valleys and plateaux, suffered the most. But some of the more remote mountain areas scarcely encountered the Red Guards. When the young zealots did make the effort to climb up into the highlands, they found few people, no one obviously wealthy to direct their attack upon and little to eat. They would then just call a meeting, harangue the villagers for a while, stage a noisy demonstration and go back down the mountain, not very eager to return.

The most isolated communities could stay aloof from most of the decade's developments, but could not completely escape the general assault on tradition in all its manifestations. Everywhere the minorities were repeatedly urged to abandon their 'special characteristics' and join the socialist mainstream, and their children were educated in the fiercely secularist temper of the times. In the border areas the ethnic exodus resumed, but in the interior counties that was never an option. There, as with their Han neighbours, the minorities made an outward appearance of adjustment and kept their resentments to themselves.

REVERSAL AND REOPENING

Even before the death of Mao and the fall of the Gang of Four in 1976, revolutionary fervour in the mountains of Yunnan had been flagging. Rallies and meetings were called less and less, while the proscription on ethnic costume stopped being enforced. Most other manifestations of ethnicity, however, were still impossible. The communes were still in place, too, and the radicals yet in positions of local authority. But with the ascendancy of Deng Xiaoping the days of both were numbered.

Real change came with the decision to launch the reforms at the end of 1978. The communes were dismantled and the family responsibility system put

(previous pages) Land erosion remains a problem not only in Yunnan but everywhere in Southeast Asia. Here, the Jinshajiang runs through dry hills around Wanbi, on the border of Chuxiong and Lijiang Prefectures.

into effect. After meeting the state's requirements at fixed prices, families could now produce surplus for sale at whatever price the market would bear. This sudden liberation caused problems, however, for hill farmers in Banna, for example, began clearing forest tracts for new farms, causing extensive deforestation. The government stepped in and imposed controls, yet at the same time introduced cash crops, like sugar cane, which were far less demanding on the soil than rice.

As for the ethnic minorities, the government reversed its policy. 'Little nation chauvinism' was dropped from the political lexicon and the minorities permitted their ethnic traditions, costumes and festivals again. Religion, ancient customs and ethnic pride commenced their comeback. The basic reforms introduced by the Party in the early 1950s remained in place, but anyway, no ethnic minorities clamoured for the revival of slavery, head-hunting, infanticide, the imposition of tribute, corvée labour or any of the other abuses of the past.

The Reform era also put an end to the ideological slant on China's foreign policy. China now sought good relations with the governments of its neighbours and stopped supporting and supplying revolutionary groups trying to overthrow them. Naga, Mizo and other Northeast Indian guerrillas lost their training bases in southern Yunnan and the government even wound down its long-time support of the Burmese Communist Party, with its largely Wa military forces, which had been using the borderlands of Lincang and Simao as bases and sanctuaries.

Reforms and infrastructure development continued cautiously but steadily in Yunnan and other remote provinces, while the southeast was put on the fast track. Business enterprises, joint ventures and tourism were all introduced sooner in the southeast, but the die had been cast and, despite incidental retreats here and there, there could be no going back to the radical era. China was determined to enter the community of nations, to expand its opening to the outside world. This also meant permitting citizens of that outside world to travel, on their own, inside China, without having to be part of an organized group shepherded everywhere by Party guides. One after the other, China's provinces opened their doors to the individual foreign tourist. Yunnan's turn came in 1985.

PART III ◆ CONTEMPORARY EXPLORATION

Open Counties

INITIAL DESTINATIONS

The first tourists to take a look at Yunnan were by no means permitted to roam freely across the province and explore every remote county that caught their fancy, as they do today. Once tourism was judged to be of economic importance in the New Long March towards modernization, it became subject to government policy controls. Tourism would continuously expand, just like other goods and services in the country, but at a steady rate, not outpacing the capacity of the nascent tourist industry to absorb the increase in business. In line with new government policy, tourism was expected to attract private investment and arouse the dormant commercial talents of an ambitious section of its people to exploit the opportunities offered by a guaranteed growth industry.

In the beginning, though, the government was the only investor in the tourist trade. It owned the hotels, the bigger restaurants and the tour agencies with their buses and cars. Coupled with the general cautious attitude that characterized the new economic policies, this meant that foreign visitors stayed in government hotels, ate in government restaurants and went on government-arranged tours. Only a few hotels were even authorized to accept foreign guests, while only a handful of destinations were open to them.

Such a policy partly reflected the lingering worries about liberalizing too fast and upsetting stability. Conservative officials would let the foreigners in now, but try to keep watch over them, shepherd them around to areas of obvious tourist interest, but in a way that would keep them from seeing things that might embarrass China. For the conservatives, evidence of poverty was an example of something that tarnished the nation's image. So as a start they restricted tourists to just four main cities in which they could wander freely, for these had the temples and old buildings that are part of any tourist itinerary, and areas of scenic beauty not far away.

Beyond the security and propaganda aspects, another consideration limiting the scope of tourism was the lack of accommodation. It's not that Yunnan had too few hotels or guesthouses. It didn't have enough that met the standards the government believed foreigners expected. As time went on, and no social or security problems developed because of tourism, lack of 'proper'

A Xiaoliangshan Yi girl, one of the 25 major minority groups that inhabit Yunnan.

accommodation became the only reason to keep a county closed. Once the new hotels or guesthouses were constructed, the county's doors were officially opened.

In the first few years, therefore, foreigners could roam all over Kunming and, of course, the Stone Forest, but not Lunan town. They could explore Jinghong, but not far beyond, Dali but no other Bai county (not even nearby Eryuan) and Lijiang and Tiger Leaping Gorge, but not Baishuitai just across the Jinshajiang. Outside Kunming, foreigners couldn't even eat where they wished. At Lijiang, for example, all guests were billeted in the No. 1 Guest House and required to dine in the hotel restaurant. Local residents were informed of the restrictions, too, so that anyone who tried to order food in an old town restaurant was politely and apologetically refused service.

Tourists were also required to exchange their foreign currency not for ordinary *renminbi*, the national currency, but for Foreign Exchange Certificates (FEC) instead, at the official rate. At that time the exchange rate was fixed at less than six yuan per US dollar. Tourists had to pay hotel, train and airline bills in FEC Yet restaurants and buses wanted only renminbi. The unofficial rate for renminbi was over eight yuan per US dollar. Black market money-changers, often Sani ladies from Lunan County, congregated near the entrances to those hotels permitted to have foreign guests. And any tourist who wished to play by the rules and only purchase FEC found out at the next meal that local businesses preferred the other. In the mid-1990s, China revalued its yuan, bringing it in line with the black market rate, and dropped the FEC system (at the same time that Myanmar adopted it).

Besides the FEC system, foreign tourists were also irked by the instances of double pricing. They were forced to pay more for train tickets, park entrance fees and sometimes hotel rooms. This can still be a problem in Yunnan, though all over China such practices are diminishing. Foreigners are not required to purchase expensive insurance policies to ride long-distance buses, as they have been in some of the northern provinces. They pay the same for transportation as local Chinese and in only a few counties do they pay for hotel rooms at a higher rate than Chinese. And in some places they must stay only in the *binguan* (hotel), the best grade of accommodation, and may not stay in the cheaper places.

OPENING MORE DOORS

In the early 1990s the government began to accelerate the opening of the province. Most of central Yunnan came first and at the end of 1992 a number of counties were declared open that have since become major tourist destinations: Zhongdian (Shangrila) and Ninglang in the northwest,

Tengchong, Baoshan and Dehong Prefecture in the southwest. At the same time it dropped restrictions in those areas that had already been open. Now tourists could overnight in Lunan town, instead of the Stone Forest only, and catch the early morning market activity, as well as visit the lakes and Sani villages on their own. Permits were no longer necessary for Baishuitai, Lugu Lake, or the remoter townships in Xishuangbanna. And signs at the bus stations, which listed the counties for which foreigners were not permitted to buy tickets, were taken down. Both ticket-sellers and foreigners had been pretty much ignoring them anyway.

Some counties remained closed in the middle of the decade. A few newly opened areas still required foreigners to lodge in the government-owned binguan. Other counties would allow foreign visitors only if they secured permits from the prefectural capital. Unwary travellers caught in such counties were fined and ordered to leave.

But the government never issued printed notices of closed areas to foreign tourists, nor did hotels and restaurants post any. With ever larger numbers of foreigners coming to Yunnan, many eager to explore away from the beaten track, this situation could not long prevail without damaging Yunnan's tourist image. So the government threw open the last closed doors and abolished the permit requirements. Only those reserved forests and protected areas that are off-limits even to ordinary Chinese citizens remain closed to foreigners.

ENCOUNTERING THE MINORITIES

Yunnan's tourism advertising has always presented the ethnic minorities with an emphasis equal to that of its scenic attractions. The first areas opened were those where both aspects combined easily: the Sani and Stone Forest, the Bai and Erhai, the Naxi and Jade Dragon Snow Mountain, the Dai and tropical Xishuangbanna. In the beginning the authorities may have restricted how far afield the foreigners could go to meet the local people, but they put no limits on their encounters within the free-access zone.

The first relaxation in the rules governing tourism came soon. Foreigners could now eat wherever they chose. The government-run hotels were filling up with Chinese guests anyway, who often travelled in groups and tended to order up big banquets in the hotel restaurants. So the foreigners were at last given liberty to eat elsewhere. As the influx continued to grow, local entrepreneurs set up restaurants catering to the foreigners, with English menus and Western-style dishes. These became the easiest places to meet local minority people, both the restaurant's staff and those adventurous locals looking for someone with whom to practise English.

The other main venue was the market. On market days, in the towns of Shaping and Wase near Erhai Lake, groups of foreign tourists became as regular a feature as the vegetable hawkers. Opportunities abounded for meeting local Bai, even if few took full advantage of this. In the street stalls of Dali and most of the shops and stalls in Lijiang's old town, however, the Bai were the ones selling the crafts and souvenirs foreigners sought, just as in Lunan it was the Sani. Later on the Naxi in Lijiang began getting into the auxiliary tourist businesses. When Zhongdian opened, local Tibetans entered the trade, too, so foreigners automatically experienced an ethnic encounter of some sort just by buying things.

The best encounters took place in those destinations that, though open, had a shortage of accommodation or perhaps none at all. Baoshan Stone City, in eastern Lijiang County, was a place where visitors stayed with Naxi families because the village had no guesthouses. And at Lugu Lake foreigners, unless in big groups, preferred to stay with individual Mosuo families in Luoshui, right on the lake. In such places the foreigner had a close-up, on-hand view of minority people's daily lifestyle, and a more intimate setting for making friends with them.

(*above*) *Wa farmers salute their foreign guest before departing for the fields.*
(*left*) *Zhuang and Miao in the market at Babao.*

THE ETHNIC SHOW

Upon arriving in Kunming, travellers are instantly aware of the emphasis placed on the minorities as a tourist attraction. Advertising posters for local tour companies highlight the minorities' colourful costumes with photos of gorgeously attired minority women either in scenic settings or in dance performances. Among the stock images are pretty Sani guides in the Stone Forest, a group of Bai guides on board a boat in Erhai, a troupe of young Naxi women dancing in the alpine meadow of Yunshanping, Dai girls bathing in a Banna creek, a lovely dancer performing the Dai Peacock Dance, and Mosuo girls in long white skirts rowing boats on Lugu Lake.

Customized minority houses, singing and dancing ethnic performers and a generally artificial setting characterizes the Minority Nationalities Park in Kunming. Visitors get a very sanitized version of minority life here, the elephant show being the highlight of the tour. But right next door is the **Minority Nationalities Museum** *(minzu bowuguan),* which is worth hours of examination. Comprising one main building with several exhibition halls and two smaller buildings, devoted respectively to geology and to the transformation of Yunnan since 1949, it is a much more ambitious venture than the tourist-oriented park.

Separate halls feature costumes, ornaments, musical instruments, material culture, religion, writing systems and festivals. Every item is identified by object name, ethnic group and location by county, albeit only in Chinese. However, the museum has a staff of minority personnel ready to assist anyone's research. Besides the tourist literature, ethnic imagery appears on street signs and posters advertising commercial products from the province. The televisions in the hotel rooms provide more. A Kunming station runs a short programme every evening about different locations in the province, which, as often as not, includes the lifestyle of the ethnic minority in that place. Occasionally other provincial and prefectural channels run half-hour documentaries on a single minority.

The national networks also regularly run documentaries on one of China's 55 ethnic minorities. As Yunnan is home to 25 of them, a good portion of these shows are set in Yunnan. Dancers in ethnic costumes are often part of big musical shows staged on major holidays for national TV. And sometimes minorities have roles in commercial advertisements, usually as customers using the product. But one advertiser made use of them culturally, running a clip of young Ximeng County village girls at festival time, waving their waist-length hair up and down and in circles for the traditional Wa Hair Dance, before the shots of the product being advertised—shampoo. Wash your hair with this stuff, girls, and your hair will be so clean and full of life you can dance with it like the Wa.

The national film studios periodically turn to Yunnan for stories and locations. Sometimes they shoot war films, wherein the PLA drives out the remnants of the Guomindang with the enthusiastic help of the border area Jingpo, Dai and Lisu. A nationally popular romantic film, *Five Golden Flowers*, shot in black-and-white in the late 1950s, told the story of Bai lovers in scenic Dali. Decades later, it was reissued in colour. The Sani epic of *Ashima* was made into a movie. Another film was set in Dulong Valley, in northwest Nujiang, about the love affair between a Tibetan boy and a lovely Dulong girl (the only female in the cast without tattoos). Their love is opposed by her family and ends in their tragic deaths.

In recent years newly established prefectural studios in Yunnan are producing films with a distinctive ethnic accent. One of the best-known of these is *Huayao Bride*, shot in Shaochong district, Shiping County, in an authentic traditional Huayao Yi village. The plot revolves around the complications of a Yi custom that newlyweds must keep separated from each other for one full year. The bride wants to join a dragon dance team that will compete in the big Yi festival, but the husband is also involved in the dances. Since they are not supposed to associate with each other, problems arise. *Huayao Bride's* national success led to two sequels.

Nujiang Canyon is the setting for *Nu Tou Ren* (Woman Headman), a story of the Black Lisu. The plot involves a special ceremony, the critical elements and ritual objects of which came from the Stone Moon, a Gaoligongshan peak in northern Fugong County with a hole near the summit. The mountain plays a large role in local Lisu mythology. Outwitting and defeating the bad guys, a young Lisu woman successfully obtains and delivers the objects, the ceremony can take place and, as a reward, the villagers select her to be their headman.

Ninglang County has served as the location for two cinematic works. One was a modern story of twin Mosuo girls, one of whom lives in Beijing. The other stays home, living in the traditional way in a Lugu Lake log cabin. The Beijing girl returns to Lugu Lake for a visit and talks her sister into coming to Beijing. She goes, alone, wanders through the subway with her pack-basket on her back, has various adventures, but in the end goes home to her anxious boyfriend back at Lugu Lake. The Beijing Mosuo marries her construction company boss and stays there.

A much more ambitious film, *Bilu Yanbao*, running in six one-hour segments, told the story of the rise and fall of a Black Yi slave-owning

(following pages) A Wa Hair Dance performance.

aristocrat in the Nationalist era. Set entirely in the mountains of Ninglang County, the film took pains to present the Yi as authentically as possible. Distinctions of dress and ornaments, depictions of weddings, funerals, dances and domestic life were all done with great accuracy. (One could complain, though, that the costumes were all brand new and, no matter what the situation, always immaculately clean.) But the Yi claimed the rituals and some of the social relationships were in error. The story itself was based on the life of a real character and the events of the film, according to the Yi in Ninglang, including the slave raids, the clan feuding, the revolt of a section of the slaves and the death of the protagonist in his burning home, were in general true and accurate.

Dancing in *Bilu Yanbao* was confined to the wedding sequence. Other films set in Yunnan devoted much more footage to singing and dancing, for these have become an integral part of the minorities' image. Happy, colourful people who excel in song and dance is the general theme that permeates not only tourist promotional material but also the image Yunnan's urban Han themselves have of the minorities. For those in the business of promoting tourism, it's the easiest, most positive image to advertise. Promise them exotic entertainment and the tourists will be eager to come. Music and dance, unlike the intricacies of social relationships, the complexities of environmental usage, or the backgrounds of religious beliefs, do not need much explanation.

*(above and right) The Huayao Yi Dance Troupe performs
at the annual Bean Curd Festival in Shiping.*

So the entertainment aspect receives the greatest prominence. Even in Kunming, many restaurants stage floor shows featuring dances of the province's minorities, even if the performers themselves are mostly Han. Elsewhere, the performers are most likely all from the minorities. Most of the dances are traditional and can only otherwise be viewed at big festivals or perhaps weddings or funerals. Dai dances are generally graceful, with lots of flowing gestures. Sani, Yi and Mosuo numbers are quite lively. Some numbers are modern creations, though they use the traditional musical instruments and are often hard to distinguish from the older ones.

As tourism increases, so does the ethnic entertainment factor. A good example is Lijiang. In the early 1990s, tourists could appreciate classical Naxi music only by attending one of the Dayan orchestra's concerts. It wasn't until 1994 that these were daily events. As this orchestra's reputation grew, it frequently performed out of town and tourists had to be satisfied buying cassette tapes.

Hotels were already beginning to hire village orchestras when an earthquake struck in February 1996. A year later, with most of the old town repaired, tourists were returning in ever-burgeoning numbers, putting new demands on the ethnic entertainment sector. Now over a dozen venues offer classical Naxi music, Naxi folk dances, even dongba dances.

At Lugu Lake dancing became part of Mosuo hospitality. Chinese tour groups, which by the mid-90s arrived daily except during the coldest weeks in winter, hired Luoshui village troupes for traditional ring dances around a bonfire. But this was not just a show to watch. The Mosuo encouraged their guests to join the ring. After this, long solos, duets, and song-and-response numbers by small groups of men and women followed. Guests were invited to sing their own songs, a request the karaoke-addicted Chinese tourists were quick to meet. In the daytime Mosuo women donned their traditional outfits and sang to the tourists as they rowed them out to the islands.

Some travellers look askance at the whole entertainment aspect of the ethnic encounter. The show seems too slick, too packaged, too commercially inspired. But there are other aspects to consider. Far from feeling exploited by the tourist trade, the minorities are proud of their reputation for music and dance. They have been enthralling outsiders with their own traditional entertainment ever since the Nanzhao embassy missions brought performers to the Tang court. For several decades the Tang capital hosted a resident troupe of Yunnan musicians and dancers. With the rise in tourist interest, too, more entertainers are needed and thus a greater number of the ethnic minorities' younger generations will now be motivated to learn their traditional songs, music and dance. The tradition may be getting commercialized, but it is definitely being preserved.

Calling On The Minorities

FOREIGNERS THROUGH ETHNIC EYES

At the start of the 21st century, no place in Yunnan was so remote and out of the way of modern communications that its inhabitants were unaware of the existence of foreigners. Maybe they hadn't met any yet, but with electricity extended to nearly every township in the province, no matter how far off the roads, they had caught a glimpse of them through television programmes. The image they have formed has for the most part been that which they have acquired from the characters seen on TV. It's a vague and superficial image, a view of the foreigner as someone from a very modern society, with a car and lots of other gadgets, and a sufficient amount of money to be able to fly halfway around the world to go sightseeing in Yunnan. Beyond these basic assumptions, nothing is crystallized.

For those minority nationalities who dwell in places of outstanding natural beauty, especially those first opened to tourism—Stone Forest, Dali, Lijiang, Xishuangbanna—that foreigners would come so far to visit their homeland is not at all unusual. They need no persuading about how beautiful their environment is. So they are not surprised that foreigners, now that they are allowed to, take so much trouble to see their areas. That some of these foreigners come to see them as well as the scenery might surprise some, but in any case if the foreigner evinces an interest in the life and culture of the minorities, the latter are more likely to be flattered by the attention than wary of the stranger.

In the remote, rarely travelled counties, where some of the most conservative, unsophisticated ethnic minorities live, the appearance of a foreigner may cause a stir and initiate speculation about what the foreigner is doing here. Perhaps he took the wrong bus and came here by mistake. Maybe she is one of those wandering missionaries proclaiming the end of the world is nigh. Or it might be someone sent by the government to make an inspection. Reactions will vary from intense curiosity, with much mass staring, to shyness so severe, especially among young girls, it provokes a flight from any possible encounter.

The minorities' reaction to foreigners trying to take their photographs can vary considerably. Some don't mind at all and appear to be rather pleased by the attention. Some turn away, or even scatter and run, as soon as a lens is pointed their way. To some degree this reluctance may be based on the belief that the photographer captures their soul as well as their portrait. Others may think the foreigner is trying to show how dirty they are, when in fact the foreigner behind the lens doesn't even notice the dirt, only the colours of the

costume. But these same people will pose proudly on festival days, when they are dressed in their finest and cleanest.

Another cause for reluctance is the fear of what will be the ultimate disposition of the photograph. The wildest rumours can compound this reluctance. One weird rumour about why foreigners took pictures of minorities, circulating for a while in the mountains in the early 1990s, was that foreigners printed the photos on their toilet paper!

CHARACTER TRAITS

Ridiculous as such a rumour is, it reflects a very real worry that the foreigners would look down on them. Historically, this has always been their worry concerning outsiders. Until recently, the outsiders have been the Han, representatives of a stronger, more sophisticated, more developed culture. Now that they are exposed to a new kind of outsider, the foreigner, whom they see also as a representative of a stronger, more developed culture, that same old fear returns. Yet as soon as they can sense that the stranger does not look down on them, their inhibitions dissolve and the encounter becomes natural and friendly.

In actuality, the minorities can be just as curious about the foreigner as the latter is about them. In some remote areas, among the least inhibited, this

(above) Jingpo dancers on stage during a minorities festival at Munao.
(left) A Xundian Yi in traditional costume.

curiosity can extend to a close-up examination of one's clothes, camera gear and other gadgets, the contents of one's shoulder bag and so forth. At the same time, they will be as careful as possible not to break, soil or damage anything they touch.

This example of care is an outgrowth of another trait—politeness and respect. Having in a sense demanded respect from the foreign outsider, without which they are disinclined to have any encounter at all, they extend it in turn. Within their own cultures, limits of behaviour and guidelines for proper interaction are a part of their everyday life. Unsure of the foreigner's cultural codes, they will be unfailingly polite so as to assure themselves of not being thought uncouth, which would lead to being looked down upon.

Honesty is also a prime characteristic, for it is a trait highly valued in traditional societies. Assuming the foreigner to share their regard for honesty, they see no reason to disbelieve anything the foreigner tells them. Not quick to make promises themselves unless they intend to keep them, they expect the same standard from others.

Finally, no traveller can fail to notice another outstanding trait the ethnic minorities have in abundance—good humour. They are quick to return a smile, enjoy a good laugh and have a propensity to turn the encounter with the foreigner into something resembling a mutually appreciated good time.

COMMUNICATION

In more established destinations, where minorities are involved in the tourist trade, the traveller will find Bai, Naxi, Yi or Tibetans who speak some English. Out in the villages this may be next to impossible, though occasionally middle school students will approach foreigners to try out their linguistic skills. One can also try meeting the local school's English teacher. Otherwise, those who do not speak any Chinese will have to rely on sign language. This may work quite well in the beginning, but it is no substitute for at least some command of basic *putonghua*—the official national dialect of China, as well as the one used on television and radio.

Except for the oldest and the youngest generations, even in the remotest areas, the minorities, at least the males, will speak basic putonghua. Often their command of it is limited, so those foreigners with only some fluency in Chinese may actually find it easier to speak Chinese with the minorities, to whom it is also a second language, than with the Han in the cities. The former are not likely to trip up the foreigner with fancy vocabulary or complex grammatical constructions.

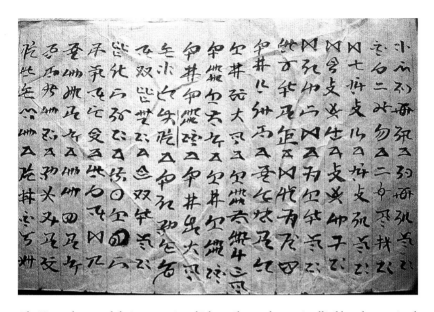

The Yi people created their own script which, until recently, was intelligible only to a ritual specialist known as a Bimaw.

The greatest possible positive impression, though, will come not from one's fluency in Chinese, but from the traveller's capacity to speak to the ethnic minorities in their own languages. The more one can say in the local language the better, of course, but even a few common phrases or words will guarantee a delightful reaction. The minorities see it as complimentary to their culture and ethnic identity, as evidence that the foreigner, for having taken the trouble to learn to speak to them in their own tongue, certainly does not look down on them. They then reciprocate by behaving in a way that will retain and enhance the foreigner's appreciation.

The easiest time for a foreigner to acquire some of the local language is in dining situations, either in a restaurant staffed by ethnic minorities or in their homes. Asking the words for food items, for example, augments the experience. Learning a few words or phrases of their language warms their hearts and wins their respect and liking. Having collected a bunch of words, the traveller can then make simple sentences by remembering the basic structure of the language involved. Those from the Tai-Kedai or Mon-Khmer linguistic families will be, like English and Chinese, subject-verb-object. The word order of Tibeto-Burman languages is subject-object-verb.

TRIBAL HOSPITALITY

In those areas used to foreign visitors, the traveller may experience, while wandering around the less frequented villages, an invitation to visit someone's house. In the remote areas, where residents only rarely see a foreigner, this may take longer, for people are apt to be so surprised that their first thought is to wonder what on earth the foreigner is doing there. This attitude paralyses most people, but eventually a bold individual will extend an invitation to step inside and have some tea. If the weather is cold, this may be phrased as an invitation to come inside and sit by the fire.

In most cases the guest will be seated near the hearth. If no others are inside already, the guest will be urged to occupy what the local culture deems the place of honour. Among the northern Yi, for example, this will be at the right rear side of the fireplace. The host will take trouble to tidy up the spot and make the guest comfortable, either on a low stool, a woven mat of split bamboo, or a folded blanket or cape of felt wool.

Tea is always part of the welcome, buttered tea in Tibetan and Mosuo areas. Other things offered depend upon the locality, the season, and even the mood of the host. Snacks range from the *tsampa,* bread or buns, walnuts, peanuts and sunflower seeds of ethnic minorities in the north to the fruits and sweets common among those in the south. Hosts also offer cigarettes and alcohol, and if a feast is going on, or the family is about to eat, they will urge their guest to stay and have a meal with them.

The moment tribal people overcome their initial natural shyness regarding strangers, which may be more pronounced if the stranger is a foreigner, their own tradition of gracious hospitality takes over and directs their behaviour. Always solicitous of the guest's comfort, they do their utmost to make a good impression and have a happy encounter.

THE GUEST'S BEHAVIOUR

It is easy for the guest to make a favourable impression by simply following the common sense rules of polite behaviour. Being respectful, avoiding loud, boisterous or rude actions, never displaying anger or impatience and making at least the appearance of being comfortable will guarantee the host's pleasure. The guest should consume the drinks and edibles slowly and not finish off the lot, or even all the food if invited to dinner, so as to avoid giving the host the impression he or she did not offer enough. Minority peoples have the same respect for elders as do Chinese, so it behooves the guest to keep that in mind and make some gesture of respect when greeting or communicating with the older generation.

What happens next depends upon the circumstances of the encounter and the personalities of the participants. The traveller could initiate some conversation with the use of photographs. But these should be of Yunnan, its people, or even those of the places and people in neighbouring provinces or countries in order to arouse a reaction. Minority people generally won't know what to say if shown pictures of one's home country, its buildings, cities and monuments, for such images are so different as to be beyond the realm of comment. Minority people are family-oriented, so photos of one's kin may spark interest. But however one carries out one's part in the encounter, with or without props, a display of politeness and appreciation will anyway ensure a friendly reception.

THE DISCOVERY OF AFFINITIES

More scenic variety exists in Yunnan than in any other province in China. One could have a very pleasant time here just travelling from one outstanding viewpoint to another. Yet neighbouring provinces and countries have their scenic attractions as well, and in the main such sights cater to the same sort of sensual and emotional response wherever and whenever they are enjoyed. What makes Yunnan potentially so much richer a travel experience is the ethnic aspect. Nowhere else offers such a diversity of lifestyles, such a range of ecological responses, such a wealth and depth of culture. Here is the chance to experience several cross-cultural encounters on a single journey, which will etch themselves more sharply in the traveller's memory than the most spectacular scenery. They may even change the way a traveller thinks and lives... for the better.

Too often the human side of travelling has been restricted to merely enjoying the company of local people. While there's certainly nothing wrong with this, in Yunnan nowadays one can be more ambitious. Minority people here long ago worked out different ways to live in different kinds of environments. Their cultural responses have largely stood the tests of many centuries. Success imbues them with the self-reliance that is the source of their ethnic pride and the self-confidence that is their charm.

One can learn much from such people. For example, in a life that is satisfactory, what are the key values worth cherishing? In cross-cultural encounters much will transpire that is strange or even unfathomable. But much else will be familiar, will resemble in a general way something in the traveller's own cultural background. Then one will discover those thoughts and feelings one truly shares with these different people. These are nothing less than the underlying values of human beings everywhere. Travellers need to remind themselves of such affinities, time and time again.

PART IV • BEATEN TRACKS

Kunming & Environs

HISTORICAL KUNMING

When the ancient kingdom of Dian dissolved and conquering Han armies from the north established new political entities in the area, Kunming became the site of a new administrative centre. Known as Yizhou under the Han and during the Nanzhao era (8th–10th centuries), it was the most important of the kingdom's cities in the east. After Kubilai Khan swept through Yunnan in 1253 and annexed it to the Mongol Empire, he selected Kunming, rather than Dali, as the new provincial capital. It has remained the political, economic and cultural capital of Yunnan ever since, as well as its largest city.

It is difficult to imagine what this bustling, sprawling, modern city might have looked like a thousand years ago. No buildings, city plans or records of the city proper exist prior to the Ming Dynasty. From 1382 on, though, the picture is much clearer. That is the year the Ming garrison commander Wu Ying began constructing a new, walled capital around Green Lake, imprinting Kunming with the classical Han-style urban layout and architecture that the Ming rulers were imposing on all parts of their empire.

The original governor's mansion stood on the big island in **Green Lake**. The walls began on the hill behind the lake, where the Yunnan University campus now stands, ran just west of the lake, more or less along what is today Dongfengxilu, turned east just above Jinbilu, then turned north around Huguolu all the way up to Yuantong Hill, site of the zoo.

This was the core of **Old Kunming**. The rich and the important lived within its walls, but a sizable population resided in adjacent suburbs. Most religious centres and monuments were outside the walls, with the notable exception of **Yuantong Temple**. Lying in a capacious compound just east of Green Lake, at the foot of Yuantong Hill, it was the largest monastery in the area. The main hall was erected in the Yuan Dynasty, over what was originally a Nanzhao temple site. Expansion and renovation in later centuries have given it its present look. Its four gardens contain specimens of all the main flowering trees in the province, each blossoming at a different time. Thus, no matter what month it is, flowers of some kind are always blooming in Yuantong Temple.

The East Temple Pagoda, a landmark of Old Kunming.

South of Jinbilu, at the end of a long rectangular grove, stood the East and West Pagodas (*Dongsita* and *Xisita*). The grove is gone but the pagodas are still there. These pagodas were not the city's first, for a different type, sculpted with figures showing a strong Indian influence, went up in the Nanzhao era. A fine example is known as the Dharani Pillar. It rises from a pedestal chiselled with classical Sanskrit inscriptions and can be viewed in the **Kunming City Museum**, near the corner of Baitalu and Tuodonglu. In the same building is a large relief model of Old Kunming, with its walls, buildings and monuments.

In the Ming era the urban area outside the city walls did not extend anywhere near as far as it does now. Forests lay beyond and in quiet, secluded spots on the slopes of the hills religious-minded patrons sponsored the building of temples. Most were too far for an ordinary excursion, though they are easy to reach by car or bus now. One such temple, Tanhuasi, built in 1634, lies just 4 km from the city centre near the end of Renminlu. Named for the ephyllium tree (a species of magnolia) in the courtyard, it was probably the

The old city of Kunming as seen by Garnier and Delaporte when they visited during their expedition in the 1860s. The city was known as Yunnanfu at that time.

ex-urban temple most frequented by Old Kunming residents. As they do today, people came to offer prayers, observe religious holidays, or just for the pleasures of the outing, the smell of the flowers and appreciation of the rockery and the entire temple setting.

Even today, with buildings, roads and overpasses occupying what was once a wood, **Tanhua Temple** retains its charm. Just far enough from the main roads to be beyond their noise and stench, the compound consists of three main sections that rise gently up a slope. The first contains several courtyards grouped around the main temple, on the walls of which are mounted individual images of the 500 Buddhist saints (*arhats*), inscribed on stone slabs. Courtyards feature rockeries, ponds, pavilions, sitting halls, flowering trees and, in the nicest one, Chinese couplets inscribed on marble and fitted into the walls in the hall along the walkway.

The next section up is laid out more like a classical park, with its pavilions, shade trees, tables, sitting halls and morning tai chi (*tai ji*) exercisers. Ascending the knoll behind brings the visitor to a seven-storey pagoda, up which one can climb for a grand view of Kunming. The city is also visible from the pond in front of the pagoda. The entire compound is an oasis of serenity in modern Kunming.

Old Kunming was a very tolerant place. Not only did Daoists erect their own temples, the Muslim residents (Hui) constructed mosques in the Ming era, despite the fact that they were brought into Yunnan by the Ming's Mongol enemies. The Hui quarter of town was the area around Jinbilu and on up to Dongfengxilu. The original mosque on Jinbilu, and another at the end of Shunchengjie, near the Provincial Museum, were in the Chinese style, which meant they resembled Buddhist temples on the exterior. The difference lay in the carved and painted decorations, wherein the mosques generally eschewed depiction of people, and in the symbol mounted in the centre of the roof—a crescent moon, not a lotus. The interiors, of course, were simple and unadorned.

No major changes in the city layout came with the founding of the Qing Dynasty. Temples and pavilions, in roughly the same style, continued to be built, while those already existing underwent renovation and expansion. Among the most imposing new buildings was **Daguan Pavilion**, now standing in the lakeside park of the same name. The early Qing governor, Wang Jiuren, decided in 1690 to initiate large-scale building expansion on a site occupied by a seven-year-old Buddhist temple. The three-storey pavilion went up first, affording a fine view across the lake to the Western Hills. A Qing poet, Sun Wanreng, composed a 180-character couplet, which is inscribed on two boards on the pavilion's lakeside facade. The upper scroll extols the beauty of the scenery, while the lower scroll offers some thoughts on the seminal events in Yunnan's history.

Governor Wang added other buildings, lotus pools, the inevitable rockery and flower garden, plus walkways and small pavilions along the water. Nowadays a hotel and other new buildings have been erected, boat services established and high-rise residential blocks have spoiled parts of the view. Still, it is a quiet and pretty place, especially at sunset and under a full moon.

In the closing decades of the Qing Dynasty small numbers of Europeans began arriving in Kunming. Missionaries were permitted to build churches in the city and by the end of the Nationalist era the city had three: on Wuchenglu, on Jinbilu and on what is now Beijinglu. The Christian congregation remained small, but the missions also provided hospitality and a degree of cultural familiarity to 19th century European explorers, business travellers and political attachés.

Life and commerce in Old Kunming ran much as it did in other Chinese inland cities. Residents lived in houses of brick and wood, with tiled roofs. The gentry built two- or three-storey homes with walled compounds. Nearly everyone else occupied smaller houses, jammed next to each other on cobbled streets. In the commercial quarters, shop owners ran their businesses on the ground floor of their houses and used the upper floor for sleeping. Most houses had ledges outside the tiny upper floor windows, where they placed pots of flowers or perhaps kept a caged songbird. Certain occupations dominated specific streets or neighbourhoods. Vestiges of this characteristic persist today in the heart of the city, with beef merchants still on Shunchengjie and sign-makers on Wenmiaozhijie, the lane parallel to Zhengyilu.

Wealthy house owners and shopkeepers often hired carvers to add decorative flourishes to their exteriors. Artisans fashioned animals and vegetation in relief on doors, shutters, roof struts, awnings and window brackets. A bit of this art has survived in those parts of the old town that have not been demolished, such as the area west of Zhengyilu.

THE TRANSFORMATION

Kunming commenced its modernization in the 1930s, especially after the Nationalist government moved to Chongqing during World War II, which the Chinese call the Anti-Japanese War. The old walls came tumbling down and the urban extension began eating up the adjacent fields. The pace continued after 1949, with the last of the city gate towers demolished in 1953. By the time Yunnan was opened to tourists in the 1980s, all basic infrastructure of a modern metropolis was in place. Yet at the beginning of the 1990s it was still a relatively tranquil, backwater provincial capital with little of the hustle and bustle of cities to the east.

More used to the cities in the plains, which sprawled out over boring flat horizons, visitors flying into Kunming were struck immediately by its setting. Mountains flank three sides of the city and the upper end of Dian Lake the fourth. At 1,893 metres altitude, the air is slightly thinner and the skies richer. The climate is mild, never too cold in winter nor too hot in summer, a condition which has earned it the nickname of Spring City. Traffic was still light back then, mostly bicycles, and many blocks of the old town, with its fascinating traditional architecture, were still intact. Kunming was an ideal place for a long, leisurely stroll.

Certain streets were especially appropriate for getting the feel of Old Kunming. On Wenchenglu one could espy some of the best decorative carvings on the two- and three-storey shophouses, along with one of the city's oldest churches. More old houses stood on Wuyilu and Guanghuajie, where the

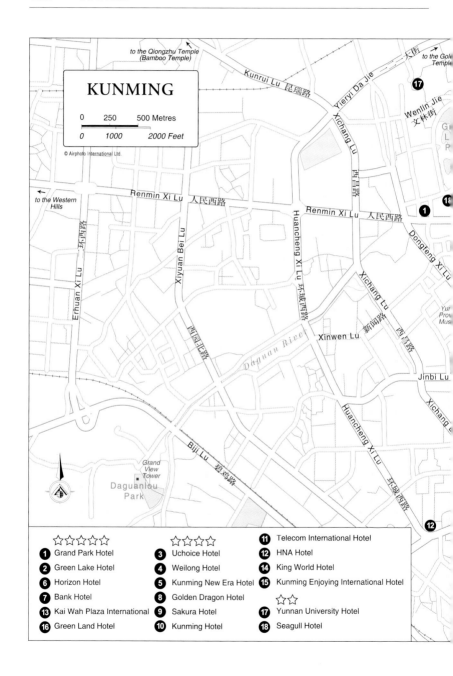

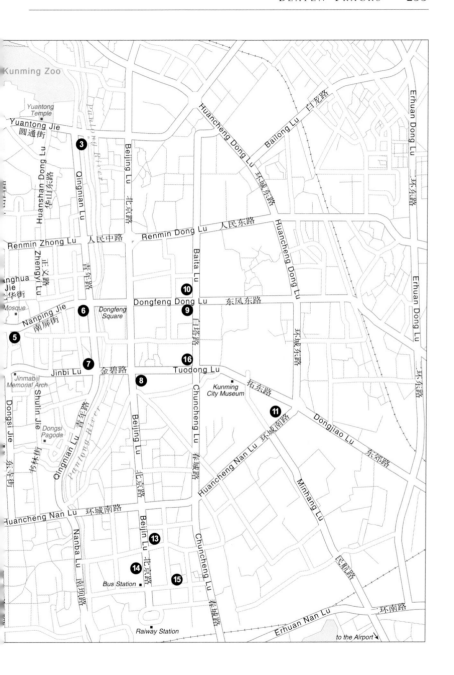

warren of shops known as the Bird Market were located. Besides birds and birdseed, shoppers could find small fish, fish food, turtles, peacock feathers, kites, fishing tackle, Dai umbrellas, jade ornaments, porcelain and antiques. The streets north of Green Lake, leading to the main gate of Yunnan University, with several nearby outdoor restaurants, and traditional tree-lined Jinbilu, with its rows of old yellow, turn-of-the-century buildings, were other popular walking areas.

Narrow lanes connecting the streets in the old town provided glimpses of what it was like to live in the heart of a Chinese city, without a shop to manage, too. In the late afternoons teahouses filled with older men chatting while smoking long pipes. In small inner-city parks they played board games. Itinerant traders wandered into town: Hui from Ningxia selling furs, Uighurs from Xinjiang with baskets of raisins, Tibetans hawking medicines, Sani peddling handicrafts.

Streets around the Bird Market were left largely unscathed during the city's modernization. Some still boast fine old traditional buildings like this three-storey drugstore.

The Jinbilu Gates of Kunming.

A few areas catered to foreigners, such as the row of restaurants on Beijinglu near the Kunhu Hotel, which are all still there, and the cluster of small restaurants at the back of the university campus. Individual shops in other quarters posted bilingual signs in a bid to attract foreign customers. Some of these were oddly phrased, like the Jewellery and Queer Stone Shop on Baitalu and the one on Huguolu that used to offer Chinese and Alien Snacks.

By the middle of the 1990s Yunnan began to develop more rapidly and the pace of Kunming's modernization accelerated. New skyscrapers rose every season. Vehicle traffic quickly multiplied and to deal with this fast-growing problem the authorities decided to widen some of the main thoroughfares, including those going through the old town. Wuchenglu, with its old church and older homes, was destroyed, and on a bright Sunday in October of 1997, the shops on Jinbilu held their final 'Everything Must Go' sale, the day before the wreckers came.

Destruction was not total, though. The new width stipulated for Jinbilu spared the Catholic Church, which was already set back far enough from the street. The new road was also made to swerve to the side of the old mosque, so that this venerable relic of Old Kunming remained untouched (though only until the new, Arabian-style mosques were completed off Dongfengxilu). Gateways in the classical style were erected on the walkway, as well as the connecting lane to the roundabout at the end of Nanpingjie. Flower beds were laid out along the road, as elsewhere in the city, in line with Kunming's preparation for the horticultural exhibits of Expo 99.

The exposition was staged in a specially constructed site not far from the Golden Temple (*Jindian*), just east of the city. A decade's worth of development money was used to spruce up Kunming as well as all the prefecture capitals. Just west of Beijinglu, the river area was cleaned up and new parks created. Street merchants on the main roads were ordered off, but many, including the blind masseurs, set up in the corridors of the underpasses. Finally, to augment the new parks and gardens and decorate the cleaner, wider streets, the city set out two million flower pots.

THE ARCHITECTURE OF NOSTALGIA

When Expo 99 concluded, the city maintained the grounds as a park, which is still a regular tourist attraction. With the new century, Kunming's transformation continued, but with a new emphasis—resurrecting some of its traditional look. The trend had already been foreshadowed in the reproduction of the two gates in the square at the end of Jinbilu. Both the eastern one,

Golden Horse Gate (*Jinmafang*), and the western one, **Green Phoenix Gate** (*Bijifang*), exactly replicate the originals in dimension and style.

For its next project the city rebuilt **Jinrilou Tower**, near the East and West Pagodas, a massive gate that served as the main entrance to Kunming during the Qing Dynasty, but which had been demolished in the 1950s. Once again, the building was a faithful reproduction of the original. At the same time, the drab buildings on the street between the two pagodas were knocked down and replaced with traditional-style shophouses. The street was paved with bricks, vehicular traffic banned and in 2002 bronze statues of vignettes of 19th century life—a marketgoer leading his pony, an egg seller with her goods wrapped in a straw case, two old men playing chess—were installed on the street.

Over on Baitalu, city authorities renovated the old Taoist temple and other venerable buildings in the Zhenqingguan compound. Besides the original temple, the compound includes teahouses, a small performance stage and family shrines, all in the classical style. In the old days, a Tibetan-style white pagoda stood in the middle of the street here. But to reconstruct it in the same spot would have made it an obstacle to traffic on one of the busiest thoroughfares in downtown Kunming. So a smaller version went up instead in the yard between the temple compound and Baitalu.

Meanwhile, workers constructed an underpass for traffic on Dongfengxilu and remade the street above into a pedestrian-only stretch, with fountains, flowers, classical monuments and bronze sculptures of life in Kunming before World War II. These included ornate chairs, a peasant bearing trays of fruit on a shoulder pole, a studio portrait photographer with his big box camera, an old man leading his grandson to the park to listen to birds, and other activities of everyday life in the early 20th century.

One might bemoan the passing of so much of Kunming's old town and regard the resurrected architecture as not quite authentic. But so many Chinese cities have all but obliterated their pre-modern look that one should be pleased that Kunming chose to recreate at least part of its heritage, rather than leave it all buried forever beneath the foundations of the shiny new skyscrapers.

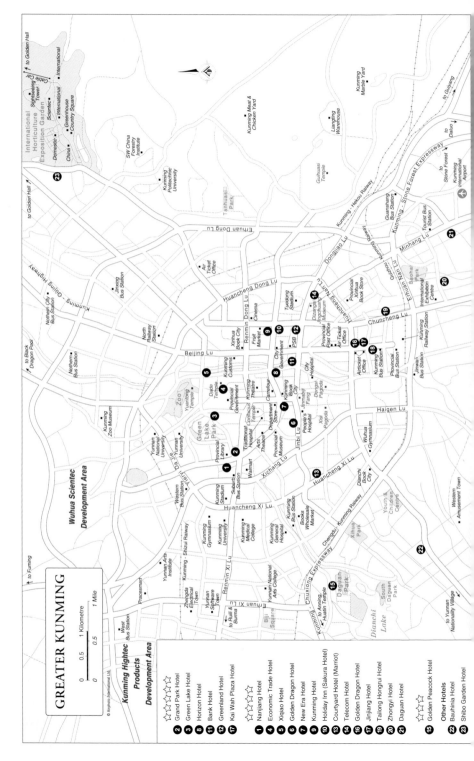

EXCURSIONS

To escape the noise, traffic and congestion of Kunming, one has a choice among several attractive alternatives in the nearby hills and along the lake. All of them are easily accessible from the city by regular public transportation. The sites in the hills are old temple compounds, occasionally with good views, but mainly notable for their seclusion, closeness to nature, ancient trees, architectural embellishments and sculptural achievements. While crowds may throng the compounds on weekends and holidays, the neighbouring forests offer a clean and tranquil refuge.

The nearest of these compounds is the **Golden Temple** (*Jindian*), 7 km east of the city centre, comprising several buildings on **Mingfengshan**—the Hill of Singing Phoenixes. In between the buildings, walkways lead past pines and cypresses to gardens of camellias or azaleas up to the Bell Tower, from the top of which one can view the distant hills behind the skyscrapers of Kunming. The three entry gates at successive points on the hill are notable for their decorative carved and painted brackets supporting the roofs.

The Golden Temple is actually a building embellished with high-quality Yunnan bronze, used on the pillars, window screens, brackets and sculptures. Originally constructed by order of the Ming Dynasty Daoist Governor Chen Yongbing in 1602, following a dream he had of the Daoist Immortal Lu Dongbin, the original was removed to Jizushan in western Yunnan in 1637. The present temple was built under the stewardship of Wu Sangui in 1671, when he ruled Yunnan for the Qing Dynasty. He is supposed to have left his own 12-kg sword here. It is housed inside the temple along with an even bigger, 20-kg double-edged sword, said to have been used by the Daoist saint Zhen Wu to defend the temple.

On Wubaoshan, 11 km north of Kunming, lies the early Ming-era Black Dragon Palace. First erected in 1394 and redone in 1454, it stands beside **Black Dragon Pool** (*Heilongtan*) and was formerly the site of temples in the Han, Tang and Yuan dynasties. These were all destroyed by war, but a Tang-era plum tree, a Song Dynasty cypress and a Ming camellia tree remain in the compound, still blossoming every Lunar New Year. A statue of the black dragon also stands in the courtyard. A companion compound in the adjacent woods, the Dragon Fountain Palace, comprises several halls dedicated to the Jade Emperor and other Daoist deities.

Daoist legend states that Black Dragon Pool is the home of a small black dragon, confined there by the Immortal Lu Dongbin after he subdued nine larger dragons that were causing floods. The last one he commanded to do good for humans and supposedly, once the ancient inhabitants started drawing its water to irrigate their fields, the little black dragon made sure the pool never ran dry, even in years of drought. About 600 square metres in area and 11 metres deep, it is divided by a bridge from a half-metre deep pool that is five times its size. Pavilions on the edge are for watching fish; the odd thing about them is that, though the water of the two ponds is connected, the fish that swim in one pool never pay a visit to the other.

Northwest of the city, about 13 km from the centre, the **Bamboo Temple** (*Qiongzhusi*) lies on a wooded slope of **Jade Table Mountain** (Yu'anshan). This Buddhist monastery was originally founded by a monk from Kunming who followed the Chan sect (otherwise known as Zen) in central China for 25 years, around the end of the Song Dynasty (13th century). Within the main hall one of the many inscribed tablets dates from the Yuan Dynasty and is bilingual—Mongolian and vernacular Chinese. Standing in the courtyard are two 600-year-old cedar trees.

The outstanding feature of this temple is its collection of 500 painted clay sculptures of Buddhist *arhats*. The work of a mid-Qing sculptor from Sichuan, Li Guangxiu, and his apprentices, the statues all differ from one another, every one modelled on real and unique contemporary originals. Faces display the whole gamut of possible expressions. Some are kindly, some fierce. Some are sedate or contemplative and others active, even chatting or laughing. No two are the same and the dress, hairstyle and props are also unique to each statue. According to local legend, if a visitor begins counting the statues, starting from the beginning of any row, and comes to the number matching his or her age, that statue will symbolically represent the visitor's dominant inner character.

Towering over 2,500 metres above the northwest shore of Dianchi, 16 km west of the city, is a group of five mountains known as the **Western Hills** (*Xishan*). Three famous temples and a climb up to a viewpoint draw visitors. Buses take them all the way to the top-lying temple, and from here to the lookout point at Dragon Gate (*Longmen*) the pathway can get crowded. But like the other ex-urban temples, one can easily walk away from the masses, out onto innumerable paths high in the hills, and search out a view of one's own.

Most visitors these days are tourists in vehicles and they head straight for Dragon Gate. Proper pilgrims were supposed to walk up the mountain, which only takes a couple of hours, stopping at the temples en route. The first, just over 2 km from the turnoff from the Kunming road, is **Huating Monastery**. This Buddhist temple was first built in 1320, renovated in the Ming and Qing Dynasties and last rebuilt in 1920. Besides the imposing guardian statues and images of the Buddha in various guises, the 500 *arhat* sculptures of the Bamboo Temple are replicated here. They are largely in high relief on the walls of the main hall and exhibit the same realism and individuality as their counterparts at the Bamboo Temple.

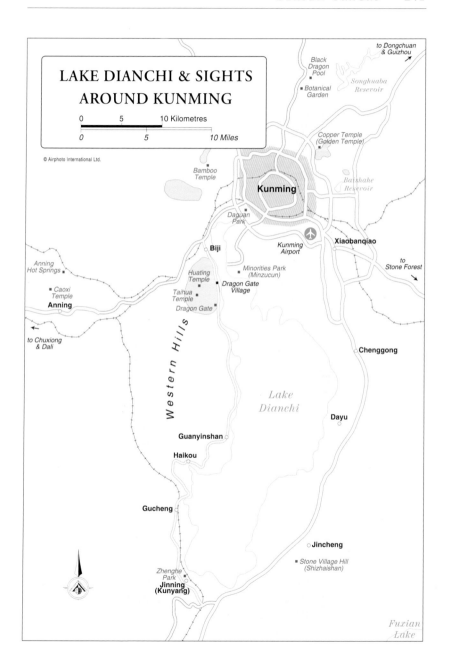

LAKE DIANCHI & SIGHTS AROUND KUNMING

0 5 10 Kilometres

0 5 10 Miles

© Airphoto International Ltd.

to Dongchuan & Guizhou

Black Dragon Pool

Botanical Garden

Songhuaba Reservoir

Copper Temple (Golden Temple)

Bamboo Temple

Baishahe Reservoir

Kunming

Daguan Park

Anning Hot Springs

Biji

Kunming Airport

Xiaobanqiao

Minorities Park (Minzucun)

to Stone Forest

Huating Temple

Dragon Gate Village

Caoxi Temple

Anning

Taihua Temple

Dragon Gate

to Chuxiong & Dali

Western Hills

Chenggong

Lake Dianchi

Dayu

Guanyinshan

Haikou

Gucheng

Jincheng

Stone Village Hill (Shizhaishan)

Zhenghe Park

Jinning (Kunyang)

Fuxian Lake

Predating Huating is the next temple up the hill, 2 km by road, slightly shorter by footpath through the forest. This Chan Buddhist temple was built in 1302 by the monk Xuan Jian and is called **Taihuasi**. A 600-year-old gingko tree rises above the gate. The complex includes pavilions beside the 1,000-square metre **Blue Pond**, itself embellished with rockeries, islets and walkways. Another pavilion, the **Sea Viewing Pavilion**, offers a long view of Dian Lake.

Even grander views are possible from the next temple up—the **Songqingge** Daoist Temple. Though one can drive up the mountain road to the entrance, the true pilgrim prefers the winding stone staircase of over 1,000 steps that begins at the base of the hill. The buildings belonging to this complex are stacked above each other on the steep side of the mountain. Even higher, in an eyrie perched on a sheer, perpendicular cliff, is **Dragon Gate**, the goal of every visitor, the greatest viewpoint in the Kunming area. The view is all the more appreciated because of the arduous task of getting there, which is by squeezing in and out of small grottoes chiselled out of the rock by Qing Dynasty monks. The slow and dangerous work took 72 years and the final passageway was completed in 1853. It replaced a hazardous, rickety plank road attached to the cliff face.

At the other end of Dian Lake are two sights popular with Chinese, one a temple, the other a kind of museum. The temple is **Panlongsi**, a restored complex with a towering pagoda in the close-eaves style (like the East and West Pagodas in Kunming). It stands on a hill behind Jincheng, 45 km south of Kunming. The buildings have been recently renovated and the location lacks the thick pine forests and bamboo groves of the temples nearer to Kunming.

More interesting is the **Zheng He Memorial Park** in Jinning, also known as Kunyang, off the south shore of the lake, 64 km from Kunming. A native Muslim of Jinning, Zheng He was the admiral who commanded seven naval expeditions in the early 15th century, ordered by the Ming Emperor Yong Le to extend the dynasty's prestige. It was the only time in history when China employed a navy for diplomatic purposes. Zheng He guided the expeditions as far as India, Arabia and Africa.

The park is on a hill above the town. Among its attractions are the main exhibition hall, with maps, a scale model of the type of ship used in those days and other items relevant to the expeditions. Outside are low-relief sculptures of scenes from the journeys, depicting the countries where the ships visited. In another part of the park is an area with sculptures of some of the strange (to Ming sailors) animals found in those faraway lands and brought back to China.

North of Jinning, about halfway up the western shore of the lake, stands **Guanyin Temple**, on a small hill not far from the lakeside. The villagers are Bai from the west, though they look and live like Han nowadays. The temple is pleasant, but not grand, the view nice, but not spectacular. Further south is the resort of **Baiyukou**, which affords better scenery and a chance to observe various boats and fishing activities. In fact, the place is named after the white fish (*baiyu*) that abound in the bay here. Baiyukou is a narrow peninsula that juts out into the lake. Weirdly shaped cliffs rise on three sides. A Nationalist-era villa, gardens and pools separated from the lake by stone embankments, as well as nearby arbours and pavilions augment the setting.

THE STONE FOREST AND LUNAN COUNTY

Just two hours east of Kunming is the best-known excursion of them all—the Stone Forest (*Shilin*). An immense natural rockery of stones and pillars, eroded by time into arresting shapes, crammed into an 80-hectare plot in Lunan County, the *Shilin* draws thousands of visitors a day. It is one of the most famous scenic attractions of Southwest China, and hence one of the most organized. Five kilometres of pathways have been constructed, maps of the park come with the ticket purchase, guides in colourful Sani costume are everywhere, as are the handicrafts markets, numerous guesthouses flank the park entrance area, while an upgrade hotel lies within the park boundaries, and Sani dance troupes perform nightly. The place can get awfully congested at times, particularly from late morning to mid-afternoon. And while the viewing pavilions are perhaps inevitable, the Chinese characters painted on some of the rocks, as well as the plethora of concession stands, do detract from ordinary appreciation.

Yet some places are popular tourist destinations because they are inherently beautiful and deserving of the attention. The Stone Forest is not always packed with tourists, for they almost all make it a day trip out of Kunming. Even if they stay overnight, they usually like to be back at the hotel for dinner long before dark. Thus to enjoy the walk and be able to marvel in peace and quiet at the weirdly shaped pillars, one need only take walks in early morning or in the last couple of hours before sunset, when the light is richest.

The geologic upheaval that created the Stone Forest some 200 million years ago did not leave it on level ground, and the pathways both wind in and out of the groups of pillars as well as up and down between them. Nor did all the water seep away. Besides the lake near the entrance, the park contains three small bodies of water: **Lion Pond** and **Lotus Pond** near the entrance and **Sword Peak Pond** further inside. The latter is easily the most picturesque, with Lotus Peak rising behind it. This pillar is supposed to resemble a lotus flower, while other strangely shaped rocks have been given names by imaginative travellers

BASIC FORMAT OF TEMPLES

In spite of variations in size, detail and topography, most temples in Yunnan follow the same layout. An entrance hall leads in to an open courtyard bounded on the sides by monastic living quarters and galleries. The main temple stands at the rear with one or two additional temple buildings behind it. The temple usually faces south with the entrance at the lowest level, flanked by two guardian figures, either animal or demonic.

The entrance hall usually contains a fat, laughing Buddha and four giant kings, guardians of the four directions. East is white, and he carries a lute. South is blue, and he carries a sword. West is red, and he carries a pagoda or a pearl. North is orange, and he carries a stylized Buddhist banner. The chief of the Four Kings is East.

Courtyards vary greatly, depending on the site, but they commonly hold ancient, sacred trees, a garden and sometimes a pool or fountain.

The main temple normally has central statues of three aspects of the Buddha, or of a single Buddha and two of his disciples. They may be attended by any number of figures representing bodhisattvas, disciples and mythological beings. Behind the main statues there is often a shrine to Guanyin, the Chinese Goddess of Mercy.

The second or third temple building often gives access to a confusing maze of outbuildings, small courtyards, vegetable gardens and so on.

Temple guardian from Huating complex, Western Hills.

in past centuries, who fancied their resemblance to living phenomena. Thus the stroller searches out and passes by stones dubbed 'Rhinoceros Looking at the Moon', 'Woman Waiting for Her Husband', 'Camel Riding an Elephant', and the anthropomorphic pillar in the adjoining Little Stone Forest named after the tragic Sani heroine Ashima.

The Stone Forest is the best, and most concentrated, example of the type of landscape phenomenon that permeates Lunan County's rolling hills. Smaller clusters of pillars, stone groves so to speak, pop up across the land, while limestone boulders litter the red-soiled farmlands. Another major collection of them lies 15 km north of Shilin, beside Cloud Lake and across the Bajiang River. Because the pillars here are darker, it is known as the **Black Stone Forest** (*Naigu Shilin*). It is less built up, but also full of suggestive shapes. More such stones line parts of the shoreline of **Oblong Lake** (*Changhu*), 24 km southeast of Lunan. Local Sani like to picnic here. The county's other lake—Moon Lake (*Yuehu*)—lies 10 km southwest of the turn-off to Naigu Shilin. Secluded and peaceful, it is only accessible from one shore, however, whereas Changhu can be easily circumambulated.

Southwest of the county seat, 10 km south to Banqiao, then 13 km west, the Bajiang River tumbles over a 30-metre-wide cliff to fall 96 metres at a spot called **Daduishui**, Yunnan's highest waterfall. It can be approached by paths leading to the pool at the base of the fall. Crossing the stream, one can ascend the steep hill opposite and sit on a ledge that puts one on a level with the top of the cataract, for a wholly different perspective.

Besides the fantastic landscape above ground, erosion was equally busy creating scenery beneath the earth's surface in the limestone caves on the approach to Shilin. For the most part these are more like grottoes, with routes entering one end and exiting another. Those parts featuring attractive stalactites, stalagmites shaped like animals, plants, etc, are all illuminated with multicoloured lights.

A finer group of karst caves, some 65 in all, lies at **Jiuxiang**, 45 km north of Yiliang, the county seat just west of Lunan. Perhaps the most impressive is **Sleeping Dragon Cave** (*Wulongdong*). From its entrance at Terrestrial Gate, the visitor peers down 120 metres to the cavern floor. A subterranean waterfall inside drops 30 metres. Just past this the trail winds around the river past a series of natural stone terraces, resembling an underground **White Water Terrace** (*Baishuitai*), except that the water in these terrace 'plots' is often several metres deep. Fish in this river are blind and an aquarium at the major rest stop on the trail displays some of them; they are a type of freshwater mackerel. As in Lunan's caves, coloured lights illuminate the weirdest shapes of stone and the most striking stalactites. The entire Jiuxiang area has several

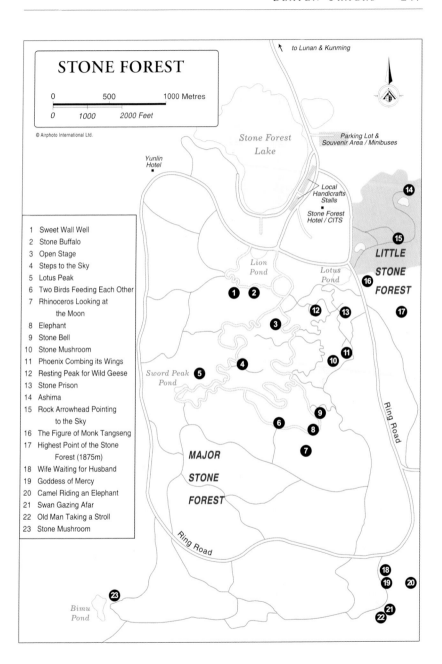

STONE FOREST

0   500   1000 Metres

0   1000   2000 Feet

© Airphoto International Ltd.

to Lunan & Kunming

Stone Forest Lake

Parking Lot & Souvenir Area / Minibuses

Yunlin Hotel

Local Handicrafts Stalls

Stone Forest Hotel / CITS

Lion Pond

Lotus Pond

LITTLE STONE FOREST

Sword Peak Pond

MAJOR STONE FOREST

Ring Road

Ring Road

Bimu Pond

1   Sweet Wall Well
2   Stone Buffalo
3   Open Stage
4   Steps to the Sky
5   Lotus Peak
6   Two Birds Feeding Each Other
7   Rhinoceros Looking at
        the Moon
8   Elephant
9   Stone Bell
10 Stone Mushroom
11 Phoenix Combing its Wings
12 Resting Peak for Wild Geese
13 Stone Prison
14 Ashima
15 Rock Arrowhead Pointing
        to the Sky
16 The Figure of Monk Tangseng
17 Highest Point of the Stone
        Forest (1875m)
18 Wife Waiting for Husband
19 Goddess of Mercy
20 Camel Riding an Elephant
21 Swan Gazing Afar
22 Old Man Taking a Stroll
23 Stone Mushroom

Karst limestone pillars of the Stone Forest. (photo by Magnus Bartlett)

scenic walks in its hills. Visitors can also take a boat ride 600 metres through a shady gorge. Hui and Yi reside in the villages and the area really comes alive the first three days of the 2nd lunar month, when the Yi stage their Hunter's Guardian Festival.

SANI LIFE

Lunan is a Yi Autonomous County. In 1998 its name was officially changed to Shilin Yi Autonomous County, but the local people still refer to their town and county as Lunan, to distinguish it from the park Shilin. Its main inhabitants are a branch of the Yi called Sani, with smaller numbers of another branch, the Axi, living on the southern fringes of the county. Because of the Stone Forest's tourist draw, the Sani are among the best known of Yunnan's ethnic minorities, and certainly one of the most publicized. Their colourful costumes are easy to recognize, for the guides don them, the crafts sellers wear them, the performers dance in them, Kunming shops sell them and portrait photographers in the parks lend them to customers so they can have their pictures taken dressed in minority (*shaoshu minzu*) style.

The woman's costume consists of a long-sleeved, side fastened jacket with a back flap that reaches to the knees. This is tied with a belt with embroidered ends hanging over the jacket flap and worn with trousers, a turban, and in cooler weather a cape of sheepskin or palm fibre. Younger women prefer bright or pastel colours, older women black or blue. Turbans indicate marital status, for the unmarried wear ones with brighter colours, actually symbolising a rainbow, and two triangular tabs, one above each ear, that the married women's turbans don't have. Arabesques in different forms and colours are appliquéd onto the tabs on the turbans and the tabs connecting the cape to its strap. The same are also attached to their shoulder bags.

Men's costume is less distinctive. The main piece is a white vest with pockets, usually of unbleached hemp or 'fireweed' cloth, wide trousers, ordinary shirt and a head scarf. Nowadays the vest may be made from cotton, for making thread from hemp or 'fireweed' (so named because it is used as tinder for starting cooking fires) is tremendously labour-intensive. Sani women claim more than 60 steps are required to turn the hemp plant into thread, mostly soakings in various baths and subsequent rinsing. They then weave it on a simple, narrow, bamboo-frame loom, standing up to do the work. The resultant cloth, however, is one of the strongest, most durable to be found in Yunnan. Sani women are also first-class embroiderers, using both the cross-stitch and the pictorial styles to create patterns on belt ends, shoulder bags and particularly baby carriers.

Because of the popularity of the Stone Forest, where many local Sani work as guides, the Sani girls' traditional costumes are among the best known in Yunnan.

Away from the tourist zone around Shilin, Sani villages usually lie near ponds, sometimes with a stone grove as a backdrop. Their houses are one- and two-storey, mud-brick, with tile roofs. Some have a beehive built into the back of the house and gather the honey in spring. Sani raise rice, maize, tobacco and vegetables and tend flocks of goats, the milk from which they turn into Lunan's *mingcai*—fried goat cheese *(rubing)*. Some villages are Christian, the result of 19th century French missionaries. The largest church stands in Guishan, in the eastern part of the county.

Guishan stages a modest Sunday market, but most business takes place in Lunan, which holds market days every Wednesday and Saturday. Then tractor-trailers and trucks bring in the villagers, with their animals, vegetables, sugar cane, bamboo poles, straw stools, grain and so on. The town is still rather quiet and pleasant, featuring a statue of Ashima in its centre. The tree-lined avenue running south ends at a huge, red brick gate, marking the entrance to the lanes of the old town.

The Sani are justly renowned for their music and dance. Every Kunming restaurant with a floor show includes at least one Sani dance, even if the performers happen to be Han. For accompaniment, the males play three-stringed guitars with a long neck and deep, bucket-shaped box, flutes and gourd-pipes. The girls may play gourd-pipes too, or else just make music whistling with leaves, making a sound like a high-pitched clarinet.

The visitor may wonder why Lunan displays a statue of the Sani heroine Ashima, why one of the stone pillars in Shilin is named after her, even why her portrait adorns packages of the local cigarette, also named after her; it's because Ashima embodies all the ideals of the Sani woman. In the long poem devoted to her, she is an adept spinner and weaver, is so close to nature she can converse with the animals, is respectful and attentive to her parents, and is good at singing, dancing and playing the *mo-sheen*, a kind of bamboo Jew's harp. Her attributes attract the attention of a local despot, who kidnaps her and tries to persuade her to marry him. With the aid of her brother she escapes, but the wicked chief controls the rivers, which he causes to flood. The pair are trapped in the Stone Forest and Ashima is swept away, then metamorphosed into the rock that bears her name.

THE LAKES

South of Kunming, set among the rolling hills of the central plateau, lie three of Yunnan's picturesque lakes. The province's deepest and third largest, Fuxianhu, lies just a few kilometres below **Chongjiang**, a small city with one major attraction—the 20,000 sq m Confucian temple in the eastern quarter. Originally built in 1571, the compound underwent extensive renovations in the Qing Dynasty and again in recent years. Now yellow glazed tiles roof the seven adjoining chambers of the 10-metre-high main hall.

The nearest shore of **Fuxian Lake** has been built up as a resort centre. On the northeast side rises a large promontory called **Elephant Trunk Hill**, after the long rock that seems to stretch into the clean blue water for a drink. The southern loop of Fuxian Lake, just east of Jiangcheng, is perhaps more attractive and certainly more tranquil. Visitors can stay in new villas in the traditional style with white walls and orange glazed tile roofs, on the small but pretty **Solitary Island** (*Gushan*) near the southern end. Further down, the lake empties into the shallow waters of Xingyun Lake, an arched stone bridge marking the spot.

The waters of this lake, as well as of **Qilu Lake** further south, are somewhat greyer than those of Fuxian. Hot springs lie in several spots in the vicinity. One set is on the east side of Fuxian. Another five are around Xingyun, with the water temperature increasing the further south the spring is situated. The biggest, a built-up local tourist destination of its own, is **Elephant Trunk Spring** in Huaning County, 28 km east of Tonghai.

Tonghai

Passing Xingyun Lake and Jiangchuan city, the road south crosses low hills and then winds into the plain around Qilu Lake. Tonghai sits a couple of kilometres beyond, backed by wooded hills. It is one of the nicest of the cities in central Yunnan, for south of the main through road lies the original urban core, where the streets are lined with shadey trees and traditional-style buildings still dominate the architecture. Fine old wood and tile buildings, originally religious but now serving secular purposes, occupy the compound of **Yuanming Temple**, at the base of the hill.

The hill behind Tonghai, rising about 200 metres higher than the town, is called **Xiushan**—Beautiful Mountain. It has long been venerated by Buddhists, who constructed five temples on its wooded slopes, the oldest dating back to the Tang Dynasty. Poets and scholars have gravitated here over the centuries. Inscribed stone tablets and over 200 couplets have been left at the temples, some perhaps composed at one of the 20 pavilions and arbours placed around the hill. Ancient trees—a Song cypress, a Yuan cedar and a Ming magnolia—are also part of the furnishings in the compounds, while the wood carving and the rows of painted sculptures of the deities are even more eye-catching.

Tonghai's residents are mostly Han, but the Hui also have a significant presence, both in the town and in several of the county's villages. The largest Hui settlement is Najiaying, on the west side of Qilu Lake, 13 km from

(following pages) Gushan Resort overlooks Fuxian Lake.

Tonghai. Separated from the lake by its farms, lying along the east side of the road, flanked by hills on its west, **Najiaying** is a strongly Hui town. The new, green-domed, white mosque in Arabian style dominates the northern part of the town, but a much older Chinese-style mosque stands in the southern quarter. A two-tiered tower rises over the compound's entrance and an Islamic Studies Centre sits beside the mosque.

Most of the houses are the same brick and tile types seen in Han villages nearby. But often the residents mount a Koranic inscription over the front door. Islamic motifs also mark the new homes of the newly rich, mainly in the northern quarter, such as plaques on the facade with Arabic inscriptions, Arabian-style cupolas on the upper balconies, etc. The Hui bury their dead. Some tombs are up on the hill slopes, but other tombstones and sarcophagi stand in the forest between the settled area and the highway. The Hui don't have an ethnic costume per se, but many women keep their hair covered. Besides farming and occasional fishing, Hui men are heavily involved in the transportation business. Hui-owned or Hui-driven vehicles usually sport a decal in the windshield of a crescent moon and a Koranic quote in Arabic script.

South of Tonghai the road passes by **Lishan**, a local tourist attraction for its modest karst cave and the jungle food available in the restaurants. Then it winds into the hills to **Gaoda**, 17 km south. The main road turns east to Jianshui and the branch road leads directly south into the hills of northern Shiping County. After about 30 km it reaches the high plain and rolling hills of **Shaochong** and **Longpeng** townships, home of the Huayao Yi, one of the most colourfully dressed branches of the Yi.

The Huayao Yi woman's costume consists of a lavishly embroidered vest over a long-sleeved jacket with a long tail that hangs to the back of the knees. Around their waist they tie a belt with two wide, diamond-shaped ends, fully embroidered in a lush floral style, draped over the buttocks. Hence the name *Huayao Yi*—Flowery Waist Yi. On their heads they wear a cap with two rectangular flaps erect in the back, also lavishly embroidered. Plain black trousers with a blue stripe at the ankles complete the costume, plus shoes, but the shoes might also be embroidered. The bonnet seems to be the one component still in widespread use, even when the women are otherwise in modern garb. But many older women wear the complete outfit and a good percentage of younger women sometimes dress up Yi-style for market days.

The Huayao Yi live in mud-brick houses with flat roofs, on which they lay out their crops to dry, and an open-air central courtyard. Behind this slightly sunken courtyard is the main receiving room, while sleeping quarters are

The Huayao Yi are one of the most splendidly attired ethnic groups in central Yunnan.

mostly upstairs. Many kilns also stand in the village area, some nicely sited on the ridges, for the Yi raise a lot of tobacco, besides rice, wheat and vegetables. Like most Yi groups they observe the Torch Festival, but even more important to them is *Jilong*—Worshipping the Dragon Ancestor—which runs for three days, beginning the first horse day of the Lunar New Year. It includes a grand dragon procession around the fields, rites at the set of three stones representing the village's ancestors, skits with men on stilts and a number of dances with dozens of women performing in their gorgeous costumes.

THE MONGOLIANS

The most interesting aspect of Tonghai is the survival of a community of Mongolians, in **Xinmeng** and two adjacent villages at the foot of **Peacock Hill**, about 15 km northwest of the county seat and several thousand from their original homeland. They are the remnant descendants of the soldiers from the steppes that Kubilai Khan left behind. Most of Yunnan's Mongolians were expelled or killed when the Ming Dynasty chased the last Yuan troops from the province in the late 14th century.

Forced to hide and later to conceal their ethnic identity for several generations, this small, tightly knit community in the end not only continued to exist, but is now thriving. Yunnan's Mongolians made historic shifts in lifestyle, first to fishing, then to farming, finally to construction. Yet they maintained the social customs and traditions they brought with them from the northern steppes. Most women still wear the traditional jackets, vests and caps, often adorning them with silver clasps, buttons and pendants. They live in sturdy houses with high, thick walls, separated from each other by narrow cobbled lanes. They worship at the Guan Yin Temple but also, in Xinmeng village, have their own splendid hall honouring, and housing large sculptures of, three of the great empire builders of their past—Genghis Khan, Mongke Khan and Kubilai Khan.

Local legends incorporate supernatural elements into the community's historic shifts in lifestyle. When the Ming troops all but eradicated their presence, the last seven fugitives sat on the shore of Qilu Lake pondering their future. Suddenly an old man emerged from the waters, standing on a rhinoceros skin. Inviting them on to the skin, he pointed to a huge fish supporting a temple. Back on shore the men realized that because the words for 'food' and 'temple' were similar, the old man had been telling them that fish could be food. And so they began drawing on the fish and eels of Qilu Lake for their sustenance.

Settling at Xinmeng at the base of Peacock Hill, the last Mongolian men had to marry Yi women and inculcate them into their language and customs. Their community began to multiply and then years later the Goddess Achala arrived at Qilu Lake, subdued a dragon responsible for flooding the plains, and dug a hole at the lakeside. Excess water dropped through this hole and emptied into the South China Sea: hence the county's name—Tonghai—'connecting the sea.' Achala then subdued more dragons and removed them to the hills to 'dragon pools'—springs—to irrigate the new fields.

Since then the Mongolians have been farmers, though they still trap eels and small fish in the canals that connect Xinmeng with the lake. In recent decades, the men have worked much of the year in the construction business, enjoying a high reputation as carpenters, stonemasons and bricklayers. Consequently, they are out of the area most of the time and Xinmeng's residents are mostly women and children. Yet the men are just as immersed in ethnic awareness as the women.

Only in 1979 were Xinmeng's people officially recognized as part of the Mongolian nationality. The male leaders of Xingmeng at once dispatched a delegation to Inner Mongolia to invite Mongolian teachers to come instruct their children in the written and spoken language and customs of the steppes. And while Yunnan's Mongolians have their own locally evolved customs as well as those they retained over the centuries, the greatest event of their year is the Nadam Festival in late summer. At this time the dances, sporting contests and equestrian shows of the northern steppes are on display in Yunnan's Tonghai County.

Yuxi and Eshan

The first major city on the Kunming-Jinghong highway is Yuxi, 88 km southwest of Kunming. The countryside of low, rolling hills is prime tobacco-growing land and cigarette production is one of the county's prime industries. Other light industries have given the city recent prosperity, reflected in the clean streets and fancy new high-rise buildings on the outskirts. The business district is dominated by its main north-south avenue (*Beinanjie*), while the side streets are still full of shophouses in the traditional style and lined with shady trees.

A small park in the southern quarter has an old pavilion, pond and rockery, but a much larger and nicer one lies along Hongtajie. At one end a two-storey, red wooden pavilion sits beside a pond. Two more ponds lie south of this, each graced with a small viewing pavilion in the centre. Behind the last pond is a small garden park where Yuxi men come to play board games under the trees, while listening to their caged songbirds.

In the southeast suburbs stands the 25-metre-tall, tapering seven-storey, close-eaved pagoda called Hongta, the Red Pagoda. Originally a Yuan Dynasty structure of light blue limestone, restored in the late Qing Dynasty, it was in recent decades painted a brilliant red. It has become the emblem for Yunnan's finest quality cigarette—Hongtashan.

Several resorts lie in the vicinity of the county seat. The closest is **Nie Er Park**, in the city's southwest suburbs. Nie Er composed China's national anthem and the park contains his residence and the lotus pool where he went swimming, along with pavilions, gardens and ponds. Nie Er drowned in Japan at age 25.

The **Nine Dragon Pond Resort**, 10 km northwest of Yuxi, dates its construction to the Ming Dynasty. The pine forest here was supposed to have been planted by a Buddhist monk around then. White Dragon Pond, 10 km northeast, owes its foundation to an ancient love story. A white dragon fell in love with a peasant girl as she fetched water from the fountain. The dragon assumed human form to woo her. She was willing enough to marry him, but worried about who would fetch water for her mother. So the white dragon created the stream that flowed into her village.

The other major park in the area is at **Black Dragon Pond**, 8 km from the city. A smaller pond in this park is known as the **Weather-Forecasting Pond**, for its colour and surface change according to an imminent change in weather. A watchman is employed there so that nearby villagers can

Muslim Hui girls in Eshan. The largest mosque in Yunnan is in nearby Wenming village.

call him up and find out whether it's going to rain, storm or be fair weather.

Continuing south, the road climbs into the heavily wooded hills, with almost no sign of habitation, and crosses into Eshan County. The county seat, 30 km from Yuxi, straddles the Ni River and is smaller and less modernized than Yuxi; also dirtier, with only a couple of pavilions at the south end of the river providing anything resembling a park or recreation area. One of the most colourful branches of the Yi live in the mountains to the southwest and occasionally they visit the city. All the women wear their traditional costumes: jacket, apron, trousers and headgear all heavily embroidered, with an emphasis on red.

The Hui presence is much more pervasive. Several Hui

Yuxi's unique red pagoda stands on a hill opposite Asia's largest cigarette factory, maker of the eponymous brand.

restaurants are in town and neighbouring villages are mostly Hui. At **Dabaiyi Hui** village, just a few km northeast, a green domed Islamic Institute dominates the buildings. An elegant, Chinese-style mosque, with a two-tiered gate tower, lies in the next neighbourhood.

The largest mosque in Yunnan is in nearby **Wenming** village, about 6 km from Dabaiyi. It is in the Arabian style, in a compound at the foot of the hill at the end of the village. The prayer hall is elevated and its floor covered in Arabian carpets.

CHUXIONG

The route west out of Kunming is the beginning of the old Burma Road to Dali and thence southwest to Dehong, following the caravan routes of former centuries. Nowadays, a superhighway has shortened the journey to Dali, while the rest of the road is being improved as well. The first major stop is at the resort city of Anning, 33 km west of Kunming. Rich salt wells in the vicinity made this one of the earliest places coveted by Han emperors as they attempted to expand south.

A further 10 km north, cradled by three high mountains, lies **Green Jade Spring**, reputedly the most salubrious hot spring in the province. Famous since the Yuan Dynasty, the spring is named for its dark green colour. Free from the usual sulphur odour, its temperature is 42 degrees C and its waters contain trace elements of several minerals, said to be an effective remedy against skin, joint, gastro-intestinal, venereal and gynaecological ailments. Chinese tourists come here in droves to use the modern bathhouses and pools that have been constructed, making use of the waters for bathing as well as for drinking.

Following that experience, the next move is to take a walk, or ride the cable car through the woods to the **Caoxi Temple**, all but hidden by bamboo groves. Its double-eaved hall dates from the Song Dynasty, the bracketed, upturned roofs being typical of the era. A small slit in the ceiling permits a ray of light to penetrate the interior. On the night of the Mid-Autumn Festival in the 8th lunar month, the first light of the rising full moon strikes the mirror set in the forehead of the main Buddha image. As the moon continues to rise, its beam moves down the tip of the nose and on to the navel.

Two smaller hot springs lie in the vicinity of Caoxi Temple. To the southeast sits **Pearl Spring**, a round pool where the water bubbles up like strings of pearls. It is also known as **Buddha's Rosary**, a name bestowed by a devotee with a more religious imagination. To the temple's south is the oddly titled **Divine Spring of Golden Toads**. It contains a geyser that gushes at midnight, noon and 6 pm, because, according to legend, these are the times the spring's resident golden toads come out of their holes.

Upon leaving Anning County the road enters Chuxiong Yi Autonomous Prefecture. The Yi are not the only minority here, nor even the largest segment of the population. They make up only about 18 percent in all of Chuxiong, but inhabit a majority of the land space in this mostly mountainous prefecture, and have left their imprint on the local lore and culture.

Chuxiong city itself, the prefecture capital, is also known as *Lucheng*—Deer City (or *Elu* in the Yi language). According to legend, long ago a spotted deer descended from Heaven, ran in a certain circumference and vanished. Taking the incident as an auspicious sign, the local people built a wall along the tracks the deer made and established Lucheng within it. The best view of Chuxiong, which has torn down its walls and old buildings and is now thoroughly modernized, is still from **Elu Park**, on a mountain west of the city. Besides the immediate scenery of cliffs with strange stone projections, the park is rich with camellia trees that begin blooming in February.

Within the city the most interesting spot is the new provincial museum, a grand, multi-building complex on a knoll in the western part of town. Different halls hold displays of the prefecture's flora and fauna, its calligraphy, minerals, minority nationalities' costumes and artefacts, ancient weapons and tools, plus a room full of dinosaur skeletons. The exhibits are well-labelled and the historical objects mounted in front of paintings depicting their use in ancient times.

Just northwest of the city lies the new recreational and cultural park with the long name of **The Park of the Ten-Month Calendar Culture of the Yi Nationality in China**. Dominating the park are several tall, carved, stone pillars, supposedly in the style of ancient Yi inhabitants of the prefecture.

Chuxiong's other small parks are hardly enough to keep a traveller in the city long. But besides traditional Yi villages, the most interesting of which are quite some distance away, the prefecture does have its share of enjoyable mountain areas, a few of them close. The camellia-lover will enjoy the forests of **Zixishan**. About 20 km west of Chuxiong a road turns south into the mountains, eventually reaching Zixishan's Camellia Research Centre, which has a guesthouse with comfortable rooms and electric blankets. Camellia trees abound here, with both red and white flowers. Forest walks pass by alpine lakes and small waterfalls. The area serves as an annual venue for the Yi people's *Chahuajie* (Putting Up Flowers), the 8th day of the 2nd moon. Yi then hike for hours from distant villages to assemble for a day of programmes and a night of music and dance.

In the northeast, closer to Kunming (100 km) than to Chuxiong (167 km), is the town of Wuding. Like most county seats it has been rebuilt in modern style, but the townships close by are still largely traditional in look. Most are Han-inhabited but the higher ones are likely to be Yi or Miao. Female dress of the two is so different one can immediately tell them apart. The Yi women wear trousers, with an embroidered apron, side-fastened jacket and turban. The Miao women wear bulky, knee-length skirts, embroidered jacket and pile their hair in a top bun.

Except for glimpses of minorities and some shopping, the town offers little of interest. But behind Wuding stands **Lion Mountain** (*Shizishan*), one of the prefecture's premier natural attractions. Several trails lead the visitor to pavilions commanding great views, verdant groves of gigantic trees and the inevitable Buddhist shrines. The most famous of these is **Zhenxu Monastery**, near the summit, built in 1311, more in the shape of a palace than a temple. At the end of the 14th century, following a violent succession struggle, the Ming Emperor Huidi was deposed by an uncle, who then became the Yong Le Emperor (who launched Zheng He's naval expeditions). Huidi allegedly took refuge in Zhenxu Monastery and became a Buddhist monk.

THE TORCH FESTIVAL

Midsummer is not a very busy time in the farmer's annual work cycle. The main crops planted earlier are still growing, or at best just beginning to ripen. Since it's still the rainy season, construction is put off until the autumn. So it is not surprising that this is the time of the year when people entertain themselves, when some of their biggest festivals take place. Yunnan's major summer celebration, thanks to its large Yi population, is the Torch Festival, held on the 24th day of the 6th lunar month (late July or early August). The Yi are not the only ones to observe it. The Naxi, Bai, and even some Hani do, too. But the Yi are more spread out in the province and the Torch Festival has become more associated with them.

Several different stories detail the origin of this festival. The most common tale among the northern branches of the Yi attributes it to the wrath of a deity and the measures taken to counter it. According to them, the first Yi ancestor, called Chikareu in Liangshan and Meigo in much of Chuxiong Prefecture, aroused the jealousy of one of Heaven's deities by his success in establishing a lifestyle for his people. The god then challenged the Yi hero to a wrestling match and lost. Angry at this defeat, the god dispatched hordes of mosquitoes to plague the Yi. But the Yi hero advised the people to light and wave torches to drive them away. Every year the Yi commemorate their triumph by lighting torches, singing, dancing and staging sporting events, like wrestling, pony races and inducing pairs of bulls or goats to square off and duel.

Besides the villages, the festival is also celebrated in many of the county seats and townships, often subsidised by local governments, which means lavish entertainment. Chuxiong city authorities bus in Yi performers from many different sub-groups, hence a variety of colourful costumes, and stages its programme in the new park northwest of the city. Downtown they stage a fireworks show and Yi and Han in the city join in ring dances in the parks.

The Sani of Lunan have a separate origin story. It begins with a fiendish monster riding roughshod over the people. Whenever the Sani rose in revolt the monster massacred all the attackers. Secure in his mountaintop stronghold, possessing magic powers against humans, the fiend carried on his devilry with impunity. But one day a Yi hero advised his people to fix torches to the horns of all their goats and drive them up the mountain from all directions. Unable to work his diabolic magic against goats, only humans, the fiend was trapped in the flames and burnt to death. On the anniversary of their victory, the Sani hold their Torch Festival.

Yi girls light torches at the start of Chuxiong's Torch Festival celebrations.

No one makes a grander show of it, for only the Sani have such a magnificent setting as the Stone Forest. Hundreds of dancers and musicians perform before tens of thousands of spectators, local villagers and tourists alike. Wrestling matches and bull-fighting contests augment the daytime entertainment, while at night the show is illuminated by bonfires and torches, casting shadows on the stone columns and pinnacles behind the dancers. Elsewhere that night, long lines of torch-bearing youths make a procession around the shores of Oblong Lake and in every village bonfires blaze and the young sing and dance. The Torch Festival is the Sani's greatest sound-and-light spectacle of the year, particularly in the Stone Forest, but to one degree or another, all over Lunan County.

Traditional house, Xishuangbanna

A Slice of Southeast Asia: Xishuangbanna

THE DAI

No other ethnic group in Yunnan is so much presented as a tourist attraction as the Dai of Xishuangbanna. The Sani, the Bai and the Naxi may be well promoted as integral aspects of their respective areas, but the promotional material often omits them in favour of scenic highlights, like the stone pillars of Shilin, the waters of Erhai Lake and the snow peaks of Jade Dragon Mountain. The imagery of Xishuangbanna, unless it's a tree, flower or pagoda, almost always includes Dai people in their tropical setting. Most often these are women, generally young, bathing in the stream, chatting under umbrellas, walking to the market carrying baskets suspended at each end of a balance pole, picking fruits in the orchards, fixing flowers in their hair, performing the Peacock Dance and fetching water from the village well. Sometimes they are men, as monks, fishermen casting nets, shirtless farmers ploughing with buffaloes and dancers in the streets beating long drums.

Publicists promote the Dai people as a major component of Xishuangbanna's charm. In the photos the Dai are always clean and healthy-looking, the women slim, graceful and often beautiful, while everybody looks happy and enjoying themselves. Displaying the Dai in a setting of lush forests, warm plains, with the exotic fruits and flowers of the tropics hints that the environment itself produces people as gentle and contented as the Dai. Moreover, and this is even more persuasive to Chinese who have never left their country, there is nothing Han-looking about the houses, the pagodas or the people's faces. It's like being in Southeast Asia, except that Xishuangbanna is part of China.

One might be a little suspicious of such positive images, yet in actuality they are not really inaccurate. It may be that an agreeable climate, fertile land and plenty of water have helped mould the Dai character. Theravada Buddhism and a strong streak of innate conservatism have been equally influential. Historically, the Dai who moved south in the face of Han expansion resisted assimilation. European travellers in the 19th century often noted that in dress, manners, food, domestic life and religion, the Dai were less like the Chinese than all but the remotest hill people.

Five kinds of Dai live in Xishuangbanna. The main group is the Shui Dai; the four smaller branches are the Huayao Dai, Han Dai, Kemu Dai and Paxitai. The Huayao immigrated to Banna a hundred years ago from the Red River area. Their women are the most splendidly dressed. *Huayao* means Flowery Waist, after the heavy use of embroidery on the women's costume around the midriff. They wear a black sarong to mid-calf, topped by a short skirt, the hems of both thickly embroidered, a short jacket over a long-sleeved one, and a silver chain turban.

The Han Dai, or Dry-land Dai, are so named because they settle somewhat away from the rivers. They have a few villages around Mengyang and near Jingne in the far north. Their women wear a black turban, long-sleeved blouse and a long apron over a tube skirt. Like the Huayao, they are animist, so no temples stand in their villages. The Kemu are originally a Mon-Khmer tribal group, called Khamu in Laos and Thailand, who have been assimilated into Dai culture. The Paxitai are Dai by race and Muslim by religion.

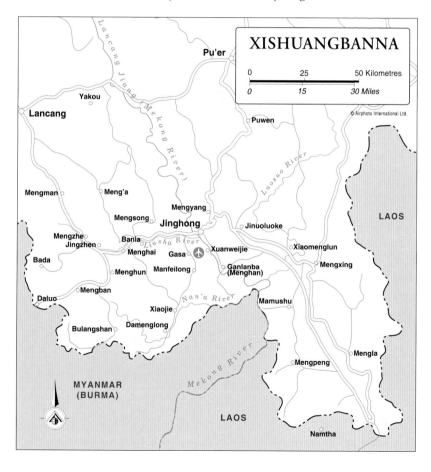

The Buddhist temple at Bulangshan.

Most of Xishuangbanna's Dai are the Shui Dai, or Water Dai, though they are also known as the Lü, or Tai Lü, as their cousins are called in northern Laos and northern Thailand. These Dai traditionally live by rivers and streams and have been Buddhist since at least the 12th century, perhaps through contact with converted Dai branches in Laos, Thailand and Myanmar (Burma). The religion stresses the law of karma and enjoins its adherents to 'make merit' as often as possible.

Equally important as a determinant of Dai behaviour is the Dai concept of keeping a 'cool heart.' This means refraining from displays of anger or great displeasure, not being insistent in one's dealings with others and avoiding rude and boisterous actions. Consequently, the Dai rarely argue in public or stumble around drunk making nuisances of themselves. But this reserve and self-control does not make them sedate or dour. On the contrary, a sense of fun and enjoyment permeates as much of ordinary daily life as possible.

One of the most enjoyable social activities among the youth is courtship (though it also has the potential to be heart-breaking). They have the freedom to choose their own spouses and have evolved customs to formalize the procedure. Traditionally every village girl learned how to spin thread. As a young woman, single and available, she might choose to do her spinning out in the open, bringing her wheel and two stools, one for her and one for any young man who is interested in her. He sits beside her while she spins. If the movement of the wheel is steady and rhythmic, indicating that the girl is trying to make a good impression, the boy stays. If the spinning is discordant and jerky, the girl is hinting at her lack of interest and the boy leaves, his place then taken by another.

Another method is possible on market days, particularly just before a big festival. The girl braises a chicken she has raised herself and brings it to the market, hoping to arouse the attention of the boy she likes. If he does indeed approach her, the pair take the chicken to a secluded place in the woods for a private picnic. If an unsuitable boy approaches and asks the price of it, she demands double the going rate and snubs him.

At festivals, too, when the girls dance they carry a small bag on a string and, during or at the end of a dance, each girl tosses it to the object of her affections, openly showing her interest in him. Anything can happen after that. If it results in a wedding this will be held at the girl's home, probably with Buddhist monks in attendance to bless the union. The moment of marriage occurs when the bride's parents tie white thread around the wrists of the bride and groom. A folk singer performs next, followed by a feast and an evening of dancing before the groom takes his bride back to his own house.

TROPICAL DISPLAYS

Dai villages mostly lie in the plains near a river or stream. Small hills rise in the vicinity and occasionally villages spread along the base and lowest slopes, to reserve the flat land for their farms. The tallest and biggest building in Buddhist villages, which is what the great majority of them are, will be the temple. There may be a pagoda mounted on the nearest hilltop, but otherwise religious activity is generally restricted to the temple compound.

Traditional Dai houses were made of wood, raised on stilts a metre and a half above the ground, had large, airy rooms, sloping roofs of wood tiles, sometimes extra gables, and always an attached open-air balcony. Houses stood close to each other and had small yards enclosed by a bamboo rail fence or thick shrubbery.

This is still the norm in the remote townships, but some changes have been introduced with the recent prosperity. Now the Dai, especially in areas along the main highways, are using brick more than wood. New houses keep the traditional shape and wood-tiled, sloping roofs. But instead of wooden stilts the house stands on brick columns. Brick is also used for house walls and for the compound boundary, replacing the bamboo rail fence. Piped water has been installed, too, so people now bathe at home instead of in the stream.

Clumps of tall bamboo stand near the villages, providing not only refuge from the sun and heat, but also a handy and useful material for tools, utensils and furniture. At least one well lies just outside the settled area. As the Dai consider such water sources sacred, they erect a small religious monument over the well. The sight of women, in long sarongs, hair tied in a bun, carrying buckets of water on a shoulder-hoisted balance pole, is one of the prettiest vignettes in Xishuangbanna.

Rice cultivation is the main occupation of the villagers. They also raise sundry fruits and vegetables. Women do most of the field work, except for ploughing, and take the surplus to the markets. Most townships have a regular market day especially for this kind of trade. Some of the women dress nicely for market day, putting on their best brocaded sarongs and fixing flowers in their hair. The Dai are never short of flowers, for if they don't grow them at their houses, they can fetch them from the forest.

About one-third of the prefecture is covered by forests, with over 5,000 species of tree, over 500 medicinal plants and herbs and 100 kinds of oil-bearing plant. Rubber tree plantations take up some of this forest coverage, but they, too, contribute to regulating the weather and holding the soil of the hills. Large swathes of virgin rainforest also exist. The bulk of these are in the east, and the easiest to see lie on both sides of the highway from Jinuoshan to Menglun.

Situated at the northern end of the tropical zone, Xishuangbanna's mean annual temperature is a pleasant 21°C. Cool mornings bring heavy dews and fog descends on the plains and valleys about one-third of the days of the year. The rainy season begins in May or June and lasts through October. Precipitation is greater in the first half of the monsoon but never so heavy as to cause floods. The first few post-monsoon months comprise the cool, dry season. These are the foggy morning days, but the bright sun burns it off by late morning. Skies are generally clear, but progressively hazier as hotter temperatures commence in late February. In the last several weeks before the rains, the thermometre hits 35°C regularly. Yet nature is kind in Xishuangbanna, for just when the hot season demands regular refreshment, mangos, lychees, longans, pineapples and melons start pouring into the markets.

Jinghong and Other Towns

Xishuangbanna is the Chinese pinyin spelling of a Dai phrase that means Twelve Thousand Rice Fields. A thousand rice fields constituted an administrative district (*banna*) under the medieval Dai princes. A couple of the *banna* were lost to French Laos, but most were incorporated into this border prefecture in the last century. The historical capital, called *Cheli* in Dai (Daybreak City) when the Mekong Expedition explorers passed through, was little more than an overgrown village at that time. Now it is the busy city of Jinghong. Sprawling west from the bank of the Lancangjiang, it is the prefecture's largest and most important city.

For the first several years after Jinghong was opened to foreigners it remained a small, quiet town flanked by traditional Dai villages, and the rural area lay within walking distance from the heart of town. Cycle-rickshaws were more common than taxis and only a handful of hotels were open for business. The main market centre was near the Banna Binguan, the only place foreigners were allowed to stay, and every morning hill people and local Dai came there

Kongque Pond in downtown Jinghong provides a respite from the city's burgeoning traffic.

to buy meat, vegetables, fruits, grains and clothing items. **Manting** village was a short stroll away, still a traditional Dai village, its farms adjacent to the city.

In the mid-1990s, Jinghong underwent rapid growth, in large part due to an almost phenomenal increase in tourism. Flight frequency out of Kunming rose from four per week to 9–12 per day, nearly every flight full. Fancy hotels sprang up all over the city and a whole new subdivision took over the rural area beside Manting village. The produce market near Banna Binguan was relocated and a new lane of shops built, their proprietors selling woodcarvings, tea, minority costume components and other local products, with some managed by Burmese traders selling jade ornaments.

Yet in spite of its growth the city retains some charm. Stately royal palms line the main avenues. Parks are still quiet refuges. In the less congested areas the Dai still set up fruit stalls and outdoor grills, often beneath huge banyan trees. In preparation for Expo 99, the city widened its downtown streets, emptied, cleaned and refilled the ponds, and passed laws that required the employment of Dai architectural motifs, such as the sloping roof, in all new high-rise buildings.

Dining remains a special experience. Buffets offer the range of Dai cuisine, both in expensive hotels and in ordinary restaurants on the streets. New restaurants vied for the tourist money by building bamboo and wood dining halls in the Dai style, placing them next to quiet ponds. Those on Manting Road offered suppers with 12 or more dishes, including rice baked in a pineapple, plus a floor show at certain hours.

A typical Dai dance set will include a variety of acts. Sometimes four or more girls will perform by themselves, sometimes with the boys. Rural life influences the choice of props like spinning wheels, carrying poles, baskets, umbrellas, etc. In some numbers the dancers mime the manners of courting, while in others the choreography is decorative rather then narrative.

The most beautiful performance, a must in every Dai dance set, is the Peacock Dance, a creation of the early 1960s that was inspired by the traditional dance of the mythical bird *kinnaree*. Wearing a long, flowing, sleeveless dress with a peacock feather pattern sewn on, the girl arches her hands to suggest the peacock's head and ripples her neck and shoulder muscles to mimic the bird's movements. Done to slow, melodious music, solo or in groups, the Peacock Dance has become part of the identity of Yunnan's Dai.

The second most popular dance is probably the *ramwong*, which often closes the set, with the performers inviting the audience to join in. Dancers

(above) A Dai food stall in Menglong serves a variety of local Dai specialities.
(right) The Peacock Dance created by the Shui Dai of Xishuangbanna.

form a line and to the beat of an elephant-leg drum (so-called for its shape) and gong, move forward in short steps, gracefully waving their arms to the sides. The line moves straightly or sinuously, depending on the space, and continues until the dancers become tired of it.

Within Jinghong County are three popular small towns, each with its own special feature. The nearest is **Menghan**, 30 km southeast, right beside the Lancangjiang, on the edge of the fertile Olive Plain (*Ganlanba*). Now the prefecture's official Dai Culture Village (with the inevitable ticket booth), the town core has been built up somewhat and a large reservoir constructed just south of the business district. A market street connects the upper and lower main roads and is active every morning. Menghan's primary feature, though, is its multi-gabled, traditional Dai houses, which make up most of the buildings. Nowhere else is the peacock motif used so extensively. Carved and painted peacocks are mounted on rooftops, on the apex of the gable or beneath, the tail feathers spreading across the triangular niche. Some are stylized peacocks, others expertly sculpted and painted with great attention to the details of the plumage.

East of Jinghong, just past the turn-off to Menghan, the road winds its way around the mountain and ascends to the plateau around **Mengyang**, 35 km northeast. On the west side is the original Dai village and on the east is the modern town and Elephant Tree, which gives Mengyang some fame.

Originally, this was a banyan tree with roots above ground in the shape of an elephant. But in the mid-1990s the area became a walled-off park, with some landscaping, teahouses, shrines and a ticket booth at the entrance. Unfortunately, the famous tree began to fall down, but now it has been propped up with wooden beams and the part resembling the elephant's trunk wrapped in planks. So if it still resembles an elephant, it's more like a crippled pachyderm on crutches, with its broken trunk in a cast.

Mengyang's genuine attraction is its people. Both the Huayao Dai and the Han Dai have villages nearby and their women, the older generation dressed in traditional garments, frequent the town market. One kilometre north of the town, a branch road heads west to **Menglun** and the first small village is Han Dai. Their women wear black turbans and sarongs and in the dry season may be seen at work on the front porches, at ground level, weaving cloth on four-shaft looms. Another kilometre east lies a much bigger Huayao Dai village, with fenced yards and brick houses, fish ponds and a winding creek at the southern edge.

South of Jinghong, 68 km across a long, flat valley, the last half watered by the Nana River, with rubber tree plantations covering the foothills, stands the town of **Menglong**. Several traditional villages lie at the bases of the hills across the river. The modern part of Menglong runs along the bottom of the hills, while the older residential section is nestled in the valley west of the main road. Its claim to tourist attraction, besides its small-town ambiance, rests on its religious monuments. On top of the hill at the south end of town is the yellow **Menglong Pagoda**. Atop the hill behind the next village north is the **Manfeilong White Pagoda**, with a large Standing Buddha and a few ornate buildings in the complex.

Both highways going east from Jinghong—the northern one going through to Jinuoshan and the virgin forest tract, the southern route via Menghan—enter Mengla County just before Menglun. This town, near the Nanhan River and backed by forested hills to its north, is noted for its Botanical Garden. The spacious park has samples of nearly all of the prefecture's tropical trees and plants, including a pond featuring gigantic floating lily pads, so big a baby could ride on one. The arrangements of the trees in their respective groves, all in perfect order, may be too artificial for some, but it does have its secluded, shady areas. For a more authentic jungle walk, one can take the trails into the hills just beyond the town's northern edge.

Mengla is one of the least densely populated counties in Yunnan. The ride to the county seat passes several protected forests and scores of rubber tree plantations. The county seat lies in the south, 58 km north of the Laos border. For travellers, it is mainly a quick stopover on the way to somewhere else and its long main street is full of hotels.

Yet the northeast quarter has some attractive Dai-style buildings and the original village lies here, next to the Namla River. In the centre of town, the local cultural centre (*wenhuaguan*) holds a small museum featuring the costumes, jewellery, material and religious objects of the county's ethnic minorities. It also houses an old boundary stone marked 'France/China.' A small hill behind the southwest quarter is the site of Mengla's largest temple, recently reconstructed, and the **Manbenggang Pagoda**. Below this hill and along the stream beside Qingnianlu lies the attractive Dai neighbourhood of Mansai, with a number of fine old houses.

Directly west of Jinghong the new highway gradually ascends through the hills of Menghai County until it reaches the broad plain around the county seat. Menghai, Xishuangbanna's second largest city, stands at a relatively cool 1,300 metres and has modernized as much as Jinghong, but less gracefully. Its central market, however, does attract colourfully dressed hill folks and its plain is home to several traditional-style Dai villages. A white or golden pagoda often stands on the hillsides behind them.

One village about 6 km east of Menghai, called **Manlonghui**, is different. The inhabitants are Paxitai, or Dai Muslims, and though the women dress the same as their Buddhist neighbours—no veil or head scarf—the houses are brick and not elevated. In front of the village stands a mosque, erected in 1993, its whitewashed walls and tiled roofs in the Chinese style, its green-domed minaret in the Arabian style.

Buddhist pagodas and temples are the main draw in the county, but it is also home to two venerable tea trees. One of them, aged around 800 years, grows on **Nannuoshan**, above a group of Aini villages halfway to Jinghong, while the other, reputedly 1,700 years old, lies in a valley near the Burmese border, in Bada township in the west. The county is famous for its Pu'er brand tea and tea plantations cover much of the cultivated area in the hills.

One spot popular with Chinese tour groups is **Daluo**, 81 km southwest of Menghai. The town still has a sizable traditional Dai quarter next to the modern business centre. Villages south of here towards the border are clean, well laid out and utilize wooden waterwheels to irrigate their streamside vegetable gardens. Near the border is the **Forest Park**, featuring a banyan tree whose forked trunk and lower branches are supported by many tall, straight roots, earning it the name 'Forest of a Single Tree.'

The principal lure in the area is the Myanmar border town of **Mengla**, which Chinese are permitted to visit. After posing for photos with their pretty Dai guides at the sign marking the border, they then cross into Mengla, only to discover it looks almost exactly like an ordinary Chinese city, perhaps richer. Big new Buddhist monuments adorn the suburban hilltops. The restaurants serve Chinese cuisine and are in fact run by Chinese. Chinese renminbi is the currency used locally and the neighbouring Dai villages look the same as in Banna.

What brings the tour groups here, besides the casino, is the mid-afternoon transvestite show. These creatures, all Thais recruited out of Bangkok, are on a four-year contract for a general in the Autonomous Wa State in Myanmar. They receive a modest salary for their daily show, which means dressing up in heavy make-up, feathers and sequins and ballroom gowns, and lip-synching while dancing to recorded music. They are permitted to keep tips from the theatre clients. Chinese tourists pay 100 yuan to touch their faces and artificial breasts. The most naive and credulous of them pay 200 yuan for the transvestite to lift his dress and prove that he hasn't gotten the operation yet and really is a boy.

Dai farmers on their way to work in Meng'a, Menghai County.

TEMPLES AND ELEPHANTS

Dai religious architecture follows the Theravadin style of its Buddhist ethnic cousins in Laos, Thailand and Myanmar. Nearly every fair-sized Shui Dai village has its own temple compound. The main hall, with its tall, sloping roofs, usually in three layers, dominates the village skyline. The roof is supported by thick red wooden pillars, often decorated with painted gold or silver patterns, as in the area just below the apex of the roof on the front facade, unless a Buddha image is mounted there.

On the exterior walls next to the entrance, and sometimes around the sides, are panels painted with Buddhist and Dai imagery. The latter includes scenes from local history, vignettes of the Dai rural lifestyle, pictures of Dai worshippers, and so on. The Buddhist imagery features not only portraits of the Buddha, scenes from his life and depiction of celestial cities, religious processions, rituals and the like, but also the local mythology of Judgement Day. The God of Death rewards some by directing them to Heaven and casts the others to the depths of Hell. Here demons perform sundry tortures on the damned according to the type of sin. The artists' imaginations are at their best in these scenes, as if they had first studied Dante's *Inferno*.

(above) A detail of roof finials and ornaments on a Dai-style temple in Bulangshan.
(left) As Banna Dai grow wealthier they spend part of their fortune on building new pagodas such as this one at Manfai village in Menghai County.

The interior of the hall houses the main Buddha image, usually seated, with a few smaller images to the sides and in front. From the rafters they hang many long, narrow cloth banners, with various designs woven into them. A few may be of paper or even currency notes. The interior wall surfaces are usually plain, but some individual posters may be mounted on the posts and decorated palanquins, used to carry images during processions, are stacked in the corner.

Monks' quarters are the smaller buildings, usually behind the temple, with spartan interiors. Older monks spend their lives here, while among the younger residents, some stay for a year or two, some study to make a career out of monkhood. The discipline is not as strict as in Myanmar or Thailand; monks do not go on morning begging rounds, nor are they forbidden to eat after noon. They can eat whenever they like, in restaurants as well, and even have a beer with the meal.

The compound may include a pagoda in the yard in front of the main hall. Or a pagoda may instead stand atop a nearby hill. The shape is usually simple, rising from a wide round or square base, tapering sharply to a point, tipped by an elaborate gilt metal crown, with little pendants flapping in the breeze around its base.

Sometimes the pagoda, such as the one at Mengzhe, tapers less, looking more like a set of bowls of ever smaller size piled on top of each other, with niches chiselled into the sides for Buddha images. On the hilltop just north of Menglong stands **Manfeilong Pagoda**, the most outstanding in the prefecture. A low wall surrounds it, with smaller pagodas at regular intervals and three-headed serpents sculpted on the staircase. Originally built in 1203, it has been restored and expanded several times since.

Nearly every small hill in the Menghai plain boasts a pagoda on the summit, with or without a temple. New ones go up every year, at least partially financed by money from Buddhists in Thailand and Singapore. Pagodas do not always stand by themselves. At Manlei, 7 km west of the city, the temple sits between two pagodas, one 7 metres high, the other 9 metres. On the hill behind Nanban village in Menghun township is a cluster of nine pagodas. The tallest rises 13 metres, the other eight 3 metres each.

A very different kind of building, unique in style and decoration, is the Octagonal Pavilion (*Bajiaoting*), on a hillock beside a large temple overlooking **Jingzhe** village, 24 km west of Menghai. So named because of its octagonal base and eight main sides, it was built in 1701 of brick and wood, used for storing Buddhist scriptures. At its base it is 10 metres wide and stands 21 metres high, the top section divided into multiple smaller sides, with altogether 32 angles and a complex set of roofs, rising in layered tiers to the top.

Whenever a new temple, pagoda or major Buddha image is to be dedicated the vicinity takes on the appearance of a festival. Many monks take part in the ceremonies and devotees turn out in the hundreds. The women wear their best blouses and sarongs, sometimes a whole contingent from a single clan or neighbourhood, in the same colours, pin flowers to their hair and put on their fanciest gold jewellery. The events at the dedication are not all solemn, for this is also a time to fire off rockets, attached to long bamboo poles and mounted on launching stands in the fields.

Occasionally along the bases of pagodas are sculptures of elephants. Not only do elephants reside in the jungles of Xishuangbanna, they figure in Buddhist mythology. Among the vignettes painted on temple walls will be one of an elephant bowing on the ground before the Buddha, for the animal in this famous story recognized him as an Enlightened One and at once paid obeisance. The elephant is also associated with royalty, for Dai princes rode them to war and in state processions.

Wild elephants still roam Banna's jungles, especially in the protected area of **Sanjianghe Park**, 62 km north of Jinghong. The park entrance leads to a long line of concrete guesthouses, restaurants and karaoke bars, but viewing towers have been erected behind the built-up area. Elephants don't recognize park boundaries, though, and occasionally passengers on inter-city bus rides can spot them lumbering along the highway. Besides the elephants, the dense forests here and elsewhere in the prefecture contain wild oxen, gibbons, bears, perhaps tigers still, but certainly smaller wild cats, otters, civets, pangolins, peacocks, hornbills, pheasants and some 400 other species of bird, amounting to a third of the total in all of China.

INDIGENOUS MOUNTAIN FOLKS: AINI AND JINUO

The Dai account for just over a third of Xishuangbanna's inhabitants. The Han are only slightly less numerous, concentrated in the three large cities, though there are scattered Han settlements in the hills. The mountains are the main abode of the other third, the non-Dai minorities, peoples like the Aini, Jinuo, Lahu, Miao, Yao, Bulang and Yi. The Aini and the Jinuo are the most publicized, partly because they inhabit the mountainous areas closest to Jinghong. While the Jinuo are a small community, confined mostly to the hills around Jinuoshan township and a few areas in northern Mengla County, the Aini are dispersed in all three counties and have the largest population of any hill people in the prefecture.

The Aini are a branch of the Hani, who split from the parent group 50 generations ago to establish themselves as a separate sub-group. People in

Banna generally know them as Aini rather than Hani, but they call themselves Akha, with some 30 sub-groups of their own. Starting out in the hills near Dian Lake, they migrated south, crossed the Red River and continued into the northern Lao provinces of Phong Saly, Luang Nam Tha and Bokeo, and slightly southwest into Xishuangbanna and southwest Simao. About 200 years ago or more they began moving into northeast Burma and in the early 20th century began establishing settlements in northern Thailand.

Their original homeland, though, the place where they evolved their traditional way of life, was in Xishuangbanna and the counties of Lancang and Menglian, just to the west. The Aini developed a complex set of rules, taboos and guidelines to embrace every aspect of their lives. The goal was to maintain the harmony which nature requires, to enable them to eke out a living in the harsh environment of the hills.

Traditionally, the Aini way of agriculture was slash-and-burn, making new rice fields every two years, letting the old ones lie fallow for a decade or more until they were ready to be used again. Most of the year's festivals were associated with key events in the rice-farming cycle. Rice had a soul, according to Aini beliefs, and the field where it grew had a spirit-owner who must be kept placated.

(above) A new Jinuo village which has replaced their traditional longhouses of old.
(right) Aini women in their traditional finery.

Spirits were innumerable. Some were potential allies, others fickle and fearsome. But there were ways to deal with these spirits, from propitiation to avoiding any unseemly behaviour that might arouse a spirit's wrath. Hence the rules, customs, social codes and special remedies. The Aini traditionally marked off their own, human world from the realm of the spirits by a pair of simple wooden gates at the entrance paths to each end of the village. Basically a crossbar over two upright poles, they could be more elaborate on top, have carved figures and objects attached to the poles, or be decorated with bamboo chain-links. Villages also erected a big swing every summer, replacing the old one, but now activated for the three-day Swing Festival.

Only the poorest and most remote Aini still practise slash-and-burn agriculture. In fact, many villages have abandoned rice farming altogether and raise the three most common cash crops in Banna—tea, sugar cane and rubber trees. Consequently the rice-associated festivals have lapsed, as well as much of the traditional belief-system, following decades of ideological assault. Nevertheless, a majority of Aini villages are more or less traditional, which architecturally means houses of wood and bamboo on stilts, with an attached open balcony, and a roof of thatch or wood tiles.

The Aini woman's costume is one of the most striking in the prefecture. Except in southeastern Mengla County, where they wear calf-length trousers, women wear a short, blue-black cotton skirt, pleated in the back and flat in the front, leggings, a halter, long-sleeved jacket, shoulder bag and lots of beads and silver ornaments. The jacket, bag and leggings are often highly embroidered and decorated with seeds, beads, shiny green beetle wings, pompoms and feathers. But the outstanding piece is the headdress. Each sub-group has its own unique style. In general it comprises a fitted round cap, lined with rows of beads or seeds, perhaps silver coins and studs, and may have an attached piece on the back or the top which is also festooned with silver studs, coins, pompoms, and so on.

Most older women still like to wear the Aini costume, the younger generation less so, though they do dress up for festivals and weddings. Some villages have reinstalled the gates and most still have the big swings. Villages nearest the big towns or enriched by rubber tree plantations (southwest Mengla County, for example) are the likeliest to have assimilated into plains culture. Further away and on into Menglian and Lancang Counties, the old traditions still dominate the lifestyle.

The same cannot be said, however, for the Jinuo. In the past their material culture in many ways resembled that of the Aini. They practised slash-and-burn agriculture to grow upland dry rice. They also grew tea, the introduction of which Jinuo myth credits to Zhuge Liang. They used the same kind of spring traps and cages for hunting in the forest and the same wood and bamboo to make their domestic utensils, baskets and containers and build their houses. But the house itself was very different. Raised on stilts, made of bamboo and wood, it was a long structure with several small rooms in the interior hall, on each side of a row of five or more hearths. Related families lived together, but each had its own hearth.

Jinuo women wore long-sleeved jackets, a white peaked cap, calf-length skirt and leggings. Both jacket and skirt feature many strips of contrasting bright colours. Men wore a light-coloured vest or jacket and white turban. The women wove the cotton cloth themselves on backstrap looms. When a girl reached maturity she started wearing a *daobi*, a half-metre wide strip of cloth around the waist and over the longer skirt.

Historically, the Jinuo were one of the most reclusive peoples in the area, staying aloof in their hills, rarely venturing out. But in 1942, reacting against a Guomindang demand for a new 'tobacco tax', the Jinuo revolted and persuaded other hill-dwelling minorities to join them. Organized and led by the Jinuo, this general uprising of the hill folks in central Banna took a year for government forces to suppress.

Afterwards the Jinuo reverted to their normal isolation until 1957, when the government built the road from Mengyang to Menglun, right through their homeland, and established the first primary school in Jinuoshan. The still mysterious Jinuo were declared a minority nationality in 1979. Schools were set up in all major villages and from then on the assimilation process picked up momentum.

Jinuo who benefited from the economic reforms began making new houses of brick and wood, in the general rural Han style. The longhouses disappeared nearly everywhere and the only ones an interested visitor could examine were the models put up in Jinghong's Minority Nationalities Park and the new re-creation erected in Longshuai, the official Jinuo Culture Village, on the highway 18 km east of Jinuoshan. Some villages still employ bamboo and wood for domestic architecture, in the Aini style and for single-family occupancy. But with the possible exception of big festival days, Jinuo women, rarely wear traditional garments, other than the cap and shoulder bag. Still, in some villages one finds the boys and girls in full ethnic gear instead of the adults. Jinuo still get together for the annual traditional celebrations, but the younger generation does not even speak the Jinuo language.

OTHER HILL PEOPLES

As a remote border prefecture in a faraway province, Xishuangbanna received scant attention from government authorities. Little money was allocated to development and the Dai princes who ruled the plains had no incentive to improve the life of the hill people. When the Red Army marched into Banna in 1950, the hill people were among the poorest in the region. Having just experienced the lawlessness of the warlord era, they were reluctant to move around much, even in the hills, or to have any interaction with outsiders.

The Kucong in southeastern Mengla County used to leave whatever animals they caught in the forest out on a publicly used trail and then hide in the nearby woods. Customers came, examined the game and left behind what they considered its equivalent in salt and cloth. After they'd left, the Kucong emerged, collected the goods and returned home. Such was the nature of trade in remote areas before roads, vehicles and market days made it so easy.

Back in the villages, life might be relatively safe, but hard. In some villages people had to take turns using the few available farming tools; metal ones like machetes, hoes and rakes, were beyond most people's affordability range. Malaria was prevalent in the plains—all the more reason to stay away. Smaller ethnic groups were on the verge of extinction, such as the Kucong, who were down to 50 households in 1950. Discovering this, Party cadres spent six years trying before they succeeded in persuading the Kucong to end their isolation and move to more fertile locations at lower altitudes. Closer to the clinics, schools and markets, the Kucong revived and now have a population in the thousands.

The Kucong have been classified as a branch of the Lahu. (Another group of them lives in Zhemi township, Jinping County.) Several ethnic groups are so small in number, a few thousand each, that they have not yet been classified as a branch of any recognized minority. Such are the Sanda, Kongge and Ake of the central hills of Jinghong County.

Among the recognized groups, small numbers of Miao live along the border in Mengla. The Yao live north of them in the same county, the Zhuang in the same area but at lower altitudes, while the northern townships of Mengla County and the hills around Puwen, 10 km south of the Simao border, are home to a branch of the Yi. West of Jinghong and in the hills of Menghai County live the Lahu and Bulang. In the far west, next to Menglian County, are a few Wa villages and in the far north, near Menga, is a single Jingpo village.

The Lahu, who inhabit the hills of the prefecture's western third, are shyer and more reserved than most hill people. Like the Aini and Jinuo, they live in houses of wood, bamboo and thatch, raised on stilts. They have a reputation for being skilled hunters and are sometimes called Musoe by Banna people, a

Dai word meaning 'hunter.' Specifically, that means tiger-hunter, for the word Lahu in the people's own language means 'specially roasted tiger meat.' According to their mythology, once hunters from several nationalities collectively killed and ate a tiger. The way one of them prepared the meat was so special that he was called the Lahu.

Although long ago they adopted farming as their primary occupation, hunting still supplements their diet. They don't go after tigers anymore, or any big animal, and mainly shoot birds. But most Lahu houses still have a crossbow and shotgun hanging on the wall near the entrance. The ancient hunting mode even influenced the style of their personal appearance, for both sexes shave their heads, leaving a small tuft of hair at the crown, and cover the head with a black turban. They say this custom originated when hunting dominated their way of life and was to prevent tigers, bears or monkeys from catching them by the hair.

Most Lahu women dress in one of two styles. The northern-dwelling Lahu wear a side-fastened, long-sleeved, waist-length jacket with contrasting colour strips along the lapel and cuffs, plus trousers and a black turban. Further south the style, trousers and turban are the same, but the coat reaches to the knees. Basically black cotton, the coat is trimmed along the hems, cuffs and lapel with small appliquéd squares, triangles and other shapes in red and white. Silver bulb clasps are often used to button the side.

The Lahu have a special cult of the drum. In common with other animist minorities, they relate the drum to the reproductive power of the earth. Traditional villages have a drum-house, where two big, metre-wide drums, one considered male and one female, are accommodated. On the 8th day of the 2nd moon the Lahu present the drums with food and wreaths of flowers. At one point, the priest tosses popped rice and tea into the air, which all present try to catch, believing it will bring them good luck.

Where the Lahu inhabit the higher slopes of the hills, and the Dai the plains and valleys, sometimes the lower slopes are home to Bulang villages. More often the Bulang's higher-dwelling neighbours are the Aini, for Bulang-dominated townships are mainly in the southern Bulang Mountains and in western Menghai County's Bada and Xiding townships. The women dress similarly to the Dai, with long sarongs, usually black, green or red, and tie their hair in a top bun. They also don loose-fitting, long-sleeved jackets, sometimes a black turban, with the younger women in white or bright blue jackets, the older ones in black.

Besides costume and house type—bamboo, wood and thatch, on stilts, with an adjoining verandah—the Dai influence is evident in Bulang music, dance and religion. Ethnically a Mon-Khmer people, the Bulang are Theravada

Buddhists, though perhaps not as religious-minded as the Dai. Every village has its own temple, similar in style to those of the Dai. Other than that, the Bulang lifestyle is roughly the same as that of their Aini and Lahu neighbours. They raise dry rice, vegetables and especially Pu'er tea, for which they have devised three ways of processing: souring, baking and loose-processing.

In the souring method they boil the freshly picked tea leaves, keep them shaded and moist until they are mouldy and sour, then bury them in bamboo tubes for a month. This is the tea they keep for themselves, for they like to chew and eat the leaves, which they say helps digestion. Tea from the other two processes they sell in the markets. One is to stir-fry the leaves, then bake them in bamboo tubes. The other is to boil or stir-fry the leaves, then spread them on a mat to dry in the sun.

Besides tea leaves, Bulang also like to chew tobacco, and smoke it. Men like the pungent variety in short pipes. Women smoke the milder stuff in long pipes. When chewed, the tobacco is mixed with quicklime and the shavings of a certain tree bark. Chewing betel is also popular among women. It blackens their teeth, but also strengthens them against decay.

The last major ethnic group in Banna's hills is the Yao. Two main branches reside in Mengla County: the Landian, the larger of the two, and the Mien. They are easy to distinguish from each other. Landian Yao women dress

(above) Banna Bulang villages largely retain their traditional look.
(right) Bulang woman husks recently harvested rice.

mainly in black—jacket, trousers and headdress—with only magenta thread lapel decorations and silver clasps and neck rings adding any colour to the costume. The Mien women wear black, too, but the entire front of their trousers is fully embroidered with intricate cross-stitch patterns. The long jacket's front lapel is decorated with a thick ruff of red or magenta wool thread, and the ends of the turban are also embroidered.

Both Yao sub-groups live across the border in northern Laos. The Landian also have villages in Honghe and Wenshan Prefectures. A portion of the Mien have migrated into Thailand and Burma, the only Yao group to move that far west. The heaviest concentrations of Yao settlements are east of Yunnan, in Guangxi, western Guangdong, southwest Hunan and southern Guizhou. Among the mountain people, the Yao are considered the most Sinicized because their literature, mostly religious texts, is written with Chinese characters and the deities and rites are recognizably Daoist. Some villages even keep a set of old paintings of Daoist deities; these are brought out and displayed at major rituals.

The Han influence is the classical one, not the contemporary one. The Yao are among the most conservative, least assimilated minorities. The females still shave their eyebrows and prefer their traditional costume for everyday activities. They just put on more silver ornaments for festivals and weddings. Yao men might also dress in traditional style, which is not as colourful as the women's—plain black vest with embroidered pockets and silver clasps on the lapel for the Mien, plain black jacket with Chinese-style fasteners and a black, Muslim-like cap for the Landian—but the Yao are one of the few ethnic minorities where a substantial portion of the men dress in ethnic style.

While the Yao raise the same crops as other hill people in Banna, and build houses out of the same materials, they set them directly on the ground, not raising them on stilts. Ancient customs still determine their relations with one another, such as who may speak to whom and how. The festivals are still observed in a big way, especially Panwangjie, the 16th day of the 10th moon, which honours their mythical ancestor. And courtship is still very formal, involving Daoist-influenced tests of the young man to determine whether he is enough of a man to have a wife. One of these, for example, involves rolling off a platform onto a plank a metre below. The initiate passes the test only if he keeps his hands clasped around his knees throughout the fall.

THE WATER-SPRINKLING FESTIVAL

The Dai calendar begins on 13 April, the day the sun enters Aries, a traditional New Year for many peoples in Asia, from the Khmers to the Punjabis, all of whom mark the occasion with celebrations and special activities. The Dai observance is shaped by three factors: religion, weather and cultural heritage. As the Dai are Buddhist, religious rites are part of the events. As it is the hottest, driest, most humid time of the year, the idea of dousing each other with water seems like a good way to celebrate anything; and because of the general ethnic renaissance in the province, the Dai are more conscious of their cultural roots. They have arranged for the festival to include highlights from other festivals, once held at other times of the year, for other reasons, but long since fallen into desuetude. Money from the government has encouraged this last aspect and so today the Water-Sprinkling Festival is not just a big Dai festival, it is a celebration of Dai culture.

In anticipation of the festival, Dai women begin dressing in their best traditional clothes and ornaments several days prior. City authorities have the streets swept and decorated, while various groups of Dai and hill people prepare their floats and costumes for the big parade. This commences in Jinghong from 10 am on 13 April, starting at the southern end of Mengle Dadao, proceeding up to Peacock Lake and turning down Xuanwei Dadao towards the river. Commercial companies and schools sponsor elaborately decorated floats, while other contingents—Shui Dai, Huayao Dai, Aini, Jinuo, Wa, Yao and Lahu, adults and children—march separately. The long procession may also include girls dressed in fancy costumes of fruits and flowers, a tribal fire-eater, huge drums on wheels, peacocks and even a black bear on a leash.

The afternoon features stage shows by the river, next to where the boat races are held. The latter event begins with a short trip downriver by all the competing vessels together. Afterwards they pair off for contests from one bank to the other and back again. Meanwhile, the stage show features group Peacock Dances, young Dai men with elephant-leg drums, various minority girl troupes in costumes based on the ethnic originals, but much gaudier. Some dances are traditional, some newly created, such as a troupe of primary school Dai girls, in tutus and spangled vests, dancing to the tune of a Chinese version of 'Frosty the Snowman'.

Most of the second day's activities take place in Manting Park, which lowers its entry fee for the day, particularly at Wat Pajai, on the hill across the lake. In the temple courtyard ritual bathing of the Buddha image begins early in the morning, while monks chant on a stage festooned with long cloth

(following pages) The water festival being celebrated with enthusiasm in the streets of Jinghong.

banners. Monks and novices pour water into a trough, which empties it onto the image. After they have all had their turn the lay people line up to do the same, while *ramwong* dancers entertain in the courtyard.

The bathing of Lord Buddha is a reenactment of the myth that at the Buddha's birth, dragons came to bathe him by spraying him with perfumed water. The act also recalls the fact that only after Gautama Siddartha—taking a break from his ascetic practices—bathed in the river did he feel refreshed and spiritually cleansed enough to be ready for Enlightenment. Yet this Buddhist aspect has been grafted on to an older festival that predates Dai conversion, with its origin in an ancient, wholly secular myth.

Accordingly, once upon an ancient time the Dai were oppressed by an avaricious, seemingly invincible demon lord, who seized the seven most beautiful women and forced them to be his wives. One night, drunk with pride and boasting of his power he let out his secret—that his neck was his vulnerable part. It could be severed by a strand of his own hair. With that fatal revelation he fell asleep. The seven wives plucked a hair from his head, wrapped it around his neck and decapitated the demon.

But the head didn't die. Instead it burst into flames and rolled around, scorching all in its path. One of the wives grabbed it and quelled the flames. But when they buried it the land became barren. When they threw it in the river a flood ensued. So each took turns holding it in her lap for one year and after seven years the head died. At the end of each round the succeeding girl splashed water on the one who'd been holding the head in her lap, in order to wash off the filth and contamination accrued in her year's turn. A variation of the myth has the head continuing to burn and the seven Dai women sprinkling water on it for 999 days, when at last the flames were quenched. The water-sprinkling at the festival (water-throwing, or water-splashing is more accurate) commemorates the seven heroines of the myth.

The festival also sometimes features, especially in the countryside, the launching of rockets from tall bamboo platforms in the fields. In the Dai communities of neighbouring countries, rocket-launching is a separate festival, also held in the hot dry season, as a signal to Heaven not to forget the rains. Included in Banna's festival activities are the dragon-boat races, which in northern Thailand and northern Laos are staged at the end of the monsoon. Teams wearing different coloured head scarves compete on the Lancangjiang in long, narrow boats with dragon-headed prows. Another event associated with different Dai festivals elsewhere is the launching of hot-air balloons at night. In northern Thailand, this is done for Loi Krathong, at the November full moon. Called *Kongming* lanterns after their supposed inventor—— Kongming being another name for Zhuge Liang—these float by the dozens over the land and water; big, fiery, orange spheres against the black night sky.

The primary activity the third day is throwing water on everyone within reach. But unlike Thailand or Laos, where the water-throwing is officially for three days, but may begin as early as 1 April in the countryside, in Jinghong it is strictly limited to the third day, from 10 am until 5 pm only. Nevertheless, even with the restrictions, it's a pretty wild day, especially around the fountains in Mengle Dadao's Culture Park. The city is full of Chinese tourists that day, many of whom rent trucks to take them and their water-pistols out into the main streets, where the action is the thickest and splashiest.

MOUNTAIN CELEBRATIONS

Among the contingents parading in Jinghong's streets during the Water-Sprinkling Festival are the Jinuo. This is one time they will likely be in their ethnic costume, rarely seen otherwise. And that's mainly because they are paid to do so by the county government, for the benefit of hosts and guests. The mood may strike them again, though, at the Jinuo's own New Year celebration in late winter, held in honour of the blacksmith.

In the unsophisticated world of traditional mountain people, anyone who had apparent control over the forces of nature merited special respect. The blacksmith, with his mastery over fire and metal, made the tools people required to farm effectively. In return, the recipients of these tools donated a certain number of days of labour in the blacksmith's fields. His role as toolmaker was thus considered essential to their well being. Consequently he was accorded a special position in the tribal hierarchy. He plays a part in selected Aini ceremonies, for example. But among the Jinuo, where he is believed to have power over rivers and seas and can lock demons behind their doors by pounding the doors shut with golden nails, the year's greatest celebration is held in his honour.

Called Temaojie in Chinese, the festival takes place on the 6th day of the 2nd lunar month. On that day the most respected male (*zhousi*) and female elder (*zhuoba*) announce the coming of New Year by beating the 'solar drums', large drums of wood and cattle hide mounted on crossed beams. Hearing the drums, people assemble at the houses of the two elders to make plans for the festival, the buffalo sacrifice and so on. Then they sing an ancient Jinuo song of how they learned to cultivate rice.

Men dispatch the sacrificial bull in a grove beside the village, butcher it on the spot and cut it into small pieces to be distributed to all village households. People then prepare a grand feast, cooking the meat several different ways and

(following pages) Baoshan Lisu dress in all their finery when they hold the Sword Ladder festival.

serving it with plenty of strong liquor. Dancing occupies the young people's time after the feast, while the drinking continues, both boys and girls imbibing.

While the buffalo dies for the sake of the whole village, another sacrifice takes place specifically for the sake of the blacksmith. Invited to have a good dream the night before the festival, the next morning, as guest of honour in the *zhuoba's* room, he is asked to narrate his dream. The *zhuoba* then interprets the dream as auspicious or not for the coming year's harvest. A feast follows and then the blacksmith, his apprentices and a senior male of the *zhuoba's* family go to the blacksmith's workshop to sacrifice a cock. Its blood and feathers are sprinkled on the bellows, furnace, hammer and tongs. The party then cooks and eats the chicken, following which the blacksmith mimes his work and shouts, 'Hammer out the old year, hammer in the new.' And with that recitation the New Year officially begins.

The Aini also ring in the New Year with a festival they call *Gatâ Pa-eu*. In Lancang and Menglian Counties they hold this in late November, beginning on a Buffalo Day with the drawing of water from a specially consecrated source. Xishuangbanna Aini have recently fixed the beginning of their *Gatâ Pa-eu* on 2 January. This is because the provincial government disburses money to the autonomous Aini townships to pay for a big celebration. Presumably it would be too difficult for outside guests to make it on the 1st, when they're still hung over from parties the night before, so it was scheduled for the 2nd.

Lasting three days altogether, the festival includes feasting, swinging, top-spinning, the settling of debts and the payment of dues into the village fund, and of course much singing and dancing, in the daylight for the guests, in the evening for themselves. Aini songs are slow to moderate tempo in general, accompanied at most by a drum, and have a choreography per number, usually uncomplicated steps and simple body-rocking. In the evenings they will be performed at an open area designated *dèhâw* in the Aini language.

This is the traditional gathering ground for the youth in the evenings after supper. Separated from each other all day in fields far apart, the *dèhâw* provided a venue for meeting each other and making merry with song and dance. In the old days this was the place in the winter months to introduce young men from other villages, who were looking for prospective wives. Schools and television have altered traditional teenage life in recent years, but young people still employ the *dèhâw* for the old reasons now and then, especially at festival time.

Some Aini still carry out the annual rice rituals and other old customs, but the situation varies from village to village. Yet all Aini stage the three-day Swing Festival in early summer. The old swing frame, which has been standing since the previous year's festival, but not with its swing installed, they tear down and erect a new one on the same spot. After the religious chief tests the swing anyone can ride. The boys put one foot in the loop at the end of the swing's rope and kick themselves into the air with the free leg. Girls insert a board through the loop, sit on it and kick their legs to swing.

Ancestral rites, feasting and an active *dèhāw* are the other features of the event. Everyone, but especially the girls, dresses in their best Aini clothes and ornaments. Dances include one with straw hats and an energetic one where youths hold bamboo poles just off the ground while the boy or girl hops over and between them. On one night the youths, as at New Year, go house-to-house drumming bamboo tubes and singing. After the third night the swing is taken down and the frame left standing until *Gatâ Pa-eu,* when the swing is reinstalled for one day.

"Heaven creates scenic wonders"—Inscription by Chu Tunan.

Heirs to Nanzhao: Dali and the Bai

THE LURES OF DALI

I t's easy to see why Dali has become such a popular tourist destination. Few places can match its setting, lying on a long plain flanked on one side by the high (over 4,000 metres) serrated peaks of the **Azure Mountains** (*Cangshan*) and on the other by the 42-km-long Erhai Lake. Eighteen brooks tumble down from Cangshan, watering the fertile plain and emptying into the lake. East of the lake, which averages just under 7 km in width, rise the smaller, ruddier, more barren hills of the Phoenix Mountains. Steamers and fishing boats ply the waters, the boats sometimes in fleets, with white triangular sails aloft to catch the wind.

The best long-range view of the valley is from the **Wanghai Pavilion** on the hill in Erhai Park, at the south end of the lake. One can see why this became an important political centre in ancient times, for it was a simple stronghold to defend. Entering **Xiaguan**, the commercial metropolis at the south end of Erhai, from the east one had to descend a high mountain via a pass that in the pre-Mongol period was walled and fortified. At the northern end of the valley, above the village of Shangguan, lookout posts provided a view north past the lake and could alert the defence well in advance of any invasion from that direction.

The posts at Shangguan are still there, as are many of the religious and secular monuments of the Nanzhao and Dali eras. Ming and Qing temples add to the area's historical legacy. The old towns of Dali and Taihe retain much of their traditional layout, so it is easy for the visitor to appreciate Dali's place in history, with so much evidence of it all around.

Dali also exhibits a strong ethnic accent. The valley is home to Han, Hui and Bai, but it is the Bai who arouse the most attention. Theirs are the elegant stone houses with wood-carved decorations. They are the women who wear the bright vests, aprons and fancy headdresses. The Hui can be equally conservative, but they don't stand out like the Bai. The latter's only real competition for tourist attention are the Yi from above Xiaguan and Midu County, who dress even more ornately than the Bai and are frequent visitors in the Xiaguan and Dali markets.

With monuments and temples to visit, a lake to sail upon, fishing life to witness, busy markets to attend, mountain trails to hike and a famous old city to wander around in, Dali offers many ways to enjoy one's time. Besides all that it is also a handicrafts centre, specializing in marble work, woodcarving, tie-dyeing,

Decorative embellishments at the Guan Yin Temple in Qiliqiao.

embroidery and painting, thus giving visitors a broad selection for their souvenirs. In recent years it has also become a place to find handicrafts from Guizhou, too, as traders from that province have established shops in Dali.

Tourism has had a decisive impact, naturally, and the core of the old town is full of bilingual or even just English signs catering to foreign travellers. The backpacker types, pleased by the array of cheap lodges, restaurants and coffee shops, tend to view Dali as a major rest and recreation centre, most of them having journeyed quite a long time in other parts of China already. This part of Dali resembles Kathmandu in the immediate post-hippie years. But for the adventurous there is plenty to see and do in Dali besides hang out.

THE OLD TOWN

A proper look at the old town begins at Tonghaimen, the South Gate that is Dali's finest extant classical building. It is the first building to catch the morning sunrays, which add a bright patina to the wood-carved struts and awnings and the sloping roofs with the curling corners. From the balcony of the first tier, one can see the straight streets and rectangular layout of the city. Parts of the old wall are connected to each side of this gate. The original stood about eight metres high and was partially dismantled after the Muslim Revolt. At the end of the 1990s, the local government reconstructed the entire length of the wall's southern section and in the following decade re-erected the eastern and western gates.

One long main street connects the South Gate with An Yuan Gate at the northern end, somewhat smaller but sporting exquisite woodcarved decorations. This is the business thoroughfare of Dali, Fuxinlu, lined on each side with shophouses in the old style, occasionally interrupted by new, taller, cement buildings. At the end of the 90s this street was widened, motor traffic banned, marble benches and ornate lamp posts set up, and the **Tower of Five Glories**, a Qing-style, three-storey building that replaced a more modest structure which had been there until World War II, was constructed to straddle Fuxinlu in the southern part of the old town.

Besides the shops, Fuxinlu is full of small stands selling handicrafts. A whole square full of these, mostly offering marble ware, is just inside the south gate. Souvenir shops and cheap, tie-dyed clothing outlets make up a large percentage of these shops all the way to Huguolu, in the centre of Dali.

Also not far from the south gate, on the left, is the **Dali City Museum**. The main hall here is actually Du Wenxiu's former headquarters. A pair of cannons used in his reign is on display in front. The exhibits inside include Nanzhao sculptures, ancient artifacts and samples of attractive marble slabs. In the gardens outside stand many stone steles, some with inscriptions in Sanskrit. It is a modest but worthwhile museum to visit for the high quality of its displays.

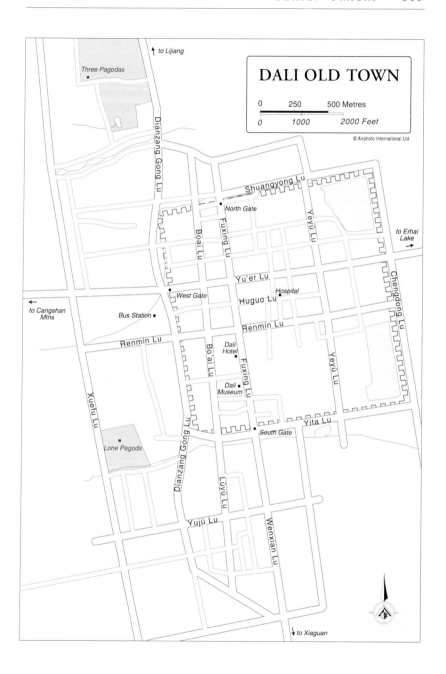

DALI OLD TOWN

0   250   500 Metres
0   1000   2000 Feet

© Airphoto International Ltd.

to Lijiang

Three Pagodas

Dianzang Gong Lu

Shuangyong Lu

North Gate

Boai Lu

Fuxing Lu

Yeyu Lu

to Erhai Lake

Yu'er Lu

Hospital

West Gate

Huguo Lu

Chengdong Lu

to Cangshan Mtns

Bus Station

Renmin Lu

Renmin Lu

Boai Lu

Dali Hotel

Fuxing Lu

Yeyü Lu

Xuefu Lu

Dali Museum

Yita Lu

Lone Pagoda

Dianzang Gong Lu

South Gate

Lüyu Lu

Yuju Lu

Wenxian Lu

to Xiaguan

Continuing down the main street beyond the Tower of Five Glories, visitors pass a city park, where the older men like to gather to listen to their caged songbirds while they converse or play mah-jong. A little further on is the Huguolu intersection, the beginning of the backpacker area. Two blocks north and one block east is **Yu Er Park**, a more secluded venue for relaxing, landscaped with flower trees, ponds and rockeries. Back up on the main street and another two blocks north is the old Catholic church. While the missionaries didn't convert many residents, the church is still there, and still holds Sunday services. A newer Catholic church, in the classic Chinese style, lies off a lane branching south from Renminlu.

Church efforts in Dali were a minor footnote to the great religious influence of Buddhism and Islam. Buddhism, the Indian Mahayana school, was the religion of Nanzhao, inspiring the magnificent pagodas around Dali and the sculptures of Shibaoshan. The most famous work of religious art is the **Three Pagodas** just north of Dali. The central one stands 69 metres tall and has 16 tiers. The two flanking it have ten tiers each and are 43 metres high. All three once adorned the Chongsheng Monastery, formerly the largest in the area, but destroyed in the Muslim Revolt. Miraculously, the pagodas were left unmolested and also survived several major earthquakes since their construction.

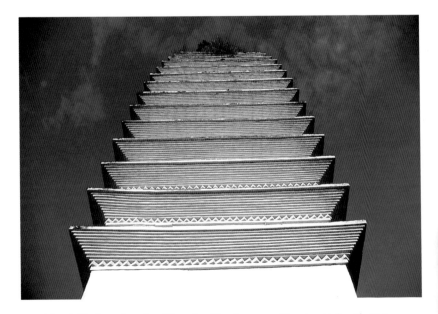

(above) The Lone Pagoda of Hongshen Temple towers 46 metres high with 16 tiers.
(right) Fuxinglu, Dali's old main street.

Two other Nanzhao pagodas merit attention. The **Lone Pagoda of Hongshen Temple**, just across the highway west of the south gate, towers 46 metres and has 16 tiers. Further south, in Yangpi village, 3 km northwest of Xiaguan, stands the **Fotu Pagoda**, or Skeleton Python Pagoda (also known as *Sheguta*). With 13 tiers, it rises 39 metres and takes its name from a Nanzhao legend. Accordingly, a python used to prey upon the local villagers until it happened to swallow the fully armed hero Duan Chicheng, who sliced the snake's insides and killed it, though he perished himself. The villagers interned both him and the python's skeleton in this pagoda they erected to commemorate the event.

Besides the pagodas, other sites in the area are connected to the Nanzhao legacy. The unusual General's Temple, on a hill just northwest of Xiaguan, honours one of the great losers in Chinese history—the commander of a strong Tang-dynasty army that invaded Nanzhao in the 8th century and was wiped out to the last man. Their bones were collected and deposited in a big stone urn in Tianbao Park in the city. General Li Mi, their commander, committed suicide, but his descendants erected the temple and the local Bai have adopted him as a protector god.

Artefacts and sculptures from the Nanzhao period, among other exhibits, are on display in the provincial museum in Xiaguan. And in recent years a recreation of the old palace has been put up on the southern edge of Dali.

More Nanzhao relics exist between Xiaguan and Dali, specifically at Taihe, which for a while served as the kingdom's capital. On the west side of the road above Taihe the stone **Nanzhao Stele** is housed in a small park. Erected by King Geluofeng in 706, its 3,800 characters narrate Nanzhao's early history, its relationship to Tang China and its differences with Chang'an, as well as its side of the current conflict. Across the road, sloping down towards the plain beside the lake, lies **Taihe**. Not much of its Nanzhao look is left, save for parts of the original wall, but, like Dali off the main thoroughfare, it is an interesting warren of stone houses and cobbled streets.

ERHAI

The literal translation of *Erhai* is Ear Sea, wherein *er* means ear and *hai* means, actually, any large body of water. The lake surface is 1,972 metres high, roughly the same altitude as Kunming. Erhai's waters are fed by the Miju and Luoshi Rivers in the north, four streams in the southeast and the 18 streams that tumble down from Cangshan to the west. At Xiaguan the waters flow through the Natural Bridge (*Tianshengqiao*) into a tributary of the Yangbi River, which eventually runs into the Mekong (*Lancangjiang*).

The publicists make much of the 'limpid blue waters,' yet the lake's colour depends on the colour of the sky. On cloudy days it is slate grey. On sunny days it is deep blue, like the sky. When the sunrise is particularly splendid, it is piebald with several shades of red, blue, purple and green. As the sun starts sinking behind the Azure Mountains, Erhai reflects the russet colour of the hills to the east. And when all the plain is in shadow, the lake is still lit by the rich rays of sunset. Yet because it is so long, the weather at one end might be completely different from that at the other end.

In the space between the western bank of the lake and the Cangshan range stretches a broad, well-watered, fertile plain. It is narrow in the south, wide in the middle and narrow again at the northern end. South of Dali most settlements are Han. North of Dali, and on the eastern shore of the lake, they are largely Bai. The best view of the plain, and of course the lake and the eastern hills beyond, can be had from temples sited high up on the Cangshan slopes.

Gantongsi, the most southerly, lies high above Qiliqiao, itself home to the Guan Yin Temple, the most popular in the vicinity. The actual shrine to the Buddhist Goddess of Mercy sits stop a boulder in the front courtyard. In the rear courtyard lies a temple honouring the Buddha, with several outstanding lamps in front of the entrance. On the 19th day of the 3rd, 6th and 9th months both Bai and Han throng the temple, for these are Guan Yin's special days.

The road behind the temple, accessible by foot, pony cart or taxi, climbs uphill to Gantong Temple. Originally a 36-hall extravaganza of the Nanzhao era, only one hall survives. Yet the setting bears evidence to its spiritual heritage. Up in the forest, away from all sound save birds, insects and the rustle of leaves in the wind, it must have nourished many meditating souls over the centuries. Paths lead both north and south, winding along the mountains.

For more exciting walks one can turn south from **Zhonghe Temple**. This lies just above Dali and can be reached by cable car. The path stays on the level and after a half-hour walk turns into a steep canyon with boulders jutting up from the chasm like monstrous fingers pointing skyward. After a bend in the path one can see these with the plain and lake as a backdrop. Affording similar long-range views, also set in the woods, is Wuwei Temple, a few kilometres northwest of Dali. And in the north, above the flower garden at **Shangguan**, from the towers perched on the slopes, one has a view of the northern pass from where Kubilai Khan's army swarmed into the plain.

The eastern side of Erhai is much less populated. The hills run close to the shore, are not fertile themselves, and most villages lie at the end of river

(following pages) The village of Shuanglang is one of the prettiest along the shores of Lake Erhai.

valleys. The largest is Haidong, just across the lake from Dali. To its south is Erhai's largest island Haidao, while on the promontory east of the bay beside Haidong perches the Luoquan Temple. Settlements are sparse north of this temple until Wase, over two-thirds of the way up the eastern shore. Just before Wase is another island, Xiaoputao, a small plot of land with a central hill and the most picturesque temple in the area on top of it.

Wase is a large village that depends as much on fishing as on farming. Its farms lie in a flat narrow valley behind the village, past the large Guan Yin temple. But dozens of tall-masted boats will be sitting in the harbour when not out on the lake. Further north, actually in Eryuan County, the village of Shuanglang is even more involved in fishing, for it is backed by hills and its narrow strip of flat land is mostly taken up by housing. A small peninsula juts out into the lake and from the hill behind Shuanglang it is obvious this is the most splendidly laid out village in the entire lake area. A small island offshore to its south has been converted into a Nanzhao theme park, so it remains to be seen whether Shuanglang's almost pristine calm can survive the coming commotion of this new artificial attraction.

The northern end of Erhai is the most beautiful section. At the very top are the villages of Haichaohe and Jiangwei, which have adjacent farms but also

The Guan Yin Temple in Qiliqiao features a shrine to the Buddhist Goddess of Mercy resting atop a boulder in the front courtyard.

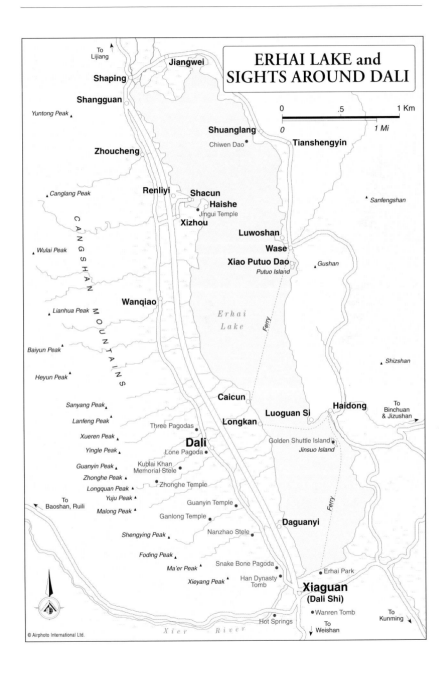

ERHAI LAKE and
SIGHTS AROUND DALI

many boats moored along the shores. Great nets are stretched along the shallows. Occasionally boats here, and more especially in the western shore villages further south, go out with cormorants to do their fishing. The Bai fix a tight collar around the bird's neck so that it cannot swallow the fish it catches, but must disgorge them. Wild cormorants can never be trained, so the Bai first trap the wild cormorants, then breed them in captivity. The offspring can be trained to catch fish.

Rounding the lake and re-entering Dali's boundary, the road passes Butterfly Spring, once a quiet pond with a big acacia tree beside it, where all kinds of butterflies visited in late spring. Now it is a major tourist attraction, with several new buildings, saleswomen galore and a special Butterfly Festival, the 15th day of the 4th moon.

Of greater interest, surely, is the Bai town of **Zhoucheng**, a few kilometres south of the spring. This is a square-shaped town lying on a slope, with its market area, shaded by resplendent trees, in the lower part near the highway. The cobbled streets, stone walls and traditional domestic architecture are uninterrupted by modern intrusions.

Nearly all Bai women dress in traditional costume—red vest over a long-sleeved blouse, apron, trousers, shoulder bag and bonnet. The Dali style is to tie the hair in a bun and top it with a white crown on a flower-embroidered band, with a long white tassel falling on the shoulder. Zhoucheng women might use a tie-dyed headscarf instead and wear an apron of the same material, for Zhoucheng is a major producer of this art. When it's not a busy time in the fields, women are likely to be at this work in their free time.

Further back towards Dali, where the plain begins to widen, 18 km north of the old city, is the mostly Bai town of **Xizhou**. This used to be a major stop on the trade route going north, before the highway was built, and its population included many rich families. They built themselves exquisite houses, with courtyards within courtyards, delicately carved gates, brackets, doors, screens and windows, commodious and comfortable rooms. The domicile of one such Xizhou merchant has in recent years been converted into an atmospheric guesthouse, retaining its original designs on the exterior and providing modern facilities in the rooms.

Another hosts the Bai song and dance show that accompanies the traditional serving of three kinds of tea. The first is bitter, but with a semi-sweet aftertaste. The second tea is sweet, flavoured with honey, ginger and walnuts. The third, called 'after-flavour tea,' includes prickly pear ash as an ingredient and is a touch astringent. Small snacks, such as the Xizhou wheat bread, accompany the servings.

Most villages between Xizhou and Dali are Bai, but even the Han and Hui settlers employ the Bai style in designing their houses. The most common is a quadrangle with rooms on three sides and a decorated screen wall. The Bai paint the roofs and pillars and use double, bow-shaped brackets, often carved with vegetation and animal motifs, mounted on columns to support the upturned eaves. On the wall below each apex of the roof they paint arabesques as a last decorative flourish. This is the Hui influence and an original Dali innovation, which has since been incorporated by rote in all Bai and Bai-influenced architecture in Yunnan.

Bai use their homes mainly for retiring. Otherwise they pass their time in the receiving room or outside in the courtyard, the women perhaps embroidering, knitting or making fish nets. That's when they are relaxing, which at first observation doesn't seem to be very often. The Bai are some of the most industrious people in the province, and around Erhai one of the most successful. They are also good at business, not averse to long-distance itinerant trade, and Bai communities exist as far away as Shanghai.

THE MARKETS

The business district in the old town of Dali is busy every day. So is the old market in Xiaguan on the lane leading to the lower bridge over the Yangbi River. But the rural folk, both in the plains and in the mountains, rely on the periodic markets, which turn sleepy townships into beehives of commerce, in a throwback to the lifestyle of their ancestors. Beyond that aspect, which is not a conscious motive anyway, rural folk like markets because that's the place these diligent farmers can sell their surplus, make money and improve their lives.

The best-known market days are those hosted at **Shaping** on Mondays and **Wase** every five days. The former draws not only Bai from all the villages on the northern end of the lake, but also busloads of tourists as well, both Chinese and foreign. Bai merchants, mostly women, compete as much for the tourists' attention as that of their own people. Lots of handicrafts, antiques and costume parts, old and new, go on sale along with farm produce.

Wase holds its market day on calendar dates ending in 0 or 5. Travellers in Dali arrange for boat rides across Erhai, combining it with a stopover in Xiaoputao. The market draws Bai villagers from the eastern shore, and mainly farm and lake produce goes on sale. Both merchants and customers largely ignore the strangers, unlike Shaping. They can get quite argumentative at times over prices or squabble over who has the right to sell goods at such and such a spot. Other villages on the northeast shore also stage market days, though they are less attended.

A very different market day takes place in **Pingpo**, 22 km west of Xiaguan, every Sunday. The township lies on a plateau above the highway and on Sundays stalls line the entire long main road, out to the promontory at the end of the buildings. Here the Yi park their ponies. The Han run most of the stands, but many Yi come down from the mountains. Their women are recognizable by the heavily embroidered aprons they wear, which are fastened above the breasts by a silver chain.

ERYUAN

The section of Erhai from Shuanglang to Shaping is actually part of Eryuan County. The county seat lies over the hills to the north, into the next major valley, 60 km north of Dali. It lies a few km west of the highway. The more traditional neighbourhoods are in the northern section, and market day is staged at the northeast corner. The women wear the same components of the Bai costume as those around Erhai, with the exception of the headdress, donning a tight-fitting bonnet instead.

Just beyond the northeast market area and across the irrigation canal is a small Bai village with cobbled streets running through a cluster of old-fashioned farm-houses. Around the first major turn-off, the scent of sulphur

(*above*) *Devout Bai women make frequent visits and offerings at major religious sites.*
(*left*) *A poster maker puts a finishing touch on a new product at his stall on Dali's market day.*

begins to permeate the air. Just past the settled area on this side lane lies a small, quaint hot spring, not built up, like a private village herbal bathing site. The other major natural attraction is **Cibi Lake** several kilometres further north. A jade colour, the waters cover eight square kilometres. The lake is noted for the unusual bubbles that emanate from the bottom.

The language and lifestyle of the Eryuan Bai resemble those of Dali. They attend the Third Month Fair and the Mid-Autumn Festival of Shaping. They also have their own festivals, such as a Farm Tool Fair on the 15th day of the 2nd lunar month, and the charming Yinyinwu, held in Fengyu village on the 5th day of the 1st moon. This festival reinforces the link between children and their elders. The latter pay special attention to the words kids speak this day, set off firecrackers when the groups of children come to call on them and send them off with small gifts.

SACRED MOUNTAINS

Many of Yunnan's towering mountains play a role in the mythology and folklore of the people who live near them. For reasons best known to diviners, sages and priests, a few mountains achieved a special reputation for spirituality. Three such mountains lie in Dali Prefecture. The nearest is

(above) Bai devotees spend hours chanting at the temples visited during Raoshanling.
*(right) Dali Bai women accustom their daughters at an early age
to wearing the traditional Bai costume.*

Jizushan, or Chicken Foot Mountain, in Binchuan County. The county seat is 73 km northeast of Xiaguan, and the entrance to the park up the mountain is another 23 km northwest. The mountain is actually visible from the Yongsheng-Binchuan highway, from where it enters Dali Prefecture, easily distinguishable from others in the range by the single pagoda that points skyward from its summit.

The mountain is so named for its location behind three ranges to its front and one to its back, giving it a shape resembling a chicken's foot. Its sanctity dates back to the Three Kingdoms era, when small nunneries were first established. With the founding of the Nanzhao Kingdom these were expanded and the first monasteries constructed. For the next thousand years successive patrons sponsored more and more monasteries until finally the mountain hosted 108, a holy Buddhist number. The desecration of recent wars, and in particular the fanaticism of the Red Guards, reduced this number to a single compound—the **Zhushang Temple**. Only the gate tower to one other ancient temple, plus the almost forlorn **Longyun Pagoda** on the summit, in the Dali close-eaves style, survived the iconoclasm.

Its tragic history has not seriously eroded its spiritual reputation, judging by Jizushan's contemporary power to attract pilgrims. Lodges and small restaurants are now set up on the mountain, for most of those taking the trouble to climb up that far want to do it at night, so as to be by the pagoda on top by dawn to watch the sunrise over the Binchuan plain. To the north **Jade Dragon Snow Mountain** is visible, as well as Erhai and Cangshan to the southwest.

Before Piluoge united the six petty states to create the Nanzhao Kingdom in 732, he and his predecessors ruled from Mengshe, the most southerly of the *zhao*. Modern Weishan is Mengshe's successor, about 70 km south of Dali. At the end of the 1990s it was still one of the most attractive towns in western Yunnan, boasting a gargantuan brick gate tower which marks the entry into the preserved traditional city centre. Fine wooden buildings, many painted blue, dominate the architecture and motor traffic is prohibited in the old quarter.

To the east behind Weishan, 15 km by road to the first temple, rises **Weibaoshan**—the Mountain of Towering Treasures. In the past it was a numinous mountain to Daoists and it is their temples that dominate the higher slopes. Formerly, Weibaoshan was home to more than 20 temples in its alpine groves and glens. Less than a third remain, which is still a better record than Jizushan. The most interesting is the **Longtan Palace**, for its murals on the walls of the stone bridge connecting the courtyard with a pavilion in the pond. The paintings, looking relatively fresh in spite of two centuries' passage, depict local Yi in a ring dance at festival time, among other subjects.

The third, and most splendid sacred mountain in the prefecture is **Shibaoshan**, the Mountain of Precious Stones, in Jianchuan County, 140 km north of Dali. The entrance is several km down the Lanping route, west of its junction 7 km south of Jianchuan. At the base of the mountain sits the Ming Dynasty **Xingjiao Temple**, with a rare set of interior wall frescoes. Winding its way up the mountain, the road comes to **Stone Bell Temple** (*Shizhongsi*), first built in the Nanzhao era. Above the compound are the grottoes, each containing exquisite stone sculptures, in good condition, some as much as 1,200 years old. The Buddha Gautama Siddartha, as well as other Buddhist deities, all exhibiting a strong Indian influence, are some of the oldest. Equally ancient are the sculptures of King Xinuluo and his family. The most unusual is the cave containing a large stone vagina, carved into the rock, where since ancient times women wanting children have come to leave offerings.

THE BAI BEYOND THE AZURE MOUNTAINS

The most visible Bai cultural achievements—art, architecture, music, festivals—are in the Dali area. The Bai are Yunnan's second largest ethnic minority, though, and besides the Erhai vicinity they occupy most of the lands to the north and west of Cangshan in western Dali Prefecture. They also reside in large areas of Lanping and Lushui Counties in Nujiang Prefecture and in small communities in Lijiang and Ninglang Counties. They are a conservative people who have blended much of the Han way into their own, but have steadfastly held on to specifically Bai customs and traits.

Such cultural traits may vary from one Bai area to another, but the similarities are greater than the differences. Bai houses may be brick instead of stone, but their shape and decorations are recognizably of the same style. The headgear changes from one sub-group to another, but the basic components of the women's costume are usually the same—side-fastened, solid-colour vest over a long-sleeved blouse, apron and trousers. Only on the fringes of Bai territory are there any major differences. The Lemu Bai women of southern Nujiang Prefecture, for example, wear an outfit inspired by that of their Lisu and Nu neighbours, featuring a beaded cap and necklaces of discs cut from shells.

Similarly, in the northern part of Jianchuan County, bordering Lijiang, the women wear the Naxi-style black and white sheepskin cape. The bonnet, though, tall and in several layers, would never be worn by a Naxi woman. Jianchuan itself is a bit larger than Eryuan, its houses and layout closer in style to Lijiang. The fine park on its western side houses the attractive, three-storey **Jingfeng Pavilion**. Except for the main street, most of the town is in the traditional style. A few kilometres east is **Sword Lake** (*Jianhu*), a small, quiet body of water that sparkles with romance on the full moon of the 8th lunar month. On this evening, called Lovers' Rendezvous, the unmarried youth go boating on the lake, singing love songs and sending candles floating to their lovers.

Jianchuan Bai hold other unique festivals that reinforce their affection for children. On the 8th day of the 2nd moon they stage the Festival of Enhancing Children's Appetites. This originated with a popular revolt against another custom long ago. This was the day when operas were staged at the Temple of the God of Letters. The rich folk wielded whips to keep the children in line. One year the parents refused to let their children attend. Instead, as today, they prepared special food for them and dispatched them for a picnic in the woods. On the 15th day of the 1st month, they honour a child-bride who drowned herself to protest her forced marriage. Bai girls parade behind a portrait of the girl, a reminder not to mistreat daughters.

South of Jianchuan, about a half-hour's ride past the Shibaoshan turn-off, lies the interesting old town of **Shaxi**. Once an important stop on the **Tea and Horses Road** (*Chama Gudao*), it has retained most of its traditional layout and architecture and in recent years rehabilitated its main temple and ancient marketplace. Market day on Fridays here draws the local Bai and Han, as well as Yi from the mountains, of the same branch as those living in Ninglang

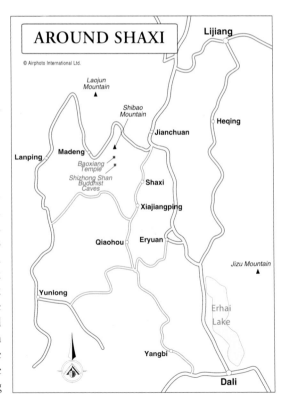

AROUND SHAXI

© Airphoto International Ltd.

Lijiang

Laojun Mountain

Shibao Mountain

Jianchuan

Heqing

Madeng

Lanping

Baoxiang Temple

Shizhong Shan Buddhist Caves

Shaxi

Xiajiangping

Qiaohou   Eryuan

Jizu Mountain

Yunlong

Erhai Lake

Yangbi

Dali

County. On the 8th day of the 2nd lunar month, Shaxi hosts its annual Taizihui festival.

West of Jianchuan the Bai occupy the valleys all the way to **Lanping**, 130 km away. Lanping itself is a small, regularly laid out city in the lap of the mountains. The down-town streets are lined with shade trees, though most of the buildings are run-of-the-mill cement boxes. The Pumi minority lives in the hills of the north, the Bai in the central and eastern parts. Fancy Bai houses, with Dali-inspired architectural motifs, stand at the northern edge of Lanping, with a large Bai village just beyond.

An old house of Shaxi.

Only the older generation of women seems to favour the Bai costume, which consequently means the dark colours like black, brown and blue predominate.

In one respect the Nama Bai of Lanping, as they call themselves, differ from other Bai communities. Here they hold festivals that emphasize the worth of their oxen. On the 18th day of the 6th lunar month the local Bai make sacrifices to the water gods and honour their oxen by kneeling for rites before stone sculptures of the beasts, and not eating any meat that day. In the 9th lunar month they sacrifice a bull to send its spirit to Heaven, re-enacting a myth that narrates how a black dragon caused floods until a yak defeated the dragon and saved the people. They wanted to make the yak their king. The animal declined the honour but accepted the food liberally bestowed by the grateful Bai. Then other oxen from Heaven came to join the feast, which angered the gods. They visited a plague upon the people until they sacrificed one of the truant bulls to send its spirit back to Heaven.

The Bai also dominate the rural population of Yunlong, the westernmost county in Dali prefecture. The county seat itself lies around the corner from a pair of steep cliffs beside the Binjiang River, which gave Yunlong its original name—Stone Gate. A venerable Qing Dynasty temple relic sits on the bank at the confluence of a stream running through the city with the Binjiang River. Across the river a white pagoda surmounts a hill. Distinctly Bai architectural motifs dominate the buildings in the business centre. Behind the town rises Dragonhead Mountain (Longtoushan), Yunlong's primary attraction. Paths lead from the town to the temple at the very top, passing small shrines, spiral pagodas, waterfalls and ever better viewpoints of the city, the valley and the mountains beyond.

In the past, Yunlong was one of Yunnan's salt sources. The wells, no longer in use, lie just to the west, on the way to the thousand-year-old Bai settlement of **Nuodeng**, whose people used to work in them. North of here, around Chongxing, are three of the county's famous **Wind and Rain Bridges**. Another lies further north, between Baishi and the Lanping County line, its walls painted red, with white towers at each end. The two across the river from Chongxing are brown and white, with tiled roofs, while 2 km north, at Baoluo, a dark grey wooden covered bridge spans the Binjiang. Such roofed bridges provided shelter in storms and nowadays are rarely seen outside Yunlong County.

Another major concentration of traditional Bai culture is in Heqing County. The county seat is actually closer to Lijiang (43 km) than Dali (145 km north-east). Heqing town lies on a long plain. The northern end, backed by steep hills, is inhabited by Naxi. Near the Lijiang airport and southward, the villages are all Bai, rather close to one another, and it's difficult to determine where the boundary marks off the fields of one village from those of its neighbour. Housing reflects the Dali style in the facades, entry gates and arabesques below the corners of the roofs. The primary material, though, is mud-brick and Heqing County Bai houses usually have high, thick, windowless back walls. And in the middle of the roof they mount a small sculpture of a lion. Often red banners with white Chinese characters on them hang on the front parts of the house. Small trees and potted flowers stand in the courtyard.

In the late-1990s, Heqing began demolishing its central section around the big, three-tiered brick tower that dominated the old skyline. The tower itself was left intact, but a contracted Kunming company rebuilt the entire business

In the Bai county of Jianchuan, north of Dali, women wear a cap composed of several layers of overlapping embroidery.

section south and west of the tower with large new buildings, in the Bai style, as well as a classical city gate at the southern end of the main street and an imposing temple in the northeast quarter. For religious-minded Bai, though, the favourite temple is **Zhaoxin Monastery**, a few kilometres southwest of the city.

On market day in Heqing, Bai from the villages dotting the plain come to sell their grain, fruit and vegetables, plus all shapes of baskets and trays made of split bamboo, rain capes of palm bark fibre, copper and brass pots, and aprons, grey Mao caps and brims for the Heqing Bai headgear. Some Yi from the other side of the mountains, from the east, will also attend, as well as Bai from further south, towards Songgui, whose women wear round black berets with jewels fixed to the brim.

Songgui, 34 km south, past rolling hills with villages set on the slopes, holds its own open market on Saturdays. It also stages a Horse and Mule Fair on the 22nd day of the 7th month, in honour of the Ming General Mu Ying's final defeat of the Mongol forces in Yunnan. Heqing Bai bring in the New Year with a ceremony called Whipping the Vernal Ox. Borne by 24 men representing each of the annual solar terms, escorted by 48 others, the clay ox sculpture is enshrined in a special tent. When the leader gives the signal, the men attack and destroy the clay ox. The pieces are strewn on the fields to ensure a good harvest.

The last of the previous year's crops the Bai save for a rite at Wufengshan on 21 March, the Spring Equinox Exhibition. Six months later, on the autumnal equinox, they stage Birds' Day in honour of the goddess Linping. She transformed her sons into 24 birds, which taught the Bai the 24 solar terms and how to plant rice. On this day the Bai feed birds with buckwheat grains.

BAI MUSIC

Bai music has absorbed much of the Han classical tradition. They have maintained it faithfully in the several village orchestras that exist in the Erhai area. An ensemble includes a dozen or so stringed instruments, flutes, bass strings, gongs and drums, with performances at major festivals and when hired for weddings and other major celebrations. It plays only the classical tunes, most of them centuries old.

Opera has also attracted the Bai taste for music. They have composed many of their own and continue to do so in contemporary times. Singing reflects the operatic influence, even when the songs are not taken from Bai or Chinese operas. Several cassette tapes are on sale in Dali and most of the songs, even the non-operatic numbers, are in the Chinese language.

Bai classical orchestras play during major temple festivals as well as for private celebrations.

Folk songs in the Bai language do exist, including a collection of love songs, some of them rather risqué. These latter tunes older women sing during the Raoshanling festival at rice-planting time. Love songs pop up spontaneously in any kind of situation, but the Bai do have a festival that features them—the Singing Contest held at Shibaoshan near the end of the 2nd lunar month.

THE HUI

The second most numerous ethnic minority in the Erhai Lake area is the Hui. When Kubilai Khan conquered Dali he left behind a contingent of his army to police the new imperial acquisition. Many of these were Muslim soldiers from northwest China and these became the nucleus of a new Hui community in Dali. Over the centuries, as Dali's commercial importance grew, the Hui became the main caravan organizers, handling most trade of western Yunnan. Perhaps it was this grip on the economy that led the Dali Hui in the mid-19th century to reckon they could revolt and set up a state of their own.

The revolt failed and savage revenge decimated the Dali Hui. They were forbidden to live within the old city and hunted down and slain if they were believed to be in any way involved in the rebellion. Some of the Hui adopted the Bai language and lived like the Bai, with no evidence of Islam to be observed, and thus escaped detection. Once the heat was off they became more openly Islamic, but still retained the Bai language in daily intercourse, even at home. An example of this linguistic adaptation survives today in the Hui village of **Chongxing**. It lies on the slopes just a few kilometres southeast of Zhoucheng, recognizable from the road by the Arabian-style mosque that dominates its centre.

The Hui are no longer forbidden to live within Dali, of course, and Hui restaurants are common in the old town. On Bo Ai Street a new mosque stands, also in the Arabian style, with an attached Islamic Studies Institute. But on Fridays Dali Hui prefer to attend prayer services at the venerable Western Mosque, on a small lane about two blocks away. The modest building is in the Chinese style. On the wall of the courtyard entrance is a painting of Mecca, the top of the wall sporting a tiled roof with upturned ends, in the typical Dali style.

Just 5 km south of Dali is the Hui village of **Wulichou**. Domestic architecture is similar to the Bai's and while walking around one cannot see much that is different from a Bai or a Han village, save for a few women in head scarves that drape over the shoulders. The 60-year-old Wulichou Mosque, however, identifies the village as Hui. Built in the Chinese style, it has an attractive, two-tiered tower over the courtyard gate.

Many Hui live in villages that are partly, and sometimes mostly, Han. One such village is Du Wenxiu's birthplace—Xiadui, a few kilometres southeast of Dali. A long, straggling village with stone houses and cobbled streets, it is the site of Du Wenxiu's tomb, in the lower end of the village. When the Qing troops entered Dali, Du took his own life. But the victors cut off his head and exposed it to the public. The decapitated body was taken to Xiadui and now is installed in a simple tomb, shaded by pines and cypresses, with an Arabic prayer on the reverse.

In Yangbi Yi Autonomous County, the Yi inhabit the mountains, especially in the north and west, but in the county seat the old-fashioned, traditional part of town largely consists of Hui neighbourhoods. One of the finest Chinese-style mosques is the most prominent building in the old quarter along the river, near the Yunlong Bridge.

This suspension bridge of wooden planks is strictly for pedestrian use and even the town's three-wheeler taxis may not use it. A new Daoist temple sits on the hill across the river. The bridge connects to the ancient **Bonan Road**, which was the trade route for pony caravans in the days before highways and trucks. Today the main traffic crossing the bridge is that of local farmers on their way to and from Yangbi markets. With a small adjacent park on the town side, and paths through the woods on the other side leading to a multi-tiered pagoda, the bridge and its vicinity is the most attractive spot in Yangbi.

THE YI

In the mountains south of Erhai and the other side of Cangshan live the Yi. Most of them rarely come to Dali, but the one sub-group that does, selling fruits and vegetables, is the most eye-catching in the prefecture, the women more colourful than the Dali Bai. These are the Duli Yi, who live in the hills immediately southeast of Xiaguan and down into the mountains of Midu County. The women all dress in their distinctive traditional costume—a green, side-fastened, long-sleeved jacket, heavily embroidered apron, trousers and embroidered shoes. Married women wear a tall, black turban, with a stone set in a silver ornament attached to it just above the forehead. Single girls wear a cap with lots of colored tassels falling down the back.

Women also wear a small round pad at the back, called a *guobei*. One kind is cotton and lushly embroidered. The other, commoner one, is of felt wool, with a pair of spiders embroidered onto it. According to Duli myth, long ago young Yi women fled the attentions of a wicked chieftain. Running into the hills, they hid inside a cave. A sympathetic spider then spun a web over the mouth of the cave. The chieftain's soldiers combed the hills and passed by the cave. But seeing the web covering the opening, they assumed the girls couldn't have gone inside. So the girls escaped and to memorialize the event they and their descendants embroidered spiders on the guobei. As a costume part it has no real function. When loading baskets on their back they push it aside so it doesn't get damaged.

Occasionally these Yi come to Dali to sell potatoes, walnuts or fruit, but more often to the food market by the river in Xiaguan. Many more attend the open markets in Midu town, which are held every four days. Residing mostly in the mountains south of Midu, they must leave their villages soon after sunrise in order to reach Midu, on foot, leading ponies packed with their produce, by late morning, the peak of activity. Huge bundles of hemp stalks and loads of firewood and sugar cane are among their goods.

Southeast of Dali, the Yi are a branch of the Lolopo sub-group that inhabits western Chuxiong Prefecture. They are less ornately dressed, distinguished mostly by the embroidered apron, which also covers the stomach and chest. West of Cangshan, in Yangbi Yi Autonomous County, live half a dozen sub-groups of Yi, each dressed very differently from each other.

In the mountains north and west of Heqing live a very traditional branch of the Yi called the Baiyi. They can be occasionally seen in Heqing's market, the women dressing in their very distinctive costume of a long-tailed tunic over

(above) Qiaotou Yi in a festive mood at Zhongdian's Horse Racing festival.
(right) Married Yi women in Xiaoliangshan wear a large, plain black hat.

trousers and a peaked, Jinuo-like cap. Colours are predominantly blue and white, with a wide, multicoloured waistband. Most of the components are handmade. They are rarely visited, but are friendly to foreigners they encounter in Heqing.

THE THIRD MONTH FAIR

The greatest event of the year in Dali is the Third Month Fair, beginning on the full moon of the 3rd lunar month. According to local mythology this is the day Guan Yin came to Dali. The festival dates its antiquity to the beginning of the Nanzhao era, but it has long since evolved into a grand commercial affair and runs at least a week. Guan Yin now has her own festival, the 19th day of the 2nd moon, so the Third Month Fair has become strictly secular.

Promising lavish entertainment as well as a plethora of trade goods, the fair attracts local people of the many ethnic groups and sub-groups in the prefecture, others from further away, Han from the western parts of the province and Chinese and foreign tourists in abundance. The usual estimate for attendance during this week is over a million. Many branches of the Bai and Yi turn up, all wearing their best traditional costumes. The fair also hosts Tibetans marketing herbs and animal parts used in medicine and Yi horse and mule

A Yi horse trader at the Third Month Fair.

traders from the northwest, recognizable by their long woolen capes. Visitors may even include the rarely seen Lisu from the western mountains above Xinwo village in Songgui township.

The venue for the commerce is a slope just west of the old town. The stone memorial tablets honouring Kubilai Khan's conquest are housed in a small, walled courtyard partway up this slope. Erected in 1304, the tablets narrate the Khan's crossing into Yunnan and his subsequent capture of the city in 1253. Shop buildings have been constructed in recent years on a new lane, from the memorial to the road, for merchants to use for the fair, while tented stalls are grouped all around the area. Livestock of all kinds are sold in an adjacent field. Besides articles of everyday use such as are sold in the area's market days, costume parts, antiques, arts and crafts of all kinds, herbal medicine and furniture are among the goods on offer.

Since this is a government-subsidized festival, the entertainment aspect gets top attention. Parades proceed through town, with dragon dances and a colourful range of ethnic minority performances. Besides these acts, in which watching the crowd observing the action can be as enthralling as the dances themselves, athletic contests, acrobatics, bulls in combat, archery tournaments and pony races are all part of the week's excitement.

OTHER FESTIVALS

Most of the big annual Bai celebrations take place in the spring, before the heavy work or rice cultivation begins, while the weather is still crisp and clear and flowers are blooming profusely. The earliest of these spring festivals is the Birthday of the Floral King, held for three days beginning on the 12th day of the 2nd month. Villagers try to gather a hundred different kinds of flowers and make mounds of them all over the plain.

Guan Yin's festival takes place on the 19th day of the 2nd month and is the only specifically Buddhist one in the Bai calendar. Bai religion is more a mix of Daoism and their own form of animism. Spirits are divided into the ancestral set (*gui*) and those associated with wells, springs, woods, lakes, mountains and other sites, collectively called *seu*. A third element in Bai religion is the veneration of the village founder, called *benzhu*. Because each village consists of more than one clan, worship of the original founder gives its people a sense of unity. In the 4th lunar month Bai villages stage operas and folk dramas in honour of their *benzhu*, in addition to chanting prayers and burning incense.

Comparable dances and folk operas are part of the ceremonies of Honouring the Sea God at the Hongshan Temple Fair, on the 15th day of the 4th month. The 'sea' is, of course, Erhai, and Bai fishing communities sponsor the fair. Eight days later, starting on the 23rd day of the 4th month, comes Raoshanling, a three-day affair that, for the Bai villages of the Erhai plain north of Dali, is the most important festival of the year, eclipsing the totally secularized Third Month Fair.

The festival is intended to fall between the end of the winter wheat harvest and the beginning of the transplanting of rice seedlings. The affair is also called Visiting Three Spirits, which is somewhat more descriptive of the events than Raoshanling, which means Winding among the Mountains. In Bai it's called *Gweusala,* but no one can give a translation of the term. In fact the festival takes place at a different temple each day, but except for the first day attendance is generally restricted to those villages that lie in the vicinity.

The festival's purpose is to promote fertility; specifically now the coming rice crop, but traditionally it also meant the fertility of women. In past generations this was the time for romantic liaisons in the woods and it was this aspect that led the Nationalist government to officially ban it in the 30s. (The ban was ignored.) Some of the original erotic features survive nowadays in the risqué songs sung by the women in the processions.

The opening day is above Qinglong village, at the foot of Wutai Peak. This is the biggest day and the path to the temple is lined with market stalls, food shops and vendors selling the paraphernalia of the festival—tassels of grains and flowers, cloth pendants of hearts and figurines and the round stickers people affix to their brows. Inside the temple devotees offer incense and

(above) Yi youth play the moon guitar at the start of the Chahuajie festival party.
(right) A Bai torch rising to the sky.

prayers, bring trays of food to be blessed and form groups that chant sutras.

At the entrance to the temple courtyard a few older men act as scribes to write prayers to the gods for the devotees. These are done on yellow paper, with the donor's name and address at the bottom. The prayer is placed into a rectangular paper box. The devotee takes this to the courtyard and sets fire to it by lighting it from the top. If the flames crackle while the box is burnt that indicates the god has already acknowledged receipt of the message.

The second day's events take place in **Hesichong**, a small village below Xichou. Market stalls line the street to the temple again, but of a more modest size, fewer in number, and without a ticket booth at the beginning. The activity within the temple is the same as the previous day's, but this day has one additional feature—a procession through the streets of Xichou. Participants sometimes wear funny masks, false noses and the like. But the groups always include several women singing and dancing. They stop to perform, making a ring, some twirling batons, others rhythmically knocking their hips against each other.

On the third day, smaller still, but perhaps the most enjoyable because of its intimacy, the host is **Majinyi**, a lakeside Bai village 6 km northeast of Dali. At least one local procession winds through the village and performs in the temple courtyard. In addition, the local orchestra plays a classical set of old tunes. The day's activities more or less conclude by noon.

The last major festival of the year, the 25th evening of the 6th month (a day behind celebrations in Chuxiong, Ninglang and other Yi areas) is the **Torch Festival**. Both the Bai in the plains and the Yi in the hills celebrate this with torchlight parades and dances around bonfires. The autonomous Yi counties of Yangbi, Weishan and Nanjian stage special programmes in the county seats. The Bai in the Dali area assemble around the torch, erected in mid-afternoon, at dusk. A troupe of women performs a few dances around its base. Then the torch is lit from the top, so it will burn slowly. Some stay around the torch, shooting off other fireworks, until it is consumed. Others light smaller torches of bamboo and carry them through the paths in the fields and the lanes of the settled areas.

But the Bai have a different origin story for the festival and consequently add a few touches to the events that the Yi don't have. Bai trace the Torch Festival to the founding of Nanzhao. According to the story, since proved apocryphal, the Weishan king invited the chiefs of the other five *zhao* to a special feast. The Binchuan queen suspected trickery and bade her husband wear an iron ring.

The host seated his royal guests in a pavilion of pine wood, closed off the exits and burned down the building. The Binchuan queen identified her husband's charred corpse by the iron ring. She refused to marry the Weishan king and drowned herself in the lake. Her body was never recovered. To commemorate the event the Bai light a big torch in each village, eat raw pork with dressing and the women paint their fingernails red, to symbolize the bleeding fingers of the Binchuan queen as she groped through the ashes in search of her husband's body.

An unmarried Yi girl in traditional costume.

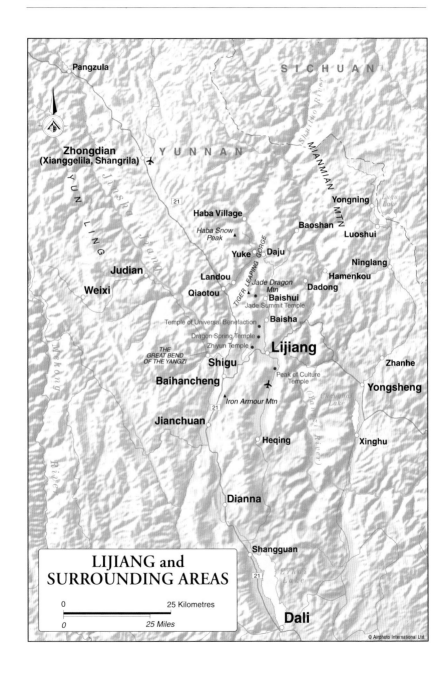

Pangzula

SICHUAN

Zhongdian
(Xianggelila, Shangrila)

YUNNAN

Shuiluo River

MIANMIAN

21

Haba Village

Jinsha Jiang

YUN LING

Haba Snow
Peak

Yuke   Daju

TIGER LEAPING GORGE

MIANMIAN MTN

Yongning   Lugu Lake

Baoshan

Luoshui

Ninglang

Landou

Judian

Weixi

Qiaotou

Jade Dragon
Mtn

Baishui

Hamenkou
Dadong

Jade Summit Temple

Temple of Universal Benefaction

Baisha

Dragon Spring Temple

Zhiyun Temple

Lijiang

Mekong River

THE
GREAT BEND
OF THE YANGZI

Shigu

Baihancheng

Peak of Culture
Temple

Zhanhe

Yongsheng

Chenghai Lake

Yangzi River

Iron Armour Mtn

21

Jianchuan

Heqing

Xinghu

Dianna

Shangguan

21

Evil Lake

LIJIANG and
SURROUNDING AREAS

0   25 Kilometres

0   25 Miles

Dali

© Airphoto International Ltd.

Snow Mountain Lands

LIJIANG: DAYAN

Nowhere is Yunnan's physical and cultural variety so concentrated as in the northwest. Each of its main geographical regions is dominated by the lifestyle and culture of a single ethnic minority. The extreme corner of the province lies on the edge of the Tibetan Plateau and is inhabited by the Khampa branch of the Tibetans. The basins around Lugu Lake are the homeland of the Mosuo. The high mountains are Yi country and the elevated plains and their surrounding hills are the abode of the Naxi. Other nationalities live in the northwest, like Lisu, Pumi, Bai, Zhuang and Miao. But they have largely adopted the cultural characteristics of their more numerous ethnic neighbours.

For travellers who came from cities in their own countries, which constitute the majority, the real gem of the region is Lijiang. More specifically, it is the old Naxi city of **Dayan**, a well-preserved traditional town with the snow peaks of Jade Dragon Snow Mountain looming to the north. With its cobbled lanes winding along the streams that run through the town, and its western quarter climbing up a small hill, it differs from the classic square grid with right-angle intersections, typified by Dali.

Dayan means 'inkstand', like the kind used in Chinese calligraphy, for that is what it resembled to its founders. The brush complimenting the inkstand is the perfectly triangular peak of Wenbishan, to Dayan's southwest. The city was founded in the wake of Kubilai Khan's campaign against the Kingdom of Dali. The Naxi had helped the Mongol army cross the Jinshajiang at Baoshan Stone City (*Baoshan Shicheng*), and when the Khan subsequently arrived in Lijiang he set up his camp around what is now the Old Stone Bridge in the town's northern quarter.

The Naxi at that time lived in the northern part of the plain. When their chieftain, the head of the Mu family, was invested with the Khan's authority to rule the area in the service of the Mongols, the Naxi moved their political centre to the vacated camp and built the city of Dayan.

For hundreds of years it remained roughly the same size, with around 50,000 inhabitants. In the 20th century a new city, the administrative capital of Lijiang County, grew up around it. The only major change to affect the old town was the introduction of electricity. When Yunnan decided to open parts of its province to foreign tourists, Lijiang was a natural first offering. Its old town intact, visitors had a chance to observe something that was becoming ever rarer in the country—traditional urban life.

(following pages) The Meili Snow Mountain group tower over the northwest corner of Yunnan's Deqin County.

Dayan's irregular layout made it easier to explore and to observe the life of the people. Naxi women used the streams to wash clothes and rinse vegetables. Farmers carried their produce through the streets and woodcutters hauled wagonloads of firewood into the town. In their leisure hours the women played cards at tables under the neighbourhood willow tree. Men brought their pet hawks to the squares and bridges to bask in the sun.

Three main streets led into the old town. The upper one, Xiahua Street, ran just above one of the streams that flow out of Black Dragon Pool into Dayan. The middle road was lined with ugly concrete buildings nearly all the way to Sifang Square. The third street, Xianfeng Street, wound its way through a quiet residential area, passed by a stream and crossed it at the Old Stone Bridge to turn to Sifang Square. The square was used daily by both Naxi and Bai merchants, the former trading farm produce, the latter hawking copperware, brass utensils and souvenirs.

Turning left at the lower end of the square, the road passed small shops, then met up with the stream that runs beneath the Old Stone Bridge. A large, three-sided building here embraced another market area, this one for the meat, vegetables, fruits and so forth consumed by local residents. Turning right past the market, this branch road, Shazu Lane, up to about a hundred metres further on, used to be the meat and poultry centre for this quarter of town. It was famous for its lady butchers.

Past this market was where many of the richer Naxi families lived, including the Mu family, and the houses boasted more decorative embellishments than in other neighbourhoods. Beyond this area, near the southern limit of Dayan, lies the Horse-Washing Pond (*Ximatang*), within a modest but attractive temple compound. The pond got its name from a local legend that the famous Buddhist pilgrim, Xuan Zang, stopped here to give his horse a bath.

From the top end of Sifang Square several streets climb up the hill, while the one turning left keeps to a height several metres above the main part of the city. From the streets going uphill paths turn off left to the wooded Lion Hill. From various points on this hill one can see between the trees and gaze on the mass of tiled roofs that make up Dayan. These viewpoints all face east and made excellent vantage points for the sunrise.

Customarily, few people venture out early in Dayan, rendering mornings especially tranquil. No motor traffic is permitted within the old town and the only post-sunrise noises heard are the songs of caged songbirds, the ripple of the streams and footsteps on the cobblestones. And those mostly belong to women, for it is the women who dominate the economic life of the town.

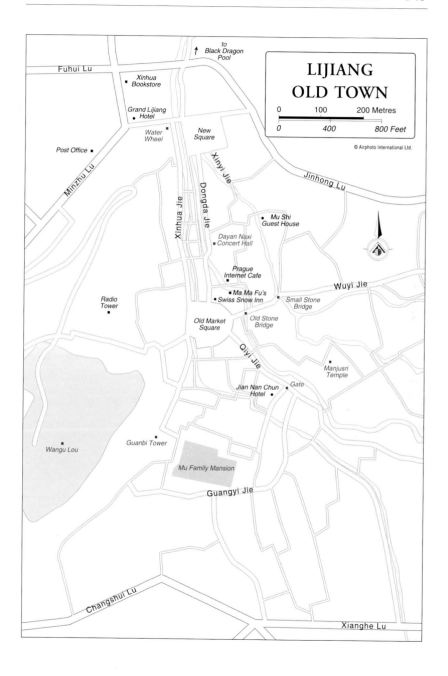

to
Black Dragon
Pool

Fuhui Lu

Xinhua
Bookstore

Grand Lijiang
Hotel

Water
Wheel

New
Square

Post Office

Minzhu Lu

Xinyi Jie

Jinhong Lu

Xinhua Jie

Dongda Jie

Mu Shi
Guest House

Dayan Naxi
Concert Hall

Prague
Internet Cafe

Wuyi Jie

Ma Ma Fu's
Swiss Snow Inn

Small Stone
Bridge

Radio
Tower

Old Market
Square

Old Stone
Bridge

Qiyi Jie

Manjusri
Temple

Jian Nan Chun
Hotel

Gate

Wangu Lou

Guanbi Tower

Mu Family Mansion

Guangyi Jie

Changshui Lu

Xianghe Lu

LIJIANG
OLD TOWN

0   100   200 Metres

0   400   800 Feet

© Airphoto International Ltd.

The older generation still preferred traditional clothing. For the men this was merely Han-style blue jackets and trousers and on special occasions long black gowns. But the women wore a distinctively Naxi item—the seven-starred sheepskin cape—in addition to trousers, apron, side-fastened jacket and simple bonnet or even Mao cap, generally in dark colours like blue, grey and maroon. The cape is half black, half white, with seven embroidered circular patches attached across the middle. It is fastened with a strap that crosses in front and ties in the back, with the ends embroidered in butterfly patterns. The cape symbolizes the diligence of the Naxi woman, as busy as the butterfly, who carries the burdens of Heaven on her back, for the seven circular patches represent the stars of the Big Dipper.

Dayan's inhabitants were Naxi, but they were not the only ethnic minority taking part in the life of the town. The Bai were regular visitors. Aside from those from Dali who ran the crafts and antiques shops and the souvenir stalls in Sifang Square, the Bai in Lijiang hail from the villages around Jinshan, several km east. Originally immigrants from Heqing County over 200 years ago, their women are recognizable by their red vests and blue head kerchiefs. The men are often employed by Naxi homeowners to build their new houses, in particular the wood-carved gates, doors and brackets.

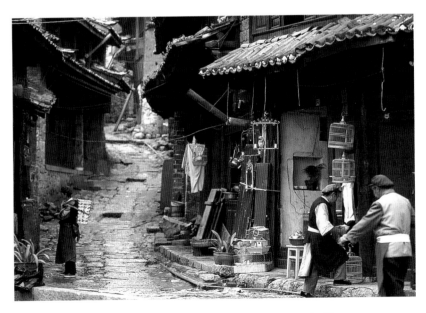

(above) A cobbled street near Xitang Square in Lijiang's old town.
(right) Naxi women have traditionally been Dayan's butchers.

Occasionally ethnic minorities from farther away came to shop in Lijiang, or even just to visit. These included Baiyi from Heqing County, Tibetans from Zhongdian and the Nosu Yi from the mountains to the north. These Yi women were the most colourful of Dayan's visitors, wearing long, three-coloured skirts, bright blouses and huge black hats.

Earthquake and Aftermath

In the early evening of 4 February, 1996, when people had come home for their evening meal, a severe earthquake struck Lijiang. Measuring 7.2 on the Richter scale, the quake toppled houses, killed over 300 and forced terrified residents into the streets and fields to put up in makeshift tents and shelters throughout the freezing night. And for several more, as aftershocks punched the surface of the earth and knocked down houses that had withstood the original quake.

The tragedy made international headlines and was a lead story on Chinese television for many days. Not only did aid of all kinds pour in at once, but many Chinese citizens became aware of Dayan and Lijiang County for the first time. Fascinated by the imagery, when in due course the reconstruction was more or less complete, a greater number of Chinese opted for Lijiang as their holiday destination. The irony of the disaster was that it led to a rather sudden change in Dayan's character and way of life because the coverage aroused so much interest and attention.

Reconstruction was rapid in the villages, but in Dayan itself many buildings were so heavily damaged their owners could not afford to rebuild them, so sold them off to companies that turned them into offices. Even these were rebuilt with traditional materials, if not always in the original's style. The local government not only insisted on it, they required that those buildings within Dayan's boundaries that did not use traditional materials must be torn down and built in the Naxi style. Hence the concrete buildings that lined the middle street leading to Sifang Square, which had survived the quake, were methodically demolished. The entire street was filled with new, Naxi-style buildings, better than almost every existing building in the old town.

The transformation went further. All the old town markets except Sifang Square, which became strictly a souvenir market, and the produce market in the courtyard of the three-storey, three-sided building by the stream, were closed. Little gardens replaced the butchers' stalls and chicken market on Shazu Lane. Meanwhile a multi-eaved viewing tower was erected on Lion Hill, and at the end of 1997 Dayan was declared a UNESCO World Heritage site.

Shortly after this about 20 square blocks below Shazu Lane were levelled. In place of the old residential neighbourhood the local government constructed a huge compound with a towering palace, built by Heqing Bai craftsmen, though billed as an example of classical Naxi art, claiming it to be a replica of the original Mu family palace in the Ming Dynasty. Xiahua Street and especially Xianfeng Street filled with shops catering to the tourists. By 2000 the commercialization of Dayan, with its new palace, multiple venues for orchestral music and folk dance shows, and growing number of guesthouses, souvenir shops, restaurants and cafés in the old town, where more than half the residents had already moved out, seemed to have reached its peak. But, as it turned out, the transformation was just getting started.

Five years later Dayan's character had changed completely. No longer was it the last traditional urban entity in the province. Scarcely a tenth of the original population still inhabited their houses, almost all in the northeast quarter, outside of which stood the only remaining local marketplace. All the other market venues in the old town had been closed and replaced by guesthouses and restaurants. And this market, too, was to be torn down and replaced by a new train station, because regional planning included the extension of the rail line from Xiaguan. Local Naxi were to be relocated to new villages beyond the new city, their houses slated for conversion into guesthouses, restaurants and souvenir shops, like those now in every other quarter of the city, run by immigrant merchants, mostly from Hunan Province.

Dayan's makeover included gigantic waterwheels straddling the stream at the entrance to the town, a wall full of thematically ethnic, but modern sculptures, ornamental gates erected at various street junctions in the town, a new park, replete with bronze sculptures of traditional life, laid out beside the old town entrance, and even a new old town erected opposite the Lijiang Grand Hotel. The Disneyfication of Dayan featured the daily appearance of 50 Naxi men and 50 Naxi women, in traditional costume, all from villages in the nearby plains assigned by rotation, at Sifang Square to dance for the tourists. Other Naxi men, garbed in old warrior clothes, took tourists on pony rides through the city. Every night it wasn't raining a Torch Festival, with bonfire and ring dancing, was staged in Sifang Square.

The city government also ordered every establishment catering to tourism, which by then came to 80 percent of the buildings, to erect a red lantern at its door. The idea was that, because of the movie *Raise the Red Lantern,* these were associated with traditional Chinese domestic architecture. But, sadly, with the old town buildings illuminated at night, red lanterns hanging everywhere and the wild sounds of tourist parties in the air, the effect is rather an unintended resemblance to a vast traditional red-light district.

Meanwhile, the transformation continues. Sledgehammers knock down old houses, which will be rebuilt in the traditional Dayan style, but with interiors redone to serve as guesthouses, restaurants and souvenir shops. Its former Naxi residents have been relocated in new neighbourhoods far from Dayan, but in quasi-Naxi-style houses, equipped with hot and cold running water and private bathrooms. Their town has been taken away from them, but, materially speaking, they all live more comfortably.

As for Dayan's future, it seems wedded to the needs of Chinese tourists. They enjoy Dali and like its scenery and so forth, but they love Dayan. The architecture of Dali is Han-influenced, but different enough to be too exotic for Chinese to feel completely at home. By contrast, the architecture of Dayan, though nominally Naxi, looks like the kind of place their grandparents grew up in. Never mind that the traditional life of the city no longer exists. The setting is still authentic and for them that is all that matters.

NAXI CULTURE

The Naxi migrated out of the highlands of eastern Tibet into Lijiang County beginning in the 1st century AD. The broad plain below Jade Dragon Snow Mountain was then occupied by the Pu people and the Naxi began contesting them for it in the 8th century. By the beginning of the 13th century they had evicted the Pu, who thereupon disappear from history. The Naxi chose to help the Mongols against Dali, rather than try to resist their advance into Yunnan. As a result, Kubilai Khan appointed their chieftain as his own governor. Throughout the Yuan Dynasty and its successor, the Ming, the Mu family remained a most dependable ally of the imperial throne. Naxi troops pacified the frontier and were the hardiest, most reliable troops in the campaigns against Burma.

Political loyalty allowed the Naxi cultural autonomy and during the Mu regency influences from both Han and Tibetan culture gradually augmented the aboriginal religion and directed the styles of its art and architecture. Native religion was based around the ritual specialist called the *dongba,* who conducted the rites honouring Heaven, various deities and natural forces. It originated with an individualist Bön shaman from eastern Tibet named Dongba Shilo, who lived in a cave near Baishuitai 900 years ago. He is said to have invented the pictographic script used in the ritual manuals.

These manuals, long and thin, not only gave instructions for the performance of the ritual, they also contained the myths, legends and history of the Naxi people. But as the pictographs are not full transcriptions of the narratives but coded summaries, it took many years to learn the system. Thousands of these books have now been collected and most are stored in the Dongba Institute in Black Dragon Pool Park. The last living dongbas from the Lijiang area are employed there to aid the translations.

Baishuita Naxi dongba dancers perform at the Tibetan Horse Races festival in Shangrila.

During the Ming Dynasty, the Mu rulers established relationships with the Black Hat (*Karmapa*) sect of Tibetan Buddhism. This resulted from the expulsion of the 10th Karmapa Lama from Central Tibet in the mid-17th century. The Naxi sponsored the construction of five main temples (known as *wuda mingsi*) in the area—today's tourist attractions—which as late as Joseph Rock's time were supporting hundreds of monks in each. Mahayana Buddhism and Daoism also found favour in Naxi culture, which simply grafted elements onto its own increasingly syncretistic religion.

Naxi sponsors lavished money on the temples. Many were embellished with interior frescoes. Most were destroyed in wars and political campaigns, but a few examples survive. The biggest and most famous set of frescoes, painted in the Ming Dynasty and restored after Red Guard damage, adorn the walls of Dabaoji Palace in **Baisha** village, several km north of Lijiang. A smaller temple in the same village has a less impressive collection from the Qing Dynasty. The other extant frescoes are in a neglected temple in Xiawu village, currently used as a stockroom for furniture and supplies belonging to the adjacent middle school. In their use of bright colours and cloud motifs the frescoes show the Tibetan influence, while in portraiture and subject they display the Han influence.

When the Qing Dynasty succeeded the Ming the Mu had no problems adjusting. The first Qing emperors continued the past policy of having local rulers govern on their behalf. But with the accession of Emperor Qianlong the Manchu court felt strong enough to start appointing its own magistrates to rule directly. This policy was inaugurated in Lijiang in 1723 and marks a major turning point in Naxi cultural history. The Naxi had been adopting elements of Han culture already, the architecture for example, but from 1723 the assimilation of Han, specifically Confucian, aspects accelerated. Burial replaced cremation, marriages were arranged, and gentlemen dressed in long black gowns and dabbled in poetry and calligraphy.

Naxi also began observing Han festivals, but occasionally they gave them a twist. The annual Han festival of welcoming their ancestral spirits, sometimes called 'Feeding the Hungry Ghosts', is held at the full moon of the 7th lunar month. But the Naxi begin three nights earlier, hanging ornate lanterns from their rafters and floating small lamps on the streams. On full moon they do nothing. They also have their own version of the Torch Festival, with a different origin story but the same activities.

For the Naxi people, though, the most important festival honours Sanduo, on the 8th day of the 2nd lunar month. Sanduo is the war god and his temple, sited below Yufengsi at Yulong village, 12 km north of Lijiang, was the first

A classical Naxi musician. The growth of the tourist trade has led many Naxi youth to take up traditional music.

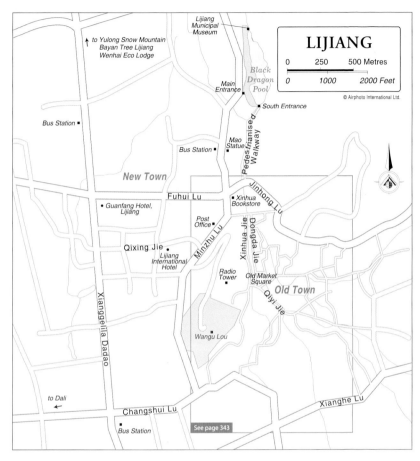

erected in the area, dating to 779. Sanduo is said to have appeared in silver armour astride a white horse in the middle of a battle to turn the tide in the Naxi's favour. A statue of the god in his mythical regalia stands in the courtyard of the Five Phoenix Tower in Black Dragon Pool Park. The one in his temple is unmounted. On festival day the temple is thronged with worshippers, who afterwards pay a visit to Yufeng Temple on the slope above and pose for photographs in front of the ancient camellia tree, in full bloom at this time.

Afterwards they may picnic or form spontaneous ring dances. Urban residents may hire a village orchestra to play the music that the Naxi have preserved since the tunes were bestowed on them by Kubilai Khan. The typical orchestra comprises men on drums, gongs, flutes and stringed instruments. The Naxi ensemble differs from a classic Chinese one in two instruments. One is the Mongolian stringed lute, played with a bow, called *sugudu*. The other is the high-pitched little flute made from the wing bone of a wild goose.

Naxi music was banned during the Cultural Revolution and the musicians forced to hide their instruments. When it was played publicly again in the early 1980s, it marked the first step in the revivalism that soon gripped the Naxi, as it did so many other ethnic groups in Yunnan. By the 90s, Dayan's orchestra was performing regularly for tourists and by mid-decade had even played abroad. Other village orchestras reformed, and in the wake of the post-earthquake tourist boom were hired for regular performances in Lijiang, both within the old town and in the city's new hotels.

Beyond music, revivalism has been marked by the extensive use of dongba art motifs in painting, hotel frescoes, souvenirs and replica ritual objects. The younger generation of women have created a new ethnic costume, more feminine than that of their mothers. It retains the seven-starred cape, but exchanges the plain trousers for a long white pleated skirt, like the Mosuo, and a round headdress with circular discs attached to it.

Even the new city has been influenced by the new ethnic awareness. Buildings going up nowadays utilise the architectural motifs and decorations inspired by Dayan houses. Foreign appreciation has abetted Naxi revivalism, to be sure, but it was already in place when Lijiang greeted its first foreign tourists.

BLACK DRAGON POOL PARK

The streams that flow through Dayan emanate from Black Dragon Pool, some 2 km to the north. Because the water here is a lucid green colour, it is also known as Jade Spring and has been a public park since the Ming Dynasty. The **Dayue Pavilion** standing in the middle of the pond, connected by the marble, five-span Belt Bridge, was originally erected in the 17th century, restored and rebuilt in 1963. When the sky is clear the snow-clad Jade Dragon Mountain reflects its peaks in the water in front of the bridge and two-tiered pavilion, for the classic postcard image of Lijiang. The smaller pavilion between Belt Bridge and the south bank of the pond serves as a complement. And tall weeping willows on either bank frame the whole picture.

On the east bank of the pond sits the 18th century Longshan Pavilion. Within its compound 500 kinds of flowers are raised. Paths from here lead one way to the Dayue Pavilion and the other way behind it to **Five Phoenix Pavilion**. This was originally the main building of Fuguo Temple, sited above

(following pages) Jade Dragon Mountain reflects in the waters of Black Dragon Pool Park.

Jade Pond, one of the five Karmapa monasteries sponsored by the Mu rulers. This one was constructed in 1661, but in recent decades was removed to the park and the Sanduo statue installed.

The 29-metre-tall building gets its name from the fact that its three tiers, with octagonal flying cornices, sport 24 angles. Accordingly, from any viewpoint the structure resembles five phoenixes taking flight. Further on, outside the park's North Gate, is the new Lijiang Municipal Museum, home to the **Naxi Dongba Culture Exhibition** and well worth a visit. An English-speaking guide will take you through the various halls displaying ritual set-ups for various ceremonies, costumes and religious paraphernalia, like the images and painted swords formerly used in funerals.

Back at the south end of the park a path leads uphill to the Dongba Institute, where the collected manuscripts are stored. Further up another building houses an art gallery. Even on cloudy days, then, the park still has its attractions. However, when the mountain is cloud-free, the option exists for an even fuller view by continuing up the path as it climbs Elephant Hill. At the summit is a pavilion from which to gaze at Jade Dragon Mountain and the dry plain that spreads between Elephant Hill and the mountain's base.

WEST OF LIJIANG

Just 13 km west of Lijiang lies picturesque **Lashi Lake**, from where comes most of the fish served in Lijiang restaurants. Lying a kilometre from the road at its nearest approach, the lake is backed by a hill that all but obscures Jade Dragon Mountain. Naxi settlements lie in the plain on both sides of the lake, while far above on the mountain sit a few Lisu villages. The road swerves away from the lake and steadily rises until not only Jade Dragon Mountain is more fully visible, so is the more distant snow peak of Habashan.

Continuing west the road crosses the hills and descends to the Jinshajiang and its First Great Bend at **Shigu** (Stone Drum), 70 km west of Lijiang. A large cyclindrical marble memorial, shaped like a drum, honours the 1548 Sino-Naxi victory over a Tibetan army in this area. This old town overlooks a narrow strip of farmland that borders the river as it makes its turn. Partway up the hill is a memorial hall to the Red Army division under He Long and Xiao Ke that made its crossing here on the Long March in April 1936— a great event in Naxi history. The views here are splendid, especially in spring when the fields beside the river shine brilliantly yellow from the mustard and rape flowers.

Another 90 km north, passing left bank mountains reflected in the river, the road comes to the small Naxi town of **Judian**, which lies back from the banks. The town has typical Naxi houses, but nowhere near as nice as in Dayan. The road west climbs into the **Hengduan Mountains**, eventually reaching **Weixi**.

Beyond Mingyin, Naxi villages are set on knolls and hills among the farmlands.

The western branch of Lijiang County is less populated, with wilder terrain and bigger patches of forest. Laojunshan, with its 99 Dragon Pools, lies west of Shigu. Halfway to Judian a lateral road turns west at Jinzhuang, passes Naxi villages in the valleys and suddenly, after about 20 km, just before **Liming**, the scenery alters. All cliffs, bald mountain summits, even boulders by the road are a very red shade of auburn. From here to **Liguang**, another 9 km, the hues of the hills are unlike any others in Yunnan. They provide a feast for the eyes of anyone who appreciates natural colours.

NORTH OF LIJIANG

Going north, the road passes **Ganhaizi** (Dry Plain), the last flat stretch of land in this direction until the plateau above the Jinshajiang at **Daju**, 96 km from Lijiang. After crossing the pass at the northern end of the Lijiang plain, the terrain is all mountainous. The road winds past Yi villages and descends to cross **White Water Creek** (*Baishui*). A cable car here takes visitors up to Yunshanping meadow, with its high, close-up view of the mountain. The road from Baishui enters thick forest and soon crosses Black Water Creek (*Heishui*). Both streams get their names from the colours of the stones in their beds.

Continuing through the highland forests another 15 km from Heishui, the road comes to a junction. The right fork leads to Mingyin. The left fork begins a slow descent to Daju. As the road winds down the mountains Naxi settlements appear on the slopes. Behind them the slopes rise steeply, bare of vegetation, with long runnels descending the cliffs. The Daju plateau, 35 km from the turnoff, is broad and besides Daju township, several villages occupy it. In the fields stand stone tumuli, containing the ashes of cremated Naxi.

Daju has long been familiar with foreigners because of its proximity to the northern end of **Tiger Leaping Gorge**, a popular trek for the backpacker set. The two majestic peaks of **Yulongshan** (Jade Dragon) and **Habashan** tower over the plateau. Its northwest edge offers a view up the gorge, while below a great riverside boulder forces the Jinshajiang into a narrow trench. It is here, according to some, that the tiger did his leaping.

Back at the fork in the road, in the hills south of Daju, the right turn leads to **Mingyin**, a regional logging centre. Passing Naxi villages perched on the slopes of high, forested mountains, the road continues for 12 km, then turns east another 16 km to Baoshan township. From this small administrative centre, the road continues towards the Jinshajiang. **Baoshan Stone City** is just an hours walk (or pony ride; they don't go any faster). The area is densely settled and several Naxi villages cling to the slopes in the vicinity. In the past this area was subject to raids by Tibetan bandits and all but one village suffered their depredations.

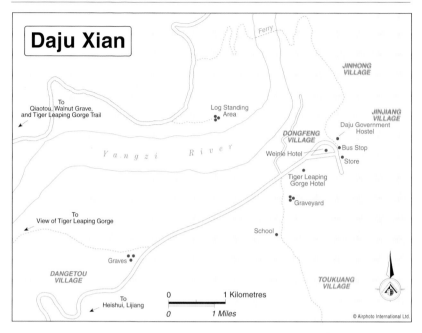

Baoshan was the one village unscathed. Situated on top of a huge boulder overlooking the Jinshajiang at one of the main crossing points taken by Kubilai Khan's forces, a thick wall surrounded its eastern side. From its western side the only approach was by a path, which wound its way up the side of the boulder to the crevice that served as village entrance. Here the gate would be shut. From the fortress on the flat summit, just above the path, Baoshan's defenders hurled stones down on the bandits. And so it remained impregnable.

The fortress has gone and the raids have long ceased, but the basic layout of the village has remained the same, except its gates are never locked shut. The name Stone City refers partly to its position on the boulder, and also the use of local stone for tables and kitchenware, like ovens, mortars, milling wheels, etc. Many houses are carved from the rock or have sections made from the red stone. Villagers did not cut steps into the boulder, though, and the steep walk down to the lower gate must be taken with care. The lower gate opens to a path down to the river.

On the opposite bank the slope rises sharply, with a few houses higher up, but few trees. Rubber dinghies ferry passengers across, replacing the inflated goat-skin rafts that conveyed the Mongol armies. The peaks along the river are high, steep and jagged. But northwest of Baoshan, on the route through the primeval forests to the Fengke-Mingyin-Lijiang road, many of the summits are round and bald. The forest features thick rhododendron trees, larch, spruce and pine, with Yi villages occupying the occasional glen.

Tiger Leaping Gorge

Once upon an ancient time, where the River of Golden Sands rushes between the steep slopes and towering cliffs of two snow-capped mountains, a tiger came hurrying through the forest. Guided by the clatter of snapping twigs just ahead of them, a band of Naxi hunters followed in hot pursuit. Their prey rushed headlong downhill until it reached the bank of the turbulent river. There was no way to swim in that current and the hunters were drawing near. Summoning all its primordial strength, the tiger made a mighty leap of over 30 metres to the other side, scampered out of crossbow range, and successfully eluded the astonished hunters.

After the hunters returned home to tell the tale, the local people began calling the place Tiger Leaping Gorge (*Hutiaoxia*). Eons later it became one of Yunnan's most famous tourist attractions, not for the legend behind its name but for the undeniable magnificence of the tale's setting. Here the river has cut an 18 km-long cleft between two of the largest mountains in the province—*Yulong Shan* (5,596 m) on the east bank and *Haba Shan* (5,396 m) on the west bank. Picturesque villages lie scattered on the west bank slopes. Birds and flowers fill the forests above them. Across on the other side, the sheer cliffs of Jade Dragon (*Yulong*) Snow Mountain rise straight up from the rapids of the river. No wonder then that when Lijiang first opened its doors to foreigner travellers in the 1980s, most included a trek through the gorge on their itineraries.

It was a popular though gruelling way to enjoy natural scenery. Conventional wisdom advised two full days of hiking from Daju down to Qiaotou, or vice versa. That was assuming you were in good shape, you didn't turn your ankle on the trail, no rockslides or rainstorms impeded you, and your travel schedule was too tight to allow for a more leisurely, less physically exacting adventure.

With villages popping into sight every two or three hours, and guest houses set up for travellers in each of them, the slower, less exhausting, more appreciative option was always available. But in general people followed the guidebook dictum and did it in two hard days. It became a fitness test to cover the route in only two days. It was something to boast about in the Lijiang and Dali cafés afterwards, until you met the inevitable maniac who did it in a single day's dawn-to-dusk mad rush.

Since the late 1990s, another option has opened for those going through the gorge—bus or car, on the new paved road that runs along the west bank all the way to the Daju ferry landing at the northern end. Close to the river for the first third of the route, the road gradually climbs up the slopes and is several hundred metres above the river by the time it reaches Walnut Grove, the northernmost village in the gorge.

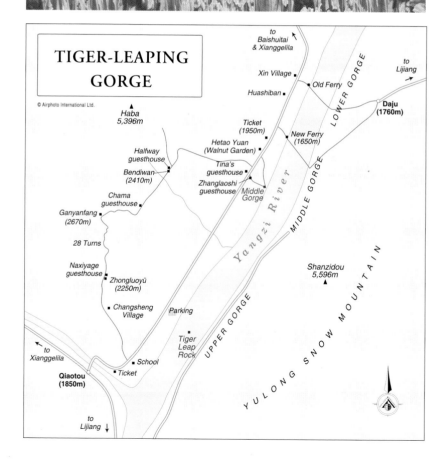

TIGER-LEAPING GORGE

© Airphoto International Ltd.

to Baishuitai & Xianggelila

to Lijiang

Xin Village

Old Ferry

LOWER GORGE

Daju (1760m)

Huashiban

Haba 5,396m

Ticket (1950m)

Hetao Yuan (Walnut Garden)

New Ferry (1650m)

Halfway guesthouse

Bendiwan (2410m)

Tina's guesthouse

Zhanglaoshi guesthouse

Middle Gorge

MIDDLE GORGE

Chama guesthouse

Yangzi River

Ganyanfang (2670m)

28 Turns

Naxiyage guesthouse

Zhongluoyü (2250m)

Shanzidou 5,596m

Changsheng Village

Parking

UPPER GORGE

YULONG SNOW MOUNTAIN

to Xianggelila

Tiger Leap Rock

School

Qiaotou (1850m)

Ticket

to Lijiang

This road has enabled a great many more people to see and appreciate the gorge, who otherwise would have neither the time nor ability to go on foot. Every day tour buses bring big groups to view the scenery, while taxis and minivans shuttle visitors and villagers back and forth between Qiaotou and Walnut Grove. Veteran trekkers from the gorge's pre-development days might assume that the new road has spoiled the adventure. But actually, except for improved facilities and the option of fancier accommodation at roadside villages like Walnut Grove, the new road has not actually interfered with the traditional trekking experience.

Tour buses generally just take their passengers to the spot where the tiger allegedly made its leap. The tourists go down to the bank to pose for pictures next to a statue of the tiger. Across the river a newly paved road ends at a creek just opposite the tiger statue and buses drop visitors here to shoot telephoto shots of the tiger from the eastern bank. Depending on the season, the river's width here is 30–35 metres. It's hard to imagine even a frog or a jackrabbit twice as large as the tiger able to make such a prodigious jump. But for people who come to bask in the aura surrounding the site of a famous legend, scientific arguments challenging the authenticity of that legend are irrelevant.

For most tourists, the gorge is just a day trip out of Lijiang. A few go on to spend a night or two at Walnut Grove and take short hikes to the waterfall above the settlement or the steep path through the farms to the spot on the bank known as Middle Tiger Leaping Gorge. The narrowest part of the entire gorge is just above, but the sheer vertical cliffs on the Jade Dragon side precluded any chance of the tiger making its leap here. The Daju plateau rises beyond this crevice and, on clear days, snowy mountains crease the horizon further on. With its traditional Naxi houses mottling the hillside, a spectacular view, and the conviviality at the guesthouse dinner tables, a trip to Walnut Grove alone can be easier on the limbs and lungs, yet amply rewarding for the eyes, ears and nose.

For the fullest experience of Tiger Leaping Gorge, nothing beats taking the trek. You tread the same high, rocky footpath the local villagers have been using since the land was first settled many centuries ago. It is well above the road and its traffic, where the air is pure and fresh, with

Tiger Leaping Gorge.

continuously changing vistas of the lines and shapes of the slopes and peaks.

The view is broader and constant on the northern half of the route, from Wenjia Stream to Walnut Grove. This is an easier stretch to hike, quite in contrast to the really rugged section between the stream and Nuo Yu village. Within this part of the route, the trail ascends sharply to the pass at 2,670 metres. On the southern side, the path zigzags up what is called the 28 Bends. The northern side, only marginally less steep, passes through a thick forest all the way to the stream. But though the trees block views of the mountains, flowers of various kinds, shapes and colours decorate the paths, including two of Yunnan's prize species—the rhododendron and the bell-shaped rough gentian.

At several points along this section of the trail, viewpoints unobstructed by trees offer a clear view of the gorge and the peaks of the eastern bank. These are ideal spots to revel in the scenery, watch eagles glide by, chat with trekkers hiking in the opposite direction and perhaps sit and fantasize upon what the gorge might look like if, as was once proposed, it had been dammed up and a huge reservoir created as a result. Would have future generations of tourists riden a cable car to this pass, sit in an expensive restaurant and sip cool drinks while enjoying the reflection of Jade Dragon's peaks in the limpid waters of a Tiger Leaping Lake?

Meanwhile, the river still flows freely and in the end the dam most likely will not be built. For the time being at least, visitors can still marvel at a spectacle wrought by time and the elements. And inevitably they will depart with the fervent hope that the powers-that-be will ultimately rate the value of the gorge not for its hydroelectric potential but for its positive effect on the hearts and souls of those who travel so far to bear witness to its beauty.

As of January 2009, authorities decided not to dam the river here but rather build 200 km further upstream in an area bordering Weixi and Deqin counties.

BAISHUITAI

The Naxi have been occupying some of the most picturesque locations in the northwest ever since they migrated to the Lijiang plain. Going east from Lijiang to Yongsheng the road climbs out of the valley and from Longshan, 18 km east, begins snaking down the mountain to the bridge over the Jinshajiang, 31 km below. Steep mountainsides are the sites of many villages, with magnificent views of the ranges across the river.

In the northwest direction, the road runs beside the Jinshajiang with villages perched on the hills above the river, all the way to Qiaotou and the junction of the river with the Chongjiang rushing down from Zhongdian. Tiger Leaping Gorge ends at this confluence and the serrated snowy peaks of Jade Dragon loom magnificently over the valley. But one of the most picturesque areas of Naxi settlement is also one of the oldest—Sanba township, north of the gorge, on the other side of Habashan, in southwest Zhongdian County.

Until recently the only access by road was from Zhongdian, from where buses ran every other day. Now a new road connects the district with Qiaotou. The old route from Zhongdian climbed to 4,000 metres, passed Yi villages in the mountains and then, crossing one last high ridge, from where Habashan is visible, it wound into the **Sanba** township valley, where several Naxi villages lie. And just a few km before passing the first village the great white lump of rock called *Baishuitai*—White Water Platform—can be seen just above the villages and below the woods, lying like it was dropped there from Heaven.

Geologists say it wasn't dropped from anywhere, but in fact took many eons to shape into a rock. Above the sprawling boulder, at the edge of the forest, a cluster of springs leaks from the ground, flows into a pool with inkblot islands, then spills over the slope. The water contains carbonate of lime and leaves particles of this behind as it flows. Slowly, ever so slowly, this built up to become Baishuitai. In many places the water spills over into natural trays that strongly resemble rice terraces.

The rock is solid and visitors can walk all over it. The water flows over the entire surface of Baishuitai, but except for the terraces here and there is rarely deeper than the soles of one's shoes. Moreover, it is not a smooth rock, but coruscated with little rills that keep footing steady, even on the slopes. A walk across the boulder, with pauses at the terraces, is one of the most pleasant experiences of nature possible in the province.

The local Naxi say the terraces were built by their gods, to inspire them how to farm the hills. In truth, Naxi rice farms resemble the terraces of Baishuitai. Yet it was local human ingenuity that built channels below Baishuitai to catch the flow and direct it to all the villages in the valley, down to Sanba, 5 km away.

Domestic architecture is the original Naxi type: log buildings with roof shingles held down by stones. The main building holds the kitchen, the elevated dining area and the sleeping quarters for the elder generation. The younger ones sleep in the adjacent building. Small animal sheds stand in the compound, as do the tall drying racks where, as in other Naxi areas, they hang their grain after harvest.

Baishuitai Naxi speak a dialect unlike that used around Lijiang. Their traditional clothing style differs, too. Men wear white jackets that cross over in front and are held in place with a sash belt. The women wear long black cloaks and instead of the seven-starred cape of Lijiang they wear one of handwoven wool, about one metre by two metres, the top end tied around the shoulders. In colder weather they don a sheepskin cape, with the fleece side out. And on festive occasions they braid and coil their hair and around it wear a crown of round discs with agate or jade pieces in the centre.

Culturally, though, the Baishuitai Naxi are like Naxi everywhere. In fact, because of their isolation they assimilated less of Han culture than those Naxi around Lijiang and retained an active dongba tradition right down to the present day. The Sanduo Festival is more spectacular here, chiefly because of the dongbas, who come in full costume for rites and sacred dances on the terraces. The dongbas feel obligated to put on a good show because this area

The calcinated rocks at Baishuitai are shaped like rice terraces.

was, after all, home to Dongba Shilo, the father of their entire tradition.

ZHONGDIAN (SHANGRILA)

Following the course of the Chongjiang from Qiaotou, the road turns past a fabulous, deep, wooded gorge, then winds past Yi villages in the high hills, makes one last ascent through the woods, and then suddenly reaches the Tibetan Plateau. A long, rolling plain bounded by thickly forested mountains stretches before the eyes. Villages checker the plain and great drying racks, shaped almost

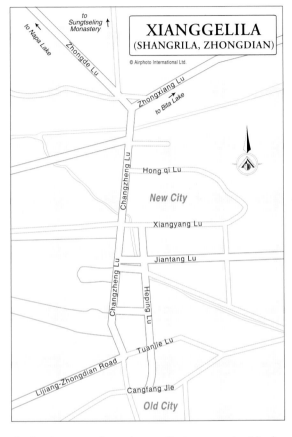

like chairs for giants, dot the landscape and stand surreally in groups beside the villages. Occasional pagodas, like small steeples mounted on domes, stand on the lanes between the settlements and off the main road.

The inhabitants of these villages are members of the Khamba branch of the Tibetans and their lifestyle has all the characteristics of highland Tibetan culture further west—barley cultivation, yaks, monasteries, etc. But Zhongdian's attributes render its Tibetans among the most fortunate of their race in all of China. Zhongdian's Tibetans can count on the annual monsoon for their barley, wheat and vegetable crops. Plenty of grazing land is available for their animals. The forests are a nearby source of timber, herbs and edible

(following pages) Snow blankets Zhongdian, a not uncommon occurrence.

(above) The monastic village of Songzhanlin sits on a knoll north of Zhongdian and is the major religious centre for the county. (left) A Tibetan women in Zhongdian.

fungi, particularly the valuable mushroom the Japanese know as *matsutake*. They particularly relish it and sponsored the development of its local trade, which dominates the summer market scene.

Being so high, an average of 3,500 metres, the plain can be cold in winter, with snowstorms possible even in late April, but more often the weather is clear at that time. The snow stays on all the lower peaks until late spring, when the fields are being sown. The rains bring the flowers, both in the mountain forests and in great swaths upon the plains. As the rains diminish the grain ripens, the fields are yellow and in the adjoining pastures a small bush turns fiery red, splashing the plain with new patches of colour.

Then when harvest commences pines and larches on the hills turn yellow-orange, while the leaves of deciduous trees turn crimson, yellow, orange, mauve and purple. The woods around the wild lakes Bitahai and Shudouhai, east of Zhongdian, nestled in the hills, are especially beautiful in early autumn.

From its opening to foreign tourism in 1993 Zhongdian began claiming that it was the model for Shangrila in James Hilton's novel *Lost Horizon*. Though the book never gives but a vague description of its location in the Eastern Himalayas, and the mountain peak described is not visible from anywhere in

Zhongdian County, the notion persisted, backed by the 'conclusions' of Chinese scholars. Eventually the government officially changed the city and county's name to Shangrila, which in pinyin comes out as *Xianggelila* (which, oddly enough, in the Black Lisu dialect of Nujiang means 'come back again someday').

THE TIBETANS

Nearly all Tibetan females, including the adolescents, and a smaller proportion of the men, yet more than most minorities, dress in local traditional style. Women wear a side-fastened vest over a long-sleeved blouse, trousers, sometimes a pleated half-skirt worn over the buttocks, and a cape of wool and fleece. They braid their hair and coil it inside a narrow, fleece-lined, open-top cap, fitted over a front brim. The fleece coming out the edges makes a pretty frame for their faces.

The men wear a loose, wide-sleeved coat that folds over in front and is held in place by a sash or belt. Often they wear it leaving one arm sleeveless. Trousers, high boots and a broad-brimmed bush hat complete the outfit. Some men wear leather belts with big fronts full of little pockets and studded with silver ornaments and semi-precious stones. In colder weather men like to wear tall, fox-fur hats.

Village houses are big, solid constructions of timber and rammed earth, two or three stories, with whitewashed walls and flat roofs with shingles weighted down with stones. People live on the upper floors. One small room is set aside for family worship services, containing an altar and an image of one of their divinities. The biggest room serves as kitchen, dining hall and receiving room. Ceilings are high enough for basketball players to stand up straight. In the most interior corner is the hearth, with its big, five-chambered cooking stove.

In the neighbourhoods of Zhongdian's old town, *Jedâw* in the local language, the space is more restricted and the compounds smaller. But the architecture is similar, except in the Naxi quarter, where the houses are in the Dayan style. Jedâw sits on and around a knoll, with a small shrine at its top. Near the base of this hill is the much larger Zanggong Hall. He Long, Xiao Ke and other Red Army officers lodged here in 1936 and a small, one-room Long March Museum occupies the smaller building left of the main hall.

The Naxi inhabitants are descendants of the troops stationed here in dynastic times, when the Han army, with many Naxi soldiers, defended the relatively prosperous Zhongdian plain against raids by Tibetan bandits from the arid, poorer, mountainous areas further north. Consequently, the two main communities, the Han of the city and the Tibetans of Jedâw and the villages, get along well, respect each other, attend each other's festivals, and even occasionally intermarry. Tibetan trade out of Zhongdian has also been mainly to the south, with the cities of Yunnan, rather than with Lhasa, which is so far away.

The Han may dominate the urban population, but even the modern buildings erected in Zhongdian often employ Tibetan architectural motifs in the roofs, windows, etc. And in the central marketplace, villagers congregate as always, oblivious to the changes in the city. Local Bai immigrants, Naxi from Sanba and Yi from the lower mountains also wander into the market, which is richly stocked with vegetables, fruits and meats, plus Bai copperware and brass pots, horse trappings, daggers, wood and silver bowls, yak tails, etc.

Zhongdian's Tibetans are a contented people, outgoing, friendly and gracious to guests. The Khambas in general are the most gregarious branch of the Tibetans and known as men of action. Rather than shy away from the strangers they often prefer to engage with them. They are thus one of the easiest people in the province to approach and befriend.

The Monasteries

Like other Tibetan peoples, the Khampas of Deqing Prefecture have always been very religious-minded. Monasteries, great and small, have been restored in recent years and are once again playing an active role in the life of the people. The most splendid of these, Guihua Temple, sits on top of the knoll, 5 km north of Zhongdian, that is the site of the monastic village of Songzhanlin. Several smaller monasteries and temples, including one old one sponsored by the former Mu rulers of Lijiang, lie on the rather steep southern slope of the knoll. The road to the top bends to the left, keeping these sacred buildings to the right, as per Tibetan custom, rounds a big chorten (Tibetan pagoda) and ends behind the Guihua Monastery.

Several older monks live in the compound, while dozens of robed novices spend the daylight hours here but retire at night to nearby home villages or in quarters outside the compound in Songzhanlin. Recitations and chanting of scriptures take place regularly three times a day, while novices sometimes hold afternoon debates on doctrine in one of the courtyards.

The colour red dominates the interior furnishings—the posts, rafters, upstairs doors, benches, cushions and of course the robes of the monks. Silk banners and *thangkas* (religious scroll paintings) hang from the rafters and ceiling. Tibetan deities line the altar tables. And in front of them the devotees have placed associated religious paraphernalia, such as butter lamps, barley dough figurines, small lion and elephant sculptures, bronze bells and *vajras* (stylized thunderbolts), and portraits of famous lamas. The exterior facades are covered with fresh, brightly painted religious imagery, in the classic, fanciful Tibetan style.

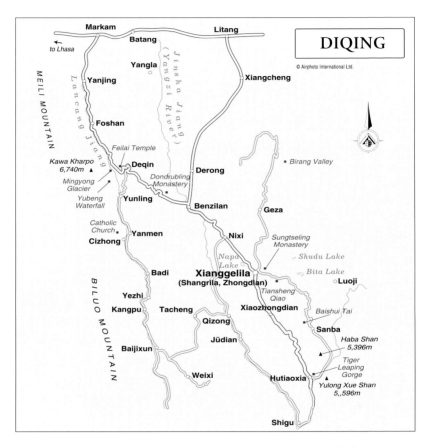

The other major Khamba monastery in Yunnan is **Dongzhulin**, 105 km northwest of Zhongdian, in the mountains above Benzilan. The original was destroyed in 1959 and this new version sited on a ridge closer to the main road. The main hall is not as big as Guihuasi's, nor as fancy inside, but its exterior murals are equally superb. Small, boxlike quarters, with whitewashed walls and flat roofs, house Dongzhulin's monks. No views of snow peaks from here, just steep, rocky cliffs with little villages at the bottom, but it probably makes an appropriate setting for those who wish to pursue a life of contemplation.

Smaller temple compounds, with at least a handful of resident monks, add to the religious life of Zhongdian County. On the hill behind the southwest quarter of Zhongdian's old town sits **White Chicken Temple** (*Baijisi*), a modest compound, also recently restored, quiet, intimate, and affording from the hill a great view all around. Somewhat larger, 10 km south of Zhongdian, is **Dabaosi**, a charming little temple on top of a wooded knoll. The entrance path is lined with chortens made of piles of *mani* stones—flat stones inscribed with the Tibetan prayer *om mani padme hum*. Prayer flags hang on the branches of nearby trees.

Like Songzhanlin, Dongzhulin and nearly every monastery, the monks belong to the Yellow Hat (*Gelukpa*) sect. But in the northern part of Zhongdian, Chengen Temple is home to Nyingmapa (Red Hat) monks, an older sect.

The other major temple compound outside Zhongdian lies just inside Weixi County, southwest of the capital. Named **Damo Temple** after an Indian disciple of Gautama Siddartha who spent ten years in the cave here before achieving Enlightenment, it was originally constructed in 1662. The spectacular masked lama dances that are an annual feature of the biggest monasteries are staged here in the fourth lunar month. Elsewhere they are winter events, held at Guihuasi at the end of the 11th lunar month and at Dongzhulin a month later.

Known locally as Gedong, the festival is the most important religious rite of the year. The elaborately costumed dances narrate a battle between the gods and the demons. The choreography is often ponderously slow, but has sequences where the performers spin around and wave their weapons. The masks themselves are works of art, wonderfully detailed, bright and grotesque. As Tibetan protective deities often assume fierce and dreadful aspects when duelling the forces of evil, it may be difficult for the uninitiated to tell the good guys from the bad, so to speak, for horrific-looking characters dance on both sides of the battle lines.

THE HORSE RACES

By the beginning of the 5th lunar month the Tibetans have finished sowing their fields. Work is slight until the rains come, nourish the crops and make the valuable mushrooms sprout in the forests. But Tibetans are busy all the same, not in the fields but at home, preparing for the great social event of the year—Saimajie, the Horse Racing Festival, staged on the 5th and 6th days of the month. Folk from all parts of the prefecture attend: Tibetans from sundry directions, even as far away as Batang and Litang in Sichuan, Naxi from Baishuitai, Lisu from Weixi, Yi from the mountains south of Zhongdian, and local Bai, Naxi, Hui and Han.

Much of the preparation, beyond riding practice, focuses on making a properly stunning appearance. New silks are cut into blouses, heirloom jewellery brought out, swords sharpened, ponies dressed up, fine old carpets cleaned and the best copperware and silver-inlaid cups and bowls polished up for the coming picnic. Capacious tents start going up around the festival site, which is in the lap of Wufengshan, a few km south of Zhongdian. Events there run in the morning and afternoon, with a long break for lunch, so families hold a feast in their tents, with meat, vegetables, snacks, fruits, jiu and plenty of buttered tea, dining on the carpets.

In the late 1990s, a new track was constructed for the festival, with a more sophisticated grandstand than the single set of bleachers in the past. Ethnic dances precede the equestrian show, beginning with an abbreviated version of the New Year masked dances. Troupes from different townships perform next, including dongba dancers from Baishuitai and local middle school troupes. When this pageantry concludes the horse show commences.

First comes a display of local horsemanship, always including a couple of female jockeys, who later pair off in their own separate race. Then four ponies advance to the starting line for the first heat. Their riders, sometimes mounted bareback, use quirts to spur them on, but Tibetan ponies are temperamental. The race is supposed to be three laps around the track, but of the four competing ponies, never do all of them complete the race. Usually two make a contest out of it, one never gets beyond a trot, while the fourth wanders off the track and refuses to run at all, to the great amusement of the crowd.

(above) Equestrian skills on display at the Horse Races.
(right) The village of Benzilan, the main town between Zhongdian and Deqing.

After a number of heats the racing takes a break and on come the individual jockeys to show off another kind of riding skill. Urging on their ponies to a full gallop they then lean way over to one side to snatch one of the white scarves laid out on the track at regular intervals. This can be exciting to witness when the pony's on a full run, but again, Tibetan ponies don't always respond to the rider's urging. A few will barely work up any speed, providing mirthful interludes in the show.

Races resume in the afternoon and all next day, though only one or two dance troupes will perform the second morning. Instead, a traditional Tibetan opera, in full costume, will be staged on the open ground near the track. In the city, besides the general bazaar scene, the streets at night are full of different groups of young Tibetans, singing and dancing, right through the traffic interruptions, until the wee hours of the morning. And the air of romance pervading these groups is all but palpable.

DEQING MOUNTAINS AND VALLEYS

Past Songzhanlin, at the northern end of Zhongdian plain, lies the small lake called **Napahai**. A broad flat pasture lies on its southern side, while hills rise behind its northern and eastern shores. Often the lake shrinks to within the lap of these hills, leaving spongy ground spreading south of it. After the rains it is larger, but shallow and, compared to Bitahai and Shudouhai, not all that pretty. However, twice a year flocks of black-necked cranes make a stopover here on their migration routes.

North of Napahai the landscape starts changing. From here on it is rugged high mountain country, dry and steep. The few villages in the valleys are small, as are their farms, without the great drying racks, but with lots more sheep and goats. The road winds down to the right bank of the Jinshajiang to **Benzilan**, the main town between Zhongdian and Deqing. The commercial area is along the main road, the residential area down below, on a riverside plateau.

From Benzilan the road zigzags up the mountain, to where one can see the Jinshajiang far below almost loop a small pinnacle in its path. The road then starts heading northwest, past Dongzhulin, towards Deqing. Houses in the area, unlike Zhongdian's, look more like fortresses, perhaps influenced by the lawlessness of the area's not too distant past.

Not long after Dongzhulin the inhabited area ends and the road ascends a little higher into the forests and soon crosses the high pastures of **Baimangshan**. A vast forest preserve of high mountains, its pastures are the grazing grounds for yaks in the summer months. Nomad herders erect temporary tents and cabins for the season, taking the animals back down the mountain when the snow begins to fall.

Another 30 km and the snow peaks of Taizishan and Meili Xueshan become visible. But then the road turns into a high valley and drops a little into the suburbs of **Deqing** city. This is a largely modernized town occupying opposing slopes above a small stream that flows into the Lancangjiang just around the mountain. Deqing has a lively market each morning, which becomes an open-air snooker stadium in the afternoon. The shops in the business district cater to the traditional tastes of the Tibetans, who comprise the great majority of the city's inhabitants. Carpets, fox fur hats, woollen blankets, swords and daggers, animal hides and skulls, silver ornaments and coral, turquoise and amber jewellery are on sale here.

A high road north out of Deqing leads to **Dong village**, from where the snow peaks are visible again. A little further on, chortens and strings of pennants and prayer flags mark the lookout point from where Meili Snow Mountain, its companion peaks and the glacier that slides down its southeastern face are visible in all their full glory.

From here the road follows the Lancangjiang straight north to the Tibetan border. The river cuts a deep gorge here, wriggling around promontories and slipping between steep, bald cliffs with streaks of mauve, purple, rust-brown and silvery blue colouring the rock. Occasional chortens by the road, flanked by tall poles with fluttering prayer flags, mark the spots where fatal accidents have occurred.

Besides Tibetan communities, a few villages are Naxi, descendants of frontier garrisons in imperial days. The last settlement in Yunnan is **Xidu**, 94 km north of Deqing and 9 km south of Yanjing, the first town in Tibet Province. The villages are by no means as poor as one might expect for such a remote location. At **Naigu**, for example, a picturesque settlement above the road, with a chorten mounted on a hill within the village perimeter, most houses are new structures. And a large percentage of them have satellite dishes on their rooftops.

Back in Deqing a road winds out of the lower part of town and around gorges cut by streams slowing into the Lancangjiang. The snow peaks of Meili and Taizi are visible at intervals. About 20 km south the road runs through three short tunnels. At the end of the last one the Lancangjiang is first visible and for the next 10 km to the settlement of Yunling makes eight distinct bends (Lancangjiang means 'Winding River' in Chinese). Gradually the snow peaks are no longer visible as the road follows the left bank of the river south.

Occasionally streams and waterfalls on the right bank slice through steep cliffs, while monasteries perch precariously on knolls above the river. Strings of prayer flags run from one side of the river to the other. **Yanmen**, the last major township in the county, 75 km south of Deqing, marks a change in

The Land of the Blue Poppy

The Mekong Valley

The weather had now set in fine, and nothing could have been more delightful than these marches up the Mekong valley, for we took matters fairly easily, making four stages from Hsiao-wei-hsi to Tsu-kou. Sometimes the narrow path was enveloped in the shade of flowering shrubs and walnut trees, the branches breasting us as we rode, the air sweetened by the scent of roses which swept in cascades of yellow flowers over the summits of trees thirty feet high; sometimes we plunged into a deep limestone gorge, its cliffs festooned with ferns and orchids, our caravan climbing up by rough stone steps which zigzagged backwards and forwards till we were out of ear-shot of the rapids in the river below; sometimes the path was broken altogether by a scree-shoot, which, dangerous as it looked, the mules walked across very calmly, though sending rocks grinding and sliding down through the trees into the river.

In one gorge through which we passed, large pot-holes were visible across the river between winter and summer water marks and yet others still higher up, forming a conspicuous feature of the otherwise smooth bare cliffs which dipped sheer into the river; but on the left or shaded bank dense vegetation prevailed wherever tree, shrub, or rock-plant could secure a foothold. The further north we went the more rich and varied became the vegetation of the rainy belt, though the paucity of forest trees, except deep down in the gullies, was always conspicuous.

Shales and slates, dipping at very high angles, and often vertical, alternated with limestone, through which the river had cut its way straight downwards; but at one spot, where an enormous rapid had been formed, huge boulders of a dark-green volcanic rock, like lava, with large included fragments, lined the shore and were piled in confusion below cliffs of slate.

It is at sunset that the charm of this wonderful valley is displayed at its best, for the sun having dropped out of sight behind the western range still sends shafts of coloured light pulsing down the valley, rose, turquoise, and pale-green slowly chasing each other across the sky till darkness sets in and the stars sparkle gloriously. It is long after dawn when the sleeping valley wakens to floods of sunlight again, and the peaks which stand setinel over it, blotting out the views to north and south, lose the ghastly grey pallor of dimly-lit snow.

A Tibetan Festival

The Tibetan festival itself seemed more in accord with the usages of nat propitiation than with lamaism, except that it was eminently cheerful, and the people, led by their priests, went to the summits of the three nearest hills to east, north, and west in turn, in order to burn incense and pray; after which they ate cakes. The first day however was devoted entirely to the amusement of the children, for Tibetan mothers, as I frequently observed, are warm-hearted creatures with a great affection for their offspring.

Dressed in their best frocks, and wearing all the family jewels brought out for the occasion, they went up into the woods in the afternoon, picked bunches of flowers just as English children love to do, romped, made swings and swung each other, and finally sat down to eat cakes, which they had been busily making for a week past.

Just as the young of different animals more nearly resemble each other than do the adults, so too are children very much alike in their games the world over; picnicking is not confined to Hampstead Heath, nor picking flowers to botanists.

In the evening they all trooped back to the village to dance in the mule square, and skip. Three of four little girls would link arms and facing another similar line of girls advance and retreat by turns, two steps and a kick, singing, in spite of their harsh voices, a not unmusical chorus; the other side would then reply, and so it went on, turn and turn about.

The Last of the Mekong

This was the last we were destined to see of the great Mekong river. I was scarcely sorry to say goodbye, for the Mekong gorge—one long ugly rent between mountains which grow more and more arid, more and more savage as we travel northwards (yet hardly improve as we travel southwards)—is an abnormality, a grim freak of nature, a thing altogether out of place. Perhaps I had not been sufficiently ill-used by this extraordinary river to have a deep affection for it. The traveller, buffeted and bruised by storm and mountain, cherishes most the foe worthy of his steel. Nevertheless there was a strange fascination about its olive-green water in winter, its boiling red floods in summer, and the everlasting thunder of its rapids. And its peaceful little villages, some of them hidden away in the dips between the hills, others straggling over sloping alluvial fans or perched up on some ancient river-terrace where scattered blocks of stone suggest the decay of a ruined civilization—all these oases break the depressing monotony of naked rock and ill-nourished vegetation, delighting the eye with the beauty of their verdure and the richness of their crops.

Happy people! What do they know of the strife and turmoil of the western world? We wear ourselves out saving time in one direction that we may waste it in another, hurrying and ever hurrying through time as if we were disgusted with life, but these people think of time not in miles an hour but according to the rate at which their crops grow in the spring, and their fruits ripen in the autumn. They work that they and their families may have enough to eat and enough to wear, living and dying where they were born, where their offspring will live and die after them, as did their ancestors before them, shut in by the mountains which bar access from the outer world.

Frank Kingdon Ward, *Himalayan Enchantment*,
Serindia Publications, London, 1990

Baishui, or White Water Creek, takes its name from the colour of the stones in its bed.

architectural style, away from Tibetan towards Naxi type housing. This is even more evident a few km south, across the bridge to Cizhong, site of the Tibetan Catholic church, now a protected state historical monument.

At **Cizhong**, a large, mostly Tibetan village above the riverbank, the houses more closely resemble the rural Naxi houses of Lijiang County. But one detail reflects the Christian nature of the community. At the apex of the roofs the suspended pair of carved fish, representing water as a defence against fire and lightning, that adorns houses in Lijiang County, have been substituted. Instead there hang painted doves—symbols of the Christian Holy Spirit.

XIAOLIANGSHAN YI VILLAGES

With the Naxi settling in the valleys and lower slopes of the mountains, and the Tibetans occupying the high plateau, it is the Yi who live in the areas between them. Those who live in Zhongdian and Lijiang Counties are part of the same branch of the Yi who are the majority of the inhabitants of Ninglang Yi Autonomous County. Northeast of Lijiang, this highland territory is part of the range called Xiaoliangshan, the Lesser Cool Mountains, as distinguished from Daliangshan, the Greater Cool Mountains, to the east in Sichuan. Ninglang's Yi migrated from Daliangshan a few centuries ago and their language, traditions and costumes are very similar. They both call themselves *Nosu*, or *Nusu* (depending on dialect differences).

Rising shortly after Yongsheng, a bustling Han city in a rich valley, the road climbs into the mountains, crossing ever higher ranges, then descends into the long plain at Ninglang, the county seat. The city lies along one main avenue, flanked on the east by a narrow, flat strip of farmland to the river and on the left by high hills. The population is mostly Yi, the market active every day. A new museum above the western side of the main road displays handicrafts, Yi alphabet manuscripts and other items of local cultural interest.

After passing a Mosuo village just north of the city, the road ascends again, crossing two more valleys, before making the last climb over the last high pass before the descent to Lugu Lake and Yongning district. Mountains rise on both sides and Yi villages are sited both high and low. Mosuo and Pumi villages lie at lower elevations, mostly near Ninglang and Xinyingpan, while the villages in the last valley south of Lugu Lake have mixed populations—Yi, Mosuo and Pumi.

Log cabins, with roofs of shingles held down by stones, characterise the traditional Yi village architecture. But in some of the wealthier areas the Yi have switched to typical Yunnanese rural houses of brick or rammed earth as the main building material. Houses are usually surrounded by a fenced yard and lie

A Tibetan gentleman.

a bit more apart from each other than in Naxi or Tibetan villages. Jinzigou, in the central part of the county, is the largest settlement, with over a hundred houses. But usually Yi villages are less than half that size. Some Yi families live practically alone in their areas, like the yak herders on top of **Medicine Mountain** (*Yaoshan*), a day's hike uphill north of **Jinzigou**, and the site of several small lakes.

Except in the lower valleys, where rice can be cultivated, the Yi raise potatoes, buckwheat, peppercorn, maize and a few vegetables. Buckwheat bread is often the main filler at a meal. Semi-pastoral, the highland Yi tend flocks of goats and sheep and shear the latter for their wool, which they turn into the felted or woven long capes both sexes wear in the cold weather. A couple of luckier villages in the eastern mountains derive an income from gold or silver mines. And in recent years an apple business has brought new income to Yi around Xinyingpan.

Xiaoliangshan Yi are one of the proudest and most conservative branches of the Yi nationality. Every sizable village has a resident *bimaw*, or ritual specialist, who conducts rites, divination and fortune-telling with the aid of ancient books inscribed in the Yi language. Domestic relationships are carried out strictly according to custom.

Most females don the traditional garments. These comprise a long, pleated skirt in three or four wide, brightly coloured sections, a black velvet vest over a long-sleeved blouse, a sash belt with a long fringed end dangling in front and a triangular purse with long tails attached to the belt. Unmarried girls wear an embroidered flat cap, held in place by her braids, or a large, rounded black one with bright trimming. Married women's hats are bigger, plain black, with right-angled corners. Men's traditional clothing consists of wide-legged trousers, plain jacket, black turban and the cape, which, like the women, they fasten around the neck.

THE TORCH FESTIVAL AND THE COUNTY FAIR

Like most Yi, those in Ninglang County make a big affair out of the Torch Festival. The Ninglang city government sponsors a public spectacle in the central stadium. Singers and dancers from the Yi, Mosuo, Pumi, Tibetan and Han nationalities perform on stage before the crowd. The show may include a *huhu* player. This is a brass mouth harp of three or four leaves, each producing a single, separate note, and some girls can play incredibly intricate and melodious tunes with it.

The sets conclude and bonfires are lit in the square. A number of Yi parade around with torches held aloft. Youth form ring dances which soon so fill up the area they turn into sinuous lines that weave in and out of each other. Flutes at the front, the dancers sing traditional, typically merry Yi dancing songs. Bigger villages in the mountains stage their own shows around bonfires in the main square and in the highlands northeast of Ninglang several village dance troupes compete in a daytime contest. Pony races and combat between bulls or goats augment the programme.

In recent years an Apple Festival has been held, usually in Xinyingpan in September, to celebrate Ninglang County's newest industry. Naturally, singing and dancing are part of the programme. A bigger, older event takes place in Ninglang city the week beginning 20 November—the Ninglang County Fair. This draws thousands of Yi visitors from all around, plus the Mosuo, Pumi, Lisu and Bai in the vicinity.

Besides the evening entertainment on the first two nights, the Fair is the venue for much market activity, including the sale of Yi clothing, Yi language books and music tapes, herbal medicines, horse trappings, tools, etc. The government puts up advisory posters on health and animal husbandry, plus agricultural displays. A field (sometimes a hill) beside the city is set aside as a large horse and mule market. Their highland owners put up with the repeated teeth and hooves inspections of potential buyers and camp with their animals for the week.

LUGU LAKE

From the high pastures above Zhifan, where the Torch Festival dance contest is held, or from the lakes on the summit of Yaoshan, range after range of Xiaoliangshan unfolds towards every horizon. The real jewel of the county, though, lies in its northernmost district of Yongning, visible soon after crossing the last pass coming up from Ninglang. This is Lugu Lake, a 52 km square, butterfly-shaped body of water with the most gorgeous natural setting in the province.

The smaller, eastern wing of the lake, most of Tubu Peninsula, the long finger of land that nearly cuts Lugu in two, and a small part of the larger wing, on a line to the Naxi village of Dazui on the northern shore, belong to Sichuan. The greater part of the lake, three of the five offshore islands, and the majestic Lion Mountain that towers over the northern shore, belong to Yunnan.

Lugu Lake lies at an altitude of 2,700 metres, with the summit of Lion Mountain another 900 metres higher. The water averages 40 metres in depth, in some places reaching 90 metres, making it Yunnan's second deepest lake. Its surface reflects the colour of the sky; a deep blue on clear days, steel grey on cloudy days, sometimes streaked with sunrise bands of red and purple, or checkered with the rose and yellow that bounces off the clouds at dusk. Villages occupy the small, flat strips of land in between the shoreline hills while various peninsulas jut out far enough to create small, picturesque coves. The prettiest village of them all, Lige on the northwest side of the lake, lies on the shore of one such cove, with a small peninsular mound protruding into the lake at the far end of the village.

Fishing, of course, plays a major role in the life of Lugu Lake villagers. It's men's work and they use dugout canoes exclusively on the water, a custom the locals date back to the origin of Lugu Lake. Once upon a time, they say, a settled valley existed here. One day a man spotted an enormous fish stuck in a hole in the big rock off the shore between Xiaoluoshui and Dazui, at the Sichuan border. Unable to pull it out himself he called on his comrades, who hitched up the fish to a team of water buffaloes.

When the animals yanked the fish from the hole, a torrent of water gushed out, quickly flooding the valley. One Mosuo woman, who was feeding her pigs at the time, saw the flood coming, kicked the pigs away and emptied the trough. In it she placed a boy and a girl, just before the water swept her away, along with everything else in the valley. But the trough stayed afloat and the children survived to become the ancestors of the Mosuo, who have used the pig trough shape for their boats ever since.

(above) Lige Village extends along a peninsula into Lugu Lake.
(right) Mosuo girls pose in front of April blossoms along the shore of the lake.

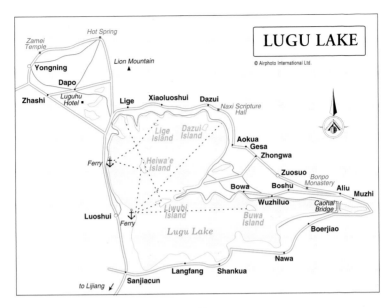

THE MOSUO AND PUMI OF YONGNING

Beyond Lugu Lake the road rises into the Yongning Basin, 100 metres higher than lakeside, and proceeds to Yongning town. This is a largely Mosuo settlement with a small Naxi quarter of Lijiang tanners who migrated here in the late Qing Dynasty. The great lamasery of **Zhameisi**, restored in the mid-90s, sits in a field just beyond the town. Yi and Pumi often come to the market here. And with the log cabins on the muddy lane that serves as the main thoroughfare, the Yi women in long skirts and big hats, and the ponies tied to the rails until they're picked up for the road, Yongning's atmosphere evokes the American West of a century ago.

From the small hill behind the town the whole length of Lion Mountain is visible. From this angle it does indeed resemble a seated lion. Far beyond the plain the snow peaks of western Sichuan loom on the horizon. One road out of Yongning heads north to Wenquan, a small village with a famous hot spring. In the old days men and women bathed in it together. But in recent years a bathhouse has been constructed, dividing the spring by sex. The other road branches northwest to Laba township, home of several ethnic groups, especially Lisu, Pumi and Zhuang.

Lugu Lake has been touted as the homeland of the Mosuo people, but, counting the Sichuan side, only half a dozen Mosuo villages lie on its shore. The plain around Yongning holds far more, though except for the absence of

Mosuo at Luoshui draw water from Lugu Lake for their domestic needs.
Lion Mountain looms in the distance.

fishing the architecture, lifestyle, farming, religion and society is the same. The Mosuo, and their less numerous Pumi neighbours, follow the Yellow Hat (*Gelukpa*) sect of Tibetan Buddhism, having been converted in the 16th century. But the deity they revere most is Goddess Ganmo, incarnated in Lion Mountain, whose paramount importance reflects the most salient feature of Mosuo culture—their matrilineality.

Not all Mosuo are matrilineal. The families of the former ruling clan, descended from Kubilai Khan's Mongol officers and the smallest of Mosuo clans, are patrilineal. So are the Mosuo further south, in the low-lying valleys of Ninglang County. But matrilineality is the norm in Yongning district. The women own the property—the house, big animals and the farms—and pass it on to daughters. And if they don't have a daughter, they'll adopt one of their sister's. All children owe their loyalty to their natal home until death, even the males, who maintain their residence there and contribute their labour to their mother's household even when 'married'.

One must use quotation marks around the word because the Mosuo don't really have marriages. Nor is there a word for it in their own language. When speaking of a non-Mosuo's marriage, they will use the Chinese words. When Mosuo establish a conjugal relationship, the man comes to the woman's house at night, for every mature Mosuo female has her own room in the family compound. He returns to his own house in the morning. All children belong to the mother, even if the relationship is terminated. Nor is the man expected to donate any child support.

The system, called by outsiders 'walking marriage', may at first seem to be inherently unstable, due to the lack of obligations in the relationship. But in a matrilineal society stability is more important in the maternal household than in the relationships between conjugal partners. In that respect the system has served the Mosuo well and survived repeated campaigns against it before the reform period, after which no one tried to oppose it.

Men, therefore, are very much in the background. They have their work roles, for they do most of the house construction, the ploughing, the long-distance trade and the fishing. But the woman's load is heavier and more constant. Men handle religious affairs, and every household has its monk who attends to its religious rites. Yet the major festival of the year, *Zhuanshanjie* (Rounding the Mountain Festival), held on the 25th day of the 7th lunar month, is in honour of Goddess Ganmo. All the minor festivals, plus the New Year events, when the young girls and boys have their rites of maturity, include Ganmo worship.

Mosuo and Pumi from all over Yongning district hike to a slope on Lion Mountain for Zhuanshanjie. And from Zhamei Monastery monks come to perform rites, beat drums and blow long alpine horns. The crowd ascends the slope to Ganmo's shrine, where they kowtow and deposit prayer flags. Afterwards they form small groups and picnic on the grass, then walk home. At night, perhaps still dressed in traditional costume—Tibetan style for the men, long white skirts, velour or silk jackets and braided turban for the women—they form a ring and sing and dance around a bonfire.

Mosuo women sing often—while rowing boats, gathering

(right) Mosuo puberty rite. At puberty a Mosuo girl ceremonially dons a long skirt for the first time. Henceforth she will be treated as an adult.

Mosuo women, as owners and heiresses of the family property, radiate more self-confidence than most minority women. Mosuo sisters prepare corn for a meal. Sisters in Mosuo society have an especially close relationship.

fodder, walking back from the fields, riding buses—whenever the urge strikes them. Their distinctive, high-pitched tunes are unlike any other and when sung at Lugu Lake the wonderful acoustics there carries them across the water. The repertoire is not unusually extensive, and a few songs have been added in recent years, yet they never tire of singing the same old songs.

It should be noted, however, that as with so many other beautiful locations that have become popular tourist destinations, tradition and local culture must now exist alongside and compete with modern influences such as karaoke, TV and Western ideals far removed from Mosou culture. Modern China, for better or worse, has reached the shores of Lugu Lake.

In terms of culture, lifestyle, appearance, even character, the Pumi of Yongning are scarcely distinguishable from the Mosuo. Sometimes several Pumi families will take up residence in a largely Mosuo village (or Yi village further south), but several villages, such as **Upper Luoshui** on the south shore road at Lugu Lake, the bigger settlements around **Wenquan** and a few in **Laba** township, are more or less exclusively **Pumi**. Their language differs considerably from Mosuo and while they venerate Ganmo as they mark the Mosuo festival calendar they do stage one big, uniquely Pumi festival in late summer.

This is held in honour of their mountain deity Suoguonaba, who resides on **Yak Hill**, the mountain just south of Lugu Lake. Local Pumi either hike up the mountain on festival day or delegate someone to do it for them. Before going up that morning the participants call on those they will represent and receive barley cakes to take along. Pumi believe that all the effects of spirits and bad karma will cling to these cakes and be absorbed by them. When left at Suoguonaba's altar all bad fortune is left there as well and the souls of the living have been purified.

Ninglang County's other sizable minority is the Lisu, of two sub-groups. A few Lisu villages lie in Laba township, northwest of Lugu Lake, but their material culture differs little from the norm in the district. The women dress similarly, except that on special occasions they wear an elaborate headdress. At such times the men, whose clothing resembles the Tibetans', may don big fur hats and vests.

Southeast of Ninglang the string of Lisu villages west of Wukai, in Fuyangping township, use rammed earth as the basic housing material and raise maize as their staple. Men like to wear goatskin vests over their otherwise ordinary clothes. Women dress like their Pumi and Mosuo neighbours: long skirt (sometimes of pleated hemp cloth), wide striped sash belts, side-fastened jackets, but with turbans rather than thickened and coiled braids.

DAYAO COUNTY

Lisu also inhabit the somewhat lower mountains south of Xiaoliangshan in Yongsheng and Huaping Counties. In Yongsheng their villages are mainly in the mountains on the right bank of the Jinshajiang, west of the county seat. Occasionally they can be seen near the bridge that crosses into Lijiang County, the women in long skirts of alternating blue and white pleats and black turbans. No one ever visits them.

In Huaping County a cluster of Christian Lisu villages lie in the hills of Lagahe township, northwest of the county seat. Their women wear one of the most attractive of the many Lisu costumes. The long pleated skirt, mostly maroon in colour, is fastened with a wide sash belt and worn with a colourful, side-fastened jacket, heavily embroidered on the cuffs, shoulders and lapel. Topping it off, they don a bright, round turban, with pendants of pearls dangling all around.

The Jinshajiang is the boundary for both Yongsheng and Huaping Counties with northwestern Chuxiong Prefecture. Ferries operate on Sundays at a crossing point several km west of **Wanbi**, the Dai riverside township at the northern limit of Dayao County. The mountains on either side of the river are big and barren, the flow quite swift and the thin, low-lying plateau on the right bank, where the Dai have settled, doesn't extend very far. Dai houses resemble those of their Yi neighbours to the south, which are basically of the standard Yunnanese rural style.

Wanbi is quite isolated, for most of Dayao County, even its mountain townships, is accessed from the south, via Nanhua on the Chuxiong-Dali route. Turning north here, the road ascends in three major stages before entering Dayao, 81 km north of Nanhua. The town is nearly all Han-inhabited, for the area was one of the earliest in Yunnan to have a continuous Han administration. **Yao'an**, 35 km south, was a Tang dynasty administrative centre of some importance until absorbed by Nanzhao in the 8th century.

Nothing of the Nanzhao era survives in Yao'an today. The town's old quarter is largely Hui. But Dayao boasts a pagoda from that era, famous for its unusual shape. Known both as the **White Pagoda**, for its colour, and the **Bell Stick Pagoda**, for its resemblance to the stick used to strike bells in a Buddhist temple, it sits atop a knoll beside the town and is visible as soon as one enters the plain from the south. Rising from an octagonal platform to a height of 18 metres, this solidly built pagoda has stood erect through major earthquakes, with its only scar a one-metre-long crack near the top.

The county's other major religious relic is the great bronze Confucius statue housed in **Shiyang** township, 36 km west of Dayao. Weighing around

(following pages) Market day at Santai in Dayao County.

1,000 kg, the 2.5-metre-high image of the seated sage, crowned and holding a tablet, is the only extant bronze Confucius in mainland China.

Shiyang, which means Stone Ram, is named after a stone ram allegedly found long ago when the great salt well in the middle of the town was being dug. It has an attractive location in a narrow valley, with old-fashioned buildings for the most part and little cave-pens for the pigs in the side of the hill. A Buddhist temple sits on the slope of the south bank hill. About 3 km east a hill just off the road has several Daoist shrines, some in small caves, with strange-looking statues, like the one of a man peeling off his face to reveal another, different one underneath.

THE PEOPLE IN GOATSKINS

Every Sunday Dayao stages its open market. As elsewhere, the townsfolk set up early. The villagers begin streaming in by mid-morning, by noon the city is packed and in late afternoon folks start going home. Most of those in attendance will be Han from the surrounding plain, but a sizable percentage will be Yi from the nearby mountains. Yi women here usually wear a colourful, long-sleeved blouse, with flowery embroidery along the shoulders, cuffs and lapel. Over this is a wide bib covering the chest and midriff, fastened in back with a belt with its embroidered ends dangling over the buttocks. Ordinary trousers and shoes complete the outfit, except for the headgear, which is a black turban with embroidered ends, fitted over a skullcap studded with silver buttons or cowry shells.

Men dress Han-style. Both sexes wear long goatskin vests and carry bright, fully embroidered shoulder bags with lots of tassels. Sometimes, like market days, they carry two or three of these bags. The vests are made from the skins of two goats, expertly stitched together, hang open in front, and last for many years. They wear them almost constantly all year round. In the cooler months they tend to wear the fur side against the body and the leather side out. When it rains they reverse the vest and wear the fur side out.

The northern part of Dayao County is dominated by mountains, the biggest being the 3,657-metre-high Tanhuashan. The Yi live on the slope of this and neighbouring mountains, raising rice, maize, wheat, potatoes, hemp and walnuts. They also keep flocks of goats and other animals. The walnuts are the best in Yunnan, especially the thin-shelled variety from Tiesuo, on Tanhuashan's western slopes. Most townships in the mountains hold weekly market days. Some merchants come up from Dayao or Shiyang, but most people in attendance, buying and selling, are Yi. Costumes may vary slightly from one township to another, the goatskins being the one item common to all.

But women in one small sub-group, in villages near Dacun in Guihua township, north of Tanhua, wear a costume totally different and unique in the region. The women's costume comprises a chicken-shaped, red-trimmed, black cloth cap with beaded tassels, skirt, long jacket and leggings. The skirt is black with appliquéd stripes in different colours. But the jacket is quite special. On the reverse rows of geometric-like patterns are arranged according to a code that tells the family history of the woman wearing it. Traditionally, the woman must be wearing the jacket when she is buried.

CHAHUAJIE: PUTTING UP FLOWERS

Dayao County Yi celebrate the Torch Festival and observe the major Han festivals like New Year, Qing Ming, etc, in the Han style. Some of the sub-groups also hold their own individual festivals. The most colourful of these is Fuzhuangjie, the Dressing Up Festival (sometimes called the Yi Fashion Show) at Santai on the 28th day of the 3rd lunar month. Santai Yi women already wear the brightest blouses in the area, with a heavy accent on gold silk. For this affair they don the most elaborately embroidered one they have and add several silk aprons in front, each slightly smaller and of a different hue than the one underneath. In the evening they give over to singing and dancing.

Festivals like Santai's attract only the Yi of the township in which it is staged. And for the Torch Festival each village has its own programme. But the one event that draws Yi from all corners of the county is Chahuajie, or Putting up Flowers, held on the 8th day of the 2nd month in a grove above Tanhua township. This festival honours the mythical Yi heroine Miyilu. At least two versions are in circulation concerning the death of Miyilu. Around Zixi Mountain near Chuxiong the Yi say that long ago a wicked lord kept demanding young Yi women for his depraved pleasure. Miyilu offered herself in marriage, but killed the tyrant after the wedding and fled. The lord's kin caught up with her and slew her under a white camellia tree. Her blood stained the tree's roots and ever since then its flowers have been red.

The Dayao version is the same up to the point Miyilu, with an azalea in her hair, promises to marry the tyrant. To toast her betrothal she offers to drink wine with him. But she has already dropped the poisonous flower into the wine and when the tyrant drinks with her they both die.

Dressed in their finest Yi costume, the women stick camellias and azaleas over their doorways before going to the grove for the official events. After rituals conducted by the local bimaw, a special programme of song and dance follows. Then the Yi break up into groups for picnics and the making of floral wreaths. Feasting, dancing and entertainment ensue. The evening party features rings of Yi youths, the boys playing the dragon-headed, round 'moon guitar', the girls singing with high-pitched, undulating voices. Dancing continues until everyone is tired. That could be long past midnight.

The Highway to Burma: Baoshan and Dehong

THE BURMA ROAD

Nowadays the new road from Kunming to Ruili, in Dehong Prefecture on the border with Myanmar 832 km away, takes less than 20 hours by sleeper bus. Only a few years ago it took nearly double the time. The new road, cut and paved over a slightly different route, is a modern, four-lane highway. The old road followed the ancient mule train track, the fabled Southwest Silk Route. Mostly cobbled rather than paved, two lanes all the way, its traffic included everything from private cars and public buses to tractor-trailers, horse carts, big logging trucks and so forth.

In the past it was even slower. European explorers in the 19th century complained about its surface and wherever possible preferred to walk on the shoulder of the road. One good reason for governments in dynastic days not to maintain the road in good condition was the fact that trade along the route was intermittent, subject to banditry and dependent upon the political power of the prospective trade partners. When the Chinese government was strong and able to extend its influence to remote areas, and when some form of stability

(above) A typical Yi village.
(right) Two kinds of Yi live in the northern part of Dayao County around Guihua. Their language and customs are the same but the women's costumes differ considerably.

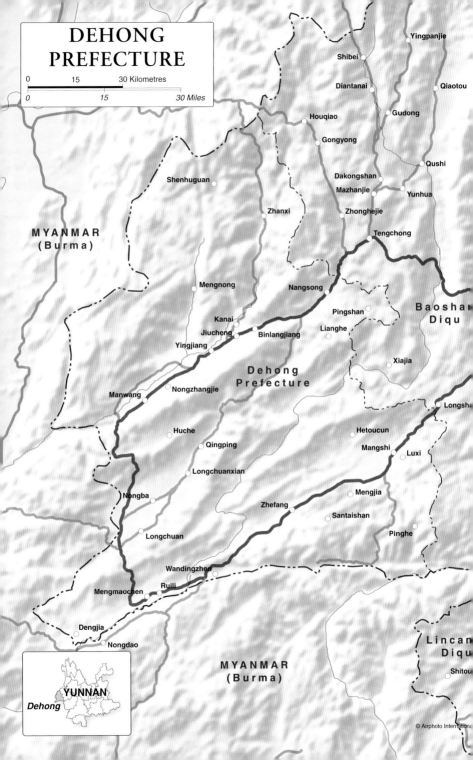

existed in northern Burma, commerce developed and the route was protected. When these conditions failed, long-distance trade ceased, not being worth the risk.

In 1937 the Japanese Army, having occupied eastern China, began blockading shipments to western China, where the Nationalist government had relocated. The old Silk Route assumed new importance. The government at once began conscripting the local population along the route, mainly ethnic minorities, to build a new road connecting Kunming with the border town of Wanding in southwest Dehong. So long as the British held Burma hundreds of vehicles, coming up from Bhamo and Lashio, crossed the bridge at Wanding, delivering thousands of tons of supplies daily.

It was not an easy task, especially since it was done under emergency pressures. Hundreds of labourers lost their lives in landslides and construction accidents. The road climbed up and down many mountain ranges, crossed the Lancangjiang and the Nujiang, as well as smaller rivers. The often wonderful scenery along the route was never in the thoughts of the road's builders, who considered only the blood, sweat and toil required for the effort.

BAOSHAN AND TENGCHONG

Beyond Xiaguan, the most important post on the Burma Road was Baoshan. Established as Yongchang in 69 AD, its site was a natural selection, for Baoshan lies on the largest plain in western Yunnan, at a comfortable altitude of 1,670 metres. Baoshan and Tengchong, the last posts in Yunnan on the ancient Southwest Silk Route, were the furthest extension of Han immigration prior to the Ming Dynasty. After the Mongols were cleared out of Yunnan the Ming rulers not only encouraged immigration to the prefecture, they forcibly transferred members of the Cuan clans in Qujing, distrusting their pre-Mongol connections with Dali.

The immediate hills and high valleys around both Baoshan and Tengchong are also the home of Han settlers. Except for the Hui, the prefecture's ethnic minorities mostly live in the mountains between these two cities, with the Dai inhabiting the lowlands along the Nujiang. Being important commercial centres, both Baoshan and Tengchong have sizable Hui communities, both in the cities and in the nearby villages. In the past the Hui organized most of the caravans that passed through here and Tengchong's Hui community used to be a bigger proportion of the city's population until the decimation visited upon them at the end of the Muslim Revolt.

Today Baoshan retains its commercial importance and is full of new buildings. The original name Yongchang was changed to Baoshan in 1911, after the small hill of that name on the western outskirts. A tall pagoda, in the Dali style, stands just above the foot of the hill and from there the road climbs to the top, site of Wuhouci, the Zhuge Liang Memorial Hall. Built to commemorate Zhuge Liang's Yunnan Expedition, it houses a statue of the Three Kingdoms era's most famous strategist, characteristically holding his feather fan. The expedition never got as far as Baoshan, but at the time Baoshan was the only prefecture to refuse to submit to Meng Huo. The campaign against Meng Huo relieved the pressure on Baoshan and perhaps that's why the hall was constructed.

The antiquity of Han influence in Baoshan can be seen in sites north of the city. In the cave at the foot of Yunyanshan, 15 km from town, lies a 15-metre-long Reclining Buddha, a copy of the original dated 716, which the Red Guards demolished. Sculptures of the 500 *arhats* also decorate the chamber. The Guangzun Monastery is another Tang relic, while the Daoist temple of the Jade Emperor (*Yuhuangge*) at the foot of Baoshan hill, was built in the Ming Dynasty.

Also in the north, 12 km from the city centre, is the rural forest park at King Dragon's Pond (*Longwangtang*). This quiet getaway spot has a couple of shrines near the pond, but a nicer venue for relaxing is by the small lake below, with a pavilion on the hillock on the bank. And in case the park ever gets crowded, the forests in the surrounding hills make a convenient refuge.

The prefecture's second major city is **Tengchong**, now 165 km southwest by the new road, which follows the highway halfway to Dehong, crosses the Nujiang, then turns northwest. The old road crossed the Gaoligong Mountains, much further north. This range, which runs north-south between the Nujiang and the Lancangjiang, boasts several peaks of over 3,000 metres and the old road passed through dense, mixed forests that are brilliant with autumn colours. The new route crosses the mountains where they've shrunken to a modest size and are less forested. However, the time it takes to reach Tengchong has been reduced by at least 25 percent.

Tengchong lies in a smaller, rolling plain at about the same elevation as Baoshan. It is somewhat smaller and contains a far greater proportion of traditional wooden buildings. Laifeng Hill rises on its eastern side. The monastery here, originally a Nanzhao temple site, is a Ming

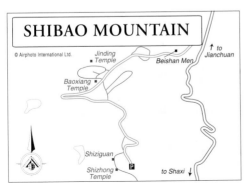

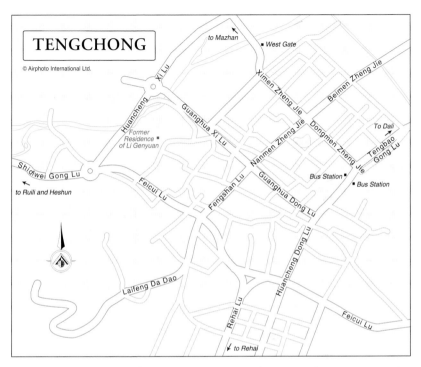

structure, the complex of which has been turned into a park. Augmenting the elegant old temple is a hall of historical figures, a model of ancient Tengchong, when it was known as Tengyueh, and a photo exhibition of the county's attractions.

In the southwest part of town a branch road leads to the **Dieshuihe waterfall**, a roaring cataract of the **Daying River**. It was over this precipice that revenge-minded Qing troops in 1879 hurled hundreds of Tengchong Muslims to their deaths.

As an outgrowth of its involvement in foreign trade, Tengchong has had a long tradition of emigration, beginning in the Ming Dynasty. The county is famous for its successful Overseas Chinese. An almost disproportionate number of these hailed from **Heshun** township, about 10 km south. Some of its native sons sent money back to sponsor local projects like the library, one of the nicest buildings in the town, built in 1922 in a combination of Western and Chinese styles. The streets that lead to Heshun's neighbourhoods, bunched together on a low, wide mound, are marked by entry arches. At various points on the lower road that runs the perimeter of Heshun, small parks have been

Outside Baoshan are several secluded parks, like King Dragon's Pond to the north, with its fine Qing-dynasty pavilion.

created around huge shade trees. Behind the town lies the pond *Yuanlongtang*. A rather ugly cement pavilion has been erected in the pond's centre, but on the hill on the north bank lie the ascending courtyards of the *Yuanlong Temple*. The architecture is in the classical style, with carved beams, painted rafters, gardens and with couplets mounted on the walls.

GEOTHERMAL DELIGHTS

Lying in a plain ringed by volcanoes and subject to frequent earth tremors, Tengchong is the capital of the most geophysically active county in Yunnan. A magnificent volcano named **Dayingshan** stands just 10 km north of the city. Rising 2,614 metres, and still active, it is easy to recognize by its cratered peak, of the kind that fits the classic image of a volcanic mountain. Dayingshan's last eruption was in 1609. Others in the vicinity look like they haven't erupted since their formation in the Cenozoic Era.

From Gongping, 20 km north of Tengchong, the land is studded with clusters of volcanoes, covering an area of 750 sq km, over 13 per cent of the county's territory. Some are not yet extinct and pumice stones and still lava streams decorate their slopes. No volcano has erupted in recent years, but as such events are unpredictable, that fact adds a tinge of excitement when hiking among them.

Besides the volcanoes, the county is famous for its 81 hot springs. The best group of these is **Rehai**, the Hot Sea, a collection of thermal springs and geysers 12 km northeast of Tengchong city, past rolling hills, picturesque villages and copses of pine and fir. Rehai is a park, becoming a resort, with hotels and restaurants in the front, marked trails to the major sites, and some of the hot springs contained in concrete vessels or engineered to flow into bath houses and pools. The star attraction is **Dagunguo**, Big Boiling Pot, over six metres in diameter, 1.5 metres deep, ringed by a guard rail, with a viewing platform nearby. In constant turbulence, it ejects puffs of steamy, vapourous clouds that waft up to the small temple above it and drift off against the dark green forest.

Rehai covers 9 sq km and only a small part of it has been built up. Most of the springs and geysers have been left intact. Trails wind up and down the hills, with most sights on the right bank of the **Zaotong River**. From the Big Boiling Pot the trail descends to the swimming pool, passing several steaming springs and a couple of stone hot wells, with animal figures carved in low relief on the sides. Along the river bank, back towards the park entrance, steam rises from the ground on the right bank, between the stones on the left bank, and jets out of a fissure in a boulder every few seconds at the site called Spouting Toad's Mouth (*Hamazui*).

Nowhere else in Yunnan are hot springs and geysers concentrated in such a circumscribed area. Dehong Prefecture has 16, but most are in Lianghe, the next county south of Tengchong, and scattered over its territory.

Big Boiling Pot is the primary thermal attraction at Rehai hot springs, near Tengchong.

THE LISU

In the northern mountains of Tengchong County, down to the border highlands of northwestern Lianghe and Yingjiang Counties, and over the border in adjacent ranges of northern Burma, live the Hua Lisu, or Flowery Lisu. They usually reside in pocket valleys or elevated plains, in simple houses of brick and wood. The architecture is unimpressive and the scenery usually unspectacular, but perhaps because of the rather drab and ordinary environment they adorn themselves with one of the most colourful costumes of any branch of this widely dispersed minority nationality. Moreover, they are the major Lisu sub-group in Yunnan which did not convert to Christianity.

Generally speaking, the Lisu live by themselves in the mountains of Tengchong and Lianghe, with Han settlements at lower altitudes. Besides farming and animal husbandry, the lumber business employs many. They sometimes come down to townships like Guyong, Gudong and Mingguang on market days, trading highland crops and hides from their animals for rice, vegetables and other articles. They are conspicuous by their splendid garments. Nearly all the women dress Lisu style and so do a large proportion of the men.

Both men and women wear wide-legged, knee-length trousers and embroidered leggings. Men's leggings are white with small red tassels, women's more colourful, sometimes wrapped with lacquered black rattan rings. Men wear a Tibetan-style jacket, wide sash belt, short sword and a broad-brimmed felt hat. When they dress up they add a bandoleer or two of cowry shells. Women wear long-tailed coats with brightly striped flaps that hang over the back. The coat is fastened down the front, often with big silver buckles, and tied at the waist with a belt with embroidered ends.

Women's headgear and jewellery vary somewhat. The traditional headdress is a thick, round band, studded with discs cut from white shells, cowry shells, silver studs or white plastic buttons. It may have a tassel hanging down the back or even an embroidered flap of cloth. Black turbans are a more informal type of headgear, but nowadays one is as likely to see wool stocking caps and red baseball caps as often as the traditional styles, though the women will otherwise be garbed entirely in Lisu style.

Jewellery may comprise a dozen or more long strands of beads looped around the neck. More popular is the round collar, decorated with cowry shells, silver studs or round shell discs, which hangs around the neck down to the collarbone. From the front of this collar many silver pendants hang, often covering the chest.

The extraordinarily colourful costume of a Baoshan Lisu woman.

CLIMBING THE SWORD LADDER

When the balmy spring weather arrives in the mountains of Tengchong and Lianghe, the Hua Lisu begin to anticipate their greatest annual event— **Daoganjie**, or Climbing the Sword Ladder. Held on the 8th day of the 2nd lunar month, preceded the night before by the feat of running through the 'sea of fire', the festival honours the Ming frontier general Wang Ji. Lisu men at that time were employed as troops in the border area and raised to value courage in warfare. General Wang Ji had a reputation for being so brave he could walk through fire and climb on swords. With Daoganjie, the most valiant men of the village emulate their historical hero.

On the night before the sword ladder is raised, fires burn on the outskirts of Lisu villages, creating the 'sea of fire' of hot, burning coals. Removing their shoes and invoking all the potential powers of mythic emulation, Lisu men dash across the glowing embers. Then, having made their run, they display the unscorched soles of their feet.

The next day the ladder goes up about noon. Meanwhile, on the adjacent grounds, a carnival atmosphere prevails among the snack stalls and the dice trays, where people lay wagers on the fall of three big dice as they are released from their position above the tray. When the ladder has been erected and secured to the stakes on the ground, the next task, which takes over an hour, is to fix the machetes, sharp side up, on the rungs. Some time after the completion, without any fanfare, the climbing begins.

The first one up is an older man, dressed in his best, with a large turban, bandoleers of cowries, a silver-encrusted bag draped over his shoulder, a sword hanging from his belt, and of course barefoot. Slowly he ascends the 60+ swords, reaches the platform at the top and yanks a couple of the flags, lights a string of firecrackers and hurls the flagpoles to the ground.

Even before he's begun his descent the next one is climbing up. About midway up the ladder is a narrow platform. As one descends he pauses at this to let the one who is coming up pass, then continues going down. When he reaches the last rung he proudly shows off both of his uncut, unscathed, unbloodied soles. The priest at the base of the ladder rubs the soles with ashes and gives the climber a small cup of refreshing liquor. No public applause accompanies the completion of the performance and in fact only a dozen or so men will make the attempt. One can only imagine their internal satisfaction when they succeed. It is one of the most amazing, inexplicable feats performed at any minority festival in the province.

A Lisu man makes the dizzying climb up the festival sword ladder barefooted and barehanded.

None of those in attendance is oblivious of the dangers involved in this act. Perhaps the crowd's silence is inspired by awe. But just to be sure, the chief priest may be seen ritually gesticulating to ward off any threats to the climbers' safety. When the last of the day's heroes makes his descent, the priest, some of the earlier climbers and their wives, form a ring and dance around the ladder, while traditional Lisu music blares over the speakers. The dance lasts about 20 minutes and at its conclusion the remnants of the crowd disperse for home. The ladder will be taken down the following day.

DEHONG LANDSCAPES

In the western part of Baoshan Prefecture the Gaoligong Mountain Range runs north to south, unusual in a province where the main mountain ranges run northwest to southeast. In Dehong, however, the ranges run from northeast to southwest, as do the two major rivers—the Dayingjiang and the Ruilijiang. The main highway from Tengchong runs southwest above and then along the Dayingjiang almost to the Myanmar border, then turns south and crosses the mountains to descend to the plain around Zhangfeng, the biggest town in Longchuan County.

From Zhangfeng the road south crosses another mountain range and then descends to the long narrow plain of Ruili. The hills are not very high

The attractive buildings on Mangshi's Youyilu Street contrast with the unimaginative grey cement buildings common to most of China's newly developed urban areas.

Attendance at an outdoor show in Mangshi produces a sea of straw hats.

and 22 km south of Zhangfeng a lateral road west stays high on the ridge to **Mengxiu**, an assimilated Jingpo village, rather modernized, but at its eastern outskirts it offers a splendid view of the plain around Ruili and the Myanmar town of Muse (Mujia) across the border. About one km from the Mengxiu turn-off, just past a Catholic church, a great view can be had of the Longchuan County plain.

Ruili is the westernmost county in Yunnan, with the county seat at its northeast quarter. The border with Myanmar runs roughly, only roughly, along the course of the Ruili River. Sometimes the river is wholly within China, sometimes its course runs through strictly Myanmar territory. The famed road continues past Ruili to Nongdao, where boats take passengers across to the Myanmar town of Nankang.

From Ruili the road goes northeast to Mangshi, sometimes called Luxi, the prefectural capital. The route follows river valleys for the most part, ascending slightly south of Santaishan, then winding down to the plain and on to Luxi. The well-made road connecting the major cities of Dehong makes travelling in the prefecture seem easy. The mountain ranges are not too high in between, and usually thickly forested, and for those using public transportation the minibuses are frequent.

Beyond the highway, though, it's a different landscape, often quite hilly, with rougher roads, some still unpaved and slow-going in the monsoon months. The highest mountains in Dehong are in the north and west above Yingjiang, where the Hua Lisu live, and in the southeast below Luxi, where a small branch of the Yi called the Limi reside. They are not as imposing as the peaks of **Gaoligongshan**, rising only to 2,500–2,800 metres. But they are viewed from lower altitudes to begin with, so can be just as impressive. One of them, just beyond the Han mountain village of Sanjiaoyan, 35 km east of Zhefang, contains a huge karst cave called Three Fairies Cave (*Sanxiandong*). A walkway has been constructed through the small chambers, passing the usual weird stalactites, tall pillars, corrugated cavern walls and anthropomorphic stalagmites common to Yunnan's subterranean scenery.

THE DAI

In the plains along the major cities and in the slightly higher valleys of the foothills, wherever the land is fairly level and near a river or stream, live the Dai. They comprise 30 percent of Dehong's population, second to the Han's 48 per cent. They are the same branch as their cousins across the border in Myanmar and in northern Thailand, where they are called Shan, or Tai Yai. Dehong's Dai are Buddhist, like the Dai of Xishuangbanna, reside in the same subtropical environment and grow the same kinds of crops. But the differences between them are as distinctive as the similarities.

Dehong Dai villages lie near streams, averaging 40–50 houses and one temple compound, with clumps of bamboo on their edges, but also magnificent peepul, banyan and other long-limbed shade trees. Villagers take their rest breaks beneath their spreading branches. Their houses sit on the ground and are made of drab-brown brick with tile roofs, sometimes enclosed by a walled compound. Auxiliary buildings, and even the main houses of the less affluent, have walls of plaited bamboo and tin roofs.

Wells are housed in consecrated shrines, as in other Buddhist Dai areas, and the women carry water in buckets suspended at each end of a pole. They use the same method to convey crops from the fields or goods from the markets, with woven baskets of split bamboo instead of buckets.

Men dress like the Han, but are often shirtless in the fields. Many tattoo their arms and chests. In former times they completely tattooed their thighs as well. Women wear the Dai sarong, usually black, with a long-sleeved, pale-coloured, side-fastened jacket. They tie their hair in a topknot and wrap it in a black silk, tubular turban or one of terry-cloth in pastel colours. Younger women may wear brighter colours and, like their counterparts across the border, apply *thanaka* powder—made from the soft outer bark of the tree of the same name—to their faces as a sunscreen and skin conditioner. Some young women wear it all the time, streaking the edges of it at the cheekbones, giving a feline accent to their facial appearance.

The Dai are skilful farmers, blessed with fertile land, and reliant and abundant rainfall every year. They easily obtain two crops a year from their fields, in some places three. The rice from the Zhefang area has a national reputation and the pineapples are the best-tasting and most nutritious in the province. Dai cuisine is similar to that in Banna, with the various dishes prepared in the restaurants in the morning and, when appropriate, reheated before being served. Baked and sour foods are popular, spiced with chilli, coriander, lemon grass, etc.

Because of its more northerly latitude, the Dai homeland in Dehong is a mite cooler than Xishuangbanna. It has not garnered the tourist attention that Banna has, but the Dehong Dai are perhaps more self-assured, polite, easy-going, refined, friendly and gracious than in Banna. A visitor feels welcome and comfortable everywhere in Dehong.

TOWNS AND TEMPLES

Simply because they are commercial centres, the major urban zones in Dehong are where most of the prefecture's Han live. Traditionally the Dai are farmers and while they did have their administrative centres where the local Dai chieftain (*sawba* in the Dai language) resided, urban occupations attracted only a small proportion of the population. Except for the tea cultivators who immigrated into the hills above Lianghe, the Han who came to Dehong sought work in the cities. Today these cities still have their native Dai neighbourhoods and some monuments and public buildings in the Dai style, and all are surrounded by the fields and fish ponds of neighbouring Dai villages.

Of the cities, Wanding and Lianghe exhibit the least ethnic Dai influence. Wanding was a sleepy border village until the late 1930s, when it suddenly became the key link between western China and the supply depots of British-held Burma. The original bridge was rebuilt after the war and is rather small and ordinary looking today. Beside it a long, wide mural depicts the 1954 crossing on foot by Premier Zhou Enlai, General He Long (of Long March fame) and the Burmese Prime Minister U Nu. Dai and Jingpo dancers and musicians flank either side of the dignitaries.

Atypical of Dehong, much of the town climbs the northern slope of the hill behind the commercial centre where the bridge is. At the top stands the **Zhengyang Gate**, entrance to a large park containing gardens, groves and the Heavenly Lake reservoir. From here one has a good view of the valley across the border and the hills of Myanmar.

Lying adjacent to Tengchong, Lianghe County drew most of the Han peasant immigrants to Dehong in past centuries. Villages on the plain are Dai and a string of Achang settlements lie in the foothills to the east, but the higher townships are Han, as are the majority of the city's population. The most interesting city building is the former sawba's residence, on the main road in the eastern sector, comprising several courtyards and a garden, with rounded entranceways. The Dai-style **Mengde Pagoda**, on a small hill in the southeast quarter, is only 20 years old, put up in the wake of the religious revivalism sparked by the launching of the reforms in 1979.

Yingjiang, 50 km southeast of Lianghe, has more of a Dai feel to it. The city is built around a reservoir and at the main intersection is a very Dai-style, three-sided elephant sculpture. Dai inhabit the adjacent village, between the city suburbs and the Daying River. At the end of this long, straggling village, past its graveyard (Dehong Dai bury their dead), a path runs to the knoll where sits one of the prefecture's most splendid pagodas—the **Yunyanta**. Rising from a square base lined with small, subsidiary pagodas, Yunyanta has a white mound, brass spire and filigreed silver crown. A plain pagoda sits across the field from it, with a small red temple behind it. As in Myanmar, the monks in Dehong generally wear red robes.

(above) Dai girls in Mangshi on their way to town.
(right) The most famous of Dehong's pagodas is in Jiele village near Ruili.

At the end of the Yingjiang valley the road turns south, crosses the **Husa River**, climbs a mountain range, then descends to the long plain of the Nanwan River, the heartland of Longchuan County. The county seat used to be at Chengzi, a small, nondescript town in the centre of the county. But the city of **Zhangfeng**, 33 km southwest, is the capital now. It is much bigger and more important commercially for its site on the main highway and its proximity to Myanmar, about 8 km west. The main market and minibus-taxi stand is beside the two huge trees just off the highway about midway through town. Open market is held every five days, attracting Dai, De'ang, Lisu, Jingpo and Burmese.

At the southern end of Zhangfeng, where a lateral road turns west to the border village of Laying, lies the city's outstanding Buddhist monument— **Sanxiangta**, a white pagoda under a peepul tree with three trumpeting elephants at its base. Northeast of the city, on a dirt road 12 km to the edge of Jinghou town, on a small hill with nearly 300 steps to its summit, stands the pagoda known as Guangmu. In the usual style of a white mound and bronze spire, it was erected in 1632 on the spot Dehong Dai believe to be the birthplace of their Buddhism. Dai villages lie at intervals on the road back to Zhangfeng, each with its own, wooden temple. Their exact positions in the village are signalled by the tall poles standing in their compounds, with long banners fluttering from them.

Just 35 km south of Zhangfeng lies the bustling border city of **Ruili**, its gleaming white skyscrapers visible from the pass 13 km north. Many of these towering buildings, however, are clustered on the small patch of Chinese territory across the Ruili River before the border post. Or they belong to the Chinese-dominated town of Muse (Mujia) inside Myanmar. Central Ruili itself is not so full of them. It has tree-lined avenues, mostly of royal palms, allowing for shady sidewalks. And at the arboreal roundabout where the main avenues meet stand stone sculptures of the Dai minority mascot—the peacock.

Most big new buildings are concrete, glass-and-tile monstrosities, but a few establishments have bamboo and wood facades and interiors, catering to the evening socialites who like a quiet drink with a magazine to read or a board game to play. The original government *binguan* is one of the most attractive buildings in town, utilizing Dai architectural motifs in a garden setting. Just a block away is the extensive market zone, with hundreds of small, mostly one-room shops and food stalls. It stays open late at night, as does the downtown area in general, with numerous outdoor grills and fruit stalls on the main avenues.

(previous pages) Partly Han style and partly Dai style, Puti Temple sits in the heart of the Dai quarter of Mangshi.

Ruili attracts lots of Chinese tourists, who come to purchase jade ornaments from the many itinerant Burmese traders in town at any given time. They also cross into Myanmar to take a quick look at the temples there and return with the satisfaction of having, albeit in a small way, visited a foreign country. Burmese residents in Ruili run several restaurants and as Burmese men wear *lungyis*, similar to sarongs, but usually plain or in checked patterns, they are an instantly noticeable presence in the city.

Beyond the border aura of Ruili, the county is blessed with attractive scenery, with low mountains flanking the northern side of the long, narrow plain, sundry streams flowing into the Ruili River, and several important Buddhist sites. Several km east of Ruili is the **Jiele Pagoda**, nearly 40 metres tall. Its thin, tapering spire is covered in glazed orange tiles and looks like a stack of bowls of diminishing size. The pagoda went up in the mid-Qing Dynasty and is supposed to contain some bone fragments of Lord Buddha.

From downtown Ruili to the border, a couple of temples lie between the southern suburbs and the river. One is typically Burmese style, on wooden stilts, tin-roofed with ornamental awning. The other is the newly constructed **Golden Duck Temple**, partly funded by money from Thailand, so its main hall is more in the Thai style, though rather spare. The central Buddha image is gold-plated bronze, in the Sukhothai style of 14th century Thailand.

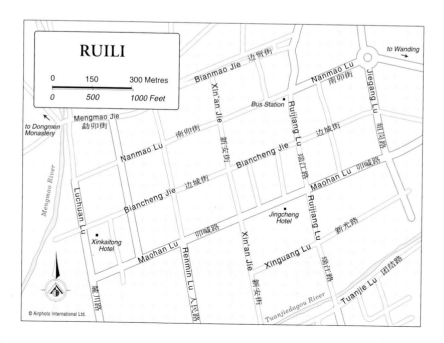

(above) The Burmese-style Yunyan Pagoda sits on a knoll outside Yingjiang.
(left) Ceremonial items in a Dehong temple.

In the southwest, off the Ruili-Nongdao road, are three more of the county's important temples. The first is in the village of Hansha, just past Jiedong, about 5 km from Ruili. The wooden building, with painted silver roofs and fancy awnings, stands beside a huge banyan tree, with a thick bamboo grove at its rear. The big painted Standing Buddha inside is in the Chinese style. But the furnishings, gilded chairs and other furniture, are typically Dehong Buddhist style. Walnuts, fruits and cigarettes are kept inside for guests, who might be surprised when the monks encourage them to have a smoke inside their house of worship.

Another 7 km down the highway at Shunha, a branch road winds across the plain for a few km and then climbs the hill to **Leizhuangxiang Temple**. The brilliant white pagoda on the south edge of the summit is visible from the highway. And from the pagoda itself the view encompasses the valley and river all the way back to Ruili and beyond. A modest temple compound occupies the back part of the summit, where five monks and 50 novices live.

The third important monastery on this route is in the village of Denghannong, about another 7 km past the Shunha turn-off. The **Damenghan Temple** compound lies to the rear of the village. It is a red wooden building with silver-painted roofs, elevated on stilts, and with a long, roofed corridor to the entrance. Inside is a gilt Standing Buddha in the Burmese style, gilt banners hanging from the ceiling and posters of events in the Buddha's life tacked on to the walls. About half as many monks and novices reside here as at Leizhuangxiang.

From Ruili it's 100 km northeast to **Luxi**, the provincial capital. The highway veers ever further away from the border, ascends slightly in the Santaishan area, then dips to the plains again, passing through Fengping, where a new temple and pagoda were constructed in 1986, and then runs the last 10 km to Luxi. The Dai name for this city is Mangshi, but most Yunnanese know it as Luxi, which means 'west of the Lu'. In western Yunnan, people frequently substitute the consonant *l* for an initial *n*. The Lu is thus the Nu River, or Nujiang.

Luxi was an important Dai administrative town in the old days, under its own sawba, with authority over the plains and hills to the north and south. Modern Luxi was simply added on to the western side of the original Dai town. Just beyond the northern entrance, marked by a stone peacock sculpture, several Dai villages dot the plains beside the Mangshi River. The northern and eastern quarters of Luxi are still mostly Dai neighbourhoods and all the temples and pagodas are east of the main business district avenue. So is the government guesthouse, tastefully built in the local Dai style in a tranquil, park-like setting near the river.

The architecture of the new city is not totally in the anonymous modern style, for Dai-style roofs cap some of the taller buildings. On Youyilu, the connecting lane along the river between the government guesthouse and Tuanjiedajie, the main business street, new rows of shophouses were recently constructed, all roofs in individual Dai styles, the facades painted in bright pastel colours.

At the south end of Tuanjiedajie the roundabout encloses a small park and two great banyans with twisting branches supported by epiphyte-grown roots that drop straight to the ground. At the north end the roundabout there features the peacock mascot monument. On a pyramidal, red pedestal, two tall, slender peacocks are mounted, one crouching, one standing in a long, elongated curve—a unique rendition among all the peacock sculptures in Dai towns in the province.

The city seems conscious of its role as the capital of a multiethnic prefecture. In the centre of the downtown area a new park replaced a market area. Besides the space needle in the centre, the southern side of the park features large stone sculptures depicting men and women of the Dai, Jingpo, Achang, De'ang, Lisu and Han nationalities. In the southwest quarter is the

Nationalities Park. In addition to the Zhou Enlai Memorial Hall, the park features a garden, small zoo, the painted poles of the Jingpo Munao Festival and a Dai village exhibit. Around a small pagoda are a few old-style Dai bamboo and thatch houses, a well, a shed and a staff of young men and women who periodically practise or perform dances in the yard.

The Dai Buddhist sites are all north and east of the new central park. The nearest is just past the Youyilu junction with Tuanjiedajie, in the compound of the No. 1 Primary School. In a corner of the schoolyard stands **Shubaota**, which means 'Tree-Wrapped Pagoda', an accurate description of what it is. One of Dehong's typically magnificent trees took root on the pagoda itself and grew around and above it. Now its roots and part of its trunk have crawled over the surface of the monument, completely covering parts of it.

The old town's three temples lie northeast of Shubaota. **Puti Temple**, on Zhengnanlu, is a red, wooden, elevated structure with silver-painted roofs, a circular entrance and interiors in the local Dai style. Similar in style, though not elevated and in a lovelier setting about 150 metres down Wuyunlu is **Wu-in Temple**. The compound sits beside a big yard with towering trees and an enshrined well. A white pagoda with painted gold spire stands within the courtyard; the temple's central Buddha image is crowned, in the *chakravartin* style (Universal Ruler). The third temple, on the main road a block east of the Wuyunlu turn-off, is Foguangsi, the Light of Buddha Temple. This one differs somewhat, constructed in the Han style in the Qing Dynasty, with ornately carved struts and roof awnings. A pagoda also stands in the courtyard.

ACHANG AND DE'ANG

Dehong is a Dai and Jingpo Autonomous Prefecture. Besides these two peoples, and the Lisu in the northern and western mountains, Dehong is also home to most members of two of Yunnan's smaller ethnic minorities—the Achang and the De'ang. The former are more numerous, about 33,000, 90 per cent of whom live in Lianghe and Longchuan Counties. The latter number close to 18,000 and are more dispersed in Dehong and reside in parts of Lincang Prefecture as well. Both have been heavily influenced by their Dai neighbours in domestic architecture, agriculture and religion. Yet they retain distinct cultural differences and are among the most conservative and traditional peoples in western Yunnan.

A main Achang area of settlement begins just 2 km east of Lianghe, on the road to Dachang township, 19 km up in the hills from the city. The road climbs at once to the first Achang village, on a long narrow plain, slightly higher than the one around Lianghe. Achang settlements continue along the plain and halfway up the hill to Dachang, an old Han township in a tea-growing area. The

Achang raise the same crops as the Dai, but they are said to be particularly good at wet-rice cultivation. The variety grown in this area is called *haogong'an* and has a reputation as the King of Wet-Rice Crops.

In Longchuan County a larger community of Achang inhabit the long valley of the Husa River, a southern tributary of the Dayingjiang. The rice variety here is slightly reddish and the Achang grind a portion of it into flour to make rice noodles for a special dish called *guoshou mixian*. Besides a big bowl of the noodles, the diner is served a bowl of chopped roast pork, ground boiled pork, peanuts, chilli and coriander, with a sauce and a bowl of turnip soup.

The Achang silversmiths and blacksmiths in Husa are famous throughout western Yunnan. The former make the jewellery the Achang women wear on festive occasions. They also inlay silver for the scabbards that hold the renowned Husa swords. The traditional beginning of this craft was in 1388 and six centuries of practice have made Achang blacksmiths the best sword-makers in the region. The most skilled can forge a blade so thin it can be wound around the waist and then straightened out perfectly for use. Shops and stands in Husa and other county towns sell the swords, as well as daggers with decorative sheaths. And all the customers will be Dehong men, of various nationalities, who want them not only for work, but also as adornment.

Achang men, when they dress traditional style, wear black trousers and usually black jackets, though some like white or blue, with a white or black turban. The women mostly prefer the Achang costume. Marital status can be determined at a glance, for the married women wear long skirts and the maidens wear trousers. Married women may wear a blue or black wraparound turban, but most pile their hair on top of their heads and don a black tubular turban, as much as 30 cm high, festooned with small pompom tassels on silver or pearl chains. Unmarried women coil their braided hair round their heads and secure it with chains of coloured yarn and pompoms. They both wear long-sleeved blouses that fasten down the front, sometimes with silver buckles.

As Buddhists the Achang celebrate the Water-Sprinkling Festival in April. They also observe other Buddhist holidays that their Dai neighbours do not. The last lunar month sees the Burning of White Firewood. The Achang construct roofed and decorated stacks of the wood near the pagodas. In the evening they set fire to them to symbolically give Lord Buddha some warmth on this cold winter night.

A much bigger festival is held in the 8th or 9th lunar month to greet Lord Buddha on his return to earth after a three-day excursion to Heaven to read scriptures to his mother. Called *Adu* in the Achang language, it involves the making and procession of two fancy palanquins. One carries the Green Dragon,

An Achang farmer woman. The tools and cultivation practices
of the Achang are similar to those of the Dai.

with fresh flowers in its mouth. The other image is a white elephant with a tall, thin pagoda on its back. Their appearance together is considered to be exceptionally auspicious.

Formerly known as the Benglong, De'ang communities exist in isolated pockets of all Dehong counties and as far east as Gengma, in Lincang Prefecture. The largest set of contiguous De'ang villages in Dehong is in Santaishan township, about 30 km southwest of Luxi. Besides the slopes near Santaishan village, a string of De'ang villages lie in the hills 6–12 km above Zhefang, on the road to Sanjiaoyan.

The next biggest concentration is over the Lincang border, in Junnong township of Zhenkang County. Some De'ang live as minority communities in Han, Dai, Jingpo or Wa villages. De'ang also reside in the mountains of Myanmar's eastern Shan States, and in the plain around Kengtung, where they are known as Palong (or Palawng). A handful of Palong villages have been established within Thailand's borders, in the wake of the ethnic wars in northern Myanmar.

They are perhaps the most ancient community in Dehong and the 'dragon bamboo' they raise in Zhenkang County has been famous in China since the establishment of Yongchang (*Baoshan*) in the first century AD. Very long, and with a stem diameter of 15–17 cm (slightly smaller in Santaishan), it makes a strong building material. Most De'ang houses are of wood and 'dragon bamboo,' raised on stilts and with tiled roofs.

Traditionally all sons lived in their father's house until he died, even after they married and had children of their own. So sometimes this extended family occupied a Jinuo-like longhouse, with separate hearths and enclosed bedrooms for the sons' families. Longhouses are rare nowadays, for the custom of each family having its own house has caught on since 1949.

Where they occupy level land the De'ang are excellent wet-rice cultivators. In the hill areas they have acquired a regional reputation for their tea. Besides the village's commercial gardens, each family has its own tea bushes in its compound, among the fruit trees and vegetable patches, and De'ang children start drinking strong tea at an early age.

The De'ang costume style varies slightly according to sub-group: the Red, Black or Colorful De'ang in Yunnan and the Gold or Silver Palong in the Shan States. Red and black are the dominant colours, with lots of silver ornaments. White cotton shoulder bags with red trim and festooned with pompoms and long fringes are common to both sexes. The men wear a black, side-fastened jacket, white turban and knee-length, loose trousers. In the old days they wore heavy silver jewellery—ear rings, torques, bangles and

Although the De'ang minority were one of Dehong's earliest settlers, they remain one of the smallest of the region's ethnic groups.

necklaces—as much as the women. This practice is reserved for festivals nowadays, but men still like to tattoo their arms and chests with dragons, tigers, Buddhist prayers and other designs.

In the old days married women used to shave their heads and wrap them in a black turban with the two ends hanging loose. Now they let their hair grow, but keep the turban. Younger women may adorn their locks with silver hair bands with pendants attached. Women of all ages wear waist hoops, usually of lacquered rattan, sometimes of silver, the more the merrier. These have customarily been a measure of a woman's attraction, so some wear up to 30 at a time.

The De'ang woman's ankle-length sarong is either black, black with a broad red band at the shins, or striped black and red. The Colourful De'ang, who wear the striped sarong, don a long-sleeved blouse of light or medium blue, red at the cuffs, and fasten it with big silver buckles down the front. The other De'ang women put on a long-sleeved blue or black jacket over a blouse, fastened below the breast, trimmed in red and sometimes sporting silver studs down the lapels.

Like their Dai neighbours, the De'ang are Theravada Buddhists. Each sizable village has its own monastery or temple. They have never been great pagoda-builders like the Dai and their temples are modest constructions. But they can be equally sincere and fervent in their beliefs, even when it seems counter to their interests. Reckoning that good Buddhists never kill animals, and that karma means acceptance of what happens 'by chance', the De'ang do not take action against wild boars that sometimes come and devastate their crops.

THE JINGPO

All but a few of Yunnan's 120,000 Jingpo live in Dehong Prefecture, mostly in the mountains at 1,500 metres or higher. Across the border in Myanmar the Jingpo are the largest of six ethnic groups (including Lisu) that are classified as *Kachin*, a Burmese word. They originated in the mountains along the eastern edge of the Tibet-Qinghai Plateau and migrated south to northern Burma and western Yunnan. By the early 15th century they were numerous enough in Dehong that the Ming government created two autonomous Jingpo districts and appointed one Jingpo nobleman in each as hereditary headman (tusi).

The following century witnessed a great migration of Jingpo to Dehong's mountains. They became the largest ethnic group in the hills and today comprise one-eighth of the prefecture's population. Around that time they learned to use iron ploughs and grow rice, a major transition from their previous economy of hunting and gathering. Living in the mountains where the soil is less fertile they generally resorted to the slash-and-burn style of farming. Contemporary governments have been weaning them away from this form of agriculture by introducing terracing, fruit orchards and crop substitution—tea and sugarcane instead of rice, as in Xishuangbanna.

The practice of slash-and-burn continues, however, though it is much reduced. But on some mountain slopes there is no other way to fertilize the soil other than with a layer of ashes. Even plains farmers burn off the straw in their fields in spring to provide nourishment for the upcoming sowing. Consequently, the air can be pretty thick in mid-spring, as the smoke enters the atmosphere on days that are already getting hazier and muggier. But at night, high in the remote mountains, long lines of carefully supervised flames make beautiful flickering patterns on the hillsides in the dark.

Most Jingpo settlements are ensconced in the forest or within bamboo groves and all but hidden from view. Traditional houses were made of wood and bamboo with thatched roofs. The walls were of plaited bamboo and a square hearth occupied the centre of the main room. The house stood on stilts or had one end against the higher part of the slope. This is still the norm in most areas, but brick housing, with tile roofs, like the Dai, are the current choice for any Jingpo family that can afford it. These rest on the ground, while separate sheds house the animals.

The Jingpo have a reputation as great drinkers, though not, it must be pointed out, as drunken revellers. But alcohol is part of a social encounter and men often carry wine flasks and cups with them. Both men and women chew tobacco, claiming it as an aid to digestion. Women like to chew catechu and betel nut, too, which darkens their teeth. In the old days this was considered a sign of beauty. The younger generation prefers sparkling white teeth though, and that particular Jingpo custom seems destined for desuetude.

The ethnic costume is still in fashion, even if nowadays the woman's wraparound skirt is more likely to be made on a knitting machine, if woollen, or a power loom, if cotton or silk. Many women still prefer to make their own and in the dry season they sit in the yard or on the porch with a backstrap loom hooked on to a house post. Older women usually wear dark sarongs and jackets, while younger women wear red, with yellow trim and inlaid patterns, or a multicoloured piece with as many intricate patterns laid in as the best of the Dai sarongs.

The side-fastened, long-sleeved velvet jacket is plain black, but on special occasions—festivals, weddings, market days, anytime a Jingpo woman wants to look her Jingpo best—it is covered with silver ornaments. These include three rows of big half-globes, stitched around the collar, shoulders and back. At the bottom of these rows hang many thin, flat pendants on chains. These drop down to the midriff in front and below the shoulder blades in back. A few round, embossed discs may also be attached to the bottom of the front of the jacket. To complete her outfit the Jingpo woman wears a red woollen tubular hat and a dozen or more lacquered rattan waist hoops.

The men don't dress up so colourfully, even on festival days. The older men tend to wear the older styles of Han clothes, the younger ones contemporary urban fashions. On special occasions they will don a black vest and a white turban, the ends coloured with many small attached pompoms. They also carry the Jingpo shoulder bag, of red wool, black strap, and covered in front with silver bulbs and pendants on chains just like the women's jacket. A sword, with a straight edge and no pointed end, in a decorated scabbard (more than likely made in Husa) is the final item. Traditionally, Jingpo men carried the sword at all times, for use in defence (rarely necessary) and as a cutting tool for chopping everything from trees to sugar cane.

THE WATER-SPRINKLING FESTIVAL

The biggest annual event in the Dai festival cycle, as in Xishuangbanna, is the Water-Sprinkling Festival in mid-April—New Year by the old Dai calendar. Celebrations are similar in Dehong, with a few major differences. Dehong Dai do not fire rockets nor stage boat races, but include all the religious activities and other aspects associated with the Banna rendition of the festival. The other

(above and right) Jingpo women at Munao. Attractive silver ornaments are stitched around their blouses.

ethnic minorities in Banna confine their participation to the dance parade through Jinghong, and perhaps a bit of water-splashing. But in Dehong the Buddhist Achang and De'ang take part in all the activities just like the Dai. The big show is in every Dai, Achang and De'ang settlement and not, as in Banna, concentrated in the prefectural capital.

Dehong's celebration especially resembles Banna's in its combination of the religious with the secular. The origin myth, about the seven Dai maidens assassinating the oppressive demon, is identical. But Dehong Dai have also grafted on Buddhist rites, such as cleaning the temples, bathing the Buddha images and making offerings of fresh flowers and clean water.

On the day before the rites begin the young men and women go to the mountains to gather spring flowers to decorate the pagodas in the temple compounds. This activity quite intentionally creates the setting for potential lovers to meet and sets the stage for the tossing of stringed purses at the fair on the third day. And the extent of one's amorous interest can be easily hinted at by how often one makes that someone the target of the water-splashing. As in Banna it begins with dipping a banana leaf in a bowl of water and literally sprinkling it. But this soon progresses to much more vigorous 'sprinkling', such as hurling the entire contents of the bowl, on up to using a hose.

The De'ang people celebrate the festival much the same as the Dai. They, too, erect a Water Dragon Pavilion to channel the water to bathe the Buddha image. Afterwards, the people use small twigs, or more often aromatic herbs, to sprinkle water on the monks and each other as a New Year greeting. They make offerings to the Buddha of flowers, fruits and grains in bamboo trays with lighted joss sticks lying at the rim. Then they resume greeting one another by water-sprinkling. This soon progresses to splashing and dousing, as in Dai and Achang villages, provoked by the impatient, rambunctious children.

In early autumn when the ripening grain turns the fields into shimmering waves of golden yellow, a number of Dehong counties and townships hold fairs. Some of these last a week and the Dai know them by the general name of *ganhai*, which means going to a gathering. The central town square fills to overflowing with kiosks and stalls selling everything one would find at a weekly market, plus clothing items, jewellery and some of the crops fresh from the fields. A stage is set up in the town centre and entertainers perform Dai favourites like the Peacock Dance and other choreographic acts, Dai operas and a contest for adepts with the Elephant-Leg Drum. The De'ang version of this instrument, by the way, is the water drum. The same size and shape, it is filled with water to give it, when struck, a softer and deeper, more resonant sound.

MUNAO

When the divine parents of Ning Gawn Na, the mythical Jingpo progenitor, lay on their deathbed, they instructed their son to give them a good sending off ceremony for their souls. Then they would metamorphose into Heaven and Earth and Ning Gawn Na would become fully human and father the Jingpo race. A proper send-off could only be a Munao Zongge, Jingpo words for 'let's dance together'. But Ning Gawn Na did not know the dance, for it was only performed by the children in the Kingdom of the Sun.

One day, however, Grandfather Sun invited a representative of the bird community to the dance. A sparrow attended and when he returned home he taught the other birds. The peacock took on the lead singing role and the hornbill organized the choreography. Ning Gawn Na and his wife happened to be watching and they took the dance home and taught others. A wild boar cleansed the corral for them and two Han brothers sent a dragon robe for the dance leader to wear. The Munao performance made the Jingpo more united, courageous and intelligent and so they have continued to stage it ever since, for four days beginning at the full moon of the first lunar month.

Because Munao symbolizes the solidarity of the Jingpo people, many separate villages join to celebrate it at one of the major festival sites. One of these is in the hills of Laying township, near Zhangfeng. Another is the knoll beside the Yunyan Pagoda on the outskirts of Yingjiang. The latter keeps the Munao poles up all year, plus a wooden hall with a buffalo skull mounted over the front door. Nearby, a white statue of a Jingpo man using his crossbow stands on a tall pedestal beside the pond. Since it is beyond the urban area, and even the adjacent Dai village, the Yingjiang Munao ground has a very rural atmosphere.

Luxi also hosts Munao in a big way, converting the athletic stadium into the staging grounds. A large corral is constructed, with gates at two sides and viewing platforms for the spirits at the other two sides. In the centre the Jingpo erect the four tall poles, painted with designs symbolizing aspects of their history and economic life. Small paintings at the top of mountains, for example, represent their mythical Himalayan origin. The crossed swords separating the two middle pillars remind them of their past battles, both against wild animals and human enemies.

At the base of the pillars in front stands a large drum, beaten during the dance to signal the pace and rhythm. To either side of this are gongs mounted in racks. Behind the pillars sits an orchestra, mostly of horns and woodwinds. Its members dress in fancy white coats with epaulets, black trousers and Jingpo headscarves. When the dance begins they play, sometimes with a singer accompanying them, sometimes without. Occasionally they pause and let an a cappella singer take the microphone or allow a long solo performance. Usually the soloist plays the flute or a specifically Jingpo instrument comprising a buffalo horn attached to a bamboo flute, which makes a sound similar to the fleugelots played in funeral processions.

Munao lasts four days, with one 90-minute dance in the morning and one in mid-afternoon. On the third night the bigger host venues like Luxi will present a stage show of songs and dances of both Jingpo and Dai, young troupes and middle-aged ones. A Lisu dance and the Wa Hair Dance may be included for good measure. A great number of Dai attend Munao, dressed in their best brocaded sarongs and pinning their jackets together with filigreed gold butterflies. A few Dai and Jingpo women take advantage of the event to open stalls by the stadium entrance, selling sarongs, silver ornaments, shoulder bags and Husa swords. Only a few Dai participate in the dance, though, preferring to watch from the grandstand or outside the corral.

Explosions and strings of firecrackers announce the beginning of the dance. The corral is empty, save for the orchestra, which strikes up its first tune. Then, slowly rocking in a two-step as they advance, the long line of dancers enters through the gate. They are led by four men in red or gold silk 'dragon robes', like the ones presented by the Han brothers at the first Munao. They hold their swords upright in front of them. On their heads they wear painted, split-bamboo helmets that symbolize the origin of Munao. On the sides wild boar tusks are attached, to remind them that the boar cleansed the first festival corral. Affixed to the top of the helmet is a hornbill beak, in honour of the organizer of the Birds' Munao, from which the Jingpo learned the dance. As a plume, the helmet uses feathers of the peacock and the hornbill, the singer and emcee at the Birds' Munao.

The line keeps to the corral railing until it has gone all the way around, then begins a more sinuous route in the open space around the poles. Eventually this fills up, too, and near the end of the dance the robed priests simply march back and forth in front of the drum.

Hundreds of Jingpo are by now in line, a group of women, then a group of men, with women slightly more in number. Every variation of the Jingpo sarong is on display, including the tight, red woollen miniskirt version. Men hold their swords aloft and sling the silver-laden bag over their shoulders. Outside the line, women attendants pour cups of rice-beer from bamboo containers to refresh the dancers. And when the dance concludes, much of the crowd stays in the corral, snapping photos of each other now that they're dressed in their Jingpo best.

Kachin Munao priests leading a procession at the Jingpo Munao Festival.

What's New in Yunnan

THE TANGULA LUXURY TRAIN JOURNEY

A luxury train service operated by the Kempinski Hotel Group will begin in Spring 2010, travelling between Beijing, Dali and Lijiang, a distance of 3,916km. The Tangula Express consists of a five-day/four-night journey with stops which include Guilin, along the famously scenic Li River, Xingyi, a cultural melting pot populated by Han and Yi minorities, the Shilin Stone Forest, Kunming, Dali, and finally Lijiang in northern Yunnan. Off-train excursions and on-board discovery programmes enrich the journey. The train accommodates a maximum of 96 guests in 12 specially designed 'suite' cars with four private bedrooms in each. Every guestroom is serviced by its own butler (on 24-hour call). Two dining cars prepare gourmet Chinese and Western food and a single vista car allows passengers to enjoy the incredible scenery along the way. The train even has its own Wi-Fi network so those who wish can stay in touch with the outside world. For more information visit www.tangulaluxurytrains.com or email info@tangula.com.cn.

The name Tangula is inspired by Thang Lha, a powerful grassland deity who watches over and protects the Tangula Pass and the Tangula mountain range.

THE KUNMING NATURAL HISTORY MUSEUM OF ZOOLOGY

32 Jiaochang Donglu, open 9am–5pm every day; www.kiz.ac.cn

This new museum in Kunming is devoted to the province's proud exhibits of ocean animal fossils—the earliest forms of ocean life—dinosaurs, reptiles from the Mesozoic period, Asian elephants and giant pandas as testimony to Yunnan's right to be called 'The Animal Kingdom'.

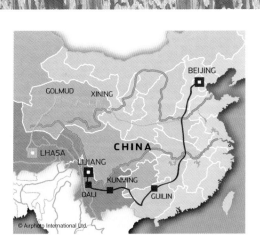

The Tangula Express has two transnational routes across China,
one from Beijing to Lhasa and one from Beijing to Lijiang.

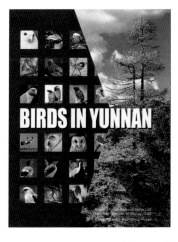

Yunnan Province is one of the most biologically diverse regions in the world.
This may be appreciated by visiting the new Kunming Natural History
Museum of Zoology or by reading one of these beautifully
produced books devoted to the fauna of the province.

PART V ◆ THE UNFAMILIAR

Up the Angry River: the Nujiang Canyon

NUJIANG AND THE MOUNTAINS

What Southeast Asia knows as the Salween River begins as the Gyamo Ngülchu in north-central Tibet, at the foot of Tanggula Mountains, near the Qinghai border (the Chinese call the river Heishui in its upper reaches). Winding south to Nagchu, it then turns east to cut through the Tibetan Plateau and bends southeast until just above Yunnan's northwest corner. With its name already changed to the **Nu River**, it then plunges directly south through the 316-km-long canyon of Nujiang Prefecture. Continuing south, the river slices through the middle of Baoshan Prefecture and at the border of Lincang makes a sharp turn west and flows into Myanmar (Burma) and, with its name changed to the Salween, eventually empties into the sea at Moulmein.

Throughout its journey through Nujiang Prefecture the river keeps a fairly straight course between two high mountain ranges. The hills often rise steeply, boxing in the river so that its width is generally 100–140 metres. Its flow is somewhat faster than that of the Lancangjiang (Mekong) and, with its many rapids, the river is hardly navigable except for a few short stretches in the north. Its constant turbulence and dangerous current seem to illustrate the literal translation of its name, which in Chinese means 'the angry river'.

However, this is not necessarily an example of the Chinese propensity to give fanciful names to the phenomena of nature. The name derives from the oldest inhabitants of the canyon—the Nu ethnic minority. In their own language, they call the river *numigua*. *Nu* means 'swarthy' and *migua* means 'river water'.

Innumerable streams tumble into the Nu River throughout the prefecture, the majority from the Gaoligong Mountains to the west. Many drop over steep cliffs just before they flow into the river. The largest waterfall is **Yinpi Falls**, opposite Zilijia, with a cataract 60 metres wide; this is atypical for the canyon, for most of the falls are much thinner and higher than Yinpi and one can hardly ride on the canyon's main road for more than ten minutes without spotting one. In addition to the natural falls, others have been created as spillage from irrigation channels cut into the cliffs, or hydroelectric projects on the river, making this a canyon of showers.

Stone Moon Mountain looms over the Nujiang Canyon. The mountain is famous for the enormous hole near its summit.

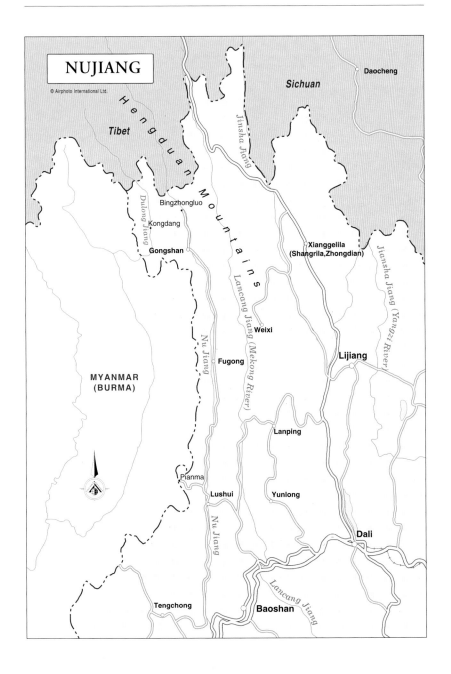

In forcing its way to the sea, the Nu River created a trench between the **Biluo Mountains** on its east and the **Gaoligong Mountains** on its west. The watershed of the latter forms the boundary with Myanmar all the way up to Gongshan County. Both ranges have several peaks over 4,000 metres high, while the elevation of the river is just over 1,000 metres. The mountains block the cold air currents from the northeast and retain the warm air from the Indian Ocean. Consequently, the canyon has several climatic zones and plenty of variety in its flora and fauna. The great diversity of flowering plants and trees inspired botanists like George Forrest and Kingdon Ward to make repeated visits. And in recent years specialists in Chinese herbal medicine have identified over 500 useful plants.

Until the government banned it in 1999, logging was an important industry in the canyon, for dense forests of larch, pine, Douglas fir, birch and dragon spruce cover vast swaths of the high mountains. Other Nujiang trees with commercial value include tung, varnish, camphor and palm, plus those with edible fruits or flowers, such as peach, pear, walnut and magnolia. In the lower elevation forests banyan, kapok, bamboo and silk-cotton trees are also found. Certain venerable trees, because of their great age, are state-protected, and the range of these, all 200–600 years old, include oak, maple, elm, bald fir, cypress, flowering peach and Chinese hemlock.

The latest count on animal species is 128 mammals, 284 birds, 25 amphibians, 44 fish and 45 butterflies. No elephant or rhinoceros lives here anymore, and perhaps the tiger has died out everywhere but Dulongjiang. But several other large mammals inhabit the montane forests and valley jungles— wild ox, takin, water deer, leopard, black bear and big-forehead ox. Large birds include the peacock, stork and three kinds of pheasant—blood, red-bellied and white-bellied. The more colourful smaller mammals are the golden monkey, white eyebrowed gibbon, macaque, red panda, muntjac, otter and flying squirrel.

Historically, the canyon has always been viewed as the remotest of the province's frontier zones. Access was only from the south, via the capital, **Liuku**. The party on the Irrawaddi Expedition, and some of the botanists, crossed the Biluoshan, which separates the Nujiang from the Lancangjiang, but on difficult trails. Even today no roads have been cut that follow the explorers' routes. But from Liuku all the way to Gongshan, 243 km north, the road is good, well-paved, rarely rising very high above the river, nor losing sight of it.

A road continuing south from Liuku along the river eventually meets the old Baoshan-Tengchong highway, though most traffic enters Liuku from the prefecture's southeastern corner, 40 km from the capital. Both the road from

(following pages) The turquoise waters of the Nu River.

Liuku Temple rests on a hill overlooking the Nu River.

Lanping and that from Baoshan meet here. Liuku straddles the river at 826 metres of altitude, just north of where a stream from the east flows into the river. Just above the confluence sits a small hill, where a large gold-coloured Buddha has in recent years been installed on the summit. A modest temple lies a little below and this is the major religious compound in the area.

An impressive bridge, 11 metres wide and 337 metres long, connects the two parts of the city, though the business section is mostly on the eastern side, as is the old city park, **Qingshan Gongyuan**, in the hilly northeast quarter of the city. Pathways climb through the woods to two pavilions, with views upriver that are at least a better sight than the collection of grey concrete boxes that comprise the bulk of the city's buildings.

One block north and four blocks north of the big bridge are suspension bridges for pedestrians. An attractive garden park lies between them on the west bank of the Nu. The southern bridge leads to the market area and so has a few peddlers at either end selling fruit, herbs, vegetables and crossbows. Those with the colourful shoulder bags with broad horizontal stripes are Lisu, but that may be the only Lisu costume component they wear. At the east bank entrance to the bridge several Lisu often assemble just before dusk to have a few cups of jiu at the stalls, enlivening the scene with a round of old Lisu songs.

From Liuku a road climbs into **Gaoligongshan**, 32 km to **Lushui**, and then zigzags through the mountains another 67 km to the border town of Pianma. Lushui is much less interesting than Liuku, being several blocks of nondescript modern buildings bounded on three sides by the mud-brick houses of Lisu neighbourhoods. Being high up on the slope, though, it does afford a good view of the mountains and Liuku in the distance.

Continuing west on the only paved road in Nujiang in that direction, the road leads to **Pianma**, high up in the mountains next to the Myanmar boundary. On the other side of the border, roads lead to destinations in the highlands of eastern Kachin State. The town is basically a transit point for the logging business done on the other side of the border. It also has a small museum and the wreckage of one of the Flying Tigers' planes from World War II. Besides Lisu, the district is home to the Chashan sub-group of Jingpo, who differ in dress and some cultural aspects from the Jingpo of Dehong. A small but colourful branch of the Bai, called the Lemo, live near Gulang, further north.

FUGONG COUNTY

For the first 30 km north of Liuku the scenery is much the same as around the capital. Hills rise up from either bank, but not too steeply, nor do they reach

The town of Liuku and its impressive suspension bridge spanning the Nu River.

the heights of those further north. Lisu villages lie next to the road wherever strips of alluvial land allow for stony but fairly level farms. Villagers dress in ordinary clothes except for the shoulder bag and occasionally a cotton cape, with thin grey and white stripes and sleeves at the shoulders. Other villages lie scattered up on the slopes

Then the scenery suddenly improves, heralded by a tall, thin waterfall on the left bank, with two major cataracts of about 20 metres each. A bit further, just before Chengga township, an even prettier fall cascades over a near-perpendicular cliff, each cataract slightly bigger and thicker than the one above it. Just beyond the settled area of **Chengga**, a huge block of bare stone sits on the right bank; the other side of the river is banked by a sheer cliff rising straight up over 200 metres.

From Chengga onwards, the mountains are progressively higher and steeper, the villages hug the slopes more densely, waterfalls spill off more cliffs and the Nu River roars so loudly it sounds like a convoy of log-laden trucks perpetually passing by. About 40 km north of Chengga, and 87 km north of Luiku, the road crosses a bridge to the left bank, enters Fugong County and runs up the eastern side of the river until just before **Gongshan**, another 161 km north. Just beyond **Pihe** township a rough branch road climbs up the

(above) The first turn of the Nu River, near Bingzhongluo.
(right) All along the Nujiang canyon waterfalls cascade from high cliffs into the river.

mountain 16 km to **Zhiziluo**, a large Nu settlement on an elevated plateau. Several smaller Nu villages cling to the surrounding slopes. Formerly known as Bijiang, this was the original administrative capital of the prefecture, though its ex-government buildings are now mostly abandoned. The township enjoys excellent views, especially of the nearby 4,206-metre peak on the watershed crest of the Biluoshan range.

Keeping to the road alongside the river, one travels 45 km from Pihe to **Fugong**, the county seat. Halfway up, on the right bank opposite Zilijia, a large Gaoligongshan stream dashes over the rocks at Yinpi Falls. It is easily accessible across the town's new suspension bridge. Such suspension bridges have largely displaced the rope-bridges of the past in the southern part of the county. They are strong enough for fully loaded tractor-trailers and have been erected near every major riverside village on the right bank, connecting the Gaoligongshan settlements with the highway.

Townships along the river en route to Fugong and beyond are small, comprising at most 20 or 30 buildings. Fugong itself is smaller than Liuku. From the centre of town, it takes only 15 minutes of walking in any direction to reach the rural areas. Peaks of over 4,000 metre rise on either side, and the Lisu village of **Shangba** climbs the nearest mountain, which slopes right down to the main thoroughfare. On the next hill north, another Lisu settlement, much smaller, hugs the slopes just below the peak.

The business district includes the main road and one running parallel between it and the river for about four blocks. The lower road leads south to the main suspension bridge, but besides the city's middle school and a small cluster of shops, the western side of the river is mainly rural. Farms and villages lie along the right bank to the south, and just above the bridge a torrential stream gushes down from Gaoligongshan into the Nujiang. Its last stretch is a popular picnic retreat for city residents. From the small village on the right bank north of the bridge a smaller, pedestrian bridge crosses the river to the top end of the market area.

Continuing north, 2 km past the settled area, the road passes **Lebuya Falls**, just to the right. Its three narrow cataracts drop over precipitous cliffs at least 150 metres high. A lateral dirt road 7 km north of the falls winds its way up the mountain, passing several small villages and hundreds of terraces for another 8 km to **Dapuluo**, a large Lisu village that serves as the administrative centre for the area. The tall peak in the immediate vicinity measures over 4,300 metres. The ridge east of Dapuluo is the border with Deqing Prefecture, with a view of the Lancangjiang valley.

From back at the turn-off to Dapuluo, the road continues along the river straight north, at intervals crossed both by pedestrian suspension bridges and the occasional old-style rope-bridge. Three of these are just past **Lumadeng**.

From here the road passes scattered settlements, a major logging camp and then suddenly begins rising higher above the river. Soon, towering dramatically to the northwest, the peak of **Stone Moon Mountain** catches the eye.

The outstanding feature of this jagged peak is the huge oval hole near the summit. The cavity measures 60 metres by 32.7 metres. According to local legend, the hole has its origin in the love affair between Adeng, the divine shepherd, and Ala, daughter of the Dragon King of the East Sea. Because her father opposed the liaison, the couple fled to Earth. But the Dragon King sent a great flood upon Nujiang, where the lovers had hidden. With his magic crossbow and arrow, Adeng shot a hole in the mountain, through which the waters escaped and receded.

Just past the Stone Moon lies the picturesque town of **Lishadi**, surrounded by majestic peaks. With Lumadeng further south and **Maji**, the next township north, and the last in Fugong County, Lishadi is in the heartland of traditional Black Lisu culture.

NU AND LISU LIFE

Almost all 25,000 members of the Nu ethnic minority reside in the Nujiang canyon. A few Nu villages lie east of Biluoshan in Lanping and Weixi Counties. In Nujiang they were for a long time the only inhabitants, moving in as early as the Nanzhao era (8th to 10th centuries), perhaps from the jungles of northern Burma, as Kingdon Ward suspected. Two branches live in the prefecture—the Anu of the north and the Nusu of the south, speaking mutually unintelligible dialects.

The canyon remained sparsely settled until the Ming Dynasty (1368–1644). Then large-scale Lisu migration commenced out of their original homeland in the mountains along the Jinshajiang, where it forms the border between Tibet and Sichuan. In the 16th century this migration reached the Nujiang canyon and the Lisu soon surpassed the Nu as the most numerous of its inhabitants. Today over 40 per cent of Yunnan's large Lisu population lives in Nujiang Prefecture, outnumbering the Nu by about 9 to 1. The Lisu are divided into two main sub-groups—the smaller White Lisu group in Lushui County and the more numerous Black Lisu of the rest of the canyon.

The salubrious climate of the valley has attracted other settlers besides Nu and Lisu. Along the river the daily temperature ranges from 17 to 26 degrees centigrade. And because the high mountains trap the warm air currents from the Indian Ocean, it is warmer in general than mountainous areas to the east. A village sited at 3,000 metres here will enjoy a slightly warmer temperature than a village at the same altitude, even the same latitude, east of Biluoshan. But except for the Jingpo, who have long inhabited some of the prefecture's

CROSSING THE ANGRY RIVER – THE OLD WAY

In China's Yunnan Province, the Salween River is known as the Nujiang (Nu River). It gives its name to the province's westernmost prefecture and derives from the name of the earliest inhabitants of the valley – the Nu minority nationality. In their own language, *nu* means dark. So the dark people live by the dark river. But the Chinese character used to represent *nu* is the word for angry. It may be the wrong choice for designating the people, for they are a small, placid, easy-going ethnic group, much outnumbered by the Black Lisu, who make up the majority of the prefecture's population. Yet it seems appropriate to call the river angry, especially during the rainy months of spring and summer, when it roars through the 300-km-long Nujiang Canyon at seven metres per second, creating long stretches of powerful, intense waves and rapids.

After the founding of the People's Republic in 1949, one of the first things the government did was to construct bridges to span the river at major towns and market sites in the three counties that make up the canyon. Until then the only way to cross the river anywhere was by rope-bridge. Mountains over 4,000 metres in height rise sharply from both sides of the river valley, sometimes meeting the water with a perpendicular wall of rock, cutting settlements off from one another. It would be too expensive to build suspension bridges everywhere people have to cross the river, so 28 rope-bridges survive today, all but a few in regular use, mostly between the towns of Fugong and Gongshan. Rope-bridges usually come in pairs, with the take-off point of each always higher than the landing point

In the old days, the bridges were made of twisted strips of split bamboo and changed every few years when they began to sag. The traveller sat in thongs strapped to a wooden slider that was mounted on the rope. Animals and packages were conveyed across the river the same way. But often the momentum gave out before the passenger reached the other side. Riders then pulled themselves across the cable the remaining distance, much like climbing a rope in a gymnasium. When that happened with packages or animals, though, locals had to slide back down the rope from the other bank, grab the package with the legs, or the animal by the straps, and pull their way back to the bank.

A woman traverses the angry Nu on a precarious rope bridge.

Nowadays the rope-bridges are made of wound steel cables and need not be changed every few years. They are also unbreakable, though the old split bamboo ones never broke, either, but still, the idea that they might scares off most visitors from trying. On the web you can find accounts that write of "hurtling to the other side at heart-stopping speed", followed by the usual speculations on how fast you would drown in the torrents below if the cable broke. One traveller wrote that the only thing that would persuade him to ride the rope-bridge would be the possibility of facing certain death if he did not ride it.

When I finally began exploring the Nujiang's northern stretches a few summers ago, I saw my first rope-bridge crossing at Lishadi, north of Fugong. The first obvious fact was that the web writers had not actually witnessed the event themselves. The speed of the passengers I saw was closer to 15 kph—not exactly "heart-stopping".

Shortly afterwards I sat by the landing point and watched two Lisu girls, aged about 10–12, roped together on the same cable hook, ride across the river several times, just for their own amusement. I drew two conclusions from this: it can't be dangerous and it must be fun Back in Lishadi I discovered that everyone who lived in a village reached by rope-bridge had their own rope harnesses and cable hooks.

When I returned to Fugong in the autumn, I purchased a strong rope and the modern equivalent of the old sliders. I called on a local Lisu acquaintance for assistance and he took me on market day to the rope-bridge at Damedi, about 12 km south of the town. On our side of the river was a tall cliff, about 30 metres above the rapids, and at the starting point I followed his instructions on how to use my new gear. I looped the rope around my body, one side in the small of my back and the other side under the thighs. The modern slider is an iron housing with a pulley wheel inside and two big hooks underneath. The slider goes on the cable, hooks facing the riverbank, and then I crossed the rope loop ends and slung them onto the hooks. Now I was ready.

With one hand on the top of the housing (not on the cable itself, which will burn the hand from friction), and the other holding my harness ropes, I simply lifted my feet off the boulder and away I went. It took about 15 seconds to reach the other side, with the movement of the pulley wheel against the cable sounding like a purring kitten. The sensation was both wonderful and unexpected. I thought my heart would beat faster, my blood rush, my skin tingle and so forth, but, on the contrary, I felt an enormous sense of serenity, rather like the high one is supposed to get from meditation exercises. The excuse I had given for wanting to cross a rope-bridge was to drink in the spirit of the Nujiang Lisu people's life. I was certainly doing that now.

After taking photos of other riders, with crossbows on their backs or a sack of grain on one of the hooks, I found on my return crossing that my own momentum gave out some 30 metres from the shore. Pulling myself the remainder of the way was rather difficult, but with Lisus watching me I couldn't very well give up and wait for one of them to come and fetch me, as they would for a pony.

So I made it to the other side, albeit breathless upon arrival, and returned to Fugong with my Lisu friend. He promptly spread the word of my feat and I became the subject of awe by all those local Lisu who have only used suspension bridges all their lives. "Wasn't I afraid?" they asked. "Not at all," said I. I'd watched the children do it at Lishadi.

In later journeys to the Nujiang, riding rope-bridges in the northern part of the canyon, I found that, since I have my own harness and cable-hook, my crossings make no special impression on the Lisu villagers who also ride rope-bridges. They are kind and hospitable but assume I live in Nujiang, or else why have the gear? Only when I return to the towns and the word has spread do I meet many Lisus who confess they have never done that because they are too afraid.

So I have developed a new ambition in Nujiang. I want to persuade one of those beautiful Black Lisu girls in the towns, who has been walking on suspension bridges across the river all her life, to hitch up with me on the same cable hook and go for her first ride ever, together with her outsider guide. Having conquered my own qualms about riding rope-bridges, I am flush with confidence that I can do anything locals anywhere do. That's the major influence the experience has had on me

It has also reshaped my own ideas, previously fuzzy, about what might make a good death. For when that time eventually comes, if I can slide out of this life as easily as I slid across the Angry River on a rope-bridge, and touch down in eternity as comfortably as I landed on the opposite bank, that would definitely make for a smooth, contented exit.

southernmost mountains, the Dai who have occupied the valley south of Liuku since ancient times, and the Tibetans in the far north, more recent immigrants like the Bai, Han and Naxi have opted for the towns or the low hills around Liuku.

The prefecture's towns and larger townships may have ethnically mixed populations, but the mountains belong to the Nu and the Lisu. So do the sections of tableland along the river, usually (but not always) where feeder streams come to meet the river. A few settlements, always close to the river, are fairly well off, with brick buildings, some with plastered and whitewashed walls, tile roofs and stone foundations. But the norm is a much simpler construction of wood and plaited bamboo, resting on stilts (the 'multi-legged house' in local parlance) or stone piles, with a thatched roof. People live on the elevated floor, pigs and cattle below.

Wooden planks or logs may be used for walls instead of plaited bamboo, especially further north. In Gongshan the roof will be made of slate. The Nu people quarry the slate from cliffs, where the rock is in vertical strata, like books on a shelf. After prying a rock loose they rip apart the layers, creating slabs as thin as half a centimetre. These they lay in a herring-bone pattern over the frame of the roof.

Formerly, the Nu and Lisu practised slash-and-burn agriculture on the slopes of the canyon, but since the 1960s this has mostly been replaced by

(above) The town of Gongshan is famous for the slate roofs that protect its buildings.
(right) Nu girls in traditional costume.

terrace farming. Nowadays terraces everywhere fill the spaces between the settlements, well irrigated from streams diverted in several directions. In some places the water runs down concrete channels with staircases beside them, enabling people to walk up and down the hill on a non-slippery, flat surface. Indeed, water engineering, from the diversion of streams to the highland farms to the many hydro-electric (hydel) projects on the river, has been the main instrument in the transformation and improvement of Nujiang people's lives.

Along the river and irrigated upper slopes, the main crop is rice, seeded in March or April, transplanted in May and harvested in September. Barley, maize, buckwheat and sorghum are the other grains cultivated. Oxen are the draught animals, with one farmer steering the animal by means of a pole attached to its neck or horns, the other guiding the plough behind. On sowing day, the Nu and Lisu customarily make offerings of grains, flowers and pine needles to the spirits protecting agriculture, and kill a small pig to feed the work crew. Hemp, vegetables, rape, fruit, especially tangerines, and walnuts are the supplemental crops.

In Fugong County the costume components of the Nu and Lisu are identical and it is only in Gongshan County, where the Anu branch dresses differently, that one can distinguish Nu from Lisu at a glance. Cotton is not cultivated in Nujiang, so traditionally Lisu clothes were made from hemp, which grows well on marginal plots and stony hillside fields. After the laborious process of turning hemp stalks into thread, the women weave the cloth on simple backstrap looms. The principal uses of this cloth were for making long skirts for the women, trousers for men and shirts for both. Nowadays cotton has largely replaced hemp, though some women still prefer to buy the thread and weave the cloth themselves.

The skirt, loose and ankle-length, is usually black, dark blue or grey-and-white pinstriped. Over this the woman wears a long-sleeved blouse and a red or black side-fastened velvet vest. On her head she wears a beaded cap of red and white sections, with a circlet of shell discs at its back. The same discs may be sewn onto a loop of narrow cloth and worn slung over one shoulder. Long strands of red or white beads are popular ornaments. A striped cloth shoulder bag, mostly red and black, with an embroidered rectangular patch in front, completes the outfit.

Men do not dress in traditional style as much or as often as the women. Some do prefer the jacket, of pinstriped grey and white, with black velvet patches on the collar, cuffs and pockets. They also use the shoulder bag, which is universal among Lisu, even the school kids. In the north men more commonly don the traditional jacket, which, among the Nu in Gongshan, is looser, robe-like, with wider sleeves, and is tied together with a cloth belt.

Nu women in Gongshan County weave a cloth of alternating sections of white and grey, with pinstripes of contrasting colours running through the broad sections. They wear this as a wraparound, shin-length skirt over trousers. A multicoloured, Tibetan-style cloth belt holds the skirt in place. A small section of hemp cloth, or plain terry cloth, is used as a head covering, which they secure by tying around it their hair braid, lengthened with brightly coloured yarn. A side-fastened vest over a long-sleeved blouse completes the costume. Beads of turquoise, coral and glass, and perhaps an engraved silver box-pendant, like the Tibetans wear, are the most popular ornaments.

In the last several years, the Nu-style striped material has been cut into sleeveless vests, which have become popular with both Nu men and women, even if that is the only ethnic item they ever wear. In general, the people of Gongshan County prefer modern clothing, while in northern Fugong County the traditional Lisu style is still popular. In Fugong itself and in the riverside townships, the trend is toward modern clothing, except for the older generation. On market day, though, which in Fugong is every calendar date ending in 0 or 5, traditional garments and accessories dominate the fashions.

Villagers from the mountains come to the city bearing firewood, poultry, vegetables and forest products like medicinal herbs or bamboo shoots. Young men sit on their stacks of firewood and play guitar while they await customers. Women examine the items in the traditional clothing and ornaments stalls. Villagers lay out for sale grubs and larva, orchids, baskets and tools, crossbows and bearskin quivers, freshly shot birds and flying squirrels. Others lead rope-leashed pigs to market, especially around planting and harvesting time. Farmers sacrifice small pigs at that time, so the market is brisk. Any pig over 10 kg, however, is saved for New Year or wedding feasts.

Elsewhere in the county, Maji in the far north has its market day on Monday, Lishadi on Tuesday, Lumadeng on Wednesday, Zilijia and Pihe on Thursday and Jiakedi on Friday. None of these displays as much variety of products as Fugong's, but those north of Fugong are more colourful still for the people and the ethnic look.

Some women wear ordinary clothing day-to-day, but dress up in their best traditional costume for market days. They want to look their finest in public places and to them the natural first choice is their clean and elegant Lisu or Nu outfit. The other venue for dressing up, with the same motivation, is the Sunday church service, for a large percentage of Nu and Lisu have been Christian since the 1920s. The Protestant church in Shangba, bare and unadorned like others in the canyon, fills up on Sundays, men on one side, women on the other, for over an hour's worth of sermons interspersed with Christian hymns, like 'Jesus Loves Me', in the Lisu language.

(following pages) Terrace farming has replaced the slash-and-burn agriculture that the Nu and Lisu formerly practised.

The conversion of the Nu and Lisu did not totally wipe out traditional beliefs in Nujiang, for villagers still hold sacrifices at sowing time and, while adding celebrations like Easter and Christmas to their festival calendar, have retained the biggest annual traditional event—the Flower Festival of the Nu and Kuosheu of the Lisu. Their form of Christianity is devout without being zealous and has little effect on their traditional material life.

Nujiang people are by nature good-humoured, self-assured and hospitable. A stranger cannot walk for long without being greeted or invited inside somewhere. The area sees foreigners only rarely and its people strain to make that visit a pleasant one. 'Tamped wine' and tobacco may be offered to guests in their homes. The wine's name comes from its process. First the Lisu boil and ferment grains of maize and sorghum and the seeds of a barnyard grass. After fermentation they put the grains in a fresh cauldron, add water and boil, all the while tamping down the grains with a wooden ladle. When sufficiently boiled, the mixture is poured into a basket of closely woven bamboo strips, which retains the mash and filters out the wine.

As per traditional custom, Lisu hosts expect their guests to get drunk and are embarrassed if a guest departs sober. They may ask the guest to join in a 'union toast', or 'one-heart drink', in which two people drink simultaneously from a single large bamboo cup. The Nu offer a milder beverage, a kind of maize beer, along with buckwheat bread, which is roasted on a heated stone slab like the ones used for roofing. With both peoples, hospitality is a duty, a notion that underlines their friendly attitude towards the curious strangers who travel so far to meet them.

GONGSHAN AND DULONGJIANG

This is the last frontier in Yunnan, the most remote and least accessible county in the province. A hump of territory extending west of the Nu River into the space between southeastern Tibet and northern Myanmar, Gongshan County has two distinct halves. The eastern half comprises the upper reaches of the Nu River and its flanking mountain ranges—Biluoshan on the left bank and Gaoligongshan on the right bank. The watershed crest of the latter neatly divides the county. The Dulong River valley runs down the middle of the county's western half, with the Dandanglika Mountains forming the boundary with Myanmar.

Peaks in this county occasionally top 5,000 metres and are altogether higher, colder, steeper and more densely forested than those in Fugong County. Yet the riverbeds of the Nu and the southern part of the Dulong are around 1,000 metres, giving the county great geographical variety. That, together with the presence of warm air currents from the Indian Ocean and its position beyond the monsoon line, endow the county with what is called a 'stereoscopic climate'. The high mountain zone is dominated by snow, thick-leafed, tough little shrubs and plants and furry animals. The middle zone is temperate, full of trees, all sizes of mammals and birds. The lowest zone is tropical, replete with flowers, bamboo, insects, reptiles and amphibians.

The Nu River enters Gongshan from Tibet and flows southeast past **Bingzhongluo**, the northernmost township, and literally makes loops nearly all the way around the two 'toes' of Biluoshan—low elevation tablelands that jut out from the base of steep mountains southeast of Bingzhongluo. The river then flows south to the county seat, turns southeast to the border of Fugong County, then cuts directly south all the way to Liuku and beyond. The highway from Fugong crosses the Nu just before Gongshan. From there the road begins rising high above the river and proceeds north to **Pengdang** and Bingzhongluo on the right bank. At the north end of Gongshan City an even rougher track leads west over Gaoligongshan to **Dulongjiang** township. Snow on the higher portions of this new road keeps it closed over six months a year.

Transportation is still in its developing stage in Gongshan. Not so long ago these roads were mere pony trails. Twenty tributary streams feed the Nu River and for centuries the only way to cross them was by rope-bridge or rattan suspension bridge. Many of these are still in regular use, but steel suspension bridges have in recent years been installed at many places along the Nu. The older generation here not only grew up without such convenient bridges, they also had to walk through tunnels cut by their ancestors into sheer cliffs on the banks. One of these is still in use just south of **Qiunatong**.

The Dulong valley is even wilder. The river's elevation is 1,200 metres higher where it enters the county than where it exits into Myanmar, 96 km due south, to eventually join the Irrawaddi. There are places where the river, bounded on each side by steep slopes covered in emerald green forests, looks like a white silk scarf laid upon a watery staircase to the sky.

Over 40 percent of the county is covered in forests that harbour a tremendous diversity of plant and animal life, including rare mammals like the tiger and takin. It is among Yunnan's least densely populated counties, home to Nu, Lisu and Tibetans in the east and Dulong in the west. Tibetans began settling in the extreme north of the county in the late 18th century. They established the **Puhua Monastery** near Bingzhongluo in 1882 and made some headway converting nearby Nu to a form of tantric Buddhism.

Competition arrived the same year in the form of the first French priest to arrive in the county. In 1904 the first Catholic church was erected in **Baihanluo**, in the Chinese style, in the Tibetan-inhabited northeastern part of the county. The original was destroyed the year after, but faithfully rebuilt and outfitted with a French bell donated from the mission's homeland. It is a one-storey wooden building with carved screen doors and windows, and tiled roofs

with upturned eaves. The bell tower stands over the front entrance, with frescoes of Christian themes on the walls and ceiling of the entrance arch.

Five more Catholic churches went up in different Nu and Lisu villages in the upper part of the canyon. Protestants were late arrivals. Not until 1925 did an American missionary begin preaching in Gongshan. In 1933 the first Protestant church was established there, followed by a half dozen more over the next few years.

The foreign missionaries left in 1949 and have not returned. The churches suffered attacks in the Cultural Revolution, but all of them have reopened and are active places of worship, not merely relics of a bygone era. Religious activity attracts a good percentage of the Christians of Nujiang, but many are non-religious by habit or even cling to traditional animism.

Remote as it is, Gongshan is not without its modern amenities. The city sits on a flat protrusion of land just above the river, with a fine view of the mountains to the north, usually snow-capped. It has an assortment of modern administrative buildings, a long market, capacious cultural centre and Dandang Park. Villages beyond the county seat are in general closer to the river or midway up the slopes beside the tributary streams. Little rice is grown in the area when compared to maize and buckwheat, the staple fillers in the local diet.

(above) A church in Gongshan, one of many that have reopened since the Cultural Revolution. A Lisu woman (left), one of the minority groups common to the Gongshan area.

Hunting supplements agriculture as a source of food. Every boy in Nujiang grows up knowing how to use a crossbow. The crossbow, and skill with it, is such a part of the local male image that at festivals and market days a young Nu or Lisu man walks around with one slung over his shoulder, and a dagger hanging from his belt. Without these he feels incompletely attired. A quiver goes with the crossbow, too, consisting of a bamboo tube to hold the arrows, which is often covered in animal hide or equipped with a strip of hide as its strap. Other quivers, sold in Liuku and in Fugong on market day, are made of bearskin, deerskin or monkey hide.

The crossbow is the main hunting tool, for Nujiang men are not trappers, except in the rivers and streams. Here they use homemade fish traps of split bamboo as well as ordinary fishing nets and poles. One other important use of the crossbow is defence; not personal defence but defence of the field. Upper Nujiang farms are close to the forests, home to bears and such animals as takin, wild ox, antelope and others that will raid a ripening crop if allowed the opportunity. Just before harvest, Nujiang farmers stay in field huts to keep watch over their crops and repel predators with the crossbow.

(above) Jungle foragers traverse a rickety bamboo bridge.
(right) Hunters in the area commonly use crossbows not only to bring down game but also to defend their fields from predators.

THE DULONG PEOPLE

The people closest to nature in Nujiang, only recently becoming acquainted with modernity and the outside world, are the Dulong. Formerly known as the Qiu, they call themselves Dulong, or Drung, in their own language, a Tibeto-Burman tongue close to the Anu dialect of the northern Nu. Western Gongshan County is their only habitat in Yunnan, where they number about 6,000, though some more live on the Burmese side of the Dandanglika Mountains. There they are known as the Nung.

Until about a generation ago, the Dulong lived primitively. This meant slash-and-burn agriculture, hunting, fishing and gathering, thus growing or collecting all their food. The forests provided materials for housing, domestic furniture and utensils and containers. Concomitant with this kind of lifestyle was a low population density, small villages, tight clan relationships and ecological harmony. Basic self-sufficiency, however, was all that could be expected.

In addition to a healthy respect for nature, a result of their total involvement with it on every level, this kind of existence produced a character that was straightforward and famously honest. Stealing is the worst of all crimes to a Dulong. They will not even keep anything that has been accidentally dropped or lost on the trail. Instead they will hang it up in plain view on the nearest tree, for the owner to pick up at another time.

Iron farming implements, such as ploughs and other tools, have been introduced to the Dulong, increasing and diversifying the agricultural output. Road construction is slowly but surely linking the far-flung villages. Hydel projects and even satellite dishes have come to the Dulong valley. Markets have introduced new gadgets and ready-made clothing to the area. But the old ways persist in many aspects of Dulong life.

The Dulong costume is basically a strip of woven hemp cloth, one metre by two metres, with a colour scheme similar to that of the Nu. This is simply wrapped around the body and tied at the neck, often leaving one shoulder bare. Personal choice is expressed in the various ways of wrapping and tying it. Jewellery, if any, will be strings of beads. In former times the main decoration for women was the facial tattoo, done in indigo pigment applied with slivers of wood. Girls got their tattoos at puberty and each clan had its own set of designs.

Nowadays in western Gongshan one still sees older Dulong women with tattooed faces. But since the extension of Chinese administration here in 1956, the custom has fallen out of fashion. It's a rare Dulong girl who has it done now. The origin of tattooing is not clear. Some claim it was a reaction to the assault of a powerful tribe who enslaved the Dulong and went after their women. Hence, they were tattooed to make them unattractive to the oppressors. Oddly, though, neither Roux, the chronicler of the Irrawaddi Expedition of 1895, nor Kingdon Ward in his reports on the area, ever mentioned the tattoos, though both saw plenty of Dulong women on their journeys.

For the non-Christian majority of the Dulong, as for their unconverted Nu neighbours to the east, the most important man in society is the *lemuya*. He is the ritual specialist, shaman, healer and diviner of the village. He is chosen, as are all shamans everywhere, by the spirits themselves. Since Dulong villages are self-sufficient households in clan alliances, no political authority or hierarchy exists. The lemuya is thus effectively the village leader. He oversees the collective rituals and is expected to be thoroughly familiar with tribal history and customs.

In his role as shaman he may recommend that his patient sacrifice a chicken to the spirits; as tribal emcee, he will officiate at the slaying of it. To exorcise ghosts he will order the slaying of a crow. To ensure good hunting he will make buckwheat dough figurines of the game animals for a ritual to the mountain god. And he is in charge of the ritual slaying of an ox at the Dulong New Year.

NUJIANG FESTIVALS

The Dulong are a happy people. They like to joke and tell funny stories. At harvest time after a long, hard day's work they get together in the evening for impromptu song and dance sessions. Laughter among them is even a part of customary politeness. As for large, organized festivities, they have only the New Year. Called Kaquewa in their own language, it is held in the 11th or 12th lunar month, the date decided each year by the village elders, depending upon the weather, the expected number of guests and other criteria.

The first day is simply a collective announcement of the start of the festival. Families decorate their houses with coloured streamers and in the evening feast, get drunk and make predictions about the coming year. Next day the lemuya conducts the rites for the mountain god, at the end of which young men with crossbows shoot the animal figurines, surrounded by a crowd of dancing, singing onlookers.

The next event is the sacrifice of an ox. The clan chief and the lemuya fetch the ox from its owner. Girls drape a Dulong cloth over it and festoon its horns with strings of beads. The two men lead the ox around the owner's house six times, then tether it to a stake. Villagers form a big circle around the animal and commence dancing. The ox's executioners then come to dance before the ox.

They first drink a measure of rice wine together from the same cup, then pierce the bull's heart with poison-tipped spears.

The animal staggers, falls to the ground and expires. One man cuts off an earlobe of the ox, impales it on a stick and waves it back and forth over the carcass as he recites prayers consecrating the sacrifice to Heaven. Then he throws away the stick and the ox is cut up for distribution. The head goes to its owner, large slices of beef to the two spearmen and smaller chunks to each of the villagers. One of the executioners then puts the ox's head on his back and performs a special dance. Dancing, feasting and drinking, with scores of 'union toasts', continue throughout the night.

The Nu people's observance of New Year shows a strong Han influence in some of the activities. They clean their houses, dump garbage far away and ceremonially open the house door to allow wealth and fortune to enter. Early New Year morning a child from each house collects a ladleful of water from each well. The family offers a cup of wine to the pine trees in the courtyard. And for the next fortnight they spread pine needles, symbols of prosperity, on

A couple share a "one heart drink" during a village ceremony.

A typical rural Lisu village home.

the main beam of the house, the hearth and the family altar. They also leave offerings at the communal altar and make processions around it.

A bigger Nu celebration takes place at Jimudeng village in Gongshan County, above Bingzhongluo, on the 15th day of the 3rd lunar month. This is the Festival of Fresh Flowers, held in honour of their mythical heroine, Areng, who constructed the first rope-bridge and the first canal. Afterwards she was murdered in a cave by her enemies. On this day, the anniversary of her death, the Nu gather great bunches of wild flowers on the mountain slopes and bring them to her altar at the mouth of the cave. In addition to the prayers and rituals, the Nu also collect water from two large stalactites, said to be Areng's breasts. Devotees first offer some of the water to visiting Tibetan lamas in attendance, then drink it themselves as a blessing from the goddess who brought them clean water.

The Black Lisu of Fugong County and vicinity once had their own peculiar calendar which, like some of the Yi branches, divided the year into ten months. New Year fell on a new moon, like the Chinese calendar, but not necessarily the same new moon, for each year village elders set the date. In recent years, though, the Lisu have fixed their New Year to the solar date of 20 December. Called Kuosheu in their own language, the festivities run for three or four days. Glutinous rice cakes and mug after mug of rice beer are consumed throughout the week, which is also marked by visiting, dancing, courting and singing from a seemingly endless repertoire of traditional songs.

It begins, like the Nu New Year, with house-cleaning, feasts, rituals and calling on relatives. The latter few days are given over to fun and games. The Lisu may construct a swing consisting of two rectangular bamboo frames, a seat suspended at each end, mounted on a crossbar resting on two sturdy, upright posts. Young men stage a competition with their crossbows, with such targets as a rice cake perched atop a pole. In former times they also lined up in a rank facing another rank of their girlfriends. On top of their heads the girls placed a bowl of rice to hold upright a thin bamboo tube. On top of the tube was an egg, the target. The set-up displayed the extreme confidence the girls had in the skill and accuracy of their William Tell sweethearts, as well as the boys' conviction they would not cause harm with their shots.

Courtship plays a major part in the Kuosheu activities. Lined up in opposing ranks, the youth sing and dance, antiphonal songs as well as solos and choruses, all dressed in their finest Lisu clothes and ornaments. The men play a lute whose body is not much wider than its neck. Girls play a bamboo mouth harp.

The other major courtship game involves burying a young man in the sand—a pit dug on the ridge of the riverbank. This is what happens: a group of young women grabs one of the young men, laughing all the way, and dumps him into the pit. They then cover him with sand up to his chest. His true love will be the one who digs him out. Much of the humour revolves around the mock suspense while the young man waits and wonders who, if anyone, will dig him out, thus declaring herself.

Laughter, joy, good humour and a sense of fun are not reserved by the Lisu for just the big festivals. They are integral aspects of the Lisu character. They need no excuse to indulge in merriment, for an ancient and oft-quoted Lisu adage says, 'None but the dead should be deprived of the mirth of life'.

Greased pole climbing is one of the activities featured during the Lisu New Year festival of Kuosheu.

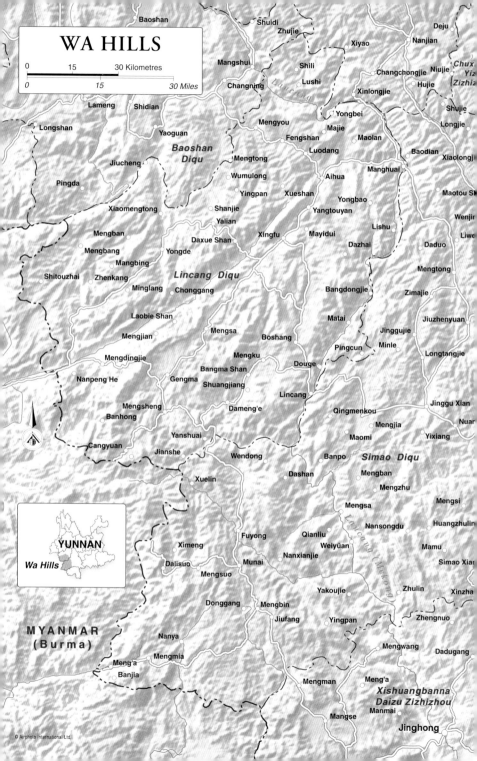

Borderlands:
The Wa and Dai of the Southwest

BETWEEN THE BIG RIVERS

Before the 19th century, when British and French possessions in Asia were still a long way from Yunnan, the status of the province's southwest region was unclear. In particular, the border with Burma between Xishuangbanna and Dehong was not defined. In these border counties, today comprising Menglian, Lancang, Ximeng, Shuangjiang, Gengma, Cangyuan and Zhenkang, the social make-up of the population was similar to Banna and Dehong. The Dai occupied the plains and valleys and various ethnic groups inhabited the hills. Though Buddhist, these Dai were mainly of a completely different branch—called the Nüa—and neither Dehong sawbas nor Banna princes ever had any authority over them.

The hill people were different, too. Some were branches of minority nationalities familiar to residents of Banna or Dehong—Aini, Lahu, Bulang in the east, Jingpo, Lisu, Yi, De'ang in the west. But the dominant ethnic group in the mountains adjacent to Burma was a people whose way of life resembled none of any other mountain folk. This was the Wa, a people who lived in fortified hilltop villages and conducted head-hunting raids throughout the area. So ferocious was their reputation that no government, big or small, had even attempted to subdue them. No trade routes passed through their territory, either.

The entire borderlands, however, were off the main trade routes connecting Yunnan with Burma. The Chinese were established in Simao and used it as a depot for trade with Xishuangbanna. The other routes into Burma were in the west, along the Southwest Silk Route first set up in the Han Dynasty. Chinese dominated the towns along the route past Dali—Baoshan, Tengchong, Longling and Luxi. Dehong Dai inhabited the last stages on the Chinese side, but there was never any doubt about the boundary in this direction. Though they belonged to the same branch of the Dai as those on the Burmese side—Tai Yai, or Shan—both the Burmese monarchs and their British successors considered the Dehong Dai as 'Chinese Shans'.

With no trade routes running through the borderland towns, no Chinese merchant moved there to open business. With malaria so prevalent in the area, no Chinese peasant migrated there to clear land for a farm. The Wa made an effective barrier against any Burmese attempt to extend their sovereignty, as they attempted in Banna, and the mosquitoes kept the Han away to their north. Dai princes ran their own mini-states in the plains and the hill people lived in their own fashion, without much interference in the form of taxes, corvée labour or other exactions.

The princes didn't get wealthy or powerful as a result, but the land itself was rich and fruitful. People didn't need to exert themselves too much to make a decent living. Their needs were easily satisfied and their wants were few. The land was fertile, the forests abundant, the climate spring-like all year round. The princes acknowledged the Chinese emperor's suzerainty, because this lip-service obeisance wouldn't alter the way they ran their realms. Content with this, the court permitted their de facto autonomy, even when taking away such freedom from other places in Yunnan, like Lijiang and Dali.

This lackadaisical attention to southwest Yunnan changed dramatically when the British started annexing parts of Burma. In the latter half of the 19th century both sides began advancing towards each other. The British annexed Upper Burma in 1881 and within a few years began surveying in the north in preparation for fixing a frontier with China. The Chinese response was to conduct their own forward policy by launching a military campaign in 1887 to conquer Lancang County, which was successfully concluded in 1892, with thousands of Lahu fleeing to Burma.

The pressure was on the sawba of Menglian to acknowledge Chinese suzerainty, which he duly did. As for the other statelets, like Gengma, Mengding and Cangyuan, the Chinese government treaded more cautiously. Worried about the inexorable British advance towards the frontier, the government did not want to alienate the Dai, lest they back the British moves by allying with their ethnic cousins across the border.

After Scott's expeditions it was time to tackle the border problem in the Wa Hills. The British made no claims on Gengma, Zhenkang or Shuangjiang, and even renounced Burma's claim on Xishuangbanna. But they insisted the Wa must not be divided, implying they should all be under British Burma's sovereignty, though their own surveyors had discovered virtually every Wa village was its own state and that these were the most disunited people in the whole region.

Eventually the Wa areas were divided, but the actual borderline remained fuzzy. Negotiations broken off by the Qing Court never resumed. The chaos of the warlord period, World War II and the use of the area as a base for leftover Guomindang troops in the early 1950s prevented any settlement. Only when Burma regained its independence and the last Guomindang troops were chased out of the area was it possible to demarcate the border and fix the sovereignty over the borderland villages once and for all.

The land between the Nujiang (Salween) and Lancangjiang (Mekong) has no flat plains or elevated plateaux of significant size. Great Snow Mountain

(*Daxueshan*), halfway between **Gengma** and the capital, dominates the central part of Lincang Prefecture at 3,233 metres. The peaks closer to the border are more in the neighbourhood of 2,400–2,800 metres, but they are never isolated, always part of ranges that criss-cross the entire area and envelop the valleys. The exception is the Big Snow Mountain in Yongde County Nature Preserve, north of Zhenkang, which rises to 3,504 metres. The preserve also contains the prefecture's Earth Forest (*tulin*), featuring tall pillars of eroded earth and stone. Between the two main rivers, the other rivers of Lincang mainly flow northeast to southwest, while those in southwest Simao run northwest to southeast.

Depending on the altitude, the entire borderlands region lies in the tropical and subtropical climatic zones and is blessed with a great variety of plant and animal life. Lincang Prefecture alone boasts 3,700 kinds of trees and 3,000 medicinal plants. Among the animals still prowling in the borderland jungles are the wild elephant, tiger, clouded leopard, leopard cat, red panda, pangolin, otter, wind monkey, water deer, lemur, wild ox, black bear, monitor lizard, peacock, golden pheasant and monkey-faced eagle.

Besides the Wa along the frontier and the Dai in the plains, several other ethnic groups make their homes in the area. In southwest Zhenkang County lives the Limi branch of the Yi. Small pockets of Miao, Lisu and Bulang inhabit other parts of the county's northeastern hills, while the largest community of De'ang outside Dehong resides in the villages of Junnong township, 22 km south of the county seat. Larger Bulang communities inhabit the hills just west of the Lancangjiang in Shuangjiang County. South of them, in central and eastern Lancang County, are the Lahu, with some Aini villages interspersed all the way to southern Menglian County.

THE HEAD-HUNTERS OF AWASHAN

The Wa seem to be the oldest inhabitants of the region. They never developed a writing system for their language and kept only the simplest of records by notching bamboo. No Wa artefacts from ancient times have survived and they have no traditional tale of once having inhabited the plains, which many mountain folk have. However, cliff paintings in Cangyuan County, identified as made by ancient Wa hunter-gatherers, are estimated to be 3,000 years old.

The biggest collection of these paintings, at a site called Ai Hua, adorns the perpendicular cliff halfway up the mountain just past **Menglai**, a nondescript little Dai township 20 km north of Cangyuan. The cliff is pale yellow, streaked with grey and rust-brown, the paintings in red-brown, mostly on the southwest face. The artists must have used ladders, for all the pictures are out of reach. They depict profiled stick figures hunting with bow and arrow, going to war with shields and spears, carrying tools, celebrating a feast, and rounding up or getting ready to slay buffaloes—in short, cameos of ancient Wa life.

Local Wa claim the ancient cliff paintings at Ai Hua were made by their ancestors.

Since the end of the 19th century, when British and Chinese expeditions were penetrating the Wa Hills, the Wa population has of course increased. More villages occupy the mountain slopes, and since the end of head-hunting, these new settlements are sited much lower than in the old days. Nowadays some tracts in the hills host villages on every ridge, as close to each other as settlements in the plains. But even a hundred years ago the area seemed densely settled to surveyors on both sides of the border.

Moreover, Wa villages were big. Since war and blood feuds were an important factor in ordering Wa life, villages tended to great size for their residents' safety. Rarely was a settlement less than a hundred houses and the norm was 200–300. The typical Wa village was stockaded, with watchtowers and strong wooden gates. It was protected by log or bamboo-riveted earthworks. A deep ditch and dense thorn hedge surrounded it. The only way in was through a tunnel 30–100 metres long, hacked out of the thorn hedge. High on the hilltops, with a panoramic view of their surroundings from their watchtowers, villagers could be sure no one could enter their village unannounced.

Wa food crops at that time were mainly maize and buckwheat. They raised rice, too, but for making liquor. They drank both rice beer and distilled spirits, as often and as easily as water. Besides pigs, they bred small dogs for meat and kept cattle and buffaloes for sacrificial occasions, never employing them as draught animals. They also grew opium poppies; opium, walnuts and liquor were their barter items with the plains Dai in exchange for salt, flintlock rifles and ammunition. For iron tools and weapons they had their own sources and blacksmiths.

Some parts of the Wa Hills had silver mines and the Wa turned the metal into an assortment of heavy ornaments and elegant tobacco pipes. Rumours of gold in the hills of Ximeng County (British maps of the Wa Hills around 1900 labeled the area Gold Tract) intensified Sino-British contention for control of Awashan. In the end Ximeng went to China. But no gold mines existed after all and today the overwhelmingly Wa-populated county is the poorest part of China's portion of the Wa Hills.

The Wa were the only people in Yunnan to indulge in the head-hunting tradition, though not the only people in Burma with the custom. Similar warrior tribes along the western border and in the mountains of northeast India, such as the Naga tribes, also practised head-hunting, for the same

While the Wa for the most part inhabit the hills, the Dai occupy the lowlands of the valleys in southwest Yunnan, such as these around Mengding.

reason. They believed a man's spiritual power resided in his skull. Decapitation and display of this skull produced a potent protective force for the village crops. Hence, sowing season was also head-hunting season.

Except for the small number of villages in the Kengtung area of northeast Burma, which converted to Buddhism, all Wa believed in the connection between the skulls and the crops. But not all the Wa carried out head-hunting raids to procure them. Outsiders divided the tribe into Wild Wa and Tame Wa. Some of the Tame Wa got their own skulls annually themselves, but only took the heads of proven rustlers and thieves, for stealing in any form was considered the gravest possible crime in Wa society. Other Tame Wa purchased human skulls from the Wild Wa or substituted wild animal skulls or those of buffaloes.

To the Wild Wa, it was the rule to conduct spring raids to collect a head or two. Sometimes warriors lay in ambush on a propitious day along a well-used, inter-village trail. More often, a party of 10–12 sneaked across the ridges to collect heads from distant villages, where nobody was related to anyone in their own village, thus avoiding a blood feud. The Wa believed the ghost of the decapitated victim stayed near wherever his skull was placed. Heads from far away were better because the ghost wouldn't know the area and thus wouldn't stray far.

When a head was taken the raiding party returned home and the village log drum was beaten to announce the good news. Shamans used chicken-bone divination to determine what animal to sacrifice to the skull. After the rite, the head was placed in a basket and mounted on a tall pole outside the log drum house. Some villages had collections of menhirs standing in a circle and mounted the heads within these. Afterwards came a feast and a night of exuberant dancing. The famous Hair Dance, in which young single women wave and swing around their waist-length locks, may have had its origin in this kind of venue.

The heads stayed mounted for two years, after which it was believed they were no longer efficacious. Then they were taken down and buried in a special plot just outside the village. Over the burial place the Wa erected carved, totem pole-like ceremonial posts. This eerie graveyard was always the first sign a traveller had that the village at hand was indeed Wa.

CONTEMPORARY WA VILLAGES

Older Wa villages, in Ximeng and Lancang Counties, and in Lincang Prefecture, stand on hilltops or lie on the slopes just below, or else straddle high ridges. To anyone familiar with the modest Aini, Lahu and Bulang villages further east, a big Wa village looks like a jungle metropolis. Save for an occasional new administrative building, school or clinic in the main townships, every building is likely to be in traditional style, built of bamboo, wood and thatch.

Housing style varies slightly. In the western areas the roofs slope more steeply and the house is only slightly elevated, with a section of the thatch cut out in front of the entrance. The small, elevated family granary stands in the yard, with a buffalo skull and horns carved on the door.

Further east the houses stand on stilts with an adjoining open balcony. The interior consists of one long main room, the hearth usually in the centre, with one or two small rooms in the corner for the elder generation to sleep in. Pigs and dogs live below. Cattle and buffaloes have their own sheds.

Head-hunting and opium-growing both disappeared from Wa life in China in the mid-1950s. Fortifications around the villages came down as well. The Wa still raise the same grain crops, but in terraces now instead of fire-fields. They also raise tea and sugarcane. Remote villages still maintain elaborate bamboo aqueduct systems and in Ximeng they use long sections of the biggest bamboo to store 100 kg of paddy.

The Wa are not rich by any standard, but relatively self-sufficient, which is a prime necessity in a mountainous area with few connecting roads. The only major town where they constitute most of the urban population is **Ximeng**, high up in the hills west of Lancang. But it is not very interesting. All the buildings are modern and include two dozen karaoke bars that stay open till the wee hours of the morning. The Wa all dress in cheap, modern clothing, except for the red and black shoulder bag. Even in the villages, though they retain the traditional architecture, aqueducts and lifestyle, the Wa only dress up for festivals.

In 2002 the county government moved to a new city of white-tiled, high-rise cement buildings and clean, wide streets beside a picturesque lake in the hills above the old Dai town of **Mengsuo**. The Wa government also set up a model of a traditional Wa village, partly inhabited, to display their people's traditions. The Wa around **New Ximeng** belong to the same branch as that in Menglian, so many of the women still favour the traditional costume.

Elsewhere, beyond Ximeng County, most of the women dress traditional style. This consists of a hand-woven cotton sarong, belt, blouse and headgear. The cloth they weave themselves in the dry season on simple backstrap looms, in striped patterns according to the style of their sub-group. Black or red usually dominates. Under the sarong they also wear cloth leggings or put on several lacquered rattan rings just below the knees.

(following pages) The relatively large Wa town of Zuodou in Lancang County.

Beads and silver dominate the jewellery. In addition to the many strings of red or white beads worn around the neck, the Wa women in the east wear wide belts of multiple strands of beads—white in Ximeng, other colours in Menglian. Ximeng Wa women also wear a wide silver hair band. Menglian Wa headgear comprises a peaked cloth cap, mostly red, held down by a ring of many strands of silver. In Lancang they wear plain, round black turbans like the men, but in Gengma and Cangyuan this turban has a flap hanging down in back. But most of the Lincang Prefecture Wa women prefer plain cotton or terry-cloth headscarves.

Wa women in Menglian and Lancang like to decorate their favourite black jacket with silver studs. Wa women everywhere like heavy silver ornaments, like thick bangles and neck-rings, strings of chunky pendants and big ear studs. In Menglian and southern Lincang Prefecture a majority of women over 30 wear them, which in Menglian are up to 10 cm long, with a 3-cm-wide tube going though the ear lobe and a large filigreed knob at the front end. To make their ear lobe holes big enough, the women insert splinters of wood, adding one every two or three days until the hole has been stretched open sufficiently to hold the ear plug. It takes at least a month.

(above) A kitchen in a Wa house in Zuodou. Except for the pots and pans, nearly everything is manufactured from jungle materials.
(right) A Wa woman of Menglian adorned with the heavy ornaments typical of their attire.

Silver is also used for the pipes. Men use short ones, women long ones, but both types are intricately designed. When not using the pipe, women stick it in their bead-belts or turbans, in Menglian slipping it under the silver chain that holds down the cap. Both men and women carry shoulder bags, usually of woven cotton, but in recent years commercial producers are making bags of acrylic wool on knitting machines. Again, red and black are the dominant colours. The eastern Wa also embellish them with pairs of Job's tears studding the bag and rows of these white seeds lining the bottom. Menglian women sometimes drape their headgear with strings of Job's tears.

As most celebrations in the past had to do with war and head-hunting, these fell by the wayside when the Wa gave up the practice. Even the log drum is only in use in a few areas, usually at the Lunar New Year festivities. Most traditional Wa celebrate the New Rice Festival, now fixed for the entire ethnic group for the 15th day of the 8th lunar month, the time of the Han Mid-Autumn (Moon Cake) Festival. In Menglian, the Wa take a break from harvest activities for the ceremonial slaying of a buffalo, a dance with its skull, an exuberant performance of the Hair Dance by the young women, and much feasting and dancing.

The usual drink at this celebration, imbibed by both men and women, is the mild rice beer, called *shuijiu* locally. Large jugs of this are fermenting at any given time in Wa houses. The host fills a large bamboo mug and, holding the mug with both hands, gives it to his guest. The guest takes it with both his hands, drinks a little, then hands it back to the host, again, as always, with both hands. This is to show respect to the host. The latter drinks a little bit, then hands it back to the guest. The guest may now consume the remainder, or pass it on to another guest afterwards, following which it goes back to the host for a refill and another round. Such is the Wa way of drinking.

DAI TOWNS AND MARKETS

Because so much of the borderlands is mountainous, Dai communities, always in the plains or nearby low-lying valleys, stand far apart from each other. In the west the Dai inhabit several villages in Yongde County, northeast of Zhenkang, the flat lands of the latter and the broad valley of the Nanding River, running through the middle of Lincang Prefecture. Both Han Dai and Shui Dai inhabit this lovely valley, the latter closer to the river. Having migrated from Xishuangbanna in the early Qing Dynasty (1644–1911), the Shui Dai have retained their traditional architecture, raising the houses on stilts or brick piles. Han Dai villages are closer to the road and the eastern foothills, with houses resting on the ground.

Now only a township headquarters, Mengding was once a separate principality, with its own sawba. The town's Dongjing Temple has long been a place of pilgrimage for the valley's Buddhists. Housing a large seated Buddha, it is also the focal point for ceremonies marking the beginning and ending of the Buddhist retreat period during the rainy season. Today, Mengding is part of Gengma County, once the largest and wealthiest of the Dai borderland principalities.

Gengma lies among rolling hills, flanked by the high mountains where the Wa live, and where a few Lahu, Lisu and De'ang have settled. Seat of an autonomous Dai and Wa county, it has two distinct sections—the business district and market, plus the original Dai quarters, slightly uphill from the market. One of the market entrances is marked by a large, Han-style ornamental gate (*pailou*), while the upper flanking street in the market zone ends in a roundabout with a huge banyan tree. Underneath, on either side, are the characteristically Dai peacock mascot statues, in concrete, painted green and blue.

Market day here, held every five days, is one of the best in the borderlands. Local Dai from the city and the nearby villages, as well as Gengma's urban Han minority, set up early in one of the three adjoining market squares, or on one of the adjacent lanes. They sell clothing, prepared food, textiles, sugar cane, vegetables, noodles, grain, fruit, thread, brooms, stools and tools. Dai women hawking bean puddings sit beside them on stools and busy themselves embroidering shoes while they await customers.

By mid-morning the hill people have arrived, mostly Wa women, selling forest produce like herbs, wild vegetables, mushrooms, firewood and bamboo, plus Wa-style textiles. They wear black jackets over shin-length, hand-woven striped sarongs, smoke long silver pipes and wear silver dollar-sized ear plugs with diamond-shaped silver pendants. Some Lahu, in bright, side-fastened, long coats over trousers, also turn up, as do a few Yi from the mountain south of the city, distinguishable from the Dai by the big black turbans and the straight-cut jacket style, usually blue.

Dai women in Gengma, the Nanding valley and Cangyuan plain mostly dress in old-fashioned style, both young and old, almost exclusively so in the rural areas. The outfit comprises an ankle-length black sarong, usually velvet, sometimes cotton or silk, a pale blue or grey, long-sleeved, side-fastened jacket with rounded corners at the bottom, slightly split at the sides. On their heads they wear a terry-cloth turban, as in Dehong. They pierce their ears with cylindrical gold plugs about 3 cm long and 1 cm wide.

Gengma's temple, **Zongfosi**, lies just above the pond in the main city park, which is adjacent to the Dai quarter. In this area each neighbourhood has a name that is posted at its main intersection. The temple, erected in 1473, has a mostly Han-style exterior, with three tiers, but in front the roofs are split and raised higher than the other roof levels, giving it a pleasing five-tiered front. Scenes from *Journey to the West* are carved on the front screen doors. The interior Buddha image is in the Dai style and the long, thin banners hanging from the rafters are typically Dai. Smaller buildings to the rear house the 25 or so resident monks and novices.

The city's other major Buddhist monument lies about 2 km away, on a hillock just above the middle school at the city's southwest edge. This is a white pagoda erected a year before the Zongfo Temple. It rises about 25 metres with eight subsidiary spires around its base. No other religious building stands near it and it is just high enough to be visible from roads approaching Gengma from any direction.

The road south follows a river valley 25 km to Mengsheng, a small Dai township in the lap of Awashan. On the hill just above the south end of town are the first Wa villages and from here until the final descent to Cangyuan, 62 km southwest of Mengsheng, the road keeps to the hills. In between the forests lie old Wa villages, averaging 250–300 houses each. A few newer, smaller Wa settlements lie at the foot of the hills where the road turns into the valley. As it gets closer to Cangyuan the villages are inhabited by Dai.

(above) A Dai woman in Mengding carries water home on a shoulder pole.
(right) A Dai monk near Gengma teaches novices how to read Buddhist scriptures.

The thatched roofs of a typical Wa hill village in Cangyuan County.

Formerly known as Mengtung, the town is the seat of Cangyuan Wa Autonomous County and it is the Wa exclusively who inhabit the county's highlands. The local monument square features stylized buffalo skull decorations; down the block, a larger-than-life statue of a Wa lady stands on a pedestal etched with reproductions of the Ai Hua cliff paintings. But most people in town and in the plain are Dai. The original town is on a knoll in the eastern quarter above the business district. Signs at each corner identify the names of the neighbourhoods, as in Gengma, and the two-storey brick houses with tiled roofs are the same.

At the end of the settled area sits the **Guangyun Temple**, a Qing-Dynasty structure with an ornate, multi-tiered entrance. Frescoes of Buddhist legends adorn the interior walls. About 20 monks and novices reside in the compound. The temple has been fully restored and the posts by the front door are embellished with gilt sculpted dragons, another motif borrowed from the Han. Near the compound gate is an unrestored, three-tiered shrine, much older than the temple.

On the whole, though, Han influence has been slight on the Dai of the western borderlands. The sawbas of old even restricted education in their statelets, fearing it as an instrument of Sinicization. On the other hand, Dai influence on the hill people, especially the Wa, is quite evident, especially in Gengma and Cangyuan Counties. The handful of Yi villages, whose people migrated 300–400 years ago from the Dali area, have been Buddhist since shortly after their arrival. Some of the Lahu are also Buddhist.

In the western half of Cangyuan County all the Wa villages are Buddhist, with their own small temples and resident monks. Dai monks converted them after the Wa gave up head-hunting in the 1950s. Wa women here dress Dai style, though they still like their thick silver bangles and long-stemmed tobacco pipes.

Further east, except for Menglian County, the Dai were in earlier and closer proximity to the Han and are today less traditional. This is immediately apparent in Shuangjiang County, where Dai villages are indistinguishable from Han.

East of the Lancangjiang the Dai inhabit the broad valleys of the Little Black River and its north-south running branch, the Weiyuan River. **Jinggu**, in the centre of Simao Prefecture, is a Dai and Yi Autonomous Prefecture. The older women wear the same long black sarong, jacket and turban, adding a long black apron, often with a blue border strip at the hem, like the Dai women east of Lancang town, and a terry-cloth turban. But the younger women dress modern-style and their generation doesn't even speak the Dai language.

*Buddhist villages in southwest Yunnan build a special enclosure
to house the village sacred pillar.*

Jinggu town lies in a large basin, developed in recent decades as a major light industry centre. Consequently, even from the best vantage points, smoke-stacks mar the scenery in every direction. The city is modern, with two Dai villages appended to the south end. The prevalence of fish ponds is typically Dai, but the architecture is ordinary Han style. Temples in each village are also Han style, yet with Dai interior motifs, like the suspended banners and sculptures in the Southeast Asian style.

The most attractive of these is **Guanmian Temple** in Dazhai, the southern village. The three-tiered temple, built in 1661, is not impressive, but its courtyard is nicely sited and has two towering trees that wrap around pagodas. Called *Shubaota* (Tree-Wrapped Pagoda) and *Tabaoshu* (Pagoda-Wrapped Tree), the latter has more of its spire visible. The pagodas stand on square stone pedestals with low-relief figures of animals, plants, scenery and people carved on the block faces.

Southwest of Jinggu, west of the Lancangjiang in Lancang County, the Dai are less numerous. Shangyun township in the north, the plain around the county seat and the low-lying valleys next to Xishuangbanna are their main areas of habitation. These are the only relatively level areas in the county.

THE LAHU OF LANCANG

The Lahu originated much further north than their present habitat in south-west Yunnan. Some scholars identify them with the ancient Kunming tribe of the Erhai area over 2,000 years ago. At the beginning of the Nanzhao era, they began migrating south and by the middle of the Ming Dynasty had settled in the hills of Lancang County. The majority of the province's Lahu—more than 400,000—live there today. Smaller communities still occupy the slopes of the Wuliang Mountains in eastern Zhenyuan County, in enough numbers to share the autonomous county government with the Yi and Hani. In Shuangjiang they share it with the Dai, Wa and Bulang, and in Menglian with the Dai and Wa. Lahu sub-groups also live in western Xishuangbanna and on the lower slopes of Ximeng's mountains, below the Wa settlements.

Lancang is strictly a Lahu Autonomous County, for here they are the majority community. Its medium-high, well-forested mountains offer the Lahu their preferred terrain—hills not too steep, away from the populous commercial centres, close to the jungle for its game, wild edibles and building materials. The higher mountains to the north and west they leave to the Wa, while parts of the eastern and central parts of the county they share with the Aini.

In the early Qing Dynasty, Han and Bai Mahayana Buddhist monks began proselytizing in the Lahu areas of Shuangjiang and northern Lancang. They made some converts both to Buddhism and to their political cause, which was to resist the imposition of Qing rule. Suppression of these uprisings included quelling the new temples and Buddhist organizations, although the religion itself was never completely wiped out. More successful at spreading a new faith were the American Christian missionaries who entered the county via British Burma early in the 20th century. They established their first Baptist church at Nuofu in the south in 1922 and today most of the Lahu of central and southern Lancang are Christian.

All the county's Lahu, however, share the same origin myth and peculiar social system. They believe the first deity was an almighty matriarch named Eh Sha. She created the couple Zha Bu and Na Bu to make Heaven and Earth and then built four temples to each to honour them. Nobody came, though, so Eh Sha planted a gourd seed and used her own sweat to water it. Three years later, the gourd, having grown to a great size, broke open and gave birth to the progenitors of the Lahu race. Today the gourd, partly because its shape resembles that of a pregnant woman, is the most sacred traditional Lahu symbol. A fertility dance uses gourds as props and a large sculpture of one, painted yellow, is the official city mascot, housed in the lot of the county government headquarters.

In the hunter-gatherer stage of their development the Lahu were matrilineal. Only with migration and the adoption of agriculture did men's status rise. Even nowadays the groom traditionally goes to live in the bride's house. In terms of inheritance, however, the Lahu evolved their own unique system called *wujiwukai*, meaning the same blood lineage divided by sex.

The mother, her female offspring and those of her sisters form one wuji, while the father, his sons and those of his brothers form a parallel wuji. Each has a head, the eldest member of the group, whose job is to convene and chair meetings, assign special tasks and arbitrate disputes. When the father dies his property is divided among his sons and other males of his *wuji*. When the mother dies, her property goes to her daughters and sisters.

The non-Christian Lahu women of the north, plus those of Menglian County, are more apt to dress in traditional style. Black is the basic colour of jacket types among the county's sub-groups. Usually the coat is long-sleeved, side-fastened and reaches to the knees. Strips or patches of coloured cloth are appliquéd to the cuffs, lower sleeves, lapel and along the split-seam hems on the side. Sometimes the lapel is studded with small silver half-globes. Some groups wear trousers, others an ankle-length sarong, the colour patterns dominated by black and red. Black turbans are the usual headgear. Some are trimmed in bright colours or have a flap hanging down the back, appliquéd or embroidered. Lahu females learn to weave and embroider while still children.

Closer to the towns, the Lahu women often wear Dai sarongs and jackets or ordinary modern blouses. Men dress modern-style, but both sexes carry big, brightly striped shoulder bags, with lots of pompoms, tassels and fringes. For ornaments the Lahu prefer silver, especially rectangular jacket buckles, Dai-style belts, filigreed pendant earrings and, in one sub-group, silver baubles and badges attached to the top of the turban.

MENGLIAN'S ETHNIC MIX

Perhaps the easiest area in the borderlands to enjoy is Menglian County. The scenery is rarely spectacular, but always pleasant. The Dai, who form the bulk of the valley and small town population, are Dai Lem, a separate sub-group, and the city's name is a Chinese corruption of the original Meng Lem. They have a greater sense of religion and the women wear a more colourful sarong, with thin stripes in shades of red on the upper third.

The Lahu are also very old-fashioned and the nearest neighbours, so the most likely of the hill folk to turn up in town when it's not specifically a market day. When such days do fall, every five days in Menglian and two days later in Meng'a, Wa and Aini stream into the towns, both of whose women are more apt to wear their full traditional costumes and ornaments than their ethnic cousins in neighbouring counties.

Leaving Lancang valley, the road runs through rolling hills southwest all the way to the border town of **Meng'a**, 97 km distant. Except for a couple of roadside Wa villages just short of Mengma, the pockets of flat land and low valleys are inhabited by Dai. Every sizable village has its own temple, usually two-storey constructions in the Burmese style. Pagodas, some new, sit atop hilltops, with a particularly pretty, gold and white one on the clifftop edge of a small hill about 5 km northeast of Meng'a.

Meng'a is right on the border, a small town of mostly modern cement buildings. Market day is staged in an attractive grove of shade trees on the southeast side of town. It draws Dai, Lahu and Wa from the Myanmar side, in addition to those of the immediate vicinity. Those from Myanmar are even more likely to dress traditional style, often without any modern items.

The other major town between Meng'a and Menglian, about the same size as the former, is Mengma. A large bamboo building at the edge of a pond at the end of the market street serves as a casino. The largest waterfall in the county is up in the hills a few km south. Menglian's other scenic spots lie closer to its southern border—Daheishan, a picturesque mountain park, and the uncommercialized hot springs in the creek beside the Dai township of Lalei, 22

Aini women dress their best for Menglian's market day.

km south of the county seat and 15 km west of Nuofu, site of the Lahu Baptist church.

The biggest pagoda in the county is in Menglian town itself, on the east bank of the Nanlei River, about a furlong (200 metres) south of the bridge. It was built only in recent years and is partly subsidized by Thai Buddhist devotees in northern Thailand. Unlike most pagodas, this one has a shrine inside the dome. The river beside it divides the original Dai town on the west bank from the new city on the east side.

The Dai half of Menglian lies on the moderate slope above the main road. Houses are of red-brown brick, two stories high, with adjoining open balcony and tiled roofs with several gables. The ex-sawba's more commodious, grander residence is now a city museum. The compound houses the most elegant of the town's secular buildings. The sawba's private shrine and a display of various traditional domestic objects, including opium weights and scales, are on view in the rear of the compound.

The only large buildings in this quarter of Menglian are the two temples, both long, three-tiered structures with moderately sloping roofs and tall supporting columns at the entrance. The lower sited one has gold painted decorations on the façade. The slightly larger one at the top of the settled area has two modest pagodas in its courtyard. Both house seated Buddhas in the Dai style of sculpture, and display long, thin banners suspended from the interior rafters; decorated festival palanquins are stacked in the corners. A somewhat smaller, less important, but equally active temple compound lies just beyond the southeast suburbs of the new city.

Local Dai Buddhism follows the same pattern of their ethnic cousins in Banna and Myanmar. They celebrate the Water-Sprinkling Festival in mid-April and include the firing of home-made rockets in the events. On the 15th day of the 9th lunar month in the Dai calendar (June or July) begins the three-month retreat for monks and novices, while the laity is expected to observe taboos on building new houses, getting married and field labour that involves cutting. Full moon day and especially the 8th days of the waxing and the waning moon are sacred, and some devotees will pray all night in the temples.

The Wa live on the ridges and higher slopes of the mountains north and south of the main road. A greater percentage of the women dress in traditional costumes than anywhere east of Cangyuan. They don't save their silver ornaments for festivals, either, wearing their ear plugs or big rings, round embossed pendants, neck rings and multiple bangles to both the fields and the city markets. They are quite approachable and hospitable. Visitors to the villages are soon invited in for tea.

Villages north of the Menglian-Meng'a road tend to be older and higher, though not the size of the Wa villages north of the county. Most of those in the south are more recent, around 25 years old, and home to Wa who fled war and famine in Myanmar. The government on that side had introduced wheat as a substitute crop for opium, but neglected to inform the Wa how to consume it. It resembled rice, so they tried to boil and eat it in the same manner. That didn't work, of course, and they were soon left with nothing else to eat.

Simultaneously, fighting erupted in the vicinity and it became too dangerous to remain. They fled to Menglian. The county government allowed them to stay and settle on some vacant land in the lower hills. In 1993 the provincial government encouraged the immigrant Wa, already granted citizenship, to stage their annual New Rice Festival, like other Wa in the county, which they had been too demoralized to observe since their flight to China. The government also disbursed money so they could have a big celebration, bused in people from other villages and payed for the sacrificial buffaloes.

The Lahu of Menglian live in the mountains at lower elevations. Their houses usually stand on the ground. Most of the women come to town wearing their traditional clothes—black jacket festooned with silver studs over a long sarong, which may be a mostly red, printed cotton one, bought in the market. Some wear a black one with bands of zigzag patterns appliquéd in red and white.

Two sub-groups of Aini live in the county. Villages are the same as in Xishuangbanna, but the women wear longer skirts and the embroidery on the jacket, leggings and shoulder bags lays heavy emphasis on the colour magenta. Some fold up the jacket and wear it as a turban. Most wear the mostly silver headdress, with an upright rounded plate at the back. Many of the Lahu and Aini men wear wide-legged, indigo-dyed cotton trousers and jackets, sometimes embroidered on the back. The presence of both these minorities, together with the traditional Wa, makes Menglian's market scene the most colourful in the borderlands.

RED RIVER VALLEY

0   20   20 Kilometres
0   20   40 Miles

Chuxiong Yizu Zizhizhou

Yuxi Diqu

Kunming Shi

Qujing Diqu

Wensha Zhuangz Miaozu Zizhizho

Honghe Ha'nizu Yizu Zizhizhou

Zhongping
Tuanjie
Jiulong
Gongshan
Songshaoguan
Cuihua
Jijie
Banqiao
Tianshengqiao
Chengfangqiao
Chanyi
Wu-ting
Qingshui Hai
Penc
Nan-ning
Zhangjiu He
Yangjie
Qujing
Yuanyongjing
Bicheng
Aziying
Songming
Ma-lung
Liac
Xindian
Guangtong
Yongding
Xiaoshao
Yanglin
Chen-nan
Lü-ho
Yipinglang
Longtan
Baiyangjie
Hongshap
Banqiao
Dashipu
Kunming
Kebao
Xiqiao
Baomanjie
Tuguan
Lubiao
Anning
Majie
Zhongyishe
Chuanjie
Baishu
Dian Chi
Lunan
Zhaokua
Danfen
Tuodian
Xiaolüzhi
Bajie
Chung-yi
Jinning
Banqiao
Shidong
Ainishan
Fabiao
Yimen
Duanqi
Xujiadu
Juece
Ejia
Haizidi
Anlongpu
Xinjie
Fuxian Hu
Xiyi
Xiyi
Zhongshu
Malong He
Zhelong
Fuliangpeng
Dajie
Mile
Longde
Shuitang
Shiyang
Tadian
Yuxi
Xiaoyangjie
Xinzhai
Shede
Jiasa
Laochang
Xinyinpan
Eshan
Sijie
Qilu
Hongxi
Rish
Zhedong
Huanian
Huaxi
Nijiao
Tuantian
Xianhe
Yangwu
Longwu
Gaoda
Jiangbianjie
Pengpu
Longpeng
Lihaozhai
Tangshang
Ganzhuang
Daqiao
Xiaolongtan
Pingyua
Baitu
Shibingzhou
Baoxiu
Baxin
Ami-hsien
Kaiyuan
Zhongheying
Jingxing
Yüankiang
Yilong Hu
Lin'an Zhen
Dehou
Bixi
Wadie
Puxiong
Mingjiujie
Tongguan
Shengli
Yangjie
Niujie
Guanting
Gejiu
Shiwopu
Datun
Wenlan
Dima
Yisa
Majie
Nansha
Kafang
Boduqing
Gegu
Yutang
Jiaqi
Shitouzhai
Niujiaozhai
Doumuge
Manhao
Baizhai
Longtan
Manijie
Niukong
Fengchunling
Manmujie
Huangcaoling
Yingpanjie
Dahezi
Jingbian
Black River
Sanmeng
Laojizhai
Adebo
Ching-pien
Wangjie
Jiangxi
Sanleng
Man-niang
Qiaotouhe
Banpo
Tongchang
Jinhe
Xiaohegou
Man-
Jiangcheng
Sha-pa
Lao Cai

VIETNAM

LAOS

YUNNAN
Red River Valley

© Airphoto Internat

Lake Dianchi

Lake Fuxian

Nan Cr

Ailaoshan: The Terrace Builders

SCULPTED MOUNTAINS

A most beautiful seasonal event in Yunnan is the arrival of the winter fog that blankets the valleys and lower slopes of the Ailao Mountains, between the Red River and the Vietnam border. The verdant mountains rise several hundred metres higher than the fog; they are mottled with villages all the way up the slopes, separated by clumps of forest and great swaths of terraced fields (*titian*). These terraces cut into every contour of the slopes, at angles up to 70 degrees, and are the most ancient and impressive in the region.

Moreover, most are irrigated and filled with water all year round. They are mostly used only to grow rice and so in the dry months of winter they are empty of crops. Filled with water, they make glistening stairways up and down the slopes, catching the colours of the clouds at sunrise all the way down to the fog line. Then, as the sun rises over the peaks, the fog begins its slow ascent over the terraces, engulfing the villages and groves before dissipating in the mid-morning warmth. Now the lines of the terrace banks, marked out by the water in their beds, lie in a plethora of swirling patterns, like the thumbprints of angels on the slopes. Every winter Chinese photographers, amateur and professional, descend on Yuanyang County in a contest to capture this essential provincial image—flooded terraces in the fog.

Terrace farming is by no means unique to the Ailao Mountains, but its long history here—in some areas the same terraces have been producing rice for over a thousand consecutive years—attests to the ecological wisdom of the ancient Dai, Hani and Yi who built them. Elsewhere in the province terrace farming depends mainly on the rain for its water. But in Ailaoshan the water from high mountain springs and creeks is channelled in ditches that are directed to run throughout the farming area. Divider stones and bamboo tubes divert part of the water from the main irrigation channel to individual terraces, from these dropping through notches in the terrace walls to feed those below and so on, all the way to the bottom of the slope.

The Ailao Mountains rise on the right bank of the Red River (*Yuanjiang*) as it flows from its origin in Dali Prefecture southeast to Hekou and on to Hanoi and the Gulf of Tonkin. Thrust up by the geologic disruptions that caused the formation of the Himalayas, the mountains stand over 3,000 metres high in the upper part of the range, in northeast Zhenyuan County. To the southeast they are not as high, but often steep, sharply etched against the skyline and flanked

(following pages) The spectacular terraces of Ailaoshan.

by other ranges cut by rivers running parallel to the Yuanjiang. Perhaps nowhere else in the province is the lay of the land, in all its possible shapes and contours, so clearly discernible. Nowhere else has terrace farming been so intensively and successfully engineered.

Besides its scenic attraction, Ailaoshan is home to a number of colourful minorities, especially in the areas close to the Vietnam border. Mostly Dai inhabit the river valleys and lower slopes, while the Hani, and to a lesser extent the Yi, dominate the highlands. Pockets of Miao, Yao, Zhuang and others occupy lands in between. Traditional costumes are most women's choice for everyday wear. Even in the cities the teenage girls prefer to dress in ethnic style. Beauty is still conceived within the bounds of tribal aesthetics.

The customs and traditions of the past are still popular here, both in day-to-day domestic life and in the observance of annual celebrations. This must be at least partly due to the time-tested success of their traditional farming methods. Terrace farming cannot be mechanized, so the organization of labour has remained constant. Improvements in fertilizer and the use of high-yield seeds have even increased annual harvests, more than matching the population growth. The old system works better than ever. Consequently, the culture built around it stays strong.

The fantastic headdresses of a Mengzi Yi girl (above) and Huoyao Dai (right).

Ethnic pride in Ailaoshan thus has its roots in the continuing efficiency of the people's traditional material culture. It also has positive effects on their general character, adding a healthy trait of self-confidence to their sociability, easy manner and good humour.

UPPER AILAOSHAN: XINPING, YUANJIANG, MOJIANG

Typical Ailaoshan scenery begins in western Xinping County, where the Chuxiong-Mojiang highway enters Yuxi Prefecture. **Xinping** city lies some 65 km east of the Red River, next to a valley cradled by rolling hills. It is not particularly interesting, with just one nice park with pools and pavilions and a small old town in the western quarter. Though it is the administrative seat of a Yi and Dai Autonomous County, few of either minority are ever in town. Most Yi live northwest of the county seat, while the Dai are the main inhabitants of the Red River valley.

The road west out of Xinping ambles through low-lying hills until it crosses the river. The high slopes of Ailaoshan rise steeply on the other side. The road joins the Chuxiong-Mojiang highway (which has surprisingly little traffic) and stays a few hundred metres above the river. Dai villages of 20–30 houses cling to the slopes, their houses of unbaked brick, like boxes, two stories high, with flat roofs. Animals live on the ground floor and people on the next.

As the river cuts a deep gorge in western Xinping County, Dai villages are sited on the slopes above. Rather than the broad fields of the riverside, characteristic of Dai settlements further downriver, Xinping Dai built narrow terraces on the slopes and contours of the lower part of the mountains and reinforced them with stone. They channelled the water from the streams tumbling from the heights and ran it through their settlements and into the terraces. Isolated from the main areas of Dai settlement in the south, they were also beyond the conversion line when the Buddhist wave swept into Dai areas in the 12th–15th centuries. Xinping Dai, and all Dai in the Red River valley, have retained their original animist beliefs.

Further downriver the valley widens and flat tablelands sometimes extend several km on the right bank. Dai villages, with the same architecture, dominate the riverside above **Yuanjiang**, especially around the market township of Dongwo. Yuanjiang town sits on the biggest right bank plain, a few km south of the bridge. It is one of the lowest and hottest cities in Yunnan. In spring strong winds sweep through the region, bending trees and raising dust along the country lanes. Except for one old stately pavilion beside a pond in the centre of the city, virtually every building in Yuanjiang is modern.

Traditionally dressed Huayao Dai from the villages upriver and Hani from the hills south are frequent visitors, however, adding a bit of colour to the streets.

The most interesting town in Upper Ailaoshan is **Mojiang**, the next stop southwest of Yuanjiang on the highway to Jinghong. Mojiang is also connected with Chuxiong and the approach from Manbang, where the road from Xinping crosses the Red River and passes through the most scenic stretch of this part of the range. The road climbs high above the river and just before the county boundary enters a high plateau in **Malu** township, home to a Yi community from the same branch as in western Chuxiong Prefecture. Both men and women wear goatskins and the women wear an embroidered apron, often embellished with silver studs, and big black turbans.

Past this plain, the road again hugs the high ridge above the river and soon offers a long view of the mountains, unfolding one after another to the southeast. A roadside market village lies just beyond this viewpoint, drawing Malu Yi and three kinds of Hani on its market day. Then the road enters a forested stretch, with the serpentine lake of Buka Reservoir, perhaps the prettiest man-made body of water in Yunnan, lying in the woods below.

Emerging from the forest, the road enters the settled highlands of Ailaoshan, home to the Woni branch of the Hani. The titian culture is visible here, with rows of terraces descending the slopes just below the villages. The latter are usually sited on ridges, promontories, or just below the woods that swathe the mountaintops. Houses are in the typical rural Yunnanese style, clustered close to one another.

Woni women tie their hair in a topknot, pile it over the forehead and cover it with a tall cloth wrap with a long black fringe hanging down the back. Over a long-sleeved blouse and trousers they wear a side-fastened, short-sleeved coat, waist-length in front, knee-length in back. Either the entire coat is dyed deep indigo blue, or only the vest part is blue and the rest white. In that case, the ends of the sleeves are embroidered in cross-stitch patterns and the back embellished with different designs and patterns stitched in red and green.

As the road descends to Bixi it passes out of Hani territory and soon enters the valley around Mojiang city. Formerly known as Talang, it is a mostly Han-populated city that the Hani largely stay away from except on market day, every five days. It lies in the lap of surrounding low mountains, with a couple of small hills within the urban area, old neighbourhoods in the eastern quarter and a shady park on the eastern outskirts, with a pond and several pavilions.

Mojiang's main claim to fame, however, is that the Tropic of Cancer runs right through the city. A park honouring and identifying the precise route of this line occupies the top of the hill on the city's southern side. Six large carved sandstone pillars stand in a niche two-thirds the way up the entrance staircase.

At the top of the stairs is a circle of Stonehenge-like pillars, about 1.5 metres high. Behind this, on the summit, a white *ziggurat* stands over the line, which is marked in red brick on the white walkway and runs under an open niche at the ziggurat's base. The brick-marked line then passes an ornamental sundial, a tall chromed pillar, and terminates at a great domed building at the end of the park.

GATEWAYS TO THE SOUTH: SHIPING, JIANSHUI, GEJIU, MENGZI

The most beautiful part of Ailaoshan, and the most expertly cultivated, lies in Honghe Prefecture, between the Red River and the Vietnam border. This is also one of the most rugged parts of the province, where even minibuses barely

The town of Luchun rests on a ridge above the terraces of Ailaoshan.

average 30 kph on the well-paved roads. Consequently, until recent decades it was a world of its own, with scarcely a Han inhabitant and no attempt at, or any real need of, government control. Other than the members of the occasional caravans, people lived largely ignorant of the existence of cities.

On the left bank (northern side) of the Red River, mountains rise at once, but they are largely too steep, rocky and infertile for cultivation. North of this range the peaks and ridges, instead of dropping off into another major river valley, gradually slide off onto the high plateau lands typical of central Yunnan. Except for small, scattered mountain groups and isolated valleys, the home of Yi, Hani and Dai, the area has long been settled by Han Chinese. The major cities of the area have been centres of Han civilization since the early Ming Dynasty, with Jianshui important even before that.

The only significant minority in these cities is the Hui, most of whose forefathers first came with the Mongols in the 13th century; they have large neighbourhoods in the old quarters. For the minorities of Lower Ailaoshan, however, these cities are closer and impressively bigger than their county seats. Ordinary commerce can be done in the latter, but the northern Honghe metropolises offer other opportunities, like secondary schooling, vocational training and temporary contract labour. These cities are much more in the Ailaoshan people's consciousness than Kunming, considered too big and too distant.

Whichever way the main highway leads, that will be the city most associated with the people of a particular county. For Jinping folks it is Mengzi, site of the old caravan terminus, or Gejiu, until recently the prefecture capital. For Yuanyang people it is Jianshui, as it is for Luchun residents, because the highway out of Luchun first bends over to Yuanyang to go north, rather than straight up to Honghe. The people of the latter county feel more of an affinity for Shiping, for a main road connects with it directly.

Shiping lies in a basin below the highlands separating it from Tonghai and the lakes to the north. It has its own lake nearby, just east of the city, called **Shilonghu**, which the county government has in recent years begun to promote as a tourist attraction by installing pavilions and other such things. This new tourist consciousness may save what is left of the old town in the heart of the city, as well as the twisting lanes and old-fashioned brick and tile houses of the adjacent eastern and southern neighbourhoods.

The county is famous for its *doufu*—tofu, soybean curd—which the locals pronounce closer to *dafu*. Numerous downtown stalls offer snacks of this to customers in the evenings, who sit around an open grill, cook the cubes to taste and dip them in sauce. In the fancier restaurants more discerning doufu connoisseurs can select from among some two dozen special preparations.

Just 50 km east of Shiping is **Jianshui**, the most attractive municipality in Honghe Prefecture in terms of architecture and historical interest. Here is a city that has not only retained extensive parts of its old town and historic buildings, but one that takes great pride in them. This attitude affects its reception of travellers. The situation is now completely the reverse of that encountered by the two 19th-century French expeditions that passed through here. Jianshui people today are friendly, polite and hospitable to their guests, only anxious that visitors appreciate the city as much as the natives do.

Over 50 structures in the county, most of them in the city and its vicinity, are under government protection. Nearly all of these are still in use, as schools, law offices, libraries, police stations, government agencies and the like. In addition, the city's old quarter has many elegant private houses in traditional style, with compound gates decorated with elaborate wood carvings. They have not been designated county monuments, but they are anyway antique, attractive and still in use.

Jianshui's most imposing building is the enormous, three-tiered **Chaoyang Tower**, formerly the eastern gateway to the city, with a long, high red wall at its base. Constructed in 1379, it is the grandest Ming-style gate extant in the

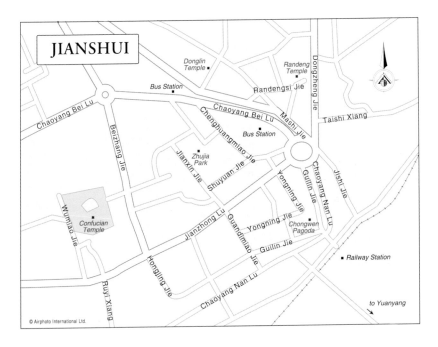

province. A green-lawned park has been appended to the front, where city residents like to relax in good weather. On the other side of the wall, Jianzhonglu heads west, lined with shade trees for the first few blocks.

At the Jianxinjie intersection, the lane to the right leads to the **Zhu Family Flower Garden** (*Zhujia Huayuan*) in the heart of the old town. Beside the entrance is a long, red, two-storey wooden house with carved doors. Pottery, jewellery, antiques and local handicraft stalls occupy the ground floor, with a painting gallery upstairs. The Zhu Garden is a vast complex of compounds within compounds, rooms with carved screen doors, ponds, flower arrangements and a hall exhibiting large colour photos of the county's attractions.

Past the turn-off to the garden Jianzhong Street continues west, passing Beizhengjie, which turns right towards the Linan Hotel, next to the roundabout with a new 'space needle'. Less than a hundred metres past the Beizhengjie turn is an entrance on the right to *Xuehai*, the Sea of Learning, a large oval water tank in front of the **Confucius Temple** (*Wenmiaosi*), the most important such temple in all of Yunnan. It was built in 1325 during the Yuan Dynasty.

Two carved stone gates flank the main entrance behind the pond. The wooden entry gate is elaborately carved and painted, with dragons winding

Chaoyang Tower was originally constructed in 1379.
Its massive gate is the largest of its kind in Yunnan.

around the two main posts. Inside the compound in front of the temple stands a beautifully forged copper incense burner, in the shape of a miniature temple, with pastoral and animal imagery as well.

Inside the temple a brightly painted statue of Confucius stands in a partly gilded wooden compartment. The walls behind are covered with portraits of the sage standing in various positions. Similar paintings hang on the walls of the two buildings on either side of the courtyard. Gilded bronze statues of Chinese deities from the Ming and Qing eras are displayed in the front room of the hall on the left. Originally the complex included more compounds, but these have been converted into, appropriately enough, classrooms and dormitories for boarding students.

Past the entrance to Xuehai stand a few more elegant old buildings, for this neighbourhood was within the old city walls. One is the **Zhilin Temple**, a formerly important Buddhist compound from the Ming Dynasty. Of the other two historic buildings, one is in use as a law office, the other as a neighbourhood police station—examples of the Jianshui feeling for their traditional architecture. In other cities the lawyers and the police occupy new cement buildings with facades of glass and tile.

The other major Buddhist sites in Jianshui are closer to Chaoyang Tower. Southeast of the tower, Guilin Lane continues two blocks to a compound of yellow-walled buildings, with carved roof struts, around the 14-tiered **Changwen Pagoda**. The largest quarter of the old town lies north of Chaoyang Tower, starting from Mashijie, across the main thoroughfare and down all the side streets.

The first turn up Mashijie goes to the **Randengsi**, Lighting the [Votive] Lamps Temple, with a colourfully ornate entrance gate and two buildings within the quiet, shady compound. A lane from here leads to the oldest city mosque, with its red wooden walls, carved doors and tiled roof. Several fancy houses lie in this quarter; a couple of the grand old mansions were expropriated and turned into a library and a primary school.

Among the county's attractions are mountain temples, classic old bridges, religious monuments, the terraced hills near the Red River and the natural phenomenon of **Swallow Cave** (*Yanzidong*), 30 km to the east. The most unusual monument is **Wenbi Pagoda**, a few km southwest. It is named for its shape, modelled on a writing brush (*wenbi*), but standing alone and unadorned on a barren knoll it could be, from a distance, mistaken for one of the many tall smokestacks over the kilns in the Jianshui vicinity.

South Lake in winter, Mengzi. Only rarely does it snow this far south in the province.

The bridges, however, are more easily appreciated—outstanding examples of their kind from the Ming and Qing periods, that today span streams which have shrunk or been rerouted. The areas are no longer so commercially active, so the motor traffic mostly keeps away and only pedestrians cross the bridges, carrying loads on their shoulder poles or tending their animals, scenes that have hardly changed since the bridges were constructed.

One such bridge, slightly arched and with a tower in the middle, is **Great Happiness Bridge** (*Daxingqiao*), just beyond Qujiang town, 50 km north of Jianshui. Another, roughly similar, is **Heavenly Elephant Bridge** (*Tianxiangqiao*), a few km east of Jianshui. But the longest (17 spans) and most picturesque is **Double Dragon Bridge** (*Shuanglongqiao*), a few km west of the city, just past a long straggling roadside village that makes gravestones. A three-tiered tower stands in the middle of the bridge and a smaller tower is at the end on the north bank. The stream is narrow and shallow and flanked by vegetable gardens. Only occasionally does a peasant cross the bridge or a pony cart trot over it. But at such moments one is transported back in time.

Gejiu, formerly the capital of Honghe Prefecture, is far less interesting than Jianshui. The vicinity is heavily industrialized, for Gejiu is the Tin Capital of China. The city's most prominent feature is its **Golden Lake** (*Jinhu*), but unfortunately all the buildings along its shore are drab, concrete, low-rise structures that look modelled on the early factories of the Industrial Revolution in Britain. A reduced old town still exists in the southern quarter and above it stands a two-tiered tower that was once part of the city walls. Just beyond this monument is the Baohua Park, which houses gardens, groves of tropical trees, pavilions and the late 17th century Baohua Temple.

The fourth of Honghe's gateway cities to the south is **Mengzi**, almost due east from Gejiu, though to get there from the latter requires first going north and then doglegging to the southeast. The city lies south of two small lakes on a large plain, with mountains rising to the east. Thus it had plenty of room to expand and in 2004 the prefecture's capital changed from Gejiu to here. The countryside sometimes resembles Wenshan Prefecture, with its limestone boulder-studded hills here and there and the group of tightly packed peaks that rises behind Zhacun, 10 km to the northeast.

Mengzi has a lake, too, on its southern outskirts and, unlike Gejiu, its **South Lake** (*Nanhu*) is the loveliest site in town. Much smaller than Gejiu's, it is nearly bisected by a long finger of land, which connects by a high, arched, marble bridge to an island. Legend says this is the site where the wife of a scholar invented *guoqiao mixian* ('over-the-bridge rice noodles') to keep her husband well fed while he studied. The dish is one of Mengzi's several *mingcai* (famous foods). At the end of the other stretch of this strip of land stands a large, pale yellow, octagonal, two-storey pavilion, with two auxiliary buildings in front at the water's edge. Other classical-style pavilions and resthouses lie at different points along the waterfront and all are reflected in the water and illuminated by lights every evening.

On the northern shore of the lake stand two French buildings erected in the 1880s, including the original consulate, with its long yellow shape and recognizably French *fleur-de-lis* on the gates. The other, much smaller, stands next to the water. About two blocks down a dirt lane past this is the old French prison, built in 1907 to house non-Chinese offenders arrested by the French police, who were responsible for the foreign community.

Mengzi is only partly modernized and the warren of streets adjacent to the lake makes up the older quarter. The town becomes especially active Sunday market day, when minorities from the surrounding countryside, hill and plain, join the urban Han shoppers in the streets and market squares. Miao of the Mengchou branch, in colourful pleated skirts and embroidered jackets and belts, are the most prominent.

An even more colourful group are the Yi from the eastern and southern mountains. Their women wear multicoloured, long-sleeved, short-front jackets over knee-length tunics and trousers; the tunic and jacket fully embroidered and appliquéd, the trousers embroidered at the shins and cuffs.

On their heads they may wear a flat, heavily embroidered rectangular cloth that folds over the hair knotted at the forehead and tilts over the back of the head. Younger girls wear a silver-studded band topped by a fan-shaped crown of red pompoms mounted on the end of sticks and with long bunches of pearl and pompom tassels on each side. Older women, however, throw a large piece of cloth over the headdress, to show that they know their youth has passed.

LOWER AILAOSHAN:
HONGHE, LUCHUN, YUANYANG, JINPING

Glimpses of the titian culture can be had on the route south from Jianshui to the Red River. The flat-roofed, mud-brick architecture typical of Yuanyang County is the feature of Yi villages beside Guanding, where the same branch of the Yi lives as in Yuanyang. A few Huayao Dai villages also lie in the township and their colourfully dressed women often come to Guanding to sell fruits and vegetables. Further south on the main road, past Baishashui, lies a long, narrow ridge, Yi and Hani villages perched on top, with others lying on the nearby hills, their terraced fields cut into the steep sides of the ridge all the way down the gorge.

Like this route, the roads from Shiping and Gejiu zigzag down the mountains to reach the Red River. All along the river valley Dai settlements occupy the flat lands, mostly on the south bank, and beside the tributary streams that have slithered down the mountains. But from the Red River to the terraced highlands of Lower Ailaoshan, each of the three approaches—from Honghe city, from Manhao and from Nansha—passes through very different landscapes.

The county seat of **Honghe** sits on a hilltop a few km above the intercity highway. The oldest part lies near the top, with a park at the summit. A Qing-era pavilion houses a huge bronze bell. Nearby is a concrete platform for viewing the mountains to the south. It is not an especially pretty view, for the foothills and nearest heights are practically barren. Not much agriculture is in the vicinity of the town, either. And unlike Yuanyang, Luchun and Jinping, the area lacks both ethnic minority villages adjacent to the urban area and terraces to gaze at from the suburbs. Dai and Yi do turn up in town, though, and the market area uptown on any particular day attracts a number of them.

The best of the county's mountain roads is the one going west, which slowly ascends into the highlands and eventually passes out of the prefecture and meets the Kunming-Jinghong highway between Mojiang and Yuanjiang.

(*above*) *Yuanjiang Yi at the market in town.*
(*right*) *The Hauyao Dai inhabit the Red River Valley beside the Ailao Mountains.*

For some 40 km or so the land is mostly dry, uncultivated and empty of people or even grazing animals. But after the ascent, the familiar Ailaoshan landscape appears. Villages speckle the mountain slopes, with bamboo groves, patches of forest and the marvelous titian in between them.

Quite the opposite scenery lies on the Manhao-Jinping route, at the other end of Lower Ailaoshan. Once across the river, the road climbs into the mountains and it is nearly all forests for the next 60 km, with scarcely a settlement visible in the hills. Then, as the road winds down to **Jinping**, Hani villages with flat-roofed 'mushroom houses' start popping up on the slopes, above their water-filled terraces. Here and there Yao villages, recognizable by their one-storey, tile-roofed houses, also cling to the hills.

Terraced slopes and traditional villages continue right up to the outskirts of Jinping town. The county seat lies on a slope above a tributary stream of the Tengtiao River, which flows through the southern part of the county. Above the settled area the forests begin, broken by Hani and Yao villages further uphill. The town itself is unattractive, with no parks, just modern, boxlike, concrete buildings. Its only saving grace is its proximity to typically beautiful Ailaoshan scenery, plus the colourful ethnic mix in the central market area. This is a daily feature, but especially well attended on horse and rat days.

Jinping is a Miao, Yao and Dai Autonomous County, yet the Hani are the most prominent ethnic minority in town. Hani women dress in loose, side-fastened black or blue jackets and trousers, augment their braids with cotton yarn and coil them on top of their heads. The Yao are the next most numerous, the women wearing embroidered trousers and tall red caps held in place with a thick silver band at the base. Yi women from the hills to the south, wearing bright, side-fastened jackets with embroidered lapels, carrying their pack-baskets, come to the town centre looking for temporary work. On market days, Miao from the hills south of Jinping also turn up, as do some of the Dai from Mengla, in long black sarongs and short jackets.

South of Jinping the road descends into another mountain range above the Tengtiao River, mostly Miao-inhabited, then at a junction close to the Vietnam border, it turns west to **Mengla**, a largely Dai township at the eastern end of a long, low valley. Market day here is two days after Jinping's and draws tribals from Vietnam as well as smaller, little-known ethnic groups like the Kucong of Zhemi township and spillover groups from across the border.

The third route into Lower Ailaoshan proceeds from Nansha, now the capital of Yuanyang County on the Red River south of Jianshui. The way climbs up to old Yuanyang, now also known as Xinjie, and on to Luchun. This is the loveliest stretch in the entire mountain range, with villages and terraces beginning just 10 km up in the hills. Beside the old Dai village of Nansha is a new city, whose high-rise concrete buildings obscure the original Dai settlement. In the late 1990s it became the administrative seat of Yuanyang County, replacing Yuanyang city, 32 km south up in the mountains.

Yuanyang itself, on a high ridge between two valleys, is mainly a new town dominated by unimaginative cement buildings and two long streets. This part was appended to a couple of existing Yi settlements, which stand beside the modern town, on either flank. In Yuanyang the outstanding scenery of Ailaoshan is just outside the narrow boundaries of the urban area, literally right around the nearest corner. Hani villages lie nearby and their women, dressed in Hani style all the time, are frequent visitors to town. With most Yi women also in their own flashy costumes, not to mention the Dai, Zhuang and even Yao who turn up, Yuanyang, despite its grey buildings, is among the most colourful cities in the whole province.

Ethnic minorities, who make up the bulk of the people in town (the Han everywhere in Lower Ailaoshan are a minority), and the rural scenery are Yuanyang's attractions. Within the town itself is a park, just beyond the southern bus terminal and above the main road. Here locals gather in the evenings for mass dance exercises while others watch, stroll around, or gaze at the mountain scenery lying just beyond the city's edge.

Behind the park the ridge continues up to a broadcasting tower and on southward. To see the western hills and the Hani villages ensconced among them, one takes the dirt road past the southern bus terminal, which quickly reaches the rural area. In winter the sun sets directly in the trough of the valley, beaming the sky's last colours onto the water in the terraces.

Back at the bus terminal, the main road bends around the hill behind Yuanyang and turns south along the eastern side of the ridge. Now the view takes in the equally well-populated, heavily terraced slopes to the east. The road wriggles over the contours of the slope for another 8 km to **Dayutang**, where a lateral road turns left to lead to the villages just espied from the road. Just beyond this village a turn right ascends a rough road past a small reservoir, comes to a high ridge, passes a Hani tea-growing village, then comes to the high pass at the Niujiaozhai junction, overlooking the Tengtiao River valley. **Niujiaozhai** is 8 km north of this junction, while **Shalatuo** is another 18 km west. Both are mixed Hani and Yi townships with many villages, sometimes with tea and tobacco plantations instead of the *titian*.

Minibuses ply this route to both townships a few times each day, but it's a rough ride. The main road south, though, is smoothly paved. It crosses the pass beyond Dayutang and winds around the mountain down to the somewhat lower promontory at Panzihua, a small administrative township grafted on to

(following pages) A winter fog swirls up the valley and over the city of Yuanyang.

a Hani village. The view from here takes in a vast panorama of terraced mountains with large Yi and Hani villages. About 70 per cent of the slopes are under cultivation. Long, thin, silvery streams ripple down the creases in the hills. More mountains, equally sculpted, loom on the northern and western horizons.

From **Panzihua** the road slowly descends to the Tengtiao River valley and the market town of **Huangmaoling**. Dai villages, rice fields and banana groves lie beside the river. The road continues south for 12 km to **Laomeng**, a larger valley township, with Dai in the lowlands and Miao in the immediate foothills. Its Sunday market is one of the biggest and most colourful in the area, drawing Miao, Yao, two kinds of Dai, three kinds of Yi and up to six different kinds of Hani.

Laomeng's commercial importance is due to its location at a junction of three main roads into the hills. The route east goes to Jinping, with largely Hani and Miao villages in between. Crossing a stream from the west, which flows into the Tengtiao at Laomeng, another road, unpaved, climbs high into the hills to the south, 21 km up to Laojizhai. This highland township is home to isolated, traditional Hani and Yi sub-groups, exhibiting cultural traits they have borrowed from each other.

The main road from Laomeng turns sharply west and follows the stream, often climbing high above it, all the way to its source in the forests at the boundary of Luchun County. Huangcaoling, the first township past Laomeng, lies on the flat top of a high, narrow spur on the north side of the stream. The high mountains rising behind it on the south side are heavily terraced and Hani-inhabited. They are the dominant ethnic group from here to Luchun. One of the largest Hani villages is right next to the road, at Habo, just before the road dips into the last valley in the county.

After ascending into the forest and entering Luchun County, the road stays at this higher elevation most of the way to Luchun city. This is a new town appended to a large existing Hani settlement, like Yuanyang, also long and narrow, with sides dropping off steeply and filled with terraces.

The county is 80 per cent Hani and the dialect of the village of **Dazhai**, at Luchun city's western end, was chosen as the standard Hani dialect for publishing and the creation of dictionaries. The eastern highlands are the most densely settled. The road west first descends into a long river valley, then rises in the western hills, turns south down to the valley at Daheishan, and passes into Jiangcheng County.

Much of the area south of the valley road is heavily forested and largely uninhabited. One branch road 50 km west of Luchun cuts though the hills to the southeast. Terraced hills and Hani villages soon give way to steep cliffs and thick forests, a few hidden Yao villages, more forests and finally, 67 km from the turn-off, the end of the road at Qimaba. This is a large Dai township on a moderate slope above its terraces, which sprawl in front of Qimaba until the edge of the slope, where there's a sudden vertical drop to the stream bed a few hundred metres below.

The agricultural reforms of the 1980s, the construction of motorable roads up into the hills and the natural diligence of the people have led to a flourishing local market scene. Every township has a market day, when hordes of villagers, mostly women in their ethnic dress, converge on the otherwise sleepy commercial area. A few energetic individuals make a good living buying goods at one market and selling them at another.

Thanks to the transportation boom, such business activity is relatively easy now, for every day or two is market day in the vicinity, especially between Yuanyang and Luchun. Some markets are weekly—Huangcaoling on Fridays, Wozha and Huangmaoling on Saturdays, Laomeng on Sundays. Others are every six days, according to the cycle of 12 days, one animal for each: Luchun, Habo and Jinping horse and rat days, Mengla monkey and tiger days, Laojizhai chicken and rabbit days.

The biggest, with the greatest variety of people, takes place every fourth day at Yuanyang—dragon, rat and monkey days. It begins around the central bus station, goes down the steps, then along the long commercial street, which runs just above the main road for vehicular traffic, nearly to the end of the city limits. Niujiaozhai, home to Yi and two colourful Hani groups, stages its market day two days after Yuanyang—horse, dog and tiger days.

HANI AND YI

The dominant ethnic group in the highlands of Ailaoshan is the Hani, who built most of the terraces. The Yi are the second most numerous and the history and culture of both nationalities are intertwined. Both languages belong to the Yi branch of the Tibeto-Burman linguistic family (along with Lahu and Lisu) and both claim to have migrated here from their original homeland in southwest Sichuan, crossing the Jinshajiang at the same time.

Though their grammar, structure and morphology are roughly the same, the vocabulary is quite different. Yi has a written form, with books kept by the *bimaw* (ritual specialist) in each community. The Hani say they, too, had an alphabet and books when they were in Sichuan. When about to cross the Jinshajiang, they asked the Yi how they intended to preserve their books. The Yi bimaw replied that he would wrap them up and keep them close to his stomach as he swam across. The Hani mistranslated the explanation and thought the Yi said to wrap the books *inside* the stomach. So the Hani ate their books before they crossed the river and ever since then their literature has been oral.

MARKET DAY IN SOUTHERN YUNNAN

The problem with most towns in the southern half of Yunnan is their drab, uninteresting appearance, consisting primarily of box-like, concrete buildings. They may have an attractive park or temple, and perhaps an old-fashioned Dai neighbourhood to wander through, but not much else maintains a visitor's interest. On market day, however, everything changes. The otherwise boring town bubbles with excitement.

Market day (*gangai* or *ganji* in the Yunnan dialect) is a periodic event common to most county seats, as well as many townships up in the hills. Some places host a market weekly, others every four, five or six days. At such times not only does the central market fill with buyers and sellers, the commercial activity spills out into the adjacent streets and lanes.

Villagers from the surrounding plains and nearest mountain ranges swarm into town, some leaving their homes at sunrise in order to arrive at mid-morning, when everything is still fresh. They carry their goods, including perhaps their afternoon rice, in baskets of split bamboo, suspended on a carrying pole, if Dai, or slung on the back, if from the hills. Others lead ponies or mules laden with full saddle baskets. Unless they rent space in the central marketplace, they will find a convenient empty spot on a nearby lane, drop their loads and set up shop. Most markets, though, do have designated areas for the poultry, the pigs, the ponies and the other animals. The rest of the streets are open for any kind of business.

The phenomenon is not restricted to the southern counties of the province. Some in the north, such as those around Dali, have long been tourist attractions. Generally speaking, though, market days in the northern counties attract only one or two ethnic minorities. In contrast, the populations in the south, particularly along the international boundaries, are ethnically more mixed, thus making market day more lively and colourful. Zhangfeng's market in Dehong, for instance, draws Dai, Jingpo, De'ang, Lisu and Burmese. At the other end of Yunnan in Jinping, market day attracts Hani, two kinds of Yao, Miao, Dai and Yi, plus Vietnamese, Yao and Giay from over the border.

Aini in a market in Menglian.

Yunnan has long had the market-day tradition. Nineteenth-century French explorers made use of it to replenish their provisions as they trekked across the province. The practice fell into abeyance after 1949, but its revival was encouraged from the onset of the Reform Era in 1979. Farmers now had the incentive to produce surpluses. And as agricultural production has expanded since then, so has the rural transportation network. Mountain roads are constantly being improved. Minibuses add new shuttle routes every year. And more farmers own tractor-trailers, used to haul people as well as goods to the market.

Trade is the primary attraction. People pile their garden produce, jungle herbs, firewood or whatever into their baskets and take the sometimes long and hilly trail to town, hoping to sell the contents and replace them with something unavailable or out of stock at home. But that may not be their only activity. If they sell out early they will take time to look around, checking what else is for sale, at what price, especially if it might be something they can grow, make or find themselves. Some even walk all that way precisely to just look around, bearing no load of goods to sell and bringing no money to purchase anything. They had nothing special to do back in the village, and anyway, market day is always pleasantly diverting.

Certainly socializing is part of the action. Relatives and old friends from outlying villages may meet, take a break from shopping, and dine together at one of the noodle stands. Neighbours make the journey in groups. Young men scout the scene for attractive young women, for courtship in village societies often begins with an introduction at the market.

Aware of this, the young women dress their best. Dai girls pin flowers to their hair. Miao girls wear newly embroidered clothes. Yao girls don their heavy silver jewellery. For most minority women in the southern counties, aesthetic standards still lie within the tribal parameters. They feel the most attractive outfit they can wear is their finest traditional costume.

For the visitor this is a bonus and makes the day replete with colour and beauty. Yet it is also an indicator of the strength of local custom and conservatism in the particular minority group concerned. Nowadays, one should expect to see only a few men dressed in ethnic style. Except for Hua Lisu in the west, older Jingpo and Wa men in the southwest, Aini in Menglian and Yao in the southeast, men tend to favour urban styles or military surplus.

Clues instead will come from the women. In relatively old-fashioned villages, the middle-aged and older women will dress ethnic style, as will perhaps a good portion of the younger married women. Mothers carry their babies on their backs in cloth harnesses (sometimes elaborately embroidered), with the child in a traditional baby's cap. But the true indicator is how young the females are who dress in the ethnic style. The stronger the ethnic tradition, the more teenage and primary schoolgirls will put on their traditional costumes. And the more local minorities prefer their ethnic style, the more likely market day will feature tables and stalls run by minority women selling traditional costumes, components and jewellery.

Much can be deduced about an area's economy by observing market-day activity. Urban vendors sell prepared food, ready-made clothing, metal containers, farm tools and other items not produced in the countryside. What the rural folk bring to sell tells the visitor something of their lifestyle and their role in the local economy. The vegetables mountain folk offer may differ from those grown in the valleys. If only the hill people are hawking firewood, bamboo, jungle herbs and other mountain products, that means valley people depend on them for such items. If the hill folk are buying rice in autumn or winter, it means they do not cultivate it themselves. If they have walked all this way to sell something that costs but a few yuan for the entire contents of their baskets, they are obviously poor people.

Ethnic diversity is the most attractive feature of market days for a visitor. In the south and southwest, the plains are populated by Han and Dai, while in the southeast the Zhuang replace the Dai. Two or more sub-groups of colourful Miao and black-clad Yao, plus the nearest branch of Yi, attend the markets in Wenshan prefecture, mainly selling vegetables and jungle produce. The Zhuang sell vegetables, grain, fish and fish traps.

In the south and southwest, the Dai are the grain merchants and run most food stalls. Xishuangbanna markets draw Aini everywhere, Yao, Yi and Jinuo in the east, Lahu in the west. Menglian's market day attracts traditional and colourful Lahu, Aini and Wa from the hills, while Menga's, on the Myanmar border two days later, draws the same folk, except Aini, from both sides. In Gengma, one of the largest markets in the southwest, Dai and Han join Wa, Bulang, Yi and Lahu, all but the Han dressed in traditional style.

In the four counties of lower Ailaoshan—Honghe, Luchun, Yuanyang and Jinping—between the Red River and the Vietnam border, the institution of market day is at its most developed. Yuanyang hosts a gathering every four days, the other three county seats every six days. In addition, every major township holds its own market day and by now enjoys regular minibus service to and from the county seat.

The Hani are the dominant mountain people, with a dozen or more sub-groups. Branches of the Yi, Miao and Yao are the next most common, while the Zhuang and Dai here are largely terrace farmers, too. The latter are animist, not Buddhist, and dress so colourfully they are

A market stall provides a feast of local delicacies.

Smoked meats on display in a market in southern Yunnan.

collectively known as Huayao Dai—the Flowery Waist Dai. Successful surplus production and improved transportation make market day in this area a real spectacle. At every market site several stalls will sell Hani or Yi jackets, trousers, embroidered belts, sashes, silver jewellery, Miao batik cloth, etc, because most Ailaoshan minority women own several traditional outfits and can thus dispense with the extra goods.

Certain Ailaoshan residents, mostly men, have become professional market-goers. Familiar with the buying and selling prices of commodities from one venue to another, they tour the townships every week, buying from one and selling for a profit at another a day or two later.

For the rural folk of southern Yunnan, market day gets better every year. Even the younger generation is enthusiastic and youth make up a large proportion of those in attendance. For not only can they make a little money through their participation, they may even find a suitable marriage partner, one with whom to set up house and field, produce more than the family can consume, and take the surplus to town on market day.

From a distance it is not possible to distinguish a Hani village from a Yi. In Upper Ailaoshan they each live in brick and wood houses with tiled roofs in the rural Yunnanese style. The same is true in Luchun and most of Honghe. But in Yuanyang and Jinping Counties they use the two-storey, flat-roofed, mud-brick style house like that of the Dai in the valleys, the only difference being a small storeroom on the roof, which is covered by a peaked, thatched roof. Hani call the style the 'mushroom house'. Some houses, even whole villages, are without this appendage, though.

Villages lie beside bamboo groves, or at the lower edge of a forest, above the terraces. Not apparent until entering the villages are the special, ritually consecrated characteristics that identify the village as Han or Yi. Traditional Hani villages will mark two of the entrance paths into the housing area with a ritually consecrated gate, separating the human world from the spirit realm. The principle is the same as that practised by their ethnic cousins, the Aini, but the gate is much simpler, basically a crossbeam with part of the sacrificial animal affixed to it during the renewal ceremony (*gatutu*) in the summer. The Yi have a sacred area within the village where three stones are set in the ground, representing their original ancestors. All important rituals take place here.

Dry fields, and freshly built terraces are used to grow maize, soybeans and cassava. The water-filled terraces are strictly for rice, one crop per year in the mountains. Ponds, springs, irrigation and drainage channels are collectively owned, even if surrounded by property privately owned or managed. Hani villages select one man to be Guardian of Channels, who is in charge of checking the flow of the main irrigation channel, cleaning it of debris and overseeing the post-harvest repairs. He is also custodian of the woodcut measures, which indicate the amount of water allowed to be channelled off for different portions of the terraced area. These he can use to determine whether anyone has surreptitiously changed the dividers in the main channel to allot more water to their fields.

The woodcut measures originate from a collective village assembly decision shortly after the foundation of the settlement. Any subsequent modification of this water-flow network requires the common consent of the village headman and the representatives in the assembly. To guarantee that every family in the village receives a fair share of the available water thus demands a high degree of cooperation among its residents.

This has affected the cultural outlook of the people, instilling a strong sense of solidarity beyond the normal kinship bonds. The very first step in organizing village life and society is to make sure everyone has equal access to

A Hani gentleman enjoys a smoke in Yuanyang.

water—the stuff that sustains and nourishes life. The Hani begin with equality and from then on any gain in status is up to individual initiative and energy.

The habit of sharing water influences their notion of hospitality; they share what they have with outsiders, believing the act will rebound in mutual benefits, just as sharing the water insures the common welfare of all. One can hardly walk around a Hani village for long in Lower Ailaoshan without being invited inside for something—tea, tobacco, jiu, maybe a whole meal. The Hani like to make social events out of ordinary meals and if they have guests they will turn dinner into a drinking, smoking, nibbling affair that can last up to two hours. Their Yi neighbours are only slightly less gregarious.

This strong sense of localism is the main ingredient in ethnic pride, which is manifested most visibly in the preference the women have for donning their traditional costume. More sub-groups of Hani than Yi live in Ailaoshan, but the women's costume of each contains similar elements. Except for the Gado Hani in western Jinping, who wear indigo skirts, the main components include a side-fastened, long-sleeved jacket, belt with the ends hanging loose over the hips, trousers and some kind of headgear. In general, the Yi jackets and belts are brighter and more heavily embroidered. The exception is the Alu sub-group in Laojizhai township, who wear black garments and a brightly coloured belt, the latter woven on a narrow bamboo loom propped up against the wall.

In Yuanyang, the Nisu sub-group appliqué several thin bands, some embroidered, in contrasting colours, on the sleeves, cuffs, around the shoulders and down the lapel. Other Nisu styles feature horizontal bands of white, or silver or nickel studs, closely packed across the entire front. Trousers are usually black and blue. The jacket hangs down the back to the knees and its lower corners and hem are decorated. Around the waist they tie a belt with big, diamond-shaped end flaps that drape over the buttocks. Called *zunyi* in Yi, these are enhanced with white pile-embroidery and coloured flowers stitched in the centre. In Honghe the ends are much smaller, without the pile-embroidery.

In Honghe, Yi women wear simple, single-colour headscarves, but in Yuanyang the everyday headscarf is a band of black cloth with embroidered ends, which they tuck into the scarf at the top of the head. Around Huangcaoling, Yi women wear an open-topped, tubular cap studded with silver half-globes. The same embellishment may be used to cover the surface of the *wubi tumaw*, the chicken-shaped cap worn by young women and little girls. Pile-embroidery, in white, with some arabesques, is more common, though the cap may have silver pendants attached.

In Yuanyang only the Yi wear the wubi tumaw, but in the hills of Honghe, especially the Lawbi sub-group in Langti township and the hills east, it's the

Hani girls who don them. Their jackets, though, are less embroidered, mainly indigo with black or other colour bands stitched along the lapel, which is fastened to the jacket with silver coin-buttons. Some of these are Republic-era Chinese coins, others French Indo-Chinese piastres, plus the occasional old Mexican silver peso or US trade dollar.

Hani in Shalatuo, Niujiaozhai and the hills southwest of Yuanyang are among the most flamboyant dressers. One group shows heavy Nisu Yi influence in the jacket style, though on the belt end-flaps they appliqué arabesques, or embroider in the cross-stitch style. Sometimes the belt ends may be straight tabs, rather than diamond-shaped, and fully embroidered. Another group dispenses with appliqué and lays a thick band of embroidery along the lapel and down to the jacket hem. They may also lengthen the jacket in front by appending a flap of indigo-dyed cloth in tie-dye patterns. Both groups wear a round headband, with a double row of silver studs all around and coloured yarn hanging down the back.

The same side-fastened, short jacket is common to other Hani groups in Yuanyang and Luchun, though the lapel and cuff decorations differ. In Luchun they use a single cloth, brighter, sometimes silk, very close to the late Qing-dynasty Han style. The Luchun turban resembles a tasseled fez, while in Huangcaoling a rectangular cloth is wrapped around the head and its end tucked into the top. Others wear a silver-studded round cap under a turban.

The little silver half-globes some Hani stitch onto their sleeve cuffs, other groups sew onto the upper lapels of front-fastened jackets. The Alu jacket has two wide bands of these running all the way down the front. Their round black caps also have a wide band of these studs all the way around, with big pompoms and tassels of bright woollen yarn attached above the ears. The Alu's neighbours, the Duni Hani, dress like Huangcaoling's Goho Hani, except that they may wear the Yi-style wubi tumaw on their heads.

THE DAI OF THE VALLEYS

The Dai in the valleys of the Red River and other streams in Ailaoshan are animists who belong to three main sub-groups: Flowery Waist (Huayao) Dai, Black Dai and White Dai. Those in Xinping, Yuanjiang and Jianshui Counties are collectively designated Huayao Dai. Their women wear the most colourful costume of any Dai group in the province. The outfit consists of a long-sleeved, short-front jacket over a long tunic, black sarong and colourful hip-wrapper, plus a variety of headgear. The lapels and hem of the jacket and the body of the tunic is heavily decorated with appliqué or embroidery, and in some cases silver studs. For festivals they add silver chains and pendants. Lots of colour is

(following pages) Entire mountainsides in Ailaoshan have been terraced.

also used on the piece covering the hips and sometimes on the hem of the sarong. It is this concentration of colour between the waist and hips that gave them the name Huayao—Flowery Waist.

Some sub-groups wear turbans. Others knot their hair and tuck it inside a round cap, embroidered on top. Some wear conical caps of split bamboo or, as in Xinping and western Yuanjiang, a round one, slightly bowl-shaped, with a small point in the centre. These women frequently tuck small baskets of split bamboo into their belts at the back of the waist when they go to the field or market.

In Lower Ailaoshan the Black Dai women dress somewhat simpler, but can be just as eye-catching. Their black, side-fastened jackets are short-sleeved, with wide strips of red and white or light blue from the shoulders to the edge of the sleeves. The collar and a broad band below the lapel are also appliquéd with bright silk, sometimes embroidered or silver-studded. The jacket is slightly split at the sides and embroidered on the side hem and the bottom. The plain black sarong drops to just below the knees, and on the calves they wear brightly embroidered leggings, in cross-stitch patterns, no two pair alike.

Throughout Ailaoshan the Huayao Dai and Black Dai live in box-like, two-storey, flat-roofed houses. They do not have the rooftop storeroom of the Yi and Hani, though. The roof is used to dry crops and laundry, of course, but it sometimes serves as an arena for relaxing or receiving guests. Some Dai villages lie a few hundred metres above the river, usually sited where the slopes are gentler. But they are terrace-builders, too, like the folks higher up, with water engineered to flow into every field.

The exception is the smaller White Dai sub-group in Laomeng and in the valley of the Tengtiao River in the vicinity of Mengla. They build houses on stilts, as in Banna, using wood, bamboo and thatch. Ancestral altars stand in their yards. The women dress like the Black Dai in Vietnam, in long black sarongs with a border strip in a bright colour, long-sleeved, pastel-coloured, front-fastened jacket, with silver buckles. The difference is the headgear, which is a simple scarf rather than the elaborate, embroidered black cloth that covers the heads of Black Dai women in Vietnam.

The Dai never choose a settlement site that is not beside running water. Not only do they want their water source close at hand, they channel it to flow though their villages. At Qimaba, a large Dai township in southwest Luchun, whose 100 families moved here from Shiping County around a century ago, the stream has been directed to flow through a network of channels that runs alongside nearly every house. From there it proceeds to irrigate the terraces just downhill from the edge of the residential area.

With their proximity to streams, the life of the Dai includes a lot of fishing. Even the flooded terraces in the dry season are a source of small fish. To catch these, and the somewhat larger species in the streams and rivers, the Dai traditionally use a variety of traps made from split bamboo. Nowadays in some areas the men use battery-operated electric rods to stun the fish and nets to sweep them up. On a walk though a Dai village one will still see bunches of fish traps of sundry shapes hanging from the house walls.

OTHER MINORITIES: ZHUANG, MIAO, YAO

While most of Yunnan's Zhuang live in Wenshan Prefecture, smaller communities live in scattered locations beyond the southeast. One such site is the northern half of Yuanyang County, home to ten Zhuang villages on the lower slopes of the mountains between Nansha and Yuanyang city. Materially speaking, the Zhuang have been heavily influenced by their mainly Yi neighbours. The villages employ the same kind of layout and architecture and their fields are terraced, though on gentler slopes and in bigger parcels than those higher up.

Differences exist. At one end of a Zhuang village lies a large water tank, with two sets of public taps. Near the tank is a place for slaughtering pigs over a big wok encased in a concrete block—this is for catching the blood.

The Zhuang women's costume is modelled on that of the Nisu Yi, with the same components—long-sleeved blouse, trousers, belt with diamond-shaped embroidered ends and head scarf. The jacket is the same, but for a much wider band of appliqué or embroidery below the lapel and on the lower sleeves. The back of the jacket, over which hangs the belt ends, is decorated from waist to hem, with an attached ruffled strip along the bottom. The headscarf and trousers are the same, but older women may wear a different cap, embroidered and silver-studded.

Ailaoshan's Miao live in the eastern part of the range, in Jinping County and adjacent townships in Yuanyang. They belong to the branch called Mengchou, or Small Flower Miao, after the dominant motif of their embroidery style. Embroidery, appliqué and batik are the methods used to add colourful embellishments to a costume and the Miao women use them all. Batik is a dry-season activity, appliqué done when assembling the final costume, but embroidery keeps them busy at spare moments throughout the year. For a proper Miao costume, lots of embroidery is required. Miao women wear a headscarf, jacket, belt, apron, pleated skirt and leggings and every piece is bright and colourful. The headscarf consists of narrow strips of cloth

(following pages) A procession of Zhuang women.

wrapped around a cloth patch that rests on their topknots. The jacket is usually solid colour, long-sleeved, waist-length, with coloured strips in broad bands around the shoulders, down the lapel and on the upper arms. The skirt, of hemp or cotton, is indigo-dyed in batik patterns, with colour strips and loads of embroidery over the lower third, and reaches to just below the knees. Similar bands of embroidered cloth make the belt, which has a wide front, under which a decorated apron hangs to the hem. From the waist in the back four or five strips of embroidered cloth, beaded and tasselled in the lower half, drape over the buttocks down to the hem of the skirt.

In Jinping, the Miao dominate the mountains south of the county seat and along the Vietnam border. But they do not confine themselves to the highlands and are just as likely to pick a valley site for settlement. In Laomeng township they live in the Tengtiao River valley right next to the Dai. Their houses do not employ the flat-roofed style, but are simple structures of mud-brick and tile. The Miao are able to wrest a living out of almost any ecological zone in the area. Where conditions are favourable, the Miao have large villages. Where farming land is minimal, Miao settlements are hamlets of a handful of houses.

The last significant ethnic minority in Lower Ailaoshan is the Yao. Two branches of them live in the area. The Landian inhabit parts of Luchun and central Yuanyang County. The Hongtou reside in Jinping. The Landian are one of the most widespread Yao branches, with several sub-groups in Honghe, Qujing, Wenshan and northern Laos. Unlike the Miao, they remain in the mountains, in forested areas that isolate them from the mainstream of commercial traffic. Hongtou Yao live in more accessible areas and participate to a greater extent in the county's markets. Both groups live in one-storey wooden houses with tile roofs, though some of the more remote Hongtou put theirs on stilts.

The costumes of the two differ considerably. The Landian prefer black as the basic colour for both men and women. The latter attach magenta thread tassels around the collar, but except for the heavy silver ornaments this is the only addition to the black of their loose jackets, gathered at the waist, and tight trousers. Young girls wear a round cap with huge red woollen pompoms on the sides and top. Married women drop this for a black cloth covering a board about 20 cm high at the back. Under this they wind a black thread coil and shave the forehead and eyebrows so that no hair shows under the hat. The rest of the hair is wound into a topknot and secured by a large and ornate silver clasp, hidden from ordinary view by the black cloth covering.

Men wear black, too, with silver studs along the lapels of the front-fastened jacket, and plain, round, flat-topped caps similar to those worn by the Hui, only black.

Hongtou women also shave their eyebrows, foreheads and temples when married, tucking the rest of the hair inside a conical red cloth cap, held in place around the base by a thick silver band. The basic colours of their clothes are also black, or deep indigo, but they embroider two strips down the front, as well as both legs, front and back, of their shin-length trousers. Unmarried women wear the same, but don a turban and don't shave their foreheads, and so forth. Embroidery, in the cross-stitch style, is a main feature of their shoulder bags as well. On market days in Jinping, after bringing in their firewood or vegetables for sale, Yao women embroider pieces while awaiting customers.

Mountain Festivals

Unlike other parts of Yunnan, spring in Ailaoshan is not the time for festivals. The cold, foggy mornings have warmed up and the weather is pleasant and balmy. But the only celebrations of importance are local rice-planting rites and the ancestral rites of the Zhuang on the 3rd day of the 3rd lunar month. In the Zhuang festival the collective feast includes red rice, red eggs and chicken. Otherwise, most minorities observe major Han festivals and participate in the government-sponsored programmes of the Torch Festival.

Ailaoshan folk plant their rice in April and May and the rains commence soon afterwards, turning the silvery terraces into steps of shimmering green. Rain soaks the steep slopes, which sometimes slip away under the weight and fall across the road. Landslides are a continuous problem in the summer, providing work for roadside villages to clear away the mud. In the hills and valleys the clouds swirl around the settlements, framing windows of rural scenery.

With the rainy season in full sway, the Hani stage Kuzhazha, though at different times in different places—a common phenomenon among these people. Yuanjiang, Honghe and Huangcaoling Hani observe their festival beginning the first pig day of the 5th lunar month. In Luchun and the rest of Yuanyang it begins on the first sheep day of the 6th lunar month.

The first day individual household heads perform rituals in the terraces to the protective spirit of the rice crop. Some villages hold a collective feast this day, too. Next day villagers construct a swing, a teeter-board and perhaps a small Ferris wheel, capable of seating four in separate chairs. The swing may be a relatively modest one, suspended on two vine-ropes from three or four long tree limbs lashed together. Or, as in Yuanjiang, it may be a pair of tall poles with a crossbeam, their positions secured by cables fixed to the ground. Swinging is done standing up, sometimes by two persons together, side by side or face to face. The teeter-board is a long beam fixed to a post about 1.5 metres tall. The beam both turns around and goes up and down, with riders at each end.

For most of the area's Yi, the Torch Festival is not part of their annual activities, except in Yuanyang city. More important are the ancestral rites, which take place three weeks afterwards, on the full moon of the 7th lunar month. On the first day the Yi repair and renovate the main road through or nearest the village. On the second day they decorate the dining area with flowers, sacrifice a pig and invite the ancestral spirits to their homes. Feasting continues for two more days. The next night the family head recites the family genealogy. On the last night they sacrifice chickens and ducks and kowtow to the ancestral spirits. A small portion of each dish goes on a tray, which they take outside, offer the ancestral spirits, and bid them goodbye.

Until 1966 the Yi celebrated the Torch Festival, but it became a Cultural Revolution casualty and its revival has been confined to the show staged by the county government in Yuanyang city. The main event here is the county wrestling tournament, which lasts three days and draws huge crowds of minorities from villages all over the county. On the 25th day of the 6th lunar month dances are staged in the stadium behind the central bus station. Individual singers and troupes of the Yi, Hani, Dai and Zhuang perform, followed by a great fireworks show. The next two mornings and afternoons feature the wrestling matches, in the same arena.

By September the rice plants in the terraces everywhere are golden ripe. Just before harvest each family plucks the first panicles and takes them home for their New Rice ceremony, involving a feast and rites for the ancestral spirits. Harvest begins after this day. Rain is intermittent by then and by October few fields remain uncut. In the post-harvest months various collective feasts are held, while in the middle of the 10th lunar month the Landian Yao stage their annual Panwangjie.

Coinciding with the lunar New Year, or the Han Spring Festival, are a couple of the most important of the annual ethnic celebrations. Ailaoshan people observe the Spring Festival in the Han manner by visiting relatives, feasting, closing shops and transportation links for three days and shooting off lots of firecrackers. The Miao, however, have their own festival over the first six days of the New Year, Caihuashan, Treading the Flowery Mountain, staged about 20 km east of Laomeng.

For this event the Miao choose the bravest young man and the most beautiful young woman. The latter presents the former with a bolt of red silk

Feasting at the Hani festival of Rhamatu.

or a banner which he is to attach to the top of the upright pole in the middle of the grounds, over ten metres high. When he concludes this feat he hands the girl a flowery umbrella. The crowd urges the couple to get closer, the couple retreats behind the umbrella and if they fall in love and marry so much the better, both for them and for the villagers.

On the third day a crowd gathers to listen to the singers at the base of the pole. Around noon attention shifts to the nearby courtyard in front of the middle school. Here Miao men conduct rituals with a pony and then a buffalo, inducing the animals to go this and that way, sit, lie on their sides, get up and hop over a bamboo pole held about a metre above the ground. Following this a number of Miao dances take place, with soloists singing in between.

The most important annual Hani festival commences a few days later, on either a buffalo day or dragon day, depending on the sub-group (Jinping Hani stage it a month later). Called Rhamatu, it involves sacrifices and rituals in the sacred grove beside or above the village, the cleaning of wells and water sources, the expulsion of evil spirits and offerings to the Dragon god of the forests at an altar before the 'dragon tree' of the grove. The following day around noon the men of the village stage a collective feast outdoors along the main street of the village. Each household provides one table, placed side-by-side in a long and sinuous, dragon-like line. The feasting continues until dark, while singing and dancing transpire nearby and again in the evening.

The Alu in Laojizhai also observe Rhamatu. Rather than a sacred grove, the Yi rites, conducted by the village bimaw, take place at the altar of the three stones within the village residential area. Though the rites and feasting occur in every Alu village, in the evening the most centrally located of them hosts the dance party for all, which continues until the next morning. Girls lose their shyness then and ask the boys to dance. A few days afterwards comes another festival, in which the boys, made up and wielding painted wooden swords, cavort through the village chasing off evil spirits. After this Alu life returns to normal and the youths pursue the romances that began with the dancing on the night of Rhamatu.

Bridges to the Middle Kingdom:
The Eastern Prefectures

LANDSCAPES AND LIMESTONE

Yunnan's eastern prefectures—Zhaotong, Qujing and Wenshan—border Sichuan, Guizhou and Guangxi, which before the Yuan Dynasty were the southwestern provinces of the Middle Kingdom. The geography and climate of the east is more like that of neighbouring provinces than the rest of Yunnan. So is the social composition. The Han are the majority in every county, but many counties have a big enough ethnic presence to give them autonomous status, including the whole of Wenshan Prefecture. Yet the bulk of the ethnic minorities in the east are migrants from further east, in contrast to those elsewhere in Yunnan, who mainly came in from the northwest, and, in the Wa and Bulang case, the south.

Coming from western and then central Yunnan, the eastern prefectures seem like a zone of transition from Yunnan proper to Guizhou and Guangxi, or to Sichuan across the Jinshajiang. Wonderful scenery, odd landscapes and colourful ethnic costumes still appear along the way, but the traveller may feel they do so after progressively longer intervals of the ordinary, the dull and the modern. And in truth, after crossing the provincial borders, the exotic becomes much less commonplace.

On the other hand, entering Yunnan from the east the traveller has the opposite impression, the feeling that the landscapes and glimpses of the ethnic minorities are getting more and more interesting, a harbinger of what's to come the further one goes into Yunnan. In fact, the eastern prefectures, taken as a whole, contain just as many features of Yunnanese exotica as they do resemblance to neighbour provinces.

The terrain varies from high, cold, steep mountain ranges in Zhaotong, down through the rolling, red-earth hills and broad plains of Qujing, to the limestone hills and subtropical climate of Wenshan. In the northeast the mountains are sometimes barren, pockmarked with limestone boulders and devoid of human habitation, much like the ranges over the border in Guizhou. The great plains of Qujing, and in Luoping County the clusters of sharply peaked mountains, are reminiscent of northern Guangxi. More of these groups of tightly packed, medium-sized, smoothly sloped mountains pop up in the highlands of southern Wenshan. In other parts of the prefecture, notably Qiubei and Babao, the hills are like domes sitting on a flat plain, again similar to Guangxi.

None of the great rivers of Yunnan pass through the east, though the Jinshajiang forms the northern boundary of Zhaotong with Sichuan. The Pearl River (*Zhujiang*) begins in Qujing, 47 km north of the city, in a fountain within a small cavern on the slope of Maxiong Mountain. The water is immediately directed into a series of pools, for the area is of course a park, and eventually leads to the Huashan Reservoir, 6 km south. From this man-made lake it trickles out to become the Nanpanjiang and flows east to Guangxi and Guangdong.

Smaller, less renowned rivers cut through the hills of the east, creating exciting waterfalls on the Huanglianhe in Daguan and the Jiulonghe and Duoyihe in Luoping. Still smaller rivers, streams most of the year, run through the picturesque hills of Puzhehei and Babao. Many streams have been used to construct reservoirs, but the region does have a couple of small but attractive lakes. One is **Qingshuihai**, in the mountains west of Xundian. The other is in Yanshan County, next to Haizibian. Called **Bathing Fairies Lake** (*Yuxianhu*), it contains a few island hills, with viewing platforms, accessible by boats from the northeast shore. Small hills rise behind every shore and Miao have settled beside the lake, the same Mengchou branch as in Ailaoshan, though the terrain is vastly different.

Zhuang, Miao, Yao, Buyi and Shui all migrated into Yunnan from the east, where substantially larger numbers of them live. From the same direction, the other main immigrant group was the Han, often from even further east, like Zhejiang and Anhui. They occupied the level lands and urban centres, as well as market towns and major transportation centres on the main roads through the mountains. They crossed into Yunnan even before the Nanzhao period.

Early Han settlers have left behind many artefacts from the past in Zhaotong, most notably the stone carvings of Guangtoushan, in Weixin County's Dapingzi, the easternmost township in the prefecture. The early Han immigrants displaced the Bo, an ancient people who have disappeared, but who left their coffins on ledges in cliff crevices at Wuchidao, Yanjin County. But no great cities grew up in the wake of immigration. Urban centres were small administrative posts or stopovers on the Southwest Silk Route, when it was in operation. Even Zhaotong, now a growing, modern city, was little more than a village until the mid-18th century.

The topography accounts for this. While Zhaotong city itself is in a plain, with easy transportation links south, north of the capital loom the mountains. Most of the prefecture is wrinkled with them and full of gorges carved by the narrow, but often swift rivers that snake among them. Once in a while a patch of level land lies beside the stream and here the towns were built. Villages hug

(following pages) Limestone hills enhance the scenery at Puzhehei in Qiubei County.

the slopes, as far up as the gradient is still habitable, to where the slope starts going straight up to the summit, a bare cliff behind the highest villages.

A couple of towns are in the mountains, like Weixin in the east and Daguan in the heart of the prefecture. On the map Daguan looks like it's right next to the river and so must be a valley town. It is beside the river, but it's a near sheer 300-metre drop from the town to the water. Daguan lies on a moderately angled part of the slope, with much more of the mountain above it.

Though almost totally modern and strictly utilitarian in its architecture, **Daguan** does have a splendid location. The mountains on each side rise steeply and the clouds often lie around the peaks or drift through the valley just below the town. Daguan's main attraction, however, is the **Huanglianhe Falls**, 7 km above the urban area. The park features several waterfalls running over the cliffs and a walkway to various caves, pavilions and cataracts. Miao villages lie on the higher slopes behind the park.

A few of the cataracts nearest the walkway are artificial, as if the park designers feared visitors might not want to descend all the way to the bottom of the cliff to admire the most beautiful fall of them all—a natural one over a precipitous cliff. So they engineered the water to cascade closer to the walkway, where it was more convenient for tourists. They even made a little rest area, with tables and benches, beneath an overhanging ledge *under* the waterfall, for a look from the inside out. A more rewarding experience is to abandon the walkway and take the paths to the natural falls, of which there are also several.

South of Zhaotong two routes are possible. One rides across the hills at the Qujing boundary, runs through the plains until hitting the mountains around Dongchuan. After winding down into this city, the road ascends again to cross the Liangwan mountains, passes Xundian and proceeds to Kunming. The mountain areas are not as rugged as north of Zhaotong, nor the hills so steep, so that both pastures and farms dominate the rural area. In vast areas the soil is deeply tinged with red. Freshly ploughed, this deep auburn colour lies beside the green of the vegetation, the yellow of the ripening fields and the blue (or grey) of the sky.

The other way into Qujing from Zhaotong is to first go southeast into Guizhou, crossing the Wumeng Mountains to Weining. The large lake called **Caohai** lies just south of here. Then the road climbs into the mountains again, turning southwest to re-enter Yunnan near the end of the range and descend into the great elevated plain that makes up most of the land in the prefecture's eastern counties. Small ranges break the horizon just east of Xuanwei and Fuyuan and north of Luoping, but otherwise eastern Qujing is fairly level ground.

Aliaoshan Miao girls.

A Tale of Yunnan

hen heaven and earth were first clearly divided, the world was not so bright as it is today. It was only a vast expanse of murky grey. The sun, moon, and stars did not exist. At that time a poor woman and her three daughters lived together in the woods. The three sisters were named Hosuni, Dosuni, and Bisuni.

One day, the mother was getting ready to go out, and before she left the house, she warned her girls, "I'm going to look for something for us to eat. Keep the door locked, and stay home. Don't go out and don't open the door. I'll be back before long." And off she went.

The three daughters waited and waited inside the house for their mother to come back, but a long, long time passed, and still she had not returned.

In the forest there was a leopard-demon who had ever been scheming how to allure the daughters to leave their house so he could eat them, but he could never find a way, simply because Hosuni, Dosuni, and Bisuni were so closely guarded by their mother. That particular day, he realized the mother had gone an awfully long while, so he passed by their door, disguised as a young man singing a folk song. At first, the three sisters were astonished to hear someone sing, and then they were scared. But the more they listened to the song, the more they liked what they heard. Surely it was a young man, after all! Convinced the leopard-demon really was a youth singing folk songs, the three girls opened the door and walked in the direction of his voice. But once they got near and had a look, they realized that their young man was none other than a leopard-demon in disguise. Then and there, they changed direction, and ran for home. Wearing a big grin on his face, the leopard-demon gave chase, intending to catch the three sisters, but they quickly scurried up a tree. The leopard-demon tried to climb up too, but he couldn't do it.

"Hey, girls!" he said, unctuously. "I'm here on a visit to see my relatives. Rest assured I wouldn't do you any harm. Won't you please just teach me how to climb a tree? If you do, I will remember your kindness my whole, entire life long."

Hosuni and Dosuni refused to trust the leopard-demon, and wouldn't tell him a thing. But their littlest sister, Bisuni, didn't know any better, and she blurted out, unthinkingly, "Why, there's nothing at all to tree climbing! All you have to do is start with your hands, and then use your feet, back and forth, back and forth." It was much too late now for the two older sisters to shush up Bisuni. The leopard-demon climbed the tree, following the little girl's advice, alternating his front paws and back legs.

Ever since that day, leopards have known how to climb trees.

When Hosuni, Dosuni, and Bisuni saw that the leopard-demon had learned to climb, they were so nervous that they headed straight for the top of the tree. But the leopard-demon followed right behind. At that point, the three girls all bawled at the top of their lungs in a fit of despair.

Now it just so happened that a god from heaven was passing by. He was enormously sympathetic. "Little girls, now stop crying. I can save you by taking you to heaven. But there is just one problem: once you are up there, you can't come back down here. How would you feel about that?" Seeing the leopard-demon was getting closer and closer, Hosuni, Dosuni, and Bisuni hastily agreed that they liked the idea very much. Raising his hand on high, the god took them up to heaven.

After they got to heaven, the three lived quite happily, but they missed their dear mother, and they longed to see the good earth again. So they earnestly pleaded with the god to let them return. The god said, "You may take turns. Since Hosuni is the eldest, let her go first. After that, Dosuni, then Bisuni." So, Hosuni went first. After she came back, Dosuni and Bisuni had a turn. Each of them got to visit their mother, and see the earth, the forest, and the river where they had once lived.

When their mother had returned home, and found that her daughters were missing, she had looked for them everywhere, but could not find them. She got to see them, however, when they came visiting. But now they were in heaven, while she was on earth, and no longer could they live together.

Every day, Hosuni and her sisters would take turns seeing their mother and the earth. In the course of time, Hosuni became the sun, while Dosuni and Bisuni became the moon and the stars. From then on, there was day and night. Sometimes, Dosuni and Bisuni appear together, and at other times, the younger sister comes out all by herself. That's why, at night, sometimes the moon and the stars appear at the same time, and at other times only the stars can be seen.

From *South of the Clouds*, edited by Lucien Miller,
University of Washington Press, 1994

In Luoping County, which borders the junction of Yunnan, Guizhou and Guangxi, a dramatic change in scenery commences. Stretches of the flat central plain are peppered with clusters of small hills roughly the same size, some connected, others standing alone, with tilled fields all around and between them. It's a hint of Wenshan's coming attractions. And turning south towards the Duoyi River, the road is soon a viewpoint for a more magnificent cluster of limestone mountains in the distance, these much bigger than the hills in the plain. The jumble of densely packed peaks, making multiple jagged lines on the horizon, is called **Wanfenglinhai**—the Sea of Ten Thousand Forested Peaks.

As the road descends from Luoping's high plain to the valley of the Duoyi River these peaks pass out of view. But along the river similar limestone hills rise high over the Buyi villages like near-perfect cones of earth, rock and trees. Further downriver, near the Guizhou border directly east of **Luoping** city, the reservoir of Lubuge is notable for its scenery. Boats take passengers on pleasure cruises past the bald, perpendicular cliffs that plunge into the water that filled what was formerly a gorge.

Cataracts big and small punctuate the course of the Duoyi River, which winds through hills inhabited by friendly Buyi farmers. A riverside hike is a mix of the social and the scenic. For scenery alone, the falls on **Nine Dragons River** (*Jiulonghe*), about 20 km northeast of the city, are more spectacular. No villages lie on the slopes rising from each bank. The river flows evenly over three great cliffs, making three fine cataracts. The biggest drops 56 metres, with a width of 110 metres. The next highest falls 43 metres, but over a narrow cliff at 35 metres. The third is 19 metres tall and 120 metres wide.

Wenshan hasn't anything as dramatic as the Jiulong Falls, but it does have one picturesque cascade—**Sanla Falls**—in the hills just northeast of Babao, in eastern Guangnan County. The stream tumbles over a series of boulders and finally drops from several points into a pond. On the eastern and southern sides of the town lay bunches of small hills on a plain as flat as a parking lot, with a small river winding among them and Zhuang villages at the bases. When winter morning mists float among them as well, these hills can be particularly enchanting.

Limestone hills jut above the plains and valleys on the way from Babao to Guangnan, but not again so attractively set until Qiubei in the northeast. There again gumdrop hills sit upon a glass-flat plain. At the Puzhehei resort, about 18 km from the county seat, many are grouped along a stream, reflecting on its surface. Local Yi row visitors on the stream in small boats on a leisurely cruise among the hills, passing villagers fishing in the shallow waters or gathering river plants. More limestone vistas in every direction are visible the further downriver the boat goes.

Boats lie in wait to take visitors for a ride on the river at Puzhehei.

A new arched bridge, a streamside pavilion in one of the villages, and a new road to distant caves and villages comprise the extent of development in the area, beyond the immediate vicinity of the resort. A stadium here stages cockfights, bulls in combat and Yi wrestling. One can also enjoy the scenery on foot, having the option to mount one of the small hills for a new perspective.

Central Wenshan is dominated by river valleys like those of the Nanlihe and Panlongjiang, which flow northwest to southeast and into Vietnam. Rolling hills, often studded with limestone boulders, lie on both sides of these rivers and their tributaries, with occasional tight groups of them like at Wanfenglinhai, though smaller. One such group stands as a backdrop to the hill town of **Maguan**, on its western side. The hills south of the Wenshan-Malipo highway are in general bigger, more contiguous and more forested than elsewhere in the prefecture. Rare and ancient tree ferns abound in the woods. White swans and white cranes pass through on their annual migrations and the area is home to rare species of animals, wild and domesticated, like the big monitor lizard and hornless goat of Maguan County.

CITIES IN THE PLAINS

A few of the eastern cities lie on highland slopes, like Daguan and Weixin in Zhaotong and Maguan in Wenshan. A few others occupy slivers of flat land beside steep river canyons, like Yiliang in Zhaotong and Malipo in Wenshan. The rest, including all the county seats in Qujing, sit on the plains. Modernization has overtaken all of them, now dominated by high-rise glass and tile office and bank buildings, fancy hotels and shopping centres. In some of the bigger cities, like Qujing and Wenshan, hardly any old buildings have survived. And with the surge in development over the last few years, construction projects—erecting big new buildings, widening the roads, making a new park—seem to be continuous.

Nevertheless, most urban areas have left at least a few old neighbourhoods relatively intact and still well integrated with the life of the city. Whatever temples, pagodas or historical monuments survived the ravages of time and politics have been restored. The creation or expansion of parks gives city residents a place of refuge from the city noise, amongst buildings, ponds and gardens in the traditional style, an ideal setting to pursue such leisure pastimes as Chinese board games, while listening to the songbirds they have brought in their cages.

The new look required by development means the creation of new symbols with which the modern city's residents can identify. Old ones like city walls and gate-towers had long since disappeared, so substitutes were necessary. Qujing in the mid-90s even built a whole new walled gate and tower in the classical style on some vacant land on the southern outskirts. Other cities satisfied themselves with the erection in a prominent downtown roundabout of a statue of the city mascot or, if they didn't have one, a space needle, on the model of the very first one at the 1970 Seattle World's Fair.

While the Han are the overwhelming majority of urban dwellers in the east, the ethnic minorities are never very far away. In the Wenshan towns they frequently live in the villages just past the urban zone. In Qujing and Zhaotong they mainly inhabit mountainous areas a bit further away and are less often seen in the towns, unless it happens to be market day.

Yet the ethnic influence does reach into even those cities rather far from the villages. Certain restaurants in the bigger cities offer ethnic-based cuisine, served by girls in their traditional costumes, perhaps including a floor show. Minority dance and music troupes are part of the programmes on big, government-subsidized holiday celebrations. And occasionally sculptures of minorities are part of a city's new 'cultural monuments', though the city's connection with that minority might be tenuous at best. In the northern quarter of Xuanwei, for example, is a statue of a Yi woman in the Daliangshan style of dress, though the nearest Yi who dress like that are about 200 km away, in the Wumeng Mountains of Zhaotong Prefecture.

The capitals of the three prefectures, plus Dongchuan, a separate administrative municipality, are the largest and most important in the east. Only **Zhaotong** has kept a sizable part of its old town, comprising the northern and eastern quarters. The city lies on a high plain at just under 2,000 metres. Though influenced by the rainier weather of Sichuan and Guizhou, the climate is mild, comparable to Kunming's and, like the latter, Zhaotong bills itself as a Spring City. The modern sections are clean, with wide streets and manageable traffic. The city mascot sculpture in the central roundabout is of a white crane, mounted on a tall pedestal.

The old town comprises wooden shophouses down narrow lanes, brick and tile private dwellings, shops selling the whole range of split bamboo handicrafts, from furniture to winnowing trays, or ceramic vessels. Though the buildings lack the carved embellishments once replete in Kunming's old town, they do create a setting of Old China. Traffic is largely pedestrian, plus some three-wheeled pedicabs with bright yellow frames and fenders. The traditional feel of the area is augmented by the old-fashioned clothing style favoured by the older generations of the Han—women in big turbans, side-fastened jackets and long aprons; men in ankle-length, side-fastened coats, slit on the sides,

(following pages) The old quarter of Zhaotong.

with long wispy beards on their chins. They are the only ones in town dressed in traditional style, save for a few Miao women marketing herbal medicines and Hui women in white headscarves.

The old town and new city meet in the north at the Qingguanting Park. Just inside the entrance is the modest but attractive Qingguan Pavilion, of grey brick and red wood, beside a big tree next to a small pond. It was built in 1809 and is the one historical structure extant in the city. A stream from this pond passes under an arched bridge to a larger one, with a long pavilion and resthouse beside it. Residents or visitors seeking more space for their recreation, closer to nature, go to one of the county's reservoir parks, such as Dalongdong to the north or Yudong to the west.

Mountains rise immediately north of Zhaotong, while the ranges to its west are progressively closer as the highway proceeds to Dongchuan. This city, originally a walled town on a square grid, lies on the Xiaojiang River in the lap of the mountains. It is one of Yunnan's major industrial cities, for the hills are rich in copper deposits. Dongchuan copper has been an export to other parts of China since the Han Dynasty. In the old days most urban households had their own little sweatshops, where family members, even women with bound feet, operated lathes to turn out copper vessels.

(*above*) *A shop in Zhaotong old town specializes in baskets and implements of split bamboo.*
(*right*) *Local Han, especially the older generation, still dress in a conservative traditional way.*

A lesser known industry then was the manufacture of felt rugs, which employed those in the western suburbs. After felting the wool and shaping it into a rug, workers applied flour paste to the surface in the desired colour pattern, dried it in the sun, then dipped the rug into the dye. The part covered by the paste did not touch the dye, so after the rug was washed and the paste removed, the pattern appeared as the undyed part.

The prefecture capital of Qujing is the most important commercial city in the east. Just two hours by the new highway from Kunming, it is connected by major roads north to Weining and northwest Guizhou, Zhaotong Prefecture, Yibing and Chengdu in Sichuan. This same highway continues south to Luliang and Honghe Prefecture. And 33 km north of Qujing a branch highway east runs into Guizhou to Anshun and Guiyang.

Historically **Qujing** is one of Yunnan's oldest and most important cities. It was a major stop on the Southwest Silk Route and an early centre of Han civilization. In the 3rd century Zhuge Liang fought the last battle of his Yunnan campaign here, beside the Baishi River in the northern suburbs, capturing Meng Huo for the seventh time. On the same field the Ming army routed the last of the Mongol forces left over from the deposed Yuan Dynasty in 1381.

The city is quite conscious of its historical legacy. It makes much of the city's connection with the ancient Cuan clan, which ruled the area prior to its incorporation into Nanzhao, though members of the clan were mostly deported to Baoshan in the early decades of Ming rule. Under Nanzhao its importance rivalled Kunming's, especially when Nanzhao expanded to the east. And it was a Qujing-based family, the Duan, that eventually came out on top in the post-Nanzhao power struggle to rule the Kingdom of Dali. A stele from the earlier Cuan rule and one from the Duan King Sushun of Dali are housed in a compound of the Mo. 1 Middle School. The Dali stele, erected in 971, records the results of the king's eastern expedition and the alliance he forged with 37 different tribal groups.

No memorial tablet commemorates the Ming triumph at Baishijiang, but a long stone wall in low relief carvings, on the main road running by the battlefield, depicts the alliance sworn by Zhuge Liang and Meng Huo. The two figures, the Han in long robes and tall hat, the Yi in cape and turban, toast each other at the centre. To Zhuge Liang's right are carved vignettes of Han life—walled towns, armoured cavalry, infantry ranks, rice planting and threshing. To Meng Huo's left are scenes of Yi life, in the costumes of contemporary Liangshan Yi, with warriors on horseback, buffaloes fighting, elephants on the loose, hunting scenes and women dancing. Constructed in recent years, it borrows heavily from the style of the Yunnan School of painting.

Despite the fact it's mainly a plains county with a Han population since ancient times, Qujing also advertises its ethnic connection. It has its own mascot sculpture, of the local Unicorn Fairy, in the fountain in the southern roundabout. Further up Qilin Street the next roundabout features statues on a high pedestal of Ashima and Ahei, the tragic protagonists of the Sani epic, in the act of fleeing the wicked demon lord. The sculpture is in the socialist realist style, however, so the pair wear properly grim, fiercely resolute expressions on their faces.

Its commercial prosperity has caused Qujing's near-total modernization of its architecture, including bank buildings done in pseudo-Greek style, with statues of Greek mythological figures in their courtyards. Classical Chinese-style structures are more or less restricted to the public parks, like the impressive new ornamental gate at the entrance to the park at **Liaokuoshan**, the hill on the southwest edge of the city. After their defeat at Baishijiang remnant Mongol forces and their commander holed up for a while here. But the Ming troops captured him here, putting an end to anti-Ming resistance. The hill's name—Peak of Victory—refers to this event.

The park area lies on the lower slopes. Pavilions, playgrounds and a mini-zoo lie further up. And above the built-up area trails lead through the woods to the summit and its view of the city. **Unicorn Park** (*Qilin Gongyuan*), in the southern quarter of Qujing, is bigger, with a lake for boating, and an arched bridge connecting the island to the shore, roofed corridors, resthouses and pavilions.

Other cities in the prefecture are smaller, less developed and perhaps less self-conscious of their place in history. They lie on broad plains, straddling rivers which have been reduced to shallow, narrow creeks, much of their water drawn off for rural irrigation before they reach the towns. None of them are as prosperous as the capital, so they still have old-fashioned neighbourhoods in addition to the burgeoning number of the glass-and-tile standards of contemporary small-city China.

A couple of towns, Shizong and Luliang, do have Buddhist legacies on their premises. In the centre of **Shizong**, an otherwise heavily industrialized city, stands a nine-tiered, brilliant white pagoda, with a column of dark arched windows on each of its eight sides. In the western suburbs lies the **Xihua Temple**, a large complex of buildings originally constructed in 1610.

Luliang has a little less of the factory town look and feel and in fact some quiet, old-style neighbourhoods with tree-lined streets and wooden shophouses. In the southern suburbs is the **Dajiao Temple**, a Ming Dynasty compound erected four years after Shizong's Xihuasi. The temple itself is a modestly decorated building. But the compound contains one of Yunnan's most interesting pagodas—the **Thousand Buddha Pagoda** (*Qianfota*). Seven stories high on a hexagonal base and pale yellow-white in colour, the pagoda gets its name because of the thousand square niches on its exterior walls, each of them containing a small Buddha image.

Luliang is the only other city in the prefecture that advertises its place in history. The county is better known as the site of the **Coloured Sand Forest**, a natural phenomenon which has been spoiled by construction of a theme park, with ancient-style battlements, altars and huge stone statues, within what was supposed to have been a nature preserve. At the village just before the turn-off to the park, signs direct the visitor to an old mansion of the **House of Cuan**, a family connected to the former Kingdom of Dali. And one of the villages in the area claims to be Meng Huo's hometown.

Further south the Buddhist influence, and for that matter that of the Han, is less widespread. In all of Wenshan Prefecture only in the capital are religious monuments major tourist attractions. **Wenshan city**, formerly called Kaihua, lies in a vast basin, at a lower elevation than Yanshan, the next city north. A sprawling metropolis threatening to gobble up the neighbouring Yi and Zhuang villages, its downtown core lies on the loop of land created by the sinuous course of the Panlong River as it makes its way through town. The city slopes from north to south, with some traditional back-alley neighbourhoods in the northern quarter between the main streets. On a hill above the northeast urban limits stands a newly built seven-tiered pagoda. A long staircase connects the site with the city.

Not far south of the city rises a steep set of mountains. The nearest of them, **Xihuashan**, is a park and its main feature, visible from the city, is the three-storey **Xishan Temple**, built in the Sanyuan Cave high up the vertical cliff-face of the mountain. A couple of crags jutting out from the cliff hold pavilions and a staircase to reach the temple has been chiselled into the rock. It is one of the most accomplished works of religious architecture in the entire province.

Besides Maguan, which has an old three-tiered pavilion called **Jade Star Pavilion** (*Yuxingge*), the only other city in the prefecture to boast of an old religious monument is Qiubei, in the northeast. The town is perhaps less than half the size of Wenshan, with slightly rolling gradients. One sizable hill stands on the southeast edge, wooded to the top. In an opening in the grove stands a seven-tiered pagoda, erected in 1854 in a much simpler, almost perfunctory style than the pagodas in Qujing. A couple of new temples have gone up in the suburbs, but Qiubei's main attraction is its ethnic mix.

Qianfo Pagoda in Luliang is named after the thousand Buddhas
placed in the pagoda's niches.

Besides the Han residents, Zhuang and Yi are frequently seen in the streets, especially market day, when some Miao and Landian Yao also turn up. The Hui are also a presence in Qiubei, not just in the town but as residents of a couple of large Hui villages about 10 km north, on the way to Puzhehei. They are recognizable by the green-domed towers of their mosques.

In northeast Wenshan the major town is **Guangnan**, lying in a long valley full of Zhuang villages. In 1276 the new Yuan government made the Zhuang chieftain of Guangnan the hereditary tusi of the prefecture, making this the most important Zhuang urban centre. The oldest government buildings in Wenshan are here, including the ex-tusi's mansion and the original government headquarters. Some old streets in the town centre, where vehicles rarely venture, are still attractive. The entrance to one market area is marked by a stone gate with low relief sculptures. Guangnan's chief draw is **Lotus Lake**, a large round pond in the heart of the town with a stately old pavilion at the end of a causeway. A minorities museum across the street exhibits artefacts and costumes of the local Zhuang, Yi, Yao and Miao.

Seventy-two km to the southeast lies **Babao**, the most beautiful small town in Wenshan. The picturesque original town lies on the north bank of a stream that runs beside the road and the new town has been appended to the land on the south bank. The cluster of Guilin-like hills that gives Babao its scenic reputation lies mostly to the east of the town. The hill on that side just across the bridge to the new town has a staircase to the top and viewing pavilions. The sight of the hills from here, that pop up from the perfectly flat plain, the river meandering among them, is unforgettable.

Hills stand behind old Babao, too, sometimes close enough to reflect in the water. A long street runs parallel to the stream. This is the venue for market day, attracting the blue-jacketed local Zhuang, two kinds of colourful Miao and the black-clad Yao. At the end of the market area the road branches one way behind the hill to a residential neighbourhood and the other way straight to the fields, turning into a path soon that passes a small shrine on a knoll and crosses a three-span stone bridge to lead back to the modern town. The misty shapes of the hills stand on the horizon.

In the heart of the prefecture, 35 km north of the capital, lies **Yanshan**, on a broad elevated plain that rolls into the mountains. The roofed sheds of pseudo-ginseng farms, a noted Zhuang agricultural product, cover the slopes of the countryside north of the city. As in Qiubei, small, steep limestone hills sit on the plains and in Yanshan a few pop up within the urban limits. One of the

(right) A Yao girl from Guangnan County, Wenshen.
(following pages) Babao lies tucked among clusters of small hills and Zhuang villages.

rocky outcrops—**Chengzishan**—has a park near its base, where the old men bring their songbirds, and steps to the broadcasting tower on top and viewing pavilions to the side. The Hui quarter lies near the base, marked by a new mosque in a new style, with sloping, pointed, orange-tiled roofs on the minarets, rather than the usual green domes.

Yanshan is about the same size as Qiubei but may perhaps be more prosperous. The architecture in the older residential quarter is in the traditional style of brick and tile, but most are of recent construction. Zhuang, Yi and Miao live in the surrounding villages and are frequent visitors to town. The city also has a central roundabout, where middle-aged *taiqi* adherents assemble in the evenings for various exercises. The sculpture of the city mascots is here, in Yanshan's case a pair of chickens. But not to forget its modern symbols, the city erected its own space needle here, too.

From Wenshan the highway continues southeast to the border county of Malipo. A branch of the Panlong River runs right through the town, with hills rising on each side. Residents in the town are mainly Han. Miao villages lie in the valley and foothills to the north and there are Zhuang settlements in the vicinity. Yao and Yi live in the mountains, along with other Miao. Except for market day, though, they are rarely in town.

Malipo's residents live on the slopes on the southeastern side of the river, both above and beyond the business district. Bilingual signs, in Chinese and Vietnamese, on downtown shops remind the visitor of the proximity of the border (by one route it's only 20 km). A covered market, well-kept and clean, lies between the main business district and the river. The river, too, is surprisingly clean and free-flowing. At the bridge near the centre of the downtown area is a small riverside park; here, even in Malipo, rises the city space needle.

People of the Northeast: Yi, Miao, Hui, Shui

As the part of Yunnan closest to the heartland of the Middle Kingdom, with the largest proportion of Han in the population, the northeast has been subject to the greatest amount of assimilation. The ethnic presence is less obvious than elsewhere in the province, for the housing in the mountains is no different from that in the plains and most minorities, including the women, dress in ordinary modern clothing. Even the Miao, generally among the most persistent in maintaining the ethnic look in everyday appearance, save their costumes for festivals and dress in contemporary rural fashions the rest of the year. In some areas, though, the minorities retain conservatives in their numbers who are reluctant to adopt the modern style.

Different sub-groups of Yi live in the highlands of Zhaotong and Qujing. In the northern and western parts of Zhaotong they are the same Nosu branch as the Yi over the Sichuan border in Daliangshan and in Ninglang County, Yunnan. Their clothing style is similar, as is the semipastoral lifestyle. They tend large flocks of sheep and herds of goats, and use the wool to make the long white felt capes worn in the colder months.

In eastern Zhaotong, Weining County in Guizhou and the mountains northeast of Xuanwei, the Yi lifestyle is the same, but the costumes differ. The men wear black turbans, black Han-style, front-fastened jackets and wide trousers. The women also don turbans, wear a side-fastened, long coat, split at the sides, apron and trousers. The lapel is in contrasting colours, the apron embroidered with flowers and other designs, and some decorative stitchwork also embellishes the lower parts of the trousers.

Qujing's Yi are concentrated in the mountains west and north of Xundian and the hills along the eastern boundaries of Fuyuan County. The women's costume is similar in both areas, dominated by a red poncho with broad white bands at the sides, tucked and tied at the waist. They braid and coil their hair and wrap it in a black headscarf, trimmed in the front with red. Yi women in Xundian County wear a loose, white, shin-length skirt. Those in Fuyuan wear a hand-woven cotton skirt, red with thin yellow stripes to the knees, medium blue from there to the hem. A brightly embroidered, fringed shoulder bag completes the outfit.

The Miao of Zhaotong are part of the Flowery Miao (*Hua Miao*) branch that inhabits Guizhou's Wumeng Mountains. Most are Christians, though their fervour has abated considerably since their conversion early in the 20th century. Nowadays the Church presence is minimal. And so are the occasions on which the Miao dress in their traditional costumes, though a few women wear at least the pleated white hemp skirts.

When they do dress ethnic style they look distinctively different from other Miao groups in Yunnan. Besides the white skirt, with black rectangular patches (representing the weaver's bench) intersecting the pleats, the women wear striped leggings, a loose, white, long-sleeved jacket and a woollen cape in bold patterns of red, black and white. An extra square piece of cotton cloth, embroidered and fringed, is attached to the back. Both men and women wear the cape and its flashy zigzag patterns are unique to this branch of the Miao. The more fully embroidered sections at the shoulders or on the sleeves employ motifs narrating the Miao migratory history. Different stitchings and shapes represent rivers, mountains, trails and fields.

Unmarried women leave their hair loose and load themselves with heavy silver ornaments. Married women wrap their hair in a cone around a stick on top of their heads. At festivals they may wear a headdress featuring a black triangular board on which are mounted several embossed discs. Once married, though, Miao women stop wearing jewellery.

The Hui are also one of the prominent minorities in the northeast. They have communities in every city, but they are also farmers and herders in the countryside south of the county seat of Xundian, which is a Yi and Hui Autonomous County, and Zhaotong. Hui villages lie just southwest of the latter city, recognizable by the green-domed minarets of the village mosques. Within Zhaotong the Hui quarter is in the old town, right next to the main street of the modern business district. A capacious mosque in the Arabian style stands in one of the alleys, housing an Islamic Studies Institute as well. Like the rural Han, the Hui of Zhaotong are very conservative. The women keep their hair covered and students at the Institute sometimes wear Arab-style *khaffiyehs* and long robes to class.

The last and smallest of the northeast ethnic groups is the Shui. Numbering just 7,000 in Yunnan, 2 per cent of the country's Shui population, they are spillovers from much larger Shui communities in Guizhou. Most live in the villages of Gagan township, on the Huangni River in southeastern Fuyuan County, in an area studded with limestone hills and karst landscapes. They live in stone houses with tile roofs. Over the entrance door they post the grotesque mask of the *tunkan,* a protective spirit that repels evil forces.

Long interaction with the Han, plus isolation from other Shui communities, has led Yunnan's Shui to adopt many of the manners and values of the Confucian tradition. This is even evident in the woman's costume—black turban, green, blue or black side-fastened jacket and trousers. For special occasions they'll wear a jacket with embroidered strips on the cuffs and along the lapel and neck. The colours are dark and the effect of the outfit is, unlike that of Miao or Yi women, *not* to attract attention, but to embody the approved female traits of quiet, reserve and elegance.

Like their Han neighbours in former generations, the Shui women spend much of their free time making and embroidering quilt covers, pillow cases, mosquito net fringes, handkerchiefs and shoes. Every woman has a few pairs of the latter. Culturally they follow the Han customs and annual ceremonies, except in weddings. Shui brides return to their natal house after the rites for six months to three years, like the Zhuang in Wenshan. And besides the Han festivals the Shui celebrate one of their own on the 3rd day of the 3rd lunar month, like the Buyi and several Zhuang groups, like them featuring the antiphonal singing that has earned them a regional reputation.

THE BUYI OF LUOPING

The northern high plain of Luoping County is Han-inhabited, as is the county seat, a nondescript, modern town that placed its new tourist hotels right next to the industrial zone. The county's ethnic minorities live in the hills and valleys south and southeast of Luoping city. The road south to the Nanpanjiang valley first passes Miao villages before making its slow, winding descent to the valley. The architecture of these villages is the same as the Han, sited on high knolls with a view east of the Sea of Ten Thousand Forested Peaks.

Miao women here wear trousers, not skirts as elsewhere. The rest of the costume consists of a bright jacket with fully embroidered sleeves and a wide tab hanging from the back of the collar to the shoulder blades, and a belt with big square panels, also fully embroidered, suspended from it in front and in back. The outfit is less spectacular than other Miao groups, but they do wear it for everyday use.

Another 30 km or so down to the valley and the landscape and people both change. Tall, steep limestone hills flank the riverbeds. One road leads to the Duoyi River, a lovely tributary of the Nanpang River, and turns up into the hills to the scenic reservoir at Lubuge. The other continues to the Nanpang at Badahe, then crosses into the extreme northwest corner of Guangxi. Coming up from the southeast, the Nanpangjiang meets the Huangnihe just past Badahe and turns east, becoming the boundary between Guizhou and Guangxi. Eventually it becomes the Pearl River of Guangdong.

From this junction of three provinces, upstream to the lower part of Shizong County, the Nanpangjiang valley is the homeland of Yunnan's Buyi people. Like the Shui, they are immigrants from much larger communities in Guizhou, where they number 2.5 million. Less than 40,000 live in southeastern Qujing, but they follow their traditional lifestyles as much as the more conservative of Yunnan's minorities. They are successful at farming both flat lands and hill slopes and are universally healthy-looking, with strong, well-proportioned limbs and clean complexions. They live in wide stone and wood houses, usually two stories high, with tiled roofs and sometimes tigers or dragons painted on the upper exterior wall or window shutters.

Every house is likely to have a loom, of the four-shaft, treadle-operated, bench type, like that used by the Dai and Zhuang, their linguistic relatives, and all the other ingredients used in textile production. Girls start learning from the age of seven how to use the cotton fluffers, spinning wheels, dye vats, looms and embroidery frames. Much of a girl's youth will be spent 'saving up for the dowry', which basically means weaving cloth and making shoes.

Female relatives must assist in this task, for between 20 and 100 sets of clothes must be made and a dozen pairs of shoes. Buyi footwear has upturned tips and embroidery on the upper parts around the ankles. A single pair takes a fortnight to produce. It is the last touch to a costume that resembles the one worn by the Shui, but sleeker and a bit more colourful. The jacket, usually in a shade of blue, sometimes dyed a deep hue with natural indigo, is cut the same way, but short-sleeved. Instead of colour strips along the lapel the Buyi use a band of black. Bright colours are attached to the lower half of the sleeves. A long-sleeved blouse is worn underneath, silver chains around the neck and a white terry-cloth turban.

The Buyi are an industrious people, but have a temperament as pleasant as the scenery. A polite and friendly manner, to outsiders as well as to themselves, is the norm. Their language, a member of the Tai-Kedai family, is very musical and spoken softly. Women assume most of the agricultural duties, men the construction work, ploughing and fishing. They also maintain the waterwheels set up along the rivers to channel water to their fields. Market days in Buyi townships are well attended, most merchants being Buyi women. They are also social occasions, when both children and grown-ups take the rafts out and pole them up and down the river.

(above) Buyi villagers pole rafting on the Duoyi River.
(right) A Miao woman draws water from Yuxianhu (Bathing Fairies Lake) in Yanshan County.

ZHUANG TRADITIONS

Yunnan's Zhuang mainly reside in Wenshan Zhuang and Miao Autonomous Prefecture, where they comprise 30 per cent of the population. As part of China's largest minority nationality they are heirs to an ancient, rich tradition that, in this part of the country, rivals the Han in depth and cultural achievements. They have always lived in the plain and low-lying hill valleys and did not develop sophisticated urban centres. Yet the basically rural slant of their culture has been no impediment to the advancement of Zhuang literature, science, arts and crafts.

Usually Zhuang prefer two- or three-storey houses of brick or wood, with tile roofs. Wenshan Zhuang are divided into many sub-groups and the prime building material and house style varies according to the sub-group. Some may be on stone foundations, others raised on stilts. Some have a side room attached to one end. Others have a balcony along the upper floor, with an open room under the roof at one corner. Livestock live on the ground floor, people above, and if the house has a third floor it is used for storage.

Many villages still retain the entrance gate, though it is no longer connected to a surrounding wall, nor bolted shut at night. Plains settlements often lie beside streams or rivers and the Zhuang have built various kinds of

(above) Zhuang carry huge baskets to the market at Babao.
(right) A Zhuang of Wenshan.

bridges to cross them. These can be simple, three-span stone bridges, like around Babao, or with a tower in the middle like at Xinjie across the Chouyang River. Or they can be constructed high above the water and be covered with a tile roof. This is the 'wind and rain bridge' style, best exemplified by the Mizhong Bridge in Malipo and the Guima Bridge in Guangnan.

For traffic in the rivers the Zhuang build long pirogues, poled rather than paddled. Along the banks they construct large waterwheels to direct water into their fields. Water is also used to power trip-hammers and pestles. Buffaloes are used to power the wooden cane or oil presses, for the Zhuang raise much sugar cane in addition to rice. Village potters supply the water jars, jugs, basins and other vessels. The Zhuang make paper from bamboo and wood pulp, white for ordinary use and yellow for funeral rites. Grave monuments in stone often have designs chiselled on them and Zhuang stonemasons are skilled in portraying human and animal figures for temple courtyards or government building ornamentation.

Men generally dress Han style, while women dress according to the fashions of their sub-group. They have two different sets: the simpler one for daily attire and a more splendid version for special occasions. The daily outfit comprises headgear, jacket and trousers and perhaps a bib or apron. The special ensemble

Farmers collect water from Yuxianhu.

includes brocaded pieces, elaborate headgear, skirt, embroidered shoes and plenty of silver jewellery. The preferred basic colour in most places is black, though in Guangnan and Funing the jacket is medium blue.

Zhuang women are excellent weavers and traditional houses all keep a loom. Their brocade has a thousand-year history and was nationally famous by the Qing Dynasty. Brocaded patches are attached to jackets, headscarves, bibs and aprons for their special occasion clothing. They are also noted embroiderers, an art used extensively for pillow cases, aprons, shoes, shoulder bags and costume parts.

Jewellery is the work of their highly talented silversmiths, who emboss, engrave, filigree and shape every conceivable kind of ornament. Wedding jewellery is particularly ornate, with wide belts, necklaces that cover the entire upper part of the body and elaborate headdresses with dozens of dangling pendants.

Zhuang religion is a syncretistic mix of Buddhism, Daoism and their own form of animism. In the past they used calendar counters inscribed on bone both to determine festival dates and the times for the key agricultural activities. They have a store of old books, written in Chinese, that narrate historical and legendary events as well as record Buddhist sutras.

They were also one of the earliest purveyors of the Bronze Drum Cult in ancient times. Some of the oldest drums have been excavated and reveal a high degree of craftsmanship. The artisans adorned the sides and top with vignettes of contemporary life, animal, human and geometric figures. The cult is still alive, so to speak, and villages still use them for New Year and other special occasions.

The Zhuang have a bigger festival cycle than most ethnic groups and singing and dancing are a part of most. They are famous for their antiphonal singing and their dances are lively. A lesser known tradition is the Zhuang drama, of three different types—Funing, Guangnan and Lexi. They are periodically staged in the village squares by touring troupes.

OTHER PEOPLE OF THE SOUTHEAST: MIAO, YAO, YI

The Miao are the second largest ethnic minority in Wenshan, but they are not as widespread as the Zhuang, nor as subdivided. While Miao reside in every county they are less concentrated in Guangnan and Funing and a greater component of the population in the south and west. Beyond Wenshan Miao sub-groups inhabit parts of Luoping, Shizong and Luxi Counties and most of Pingbian Autonomous Miao County, southwest of Wenshan city. As in Honghe Prefecture the Miao live in both the plains and the highlands, in between Yi and

Zhuang villages in the valleys and up in the hills where Yao and mountain-dwelling Yi reside.

Unlike Zhaotong the Miao women of the southeast all prefer to wear their traditional garments. For the Mengshua branch in Guangnan and Funing Counties the outfit is atypical for the province's Miao groups. It comprises a long-sleeved, open-front jacket over a blouse and an ankle-length, black pleated skirt. The sleeves and lower half of the jacket, plus the top half of the skirt are heavily embroidered in red and yellow. Their hair they coil into a top-knot, secured by a comb.

Other Miao women wear jackets, skirts, leggings, and aprons, all highly embellished with embroidery and appliqué, in varieties of the Mengchou style of Jinping County. The skirts may be all black, all white, or even pink, but pleated the same way. On festivals, besides jewellery, some Miao girls wear a round turban with pearl pendants dangling all around the base. For everyday wear most Miao women wear simple headscarves. Altogether, even the ordinary daily wear is so striking and unique that a Miao woman hoeing a field on a distant slope or walking along a faraway road is instantly recognizable as Miao, for no one else wears a skirt quite like the Miao's.

Perhaps Miao women favour wearing their full traditional costume even for everyday use because it takes them so much time and skill to make it, particularly the key component the skirt. These are still usually made from hemp and the process of making thread from this fibre is far more laborious than from cotton. It is, however, more durable and an easy plant to cultivate. Twisting, spinning and winding hemp thread is the Miao woman's commonest, pre-weaving, spare-time activity.

Weaving is done on a small, two-shaft loom while seated on a bench. The cloth is only about 25–30 cm wide and 20 metres or more long. Lengths of this white cloth are laid on a flat surface where the woman applies the design by covering in wax the parts making up the pattern. The belt is then dipped in the indigo dye bath and when the desired shade of blue is attained the wax is removed and the pattern appears in white. Next step is to cut the bolt into pieces to make the skirt and add the strips of embroidery. The last step is to make the pleats, by making the folds when the skirt is wet, sewing the folds together and removing the threads when the skirt is fully dried. After months of preparation the skirt's ready to wear and its maker reluctant to put on anything instead of it.

The Yao have small communities in central and southwestern Wenshan, but the largest concentrations are in Guangnan, Funing and Malipo Counties. Most Yao are Landian, with several sub-groups in the prefecture. All dress basically in black, with colour additions in the belt and the bright woollen tassels and fringe they attach to their collars or headgear. The young girls' caps are full of decorative pompoms, pendants, chains and bands of appliqué. In the northern half of the prefecture Yao women wear a broad white collar nearly covering the shoulders and under it in front an embossed silver plaque and silver chains.

Traditional fashion rules dictate that females change costume components like headgear during rites of passage. The first item is the coloured cap, given the babies on the third day after birth. This is a grand occasion for the family's relatives, who all come bearing gifts and invoking their ancestors' protection for the child. The size changes as the girl grows up, but the style stays the same.

Then at 15 or 16 she exchanges this for the black headscarf that wraps her hair like an adult's. This is done by the older girls, who already wear the head scarf, in a nocturnal ceremony. In Guangnan the wrapped hair bun is topped with a decoratively inscribed silver disc. They also don a special headdress for their weddings, featuring a broad cloth that covers her face and hides her shyness. But afterwards they continue to wear the headscarf they got as adolescents.

The Yao claim descent from the six sons and six daughters of Pan Hu. The Yao progenitor was originally a watchdog in ancient times who guarded King Gao Xin. But over time this king became lax in his rule and his weakened state aroused the cupidity of a neighbouring king, who amassed an invasion force. Learning of this, King Gao Xin ordered his ministers to spread the word that whoever kills the rival king will be rewarded with wealth and the hand of one of his beautiful daughters.

The only one to respond was Pan Hu, the guardian dog. So the king held a banquet in the dog's honour and next day the dog left for the enemy camp. Pan Hu played on the rival's vanity, pretended to have left his master because of the impending defeat of his state and won the rival king's confidence. Then when the king went to relieve himself Pan Hu attacked and killed him, bit off his head, swam across the sea with it and dropped it at the feet of King Gao Xin. The grateful monarch, true to his word, bestowed the princess in marriage to Pan Hu. But first, as the story goes, he transformed Pan Hu into a human. It is this Pan Hu, Pan Wang or King Pan to the Yao, whom the Yao honour in their greatest annual festival.

The Yao, Miao and Zhuang all came into Wenshan from the east. The Yi migrated here from the northwest and may be the oldest settlers in the prefecture. Most live in the central and western areas, but sizable pockets of Yi villages lie in Funing County and in the mountains of southern Maguan and

Malipo Counties. In central and western Wenshan they inhabit the plains and foothills, like their Zhuang neighbours, in villages with similar layout and architecture.

Yi women's jackets are often cut like the Zhuang's, but they use brighter colours and sometimes jackets employ more than one. In central Wenshan, for example, the body might be blue, the upper back yellow, the arms red. On top of this they wear an apron embroidered along the top, side hems and the tabs at the end of the belt, which drape over the buttocks. The headscarf is also embroidered and festooned with red pompoms.

In northern Wenshan the jacket is black with blue and red sleeves and large bands of blue and red or a wide band of embroidery across the lower front. In Qiubei's Puzhehei area the older Yi women wear plain blue jackets tied with a cloth belt, with bunches of red pompoms hanging down the back. The young girls wear costumes identical to the Sani of the Stone Forest, for this group of Yi migrated here from Lunan and still identify with their more famous cousins back in the original homeland.

In the mountains south of the capital the Yi women's costumes more closely resemble local Zhuang clothing. Some wear tight round caps with silver studs along the base and black bib-aprons with embroidered flowers at the top. In Maguan the Yi woman's cap is black and heavily decorated with silver studs, pendants and discs. The side-fastened jacket is bright silk and worn with a separate collar piece with long suspended tabs. West of Maguan, in Honghe's Pingbian County, women wear black skirts and long-sleeved, side-fastened jackets, with a wide embroidered panel across the lower half. Black skirts are also worn by Xichou County Yi, plus a blouse pieced together from bits of coloured cloth cut into geometric patterns.

In Funing the Yi have, like their Miao neighbours, became skilled at batik, though the jackets made with this kind of cloth are only worn at festivals, by both men and women. The men wear three-layered jackets, with the sleeves of each slightly shorter. Round sun motifs and geometric strips cover the entire surface of the outer layer. The women's jacket has the patterns only on the hems, collar and down the front. Ordinary wear is a white, open-front jacket with dark bands on the cuffs and lapels, worn with trousers and a pin-striped, white apron.

Ethnic Festivals

For the Miao of the eastern prefectures the biggest annual festival is Treading the Flowery Mountain. Unlike Jinping County, though, the eastern Miao stage theirs on the 6th day of the 6th lunar month, with a slightly different programme. Rituals are restricted to the sacrifice of a cock at the base of the pole, bull fights and dragon dances are included, and youths sing to each other through bamboo tubes. The dance show features men on long reed pipes and in Zhaotong they will wear their big white capes with red and black designs.

The annual Miao ancestral rites are held at different times in different communities, according to dates fixed by the village shamans. The private household ceremony involves only the family head and his brothers and paternal cousins. It is staged at midnight, with a single singer and reed-pipe player. The public ceremony includes an orchestra and a troupe performing dances in honour of the ancestors. The lead reed-pipe player performs various feats with the 81 knives used as props for his act.

Among the Yao the greatest yearly event, and the most important song and dance, are in commemoration of their mythical ancestor Pan Hu. The Yao progenitor died on a hunting expedition with his sons when he was gored by a mountain goat. His widow commanded the sons to turn the skin of the goat into a drum. This they did, adding a layer of yellow clay to the surface, then beat the drum continuously in honour of their father. The Yao have maintained the custom ever since, fashioning slender drums with wide ends from the wood of the catalpa and paulawnia trees. Male drums are long and thin, female short and round.

During the evenings of the first fortnight of the first lunar month the Yao stage dances with the yellow-clay drum. The men play the drums, the women dance around them like butterflies, waving coloured ribbons. Dancing is an integral part of every Yao festival, including the Dragon Worm Dance on the 3rd day of the 3rd lunar month and the Harvest Dance and Dance for King Pan performed at Panwangjie, the 16th day of the 10th lunar month. Pigs and chickens are sacrificed this day to honour Pan Hu and songs sung of his life and achievements.

Some Yao communities choose this festival for the boys' rite of passage called Dujie. A week before the rite the boys bathe, shave off their hair and don a hat made of bamboo leaves, symbolizing a return to the embryo state. The boys stay quietly in their homes, may not lie on their backs, and listen to the elders tell them stories of Yao history and tradition. On the day of the rite the boys, dressed in red robes, one by one mount a platform representing the sacred mountain Wutaishan. They assume a fetal position and fall off the platform into a net below, now officially reborn as an adult Yao.

For the Yi in western Wenshan, Qujing and Zhaotong the most public annual event is the Torch Festival, celebrated with wrestling matches, bull fights and pony races by day, dancing by the illumination of torches at night.

In northern and eastern Wenshan a more important occasion is Dagongjie, held for three days beginning on the 7th day of the 4th lunar month. The festival honours an ancient Yi victory over their enemies and features mock battles and the capture and trial of the enemy chieftain. Other themes expressed in Dagongjie include ancestral rites, the expulsion of evil spirits, sacrifice to the sacred sword and rites honouring the golden bamboo, which saved the race in mythic times. Horse races, parading with umbrellas and large-scale group dancing are activities drawing great crowds of festival celebrants. The women, of course, load themselves with silver ornaments at this time, but even the men dress traditional style in batik jackets or long black cloaks, with tall mitres on their heads.

Much of the singing done at this festival, as at the Yao and Miao events, is the antiphonal type, where the females sing a verse and the males respond with a verse. The Buyi and Zhuang are particularly noted for this, for it plays a big part in the courtship manoeuvring that accompanies the festival gatherings. The 3rd day of the 3rd lunar month is a big day among the Buyi and some Zhuang groups for this activity.

Buyi youth sing to each other in the presence of elders and follow a formula. They begin with mutual praise, then poke mild fun in jest, proceed to expressing their determination to demonstrate their love and conclude in pledges of loyalty. The tunes and rhythms follow a fixed style and the content of the songs must be approved by the invited elders before the singing starts. If the courtship singing does in fact lead to marriage, singing will be part of the preparation made by the bride's mother, as she sings to her daughter how to become a good Buyi wife, respect her elders and get along with her in-laws.

Antiphonal singing is a highlight of most Zhuang festivities, including the Spring Festival of the Lunar New Year. Zhuang tradition contains a variety of costumed dances, too. The Longduan Festival in the eastern areas, held on the 1st and the 4th lunar months, honouring a Zhuang military hero of seven centuries ago, is the venue for several, especially the girls' Fan Dance. Longduan also features the performances of Zhuang dramas, held day and night. Those staged at night include fighting scenes, while those by day do not. Villagers hold picnics in between the daytime shows and dances following the evening acts. The dramas remind them of their history and tradition, while the dances reaffirm their solidarity and proclaim the spirit and joy of being Zhuang.

FESTIVAL CALENDAR

SOLAR DATE FESTIVALS

date	festival	place	people
2 January	Gatâ Pa-eu	Banna, sw Simao	Aini
21 March	Equinox Exhibition	Heqing	Bai
13–15 April	Water-Sprinkling	all Dai areas	Dai, De'ang, Achang
20–26 November	County Fair	Ninglang	Yi
21–23 December	Kuoshi	Nujiang	Lisu

LUNAR DATE FESTIVALS

1st month

day	festival	place	people
1	Spring Festival	everywhere	all
2–4	Call Back the Bovine Soul	Yongren	Yi
3	Tread the Flowery Mountain	Jinping	Miao
3	Tree Bud Festival	Weixi	Bai
5	Yin Yin Wu Children's Fest.	Eryuan	Bai
1st tiger day	Rhamatu	Yuanyang, Luchun	Hani, Alu
1st horse day	Jilongjie	Shiping	Huayao Yi
10	Dabao Temple Fair	Zhongdian	Tibetan
10	Posting Oxen Horns	Jinping	Miao
12	Honour the Herding God	Yongning	Mosuo
13	Street of Flowers	Mosha, Xinping	Huayao Dai
14–16	Hunting God's Birthday	Dali	Bai
14	Mid-January Festival	Yongning	Pumi
14	Tiger Masquerade	Shuangbai	Yi
15	Milao Stick Fair	Lijiang	Naxi
15	Kitchen God Festival	Lanping	Pumi
15	Zhiju Yi Fashion Show	Yongen	Yi
15	Young Girls' Festival	Jianchuan	Bai
25–28	Munao	Dehong	Jingpo

2nd month

day	festival	place	people
1	Hunter's Guardian Festival	Yiliang	Yi
1	Bird Diversion Festival	Hekou	Yao
5–7	Calling Back the Rice Spirit	Weishan	Yi
8	Climbing the Sword Ladder	Tengchong, Lianghe	Lisu
8	Sanduojie	Lijiang, Baishuitai	Naxi
8	Putting up Flowers	Chuxiong, Dayao	Yi
8	Taizihui	Shaxi	Bai
8	Dragon's Pool Fair	Lanping	Pumi
8	Drum Festival	Jinggu, Banna	Lahu
8	Pinning up Flowers	Shuangjiang	Bulang
9	Flower Festival	Xinping	Yi
1st dragon day	Rhamatu	Jinping	Hani
12–14	Floral King's Birthday	Dali	Bai
15	Farm Tool Fair	Eryuan	Bai
15	Gongmajie	Lancang	Lahu
28	Singing Festival	Shibaoshan	Bai

3rd month

3	Jilongjie	Qiubei, Funing	Zhuang
3	Jilongjie	Luoping	Buyi
15	Festival of Fresh Flowers	Fugong, Gongshan	Nu
15–21	Third Month Fair	Dali	Bai
28	Fuzhuanjie	Santai	Yi

4th month

2	Honour the Carpentry God	Tonghai	Mongolian
5	Wheat Brew Festival	Lanping	Pumi
7–9	Dagongjie	Funing	Yi
1st rabbit day	Ox King's Birthday	Funing	Zhuang
8	Horse Races	Dali	Bai
15	Xiaoputao Temple Fair	Dali	Bai
15–18	Benzhu Village Operas	Dali	Bai
16	Memorial: the Slain of 1856	Dali	Hui
20	Burying the Bamboo	Funing	Yi
23–25	Visiting Three Spirits	Dali	Bai
28	Ancestral Rites	Ninglang	Lisu

5th month

5–6	Horse Racing Fair	Zhongdian	Tibetan
1st pig day	Kuzhazha	Yuanjiang, Honghe	Hani
8	Seeing Off Lamas	Yongning	Mosuo

6th month

day	festival	place	people
6	Tread the Flowery Mountain	Zhaotong, Wuding	Miao
1st sheep day	Kuzhazha	Luchun, Yuanyang	Hani
15	Guanmenjie	Simao, Lincang	Dai
16	Grass Worship	Tonghai	Mongolian
22–24	Honour the Mountain God	Fuyuan	Shui
24	Torch Festival	most Yi areas	Yi
24–25	Torch Festival	Lijiang	Naxi
25	Torch Festival	Dali Prefecture	Bai, Yi

7th month

12–14	Feeding the Hungry Ghosts	Lijiang	Naxi
15	Welcoming the Ancestors	Yuanyang, Honghe	Yi
15	Zhongyuanjie	Dali	Bai
15	Niru Danbajie	Zhongdian	Tibetan
22	Horse Racing Fair	Songgui	Bai
23	Making Merry on the Waves (one month)	Dali	Bai
25	Rounding Lion Mountain	Yongning	Mosuo, Pumi

8th month

15	Mid-Autumn Fair	Shaping	Bai
15	Offerings to Sun and Moon	Lancang	Lahu
15	New Rice Festival	Zhaotong	Miao
15	New Rice Festival	Ximeng, Menglian	Wa

9th month

15	Street Meeting Festival	Longchuan	Achang
15	Kaimenjie	Simao, Lincang	Dai

10th month

1	Bull's Dance	Zhaotong	Yi
16	Panwangjie	Wenshan, Honghe	Yao

11th month

19	Birds' Day	Heqing	Bai
26–29	Lama Dances	Songzhanlin	Tibetan

12th month

25	Jizushan Temple Fair	Jizushan	Bai
26–29	Lama Dances	Dongzhulin	Tibetan

MINORITY NATIONALITIES

Name	Language Group	Population	Locations (Prefectures, Cities)
Yi	Tibeto-Burman	4,705,658	all
Bai	Sino-Tibetan	1,505,644	Dali, Lijiang, Nujiang, Kunming
Hani	Tibeto-Burman	1,424,990	Simao, Xishuangbanna, Yuxi, Honghe
Dai	Tai-Kedai	1,142,139	Baoshan, Dehong, Lincang, Chuxiong, Lijiang, Simao, Yuxi, Xishuangbanna, Honghe
Zhuang	Tai-Kedai	1,144,021	Wenshan, Qujing, Honghe, Lijiang, Xishuangbanna
Miao	Miao-Yao	1,043,535	Zhaotong, Qujing, Wenshan, Honghe, Chuxiong, Xishuangbanna, Lincang, Simao, Kunming
Lisu	Tibeto-Burman	609,768	Deqing, Lijiang, Chuxiong, Nujiang, Dehong, Lincang, Dali
Hui	Sino-Tibetan	643,238	all
Lahu	Tibeto-Burman	447,631	Lincang, Simao, Honghe, Xishuangbanna
Wa	Mon-Khmer	383,023	Lincang, Simao, Xishuangbanna
Naxi	Tibeto-Burman	295,464	Lijiang, Deqing
Yao	Miao-Yao	190,610	Qujing, Wenshan, Honghe, Xishuangbanna, Simao
Jingpo	Tibeto-Burman	130,212	Dehong, Baoshan, Nujiang
Tibetan	Tibeto-Burman	128,432	Deqing, Lijiang, Nujiang
Bulang	Mon-Khmer	90,388	Xishuangbanna, Lincang, Simao
Buyi	Tai-Kedai	54,695	Qujing
Pumi	Tibeto-Burman	32,923	Lijiang, Nujiang
Achang	Tibeto-Burman	33,519	Dehong
Nu	Tibeto-Burman	27,738	Nujiang, Deqing
Jinuo	Tibeto-Burman	20,685	Xishuangbanna
De'ang	Mon-Khmer	17,804	Dehong, Lincang
Mongolian	Altaic	28,110	Yuxi
Shui	Tai-Kedai	12,533	Qujing
Manchu	Altaic	12,187	Kunming, other large cities
Dulong	Tibeto-Burman	5,884	Nujiang

Yunnan Minorities in Autonomous Prefectures

Deqing (Tibetan), Nujiang (Lisu), Dehong (Dai, Jingpo), Xishuangbanna (Dai), Honghe (Hani, Yi), Wenshan (Zhuang, Miao), Dali (Bai), Chuxiong (Yi).

Yunnan Minorities in Autonomous Counties

Deqing–Weixi (Lisu); Lijiang–Lijiang (Naxi), Ninglang (Yi); Nujiang–Gongshan (Dulong, Nu), Lanping (Bai, Pumi); Dali–Yangbi (Yi), Weishan (Yi, Hui), Nanjian (Yi); Lincang–Gengma (Dai, Wa), Cangyuan (Wa), Shuangjiang (Lahu, Wa, Bulang, Dai); Simao–Jingdong (Yi), Zhenyuan (Yi, Hani, Lahu), Jinggu (Dai, Yi), Pu'er (Hani, Yi), Mojiang (Hani), Jiangcheng (Hani, Yi); Yuxi–Yuanjiang (Hani, Yi, Dai), Xinping (Yi, Dai), Eshan (Yi); Kunming–Luquan (Yi, Miao), Lunan (Yi); Qujing–Xundian (Hui, Yi); Honghe–Pingbian (Miao), Jinping (Miao, Yao, Dai), Hekou (Yao).

Yunnan Minorities in Other Provinces

Yi (Sichuan, Guizhou, Guangxi), Bai (Sichuan, Guizhou), Zhuang (Guangxi, Guizhou, Guangdong, Hunan), Miao (Sichuan, Guizhou, Guangxi, Hunan, Hubei, Hainan), Lisu (Sichuan), Hui (most of China), Naxi (Sichuan, Tibet), Yao (Guangxi, Guizhou, Hunan, Guangdong, Jiangxi), Buyi (Guizhou), Pumi (Sichuan), Mongolian (Inner Mongolia and eleven northern provinces), Tibetan (Tibet, Sichuan, Qinghai, Gansu), Shui (Guangxi, Guizhou).

Yunnan Minorities in Neighbouring Countries

Yi (Burma, Laos, Vietnam), Hani (Burma, Laos, Thailand, Vietnam), Dai (India, Burma, Laos, Vietnam), Zhuang (Vietnam), Miao (Burma, Laos, Thailand, Vietnam), Lisu (India, Burma, Thailand, Laos), Lahu (Burma, Thailand, Laos, Vietnam), Wa (Burma), Yao (Burma, Laos, Thailand, Vietnam), Jingpo (India, Burma), Bulang (Burma), Mongolian (Mongolia, Russia), De'ang (Burma), Tibetan (Nepal, India).

Also see map on pages 48–49.

RECOMMENDED READING

An Chunyang and Liu Bohua (eds), *Where the Dai People Live,* Beijing: Foreign Languages Press, 1985.

Anderson, John, *A Report on the Expedition to Western Yunnan and Bhamo,* Calcutta: Office of the Superintendent of Gov't Printing, Calcutta, 1871.

Atwill, David G., *The Chinese Sultanate: Islam, Ethnicity, and the Panthay Rebellion in Southwest China, 1856-1873,* Stanford: Stanford University Press, 2005.

Baber, E. Colborne, *Travels and Researches in Western Yunnan,* London: John Murray, 1882.

Backus, Charles, *The Nan-chao Kingdom and T'ang China's Southwestern Frontier,* Cambridge: Cambridge University Press, 1981.

Benedict, P., *Austro-Thai Languages and Culture,* New Haven: Yale University Press, 1975.

Bigland, Eileen, *Into China,* New York: MacMillan Company, 1940.

Bossen, Laurel, *Chinese Women and Rural Development: Sixty Years of Change in Lu Village, Yunnan,* Lanham, MD: Rowman & Littlefield Publishing, 2002.

Broomhill, A.J., *Strong Tower,* London: China Inland Mission, 1948.

Cai Hua, *A Society without Fathers or Husbands: The Na of China,* Cambridge, MA: MIT Press, 2001.

Carné, Louis de, *Travels on the Mekong: Cambodia, Laos and Yunnan,* Bangkok: White Lotus Press, 1995 (reprint of 1872 edition).

Chen Jihai, *A Tour of Forests in Yunnan,* Kunming: Yunnan University Publishing House, 1998.

Clarke, Samuel R., *Among the Tribes of Southwest China,* London: Morgan & Scott, Ltd., 1911.

Davies, H.R., *Yunnan: the Link between India and the Yangtze,* Cambridge: Cambridge University Press, 1909.

Davis, Sara L.M., *Song and Silence,* Chiang Mai: Silkworm Books, 2005.

Deng Qiyao and Zhang Liu, *The Festivals in the Mysterious Land of Yunnan,* Kunming: Yunnan People's Publishing House, 1991.

Dessaint, Alain Y., *Minorities of Southwestern China,* New Haven: HRAF Press, 1980.

Dingle, Edwin J., *Across China on Foot,* New York: Henry Holt & Co., 1911.

Dodd, William C., *The Tai Race*, Bangkok: White Lotus Press, 1996 (reprint of 1923 edition).

Duan Jinlu (ed.), *Social and Scenic Tourism to Yunnan Nationalities*, Kunming: Yunnan Nationalities Publishing House, 1992.

Dupuis, Jean, *A Journey to Yunnan and the Opening of the Red River to Trade*, Bangkok: White Lotus Press, 1998 (reprint of 1880 edition).

Fei Hsiao-tung, *Earthbound China*, London: Routledge and Kegan Paul, 1949.

Fitzgerald, C.P., *The Southward Expansion of the Chinese People*, Bangkok: White Lotus Press, 1993 (reprint of 1972 edition).

Fitzgerald, C.P., *The Tower of Five Glories: a Study of the Min-chia of Tali*, New Haven: Hyperion, 1973.

Forbes, Andrew and Henley, David, *The Haw: Traders of the Golden Triangle*, London: Teak House, 1997.

Franck, Harry A., *Roving through Southern China*, London: Fisher-Unwin, 1926.

Gao Fayuan, *Women's Culture Series: Nationalities in Yunnan* (26 volumes), Kunming: Yunnan Education Publishing House, 1995.

Garnier, Francis, *Further Travels in Laos and in Yunnan: 1866–1868*, Bangkok: White Lotus Press, 1996 (reprint of 19th century editions).

Giersch, C. Patterson, *Asian Borderlands: the Transformation of Qing China's Yunnan Frontier*, Cambridge, MA: Harvard, 2006.

Gill, William, *The River of Golden Sand* (2 vols), London: John Murray, 1880.

Goodman, Jim, *The Akha: Guardians of the Forest*, London: Teak House, 1997.

Goodman, Jim, *Children of the Jade Dragon: the Naxi of Lijiang and their Mountain Neighbours the Yi*, London: Teak House, 1997.

Goodman, Jim, *Joseph F. Rock and his Shangrila*, Hong Kong: Caravan Press, 2006.

Goullart, Peter, *Forgotten Kingdom*, London: John Murray, 1957.

Graham, David Crockett, *Folk Religion in Southwest China*, Washington, D.C.: Smithsonian Institution, 1961.

Han, Carolyn, *Tales from within the Clouds: Nakhi Stories of China*, Honolulu: University of Hawai'i Press, 1997.

Hansen, Mette Halskov, *Lessons in Being Chinese: Minority Education and Ethnic Identity in Southwest China*, Seattle: University of Washington Press, 1999.

Harrell, Stevan (ed.), *Cultural Encounters on China's Ethnic Frontiers*, Seattle: University of Washington Press, 1995.

Harrell, Stevan, Bamo Qubumo and Ma Erzi, *Mountain Patterns: the Survival of Nuosu Culture in China,* Seattle: University of Washington Press, 1999.

Harrell, Stevan (ed.), *Perspectives on the Yi of Southwest China,* Berkeley: University of California Press, 2001.

Harrell, Stevan, *Ways of Being Ethnic in Southwest China,* Seattle: University of Washington Press, 2002.

Hayes, Ernest H., *Sam Pollard of Yunnan,* Wallington, Surrey: Carwal Publications, 1946.

He Liyi, *Mr. China's Son,* Boulder: Westview Press, 1993.

He Zhengting, *Yunnan Zhuang Nationality,* Kunming: Nationalities Publishing House, 1998.

Hoenstadt, Gabrielle von, *In and Round Yunnan Fou,* London: Heinemann, 1922.

Hosie, Alexander, *Three Years in Western China,* London: George Philip & Son, 1890.

Hoskin, John and Walton, Geoffrey, *Folk Tales and Legends of the Dai People,* Bangkok: DD, 1992.

Hsu, Francis L.K., *Under the Ancestors' Shadow: Chinese Culture and Personality,* New York: Columbia University Press, 1948.

Huang He (ed.), *Xishuangbanna Fengjing,* Beijing: Huayi Publishing House, 1986.

Jack, R. Logan, *The Back Blocks of China,* London: Arnold, 1904.

Jackson, Anthony, *Na-khi Religion,* The Hague: Mouton, 1979.

Johnston, R.F., *From Peking to Mandalay,* London: John Murray, 1908.

King, Victor T. (ed.), *Explorers of South-East Asia: Six Lives,* Kuala Lumpur: Oxford University Press, 1955.

LeBar, Frank M., Hickey, Gerald C. and Musgrave, John K., *Ethnic Groups of Mainland Southeast Asia,* New Haven: Yale, 1964.

Lewis, Paul W. and Bai Bibo, *Hani Cultural Themes,* Bangkok: White Lotus Press, 2002.

Liang Shutang, *Yunnan Marching Towards the World,* Kunming: Yunnan Fine Arts Publishing House, 1994.

Lintner, Bertil, *The Kachin: Lords of Burma's Northern Frontier,* London: Teak House, 1997.

Little, Archibald John, *Across Yunnan: A Journey of Surprises,* Boston: Adamant Media Corporation, 2002 (reprint of 1910 edition).

Lu Qunhe, *The Yao Nationality,* Nanning: People's Publishing House, n.d.

Ma Yin (ed.), *China's Minority Nationalities,* Beijing: Foreign Languages Press, 1989.

Ma Yin (ed.), *Questions and Answers about China's Minority Nationalities,* Beijing: New World Press, 1985.

Mansfield, Stephen, *China: Yunnan Province,* Bradt Travel Guides, 2001.

Mayhew, Bradley, *South-West China,* Lonely Planet Publications, 2002.

McDonald, Angus, *The Five Foot Road: in search of a vanished China,* San Francisco: HarperCollins West, 1995.

Metford, Beatrix, *Where China Meets Burma: Life and Travels in the Burma-China Border Lands,* London and Glasgow: Blackie & Son Ltd., 1935.

Miller, Lucien (ed.), *South of the Clouds: Tales from Yunnan,* Seattle: University of Washington Press, 1994.

Mitchell, Sam (ed.), *Yunnan through Foreign Students' Eyes: Tourism and Development in Yunnan,* Kunming: Yunnan Fine Arts Publishing House, 2004.

Mitchell, Sam (ed.), *Yunnan through Foreign Students' Eyes: Ethic Minority Issues in Yunnan,* Kunming: Yunnan Fine Arts Publishing House, 2005.

Moseley, George V.H. III, *The Consolidation of the South China Frontier,* Berkeley: University of California Press, 1973.

Mueggler, Erik, *The Age of Wild Ghosts: Memory, Violence and Place in Southwest China,* Berkeley: University of California Press, 2001.

Namu, Yang Erche and Mathieu, Christine, *Leaving Mother Lake: A Girlhood at the Edge of the World,* New York: Little Brown, 2004.

Neis, D. P., *The Sino-Vietnamese Border Demarcation, 1885-87,* Bangkok: White Lotus Press, 1998 (reprint of 1887 edition).

d'Ollone, Vicomte, *In Forbidden China,* London: Fisher-Unwin, 1912.

Oppitz, Michael and Hsu, Elizabeth, *Naxi and Mosuo Ethnography: Kin, Rites, Pictographs,* Zurich: Volkerkundemuseum, 1998.

Osborne, Milton, *The Mekong: Turbulent Past, Uncertain Future,* London: Allen and Unwin, 2000.

Osborne, Milton, *River Road to China: the Mekong River Expedition, 1866–73,* London: Allen and Unwin, 1976.

Pan Longdong et al., *Kunming,* Beijing: New World Press, 1981.

Parris, John, *Roaming Yunnan* (2 vols), Kunming: Yunnan People's Publishing House, 1992.

Pichon, Louis, *A Journey to Yunnan in 1892,* Bangkok: White Lotus Press, 1999 (reprint of 1893 edition).

Rees, Helen, *Echoes of History: Naxi Music in Modern China*, New York: Oxford University Press, 2000.

Rock, Joseph, *The Ancient Na-khi Kingdom of Southwest China*, Cambridge: Harvard University Press, 1947.

Rock, Joseph, *The Life and Culture of the Na-khi Tribe of the China-Tibet Borderland*, Wiesbaden: Franz Steiner, 1963.

Rock, Joseph, *The Na-khi Naga Cult and Related Ceremonies*, Rome: Seria Orientalia Roma, 1952.

Santasombat, Yos, *Lak Chang: a Reconstruction of Tai Identity in Daikong*, Canberra: Pandanus Books, 2001.

Shen Che, *Life among the Minority Nationalities of Northwest Yunnan*, Beijing: Foreign Languages Press, 1989.

Shi Songshan (ed.), *The Costumes and Adornments of Chinese Yi Nationality Picture Album*, Beijing: Arts and Crafts Publishing House, 1990.

Slader, Edward R. and Brown, Horace, *Mandalay to Moulmein: a Narrative of the Two Expeditions to Western China of 1868 and 1875*, London: MacMillan, 1876.

Sutton, Donald S., *Provincial Militarism and the Chinese Republic: the Yunnan Army, 1905-25*, Ann Arbor: University of Michigan Press, 1980.

Sutton, S.B., *In China's Border Provinces: the Turbulent Career of Joseph Rock, Botanist/Explorer*, New York: Hastings House, 1974.

Tan Pei-ying, *The Building of the Burma Road*, New York: McGraw-Hill, 1945.

Tang Zhilu and Jin Zhuotong, *Lijiang*, Beijing: New World Press, 1988.

Tapp, Nicholas and Cohn, Don, *The Tribal People of Southwest China: Chinese Views of the Other Within*, Bangkok: White Lotus Press, 2003.

Taylor, Mrs. Howard, *Behind the Ranges: Fraser of Lisuland*, London: China Inland Mission, 1944.

Thrasher, Alan R., *Ka-Li-Luo Dance: Songs of the Chuxiong Yi*, Danbury, CT: World Music Press, 1990.

Unger, Ann Helen and Unger, Walter, *Yunnan: China's Most Beautiful Province*, Munich: Hirmer Verlag, 2002.

Walker, Anthony (ed.), *Mvuh Hpa Mi Hpa – Creating Heaven, Creating Earth: an Epic Myth of the Lahu People in Yunnan*, Chiang Mai: Silkworm Books, 1995.

Wang Zhusheng, *The Jingpo: Kachin of the Yunna Plateau,* Phoenix: Arizona State University Press, 1997.

Ward, F. Kingdon, *From China to Hkamti Long,* London: Arnold, 1924.

Ward, F. Kingdon, *The Land of the Blue Poppy,* Taipei: Ch'eng Wen, 1971 (reprint of 1913 edition).

Ward, F. Kingdon, *Mystery Rivers of Tibet,* London: Cadogan Books, 1986 (reprint of 1923 edition).

Webster, Donovan, *The Burma Road,* New York: Farrar, Strauss and Giroux, 2003.

Wiens, Harold J., *Han Chinese Expansion in South China,* New Haven: Yale University Press, 1967.

Williams, Clement, *Through Burma to Western China,* London, 1868.

Winnington, Alan J., *Slaves of the Cool Mountains,* London: Lawrence & Wishart, 1959.

Yang, Gladys (trans.), *Ashima,* Beijing: Foreign Languages Press, 1981.

Yang Hengcan, *Dali,* Beijing: New World Pres, 1989.

Yang Jizhong et al., *Chuxiong,* Beijing: New World Press, 1989.

Yukio, Hayashi and Yang Guangyang (eds), *Dynamics of Ethnic Culture Across National Boundaries in Southwestern China and Mainland Southeast Asia,* Chiang Mai: Ming Muang, 2000.

Yunnan Nationalities Publishing House, *The Rhythmical Move of the Red Soil Land,* Kunming, 1995.

Yunnan Provincial People's Government, *Highlights of Minority Nationalities in Yunnan,* Kunming, n.d.

Yunnan Provincial Travel and Tourism Administration, *A Tourist Guide to Yunnan,* Kunming, 1991.

Zhang Weiwen and Zeng Qingnan, *In Search of China's Minorities,* Beijing: New Wold Press, 1993.

Zheng Lan, *Travels through Xishuangbanna,* Beijing: Foreign Languages Press, 1981.

Zhong Xiu, *Emerging from Primitivity: Travels in the Liangshan Mountains,* Beijing: New World Press, 1984.

Zhong Xiu, *Yunnan Travelogue – 100 Days in Southwest China,* Beijing: New World Press, 1985.

Zhu Liangwen, *The Dai,* Bangkok: DD, 1992.

PRACTICAL INFORMATION

Baoshan

TRANSPORTATION

Baoshan is located 600 km from Kunming and 120 km from Xiaguan. The entire route is now an expressway and can be reached from Kunming in eight hours. Baoshan airport, 10 km from the city, has flights to Kunming and Guangzhou.

ACCOMMODATION

Landu Hotel
Bao Xiu Xi Road
Tel: (0875) 212 1888
Fax: (0875) 212 1990
Baoshan's finest, with night club, gym and indoor swimming pool. Four stars, 150 rooms.

Longyang Hotel
Jiulong Road
Tel: (0875) 214 8888
Fax: (0875) 214 9999
A comfortable two-star hotel near the bus station.

Dali

Although the name Dali refers to the entire prefecture, most travellers commence their explorations in the old city of Dali (*Dali gu cheng*) which lies 13 km north of the prefecture's capital city of Xiaguan.

TRANSPORTATION

Dali is accessible by air from Kunming with China Eastern Airlines flying the route several times daily. There are also direct flights to Jinghong and Guangzhou. The airport is 40 km from old Dali. The road from Kunming which the buses use qualifies as an expressway—the five-hour trip bypasses the small towns and passes through several tunnels. Unfortunately, most buses only go as far as Xiaguan, leaving the traveller almost but not quite there. Unless you don't mind taking a bus or taxi the remaining 13 km, make sure your bus from Kunming goes to Dali *gu cheng*. Kunming and Xiaguan are also linked by train.

Leaving Dali for Lijiang or points further northwest via bus is less complex; the many buses which originate in Xiaguan stop to take on passengers. All the tour agencies around town sell tickets.

ACCOMMODATION

Landscape Hotel
96 Yuer Road
Tel: (0872) 266 6318
Fax: (0872) 266 6189
Located in the heart of old Dali, a low-rise hotel, modern but with Bai architectural style. Attractive, clean and moderately priced.

Dali Wangfu Hotel
175 Bo Ai Lu
Tel: (0872) 315 6888
A new and deluxe Bai-style low-rise hotel in the old city.

Tang Dynasty Guesthouse
37 Huguo Road
Tel: (0872) 266 3698
Off the street, but in the middle of the area known to locals as Foreigner's Street, with many Western restaurants and bars. Simple but clean rooms around a courtyard.

Higherland Inn
Tel: (0872) 266 1599
Email: higherlandinn@yahoo.com
Website: www.higherland.com
Located above the Zhonghe Temple on Cangshan Mountain. Great hikes to the Wuwei and Gantong temples. Accessible only by chair lift, pack horse, or a long walk up the mountain. Simple but special.

Yu Yuan Inn
8 Honglongjing Road
Tel: (0872) 267 3267
Email: ynkelan@yahoo.com.cn
A Bai family-run garden inn on a quiet street with a stream running through the middle of old Dali.

New Asia Star Hotel
Dian Zang Road
Tel: (0872) 267 0009
Fax: (0872) 267 2229
Located at the base of the Cangshan Mountains between Dali and Xiaguan, this is Dali's modern four-star hotel with 300 rooms, atrium lobby and all the facilities. Good views of the mountains, but a long walk from the old town.

Jim's Tibetan Guest House
Lu Yu Xiao Qu
13 Yuxiu Lu
Tel: (0872) 267 7824
Fax: (0872) 267 7823
Email: jimstibetanhotel@gmail.com
Website: www.china-travel.nl
Located just outside the south gate of the old city. Moderately priced, modern building but tastefully furnished, in a quiet neighbourhood. Excellent tour service for all of northwestern Yunnan and Tibet.

Jade Emu International Guesthouse
West Gate Village
Tel: (0872) 267 7311 or 01388 7232726
Email: reservations@jade-emu.com
Website: www.jade-emu.com

A large new hostel close to the West Gate with nice airy rooms, plenty of communal space and free WiFi—well priced.

Tibetan Lodge
58 Renmin Lu
Tel: (0872) 266 4177 or 267 8917
Email: tibetan_lodge@yahoo.com
Nice loft-style rooms. Good tour and travel information, especially for Tibet.

Bu Luo Ren Hotel
6 Fuxing Lu
Tel: (0872) 267 6399
Quiet and simple, with nice mountain views, off Fuxing Lu.

FOOD AND DRINK

Dali offers a wide variety of culinary choices. From steaks and pizzas, Korean barbecue, standard Han Chinese dishes, to Hui Muslim (try the *ru bing*—fried cheese) and the local Bai fish specialties, it's hard to get a bad meal here. Upper Huguo Lu and Renmin Lu between Bao Ai Lu and Fuxing Lu have dozens of good places popular with foreigners. For something more local, go to any of the restaurants on Renmin Lu below Fuxing Lu. Most of the night life which appeals to foreigners is on the upper section of Huguo and Renmin Roads.

Marley's Café
105 Boai Lu
Tel: (0872) 267 6651
A pleasant and well-furnished place to sit and watch the world go by. Western and Chinese dishes.

Mandalay Garden
137 Renmin Lu
Tel: (0872) 267 0266
Website: www.mandalaygarden.com
Located on lower Renmin Lu, serves good Indian, Burmese and Thai food.

Lijia Bai Restaurant
301 Fuxing Lu
Tel: (0872) 267 7400
Located in a hotel on the main drag of Fuxing Lu, but a good place to try local Bai food.

Stella's Pizzeria
21 Huguo Lu
Tel (0872) 267 9251
Wood-fired pizza and steaks.

Jim's Peace Café
63 Bo Ai Lu
Tel: (0872) 267 1822
Managed by Jim, the tour guide/hotelier/man who knows Dali, this restaurant is strong on both Tibetan and other cuisines. Guesthouse attached.

Lazy Lizard Bar
223 Renmin Lu
www.jointhelizard.com
Local and exotic imported beers, flavoured vodkas, light food and a rooftop with mountain views make this a chill-out favourite.

TRAVEL AND TOURS

Many small tour and travel shops line Huguo Lu. They can make bus and airline bookings and arrange local tours. Many hotels and guesthouses can do the same. For more personalized advice see:

Michael Yang Tours
68 Boai Lu
Tel: (0872) 267 8189

China Minority Travel
Lu Yu Xiao Qu
13 Yuxiu Lu
Tel: (0872) 267 7824
Fax: (0872) 267 7823
Email: jimstibetanhotel@yahoo.com
Website: www.china-travel.nl

For fully organized adventure tours around Dali prefecture and beyond, far off the beaten track, this is the best choice.

Damenglong

TRANSPORTATION

Sometimes called simply Menglong, this town is located 70 km southwest of Jonghong— buses take about an hour.

ACCOMMODATION

Lai Lai Hotel
Simple but clean, located near the bus station.

Deqin

TRANSPORTATION

The 190-km road from Zhongdian is nothing short of spectacular with majestic views of ever taller mountain ranges in the distance. Until recently, it was also highly dangerous, a rutted track subject to landslides. Chinese engineering (and lots of hard labour) have solved that and the road is now all fully surfaced, although the most precipitous sections have been wisely done in tyre-gripping cobblestone rather than asphalt. The bus from Zhongdian takes six hours. There are other connections, including a 13-hour sleeper bus to Dali. The airport called Deqin is actually located in Zhongdian. From Deqin, it is possible to continue on to Lhasa or elsewhere in Tibet, but only with the proper travel permit, which takes up to a week to obtain. This is best arranged by a tour agency in Zhongdian.

ACCOMMODATION

Rainbow Grand Hotel
Nanping Road
Tel: (0887) 841 4248
A modern three-star hotel in downtown Deqin.

Deqin Hotel
86 Nanping Road
Tel: (0887) 8412031
Email: qmdj@hotmail.com
Moderately priced and quiet. Trekking information.

Once Upon A Time In Meili Snow Mountain
A guesthouse above the chortens at Feilaisi, 10 km out of Deqin. Great sunrise views of the mountain.

FOOD AND DRINK

Deqin's commercial district consists of one main street a few blocks long; restaurants are numerous but undistinguished.

Maosheng Restaurant
Tel: (0887) 841 3186

Gejiu

TRANSPORTATION

Located 320 km south of Kunming, it takes six hours to reach Gejiu by bus.

ACCOMMMODATION

Golden Lake Hotel
Jinhu Xi Lu
Tel: (0873) 235 8967
Located on the lake shore, it's clean and modern.

Shibaolou Hotel
Jinhu Dong Lu
Tel: (0873) 212 2514
Mid-range, good value.

Jianshui

TRANSPORTATION

Jianshui is 230 km south of Kunming, which takes six hours by bus.

ACCOMMODATION

Zhu Family Garden Hotel
133 Jianxin Jie
Tel: (0873) 766 7988
Fax: 0873/766 7989
A restored courtyard-style Qing Dynasty mansion. Unique and impressive. 28 rooms, moderately priced.

RESTAURANTS

Huayuan Binguan (Garden Hotel)
36 Jianzhong Lu
Tel: (0873) 765 6285

Jinghong

TRANSPORTATION

Jinghong Airport, 10 km from the city centre, offers flights to Kunming, Dali, Lijiang, Zhongdian, Beijing and other major Chinese cities. The only direct international connection is to Bangkok, via Chiang Mai. Long-distance buses to Kunming (12 hrs) and beyond leave from the Long Distance Bus Station on Manming Lu. For destinations within Xishuangbanna, go to the No. 2 Bus Station near Baixiang Lake.

ACCOMMODATION

Tai Garden Hotel
8 Nanglin Nan Lu
Tel: (0691)212 3888
Fax: (0691) 212 6060
www.xsbn-taigardenhotel.com
Quasi-luxurious and comfortable, with pleasant gardens and a pool, but located a bit far from the centre of town.

Banna Guesthouse
Ganlan Lu
Tel: (0691) 212 3679
Fax: (0691) 212 6501
Moderately priced, nice garden. A wide selection of rooms, some with air conditioning and river views.

Banna College Hotel
XuanWei Dadao
Tel: (0691) 213 8365
Located adjacent to and managed by a local college. Modern and clean, inexpensive.

Jinghong Guest House
Xuan De Da Dao
Central and inexpensive.

Crown Hotel
Huang Lu
Tel: (0691) 219 9888
Moderately priced, three-star with a swimming pool.

RESTAURANTS

Thai Restaurant
193 Manting Lu
Tel: (0691) 216 1758
Good Thai food, English menu.

Mei Mei's
Manting Lu
Good Western and Chinese food as well as travellers' information centre.

Forest Café
Manting Lu
Good bakery, excellent breakfasts and even hamburgers. Owner shares a wealth of local information with travellers and arranges treks.

TOURS AND TRAVEL

Forest Café
Manting Lu
www.forest-cafe.org

Arranges trekking and other travel experiences in Xishuangbanna and beyond.

Kunming

TRANSPORTATION

Kunming has direct air links with all the capital cities of Southeast Asia, as well as Hong Kong, Calcutta, Chiang Mai, Mandalay, Dhaka, Luang Prabang and Seoul. Domestically, flights arrive in Kunming from all the provincial airports of Yunnan, and all the main cities in China. Trains arrive from Guangzhou in the south, passing through Nanning, and from Chengdu and Chongqing in the southwest, from Xi'an in the northwest, and from Shanghai in the east. A new rail line which already connects Kunming and Dali is scheduled to reach Lijiang by the end of 2009.

ACCOMMODATION

Grand Park Hotel
20 Hong Hua Qiao
Tel: (0871) 538 6688
Fax: (0871) 538 1189
Good location near Green Lake Park. Japanese, Cantonese and Western restaurants. Revolving restaurant on top floor. 300 rooms, five stars.

Green Lake Hotel
6 Cuihu Nan Lu
Tel: (0871) 515 8888
Fax: (0871) 515 3286
Email: contact@greenlakehotel.com
www.greenlakehotel.com
The splendidly refurbished old building now houses a spa and good restaurants; guest rooms are in the adjoining high rise. Nice location, 300 rooms, five stars.

Greenland Hotel
80 Tuodong Lu
Tel: (0871) 318 9999
Fax: (0871) 319 5888
In central Kunming, close to interesting neighbourhoods for wandering. Popular with locals for sumptuous wedding banquets. 300 rooms, five stars.

Horizon Hotel
432 Qingnian Lu
Tel: (0871) 318 6666
Fax: (0871) 319 2118
www.horizonhotel.net
Kunming's newest five star, with top-floor revolving restaurant, indoor pool and nightclub. Close to Nanping walking street. 440 rooms.

Kunming Hotel
145 Dongfeng Dong Lu
Tel: (0871) 316 2063
An older hotel in the city centre. Good Chinese seafood restaurant, 300 rooms, four stars.

Golden Dragon Hotel
575 Beijing Lu
Tel: (0871) 313 3015
Fax: (0871) 313 1082
Email: gdhotel@gdhotel.com.cn
www.gdhotel.com.cn
Well managed, outdoor pool, located near the train station. 300 rooms, four stars.

Sakura Hotel
25 Dong Feng Dong Lu
Tel: (0871) 316 5888
Fax: (0871) 313 8585
Centrally located four-star hotel with 235 rooms. Noted for its Thai and Mexican restaurants and live music in Charlie's Bar.

Kwai Wah Plaza
157 Beijing Lu
Tel: (0871) 356 2828

Email: reservations@kaiwahplaza.com
Website: www.kaiwahplaza.com
A modern five star in a central location with 525 airy, stylish rooms.

Spring City Inn
241 Baita Lu
Tel: (0871) 616 1666
Fax: (0871) 312 7379
Centrally located near the Nanping walking street. Quiet and not expensive.

Kunming Jin Jiang Hotel
98 Beijing Lu, Panlong District
Tel: (0871) 313 8888
Email: tprsvns@hubs1.net
Website: www.kunmingjinjianghotel.com
Jin Jiang Group's flagship hotel in the city near the railway station, with luxurious rooms, four stars.

Zhen Zhuang Ying Binguan
514 Beijing Lu
Tel: (0871) 316 5869
Former family home of a Yunnan governor with vast traditional gardens. Used by top cadres when they visit Kunming. Showing its age, but for some the history on show outguns the lack of modern amenities. Only 86 rooms, four stars.

MUSEUMS

Yunnan Provincial Museum
Dongfeng Xi Lu, corner of Wuyi Lu
Tel: (0871) 364 5655
Recently opened after renovations, the museum has an excellent display of bronze artefacts from the Dian civilization which flourished near Kunming from 400 BC, as well as Buddhist art from the Nanzhao and Dali Kingdoms. A third gallery holds beautiful jade and gold art objects from the Ming and Qing periods.

Kunming City Museum

Tuodong Lu
Tel: (0871) 315 3256
A magnificent carved stone pillar from the Nanzhao period, relics from the Dian era, and dinosaur displays.

Yunnan Nationalities Museum

Dianchi Lu
Near Haigeng Park
Tel: (0871) 431 1216
Excellent display of all aspects of China's minorities, including those from outside Yunnan, such as the Turkic peoples of the northwest. Not to be confused with the Yunnan Nationalities Village across the street which offers elephant shows and minority dance performances of dubious authenticity.

CULTURAL PERFORMANCES

Dynamic Yunnan

Monday-Saturday 20:00–22:00 pm
Kunming Huitang
Beijing Lu near Dongfeng Lu
Tel: (0871) 313 4218
Modern interpretation of traditional dances. Quite a spectacle.

Jixin Epulary Dance

431 Bailong Lu
Tel: (0871) 501 3777, 501 2993
Yunnanese banquet and a large-scale performance of ethnic culture, receiving governmental and international tourist groups.

Fubao Cultural City

Daily performance 19:00–20:00 pm
Fubao Village
Guandu District
Tel: (0871) 732 8000, 732 8997
Creative performances, water sports and Yunnanese cuisine, usually receiving local customers and weekend spenders.

SPAS

Brilliant Spa & Resort

Yangzonghai Brilliant Resort
Tel: (0871) 767 2666, 767 1666
Fax: (0871) 767 3666
www.brilliantspa.com
Located on Yanzong Lake, 40 km from Kunming on the road to the Stone Forest. Both day treatments and accommodation available. Luxurious and expensive.

Jingfang Forest Hot Spring Resort

Anning Hot Spring Tourism Vacation Area
Tel: (0871) 863 2788
Fax: (0871) 863 2799
A half-hour drive from Kunming, it has outdoor hot-spring pools in the forest, massage, sauna, and Japanese-style holiday villas.

Dianchi Spring Spa

1290 Dianchi Lu
Tel: (0871) 806 6094
Outdoor hot spring pools, sauna, massage, tea tasting and a bar.

Swatec

539 Baiyun Lu
Tel: (0871) 624 1888
Sauna, massage, fitness centre and mahjong rooms.

GOLF COURSES

Spring City Golf and Lake Resort

Lake Yang Zong Hai,
Tangchi, Yiliang
Tel: (0871) 767 1188
www.springcityresort.com
Two 18-hole championship golf courses designed by Jack Nicklaus and Robert Trent Jones Jr. Rated as one the best courses in Asia. Forty km south of Kunming.

Kunming Sunshine Golf Club
Kilometer 14
Anxi Road
Tel: (0871) 742 6666
Closer to the city and less expensive.

RESTAURANTS

Chinese Food

Ai Ruo Chun
Jinbi Park, Jinbi Lu
Tel :(0871) 363 2118, 363 2128
A traditional courtyard building, serving Yunnanese specialities.

Xiangyun Huiguan
43 Xiangyun Jie
Tel: (0871) 362 2929
Old-style villa serving Yunnanese food. A favourite of Kunming's downtown office staff for lunch.

Renwu Huiguan
415 Bailong Lu
Tel: (0871) 561 4111
Villa restaurant, serving Yunnanese and Hunanese dishes.

Cuo Yi Dun
Dongfeng Xiang
Tel: (0871) 317 0638
Yunnanese specialities, good location near the Kunming Hotel and Sakura Hotel.

Shipin Huiguan
24 Zhonghe Xiang, Cuihu Nan Lu
Tel: (0871) 352 7222
Old-style courtyard building serving Yunnan cuisine, well known for its bean curd dishes.

Joyously Time Teahouse
Cuihu Nan Lu
Tel: (0871) 536 0866
Serving Yunnanese food, Chinese teas and coffee. Nice atmosphere, surrounded by a bamboo grove.

Stone House Restaurant
Chahua Park, Beijing Lu
Tel: (0871) 318 3388
Old-style villa, the former residence of the mayor of Kunming in the 1940s and 50s, serving Yunnanese and Western food.

Yejun Yuan
Guanshan, Guanxing Lu
Tel: (0871) 716 7476
Near the airport, they specialize in wild mushroom hot pots.

Jade Spring Vegetarian Restaurant
Yuantong Zhong Lu
(Opposite Yuantong Temple)
Tel: (0871) 511 1672
Substantial vegetarian restaurant serving both traditional vegetarian dishes for the health conscious, as well as the "tastes like meat but isn't" for those maintaining a vegan lifestyle for spiritual reasons.

Western Food

Espana Restaurant
24 Cuihu Bei Lu
Tel: (0871) 519 9696
Serving Spanish-style roast, pizza, sea food and foreign wines.

Yizuola Grill Dinner
186 Wuyi Lu
Tel: (0871) 362 3946, 363 7173
Brazilian-style roasts and buffet food.

Red Star
Jinhuapu Lu
Tel: (0871) 822 8345
Italian, Thai and Yunnanese food.

Teresa's Pizza
40 Wenlin Jie
Tel: (0871) 537 6725
Good pizza here and also home delivery. Near Yunnan University.

Blue Bird
132 Cuihu Nan Lu
Tel: (0871) 531 5507
Western-style food, coffee and drinks.
Popular with visiting Thais and students.

Wei's Pizzeria
27 Xiaodong Jie
Tel: (0871) 316 6189
Located off the Nanping Jie walking
street in a nice courtyard building. In
addition to the pizza, an extensive
choice of Western, Mexican and
Chinese food. Pool table and play area
for children. A long-time traveller and
expat favourite.

TEA

Ten Fu's Tea
Corner of Beijing Lu and Shangyi Jie
Tel: (0871) 313 9138
The best place in Kunming for the tea
connoisseur. Quality tea leaves from all
of China. Teapots and other utensils.

CAFES & BARS

Fennel Pub
3 Cuihu Nan Lu
Tel: (0871) 512 9359
Cocktails, coffee and light meals.
Young, chic clientele.

Prague Café
40 Wenlin Jie
Tel: (0871) 533 2764
Long-standing favourite University area
café.

French Café
70 Wenlin Jie
Tel: (0871) 538 2391
Specializes in strong espresso and
authentic baguette sandwiches. Good
pastries. French books and magazines.

Chapter One
146 Wenlin Jie
Tel: (0871) 536 5635

Another student/teacher restaurant and
hangout. Small library and book
exchange. Lively in the evenings.

Lai Zhe Bu Zou
Qingyun Jie
Tel: (0871) 510 6098
Cocktails, coffee, tea and fast food.
Popular with local yuppies.

Yunjoy Café
45 Wenhua Xiang
Tel: (0871) 551 6364
Western and Yunnanese-style coffees,
using freshly roasted Yunnanese beans.
This small street behind the University
has many small restaurants and
boutiques.

Café de Camel
4 Tuodong Lu
Tel: (0871) 319 5841
Near the intersection of Beijing Lu and
Tuodong Lu. Serves Western and
Chinese food. During the day it's quiet,
but in the evenings gets quite lively.
Live music or DJ parties with dancing
on weekends.

Cha Ma Bar
Camellia Hotel
154 Dong Feng Xi Lu
Tel: (0871) 316 3000-7
Coffee, tea and light food. Internet serv-
ice.

Salvador's Coffee House
76 Wen Lin Jie
Tel: (0871) 536 3525
Near the university. Good baked goods
and homemade ice cream.

DOMESTIC AIRLINES

China Eastern Airlines
28 Tuodong Lu
Tel: (0871) 312 1223
Fax: (0871) 318 8437
This is Yunnan's biggest airline, with
most domestic destinations covered.

China International Airlines & China
Southwest Airlines
(Kunming Ticket Office)
1st Floor, Huaerbei Building
448 Qingnian Lu
Tel: (0871) 315 9171
For international flights on Air China.

China Southern Airlines
(Kunming Ticket Office)
62 Chuncheng Lu
Tel: (0871) 310 1831, 310 1832
Flights to many cities in Southeast Asia.

CHINA EASTERN AIRLINES
(Overseas Representative Offices)

Los Angeles
55 South Lake Avenue Suite 120
Pasadena, CA 91101
Tel: (213) 583 1500

London
27-29 George Street
London, W1U3QD
Tel: (20) 7935 2676

Sydney
Level 9 39-41 York Street
Sydney NSW 2000
Tel: (00612) 9290 1148

Singapore
240 Tanjong Pagar Orad
#-1-02 GE Tower
Singapore 088540
Tel: (0065) 6222 3458

Bangkok
439/6 Naradhiwastrajanagarindra Road
Bangkok 10500
Tel: (00662) 636 6958

Tokyo
1F, Toranomon Sakurada-Dori Bldg.
1-2-10 Toranomon, Minatoku
Tokyo 105
Tel: (00813) 3506 1166

Ho Chi Minh City
Bldg. F, 2/F OSIC Office Building
8 Yuanjiang Road
First Prefecture
Ho Chi Minh City
Tel: (008490) 883 4618

Vientiane
Kundatong Village
Luang Prabang Road
Vientiane
Tel: (0085621) 212 300

INTERNATIONAL AIRLINES

Hong Kong Dragonair
Rm 1405-06
Hongta Mansion
155 Beijing Lu
Tel : (0871) 356 1208-9
Fax: (0871) 319 3888

Korean Air
2F Bank Hotel
Qingnian Lu
Tel: (0871) 315 8299

Malaysian Airlines
Sakura Hotel
25 Dongfeng Dong Lu
Tel: (0871) 316 0676

Silk Air
Rm 2002, 20/F, Building B
Yinhai Soho
612 Beijing Lu
Tel: (0871) 316 6450, 313 2334

Thai Airways
King World Hotel
98 Beijing Lu
Tel: (0871) 351 1515
Fax: (0871) 316 7351

Vietnam Airlines
2/F, Building C
Kaiwah Hotel
157 Beijing Lu
Tel: (0871) 351 5850, 351 5851
Fax: (0871) 351 5852

CONSULATES

Lao PDR
Camellia Hotel
154 Dongfeng Xi Lu
Tel: (0871) 317 6623, 3176624

Malaysia
Sakura Hotel
25 Dong Feng Xi Lu
Tel: (0871) 316 5888

Myanmar
Camellia Hotel
154 Dong Feng Xi Lu
Tel: (0871) 317 7368

Thailand
Kunming Hotel
52 Dong Feng Xi Lu
Tel: (0871) 316 8916, 3149296

Vietnam
Kaiwah Hotel
157 Beijing Lu
Tel: (0871) 318 3092

TRAVEL SERVICES

Yunnan Overseas Travel Corporation (YNOTC)
Dongfeng Xi Lu
Tel: (0871) 318 8833, 312 9887
Fax: (0781) 318 8904
www.ynotc.com

Kunming China International Travel Service (KMCITS)
285 Huanchengnan Lu
Tel: (0871) 356 6626, 356 6627
www.kmcits.com.cn

CYTS Group–Yunnan CYTS Ltd
101 Tuodong Lu
Tel: (0871) 338 3188, 338 1788
Fax: (0871) 336 9111
www.yn818.com

Kunming China Comfort Travel Service Co, Ltd
CCT Tourism Building
Yongan Lu
Tel: (800) 889 7666 or
(0871) 358 5912, 358 5922
www.21cnyn.com

Yunnan China Travel Service
Zhongming Mansion
152 Beijing Lu
Tel: (0871) 351 4788
Fax (0871) 317 9878
www.yunncts.com

USEFUL ADDRESSES

Kunming Airport
Eight km southeast of the city, taxi fare about 20 yuan.

Public Security Bureau
411 Beijing Lu
Tel: (0871) 301 7878
24-hour emergency line:
(0871) 316 6191
Issues visa extensions, and can help you navigate the police bureaucracy if you have a problem.

BUS & TRAIN STATIONS

Long Distance Bus Station
Near the southern end of Beijing Lu
Tel: (0871) 351 0617
Buses to all major cities in Yunnan and beyond.

Kunming Train Station
Located at the southern end of Beijing Lu. Trains to and from Guangdong, Guilin, Chengdu. Beijing and all other major Chinese cities. Overnight train to Dali. The train station was rebuilt in 2004, but this is still an area to be careful of your belongings.
Tel: (0871) 316 2321

POST OFFICES

International Post Office
231 Beijing Lu
All postal services, including poste restante, EMS, and Western Union for non-bank financial transfers.

Post and Telecommunications Office
China Telecom Building
Corner Beijing and Dongfeng Dong Lu.
Closer to the centre of town, but fewer services. International phone service.

OUTDOOR EQUIPMENT

Yunnan Mountain 360 Degrees
Floor 1 Congshan Bldg.
Jinbi Lu
Tel: (0871) 313 6145
Good selection of high-end mountaineering and trekking clothing and equipment. Good for last-minute purchases, but prices for top brands are not cheaper in China, even if they are locally made.

BANKS

The best bank for ATM cash withdrawals from credit cards is the **Bank of China** with branches throughout the city. Their main office is at 448 Renmin Dong Lu. Almost all banks can exchange foreign cash for Chinese currency.

BOOKS

Mandarin Books
9-10 Wen Hua Xiang
Tel: (0871) 551 6579
Next to Yunnan University, this is your best source of foreign language books in Yunnan. Also has smaller branches in Dali and Lijiang.

HANDICRAFTS

Jingxing Bird and Flower Market
Jingxing Jie
Just north of Dongfeng Xi Lu and west of Zhengyi Lu, this is your best source for handicrafts in Kunming. The Jingxing Culture and Art Plaza, a five-storey building on Jingxing Jie, has a good selection of local handicrafts, antique furniture, jewellery and Chinese paintings at bargainable prices.

HOSPITAL

Yanan Hospital Foreigners Clinic
Renmin Dong Lu
Building 6
Tel: 317 7499 ext. 311

Lijiang

Lijiang consists of two adjacent parts, the old Naxi city, also called Dayan, and the new modern area of the city, which mainly lies to the north and west of the old town.

TRANSPORTATION

Within Yunnan province, Lijiang is accessible by air from Kunming and Jinghong. Other direct flights from major Chinese cities originate from Beijing, Shanghai, Guangzhou, Chengdu and Shenzhen. The airport lies 30 km from the city. Buses from Dali take about four hours to cover the scenic 200 km route. Further north to Zhongdian is another four-hour trip. Buses also leave for Lugu Lake, Qiaotou (for Tiger Leaping Gorge), Deqin and Kunming from Lijiang. Lijiang has three separate bus stations. For local trips (such as Baisha or the Jade Dragon Snow Mountain) use the Northern Bus station. For trips to Tiger Leaping

Gorge, Zhongdian, Lugu Lake or Dali, use the Southern Bus Station. The Express Bus Station serves Kunming.

ACCOMMODATION

Although perfectly acceptable hotels abound in the modern part of town, the clear preference of most travellers is to stay in the atmospheric old city. Dozens of old courtyard homes have been turned into small inns, and larger hotels which attempt to capture the Naxi style are found on the edges of the old town. If ultra modern is your preference, there are many good hotels in the new city.

Banyan Tree Lijiang
Tel: (0888) 533 1111
Fax: (0888) 533 9999
www.banyantree.com
North of town on the way to Shu He village, this five-star resort property has 55 individual pavilions, a spa, swimming pool, and a view of the Jade Dagon Snow Mountain. Tasteful, immaculate, expensive.

Jian Nan Chun Hotel
8 Guanyi Street
Tel: (0888) 510 2222
Fax: (0888) 510 2988
Email:hotel@jnchotel.com
www.jnchotel.com
A four-star hotel located in the centre of the old town. Favoured by visiting dignitaries, it is built in traditional Chinese style, but the rooms are decidedly modern.

Swiss Snow Inn
34 Sifangjie
Tel: (0888) 518 4862
Fax: (0888) 518 4851
Email: swisssnowinn@yahoo.com.cn
Website: www.swisssnowinn.com

A beautifully renovated old Naxi courtyard house in the centre of the old town.

Mu Shi Guest House
22 Ji Shan Alley
Xin Yi Street
Tel: (0888) 512 6492
www.lijiangmuzi.com
A typical courtyard house converted into a guesthouse in the old town.

Ping An Inn
64 Xin Yi Street
Tel: (0888) 5125834
Another nice old Naxi courtyard house. Simple but authentic and pleasant.

Grand Lijiang Hotel
Xinyi Street
Dayan Town
Tel: (0888) 512 0888
Fax: (0888) 512 7878
Located next to the waterwheel square on the way to the Black Dragon Pool, the four-star Grand Lijiang is modern and tastefully managed by a Thai company.

Wenhai Ecolodge
www.responsibletravel.com
This mountain lodge retreat is run by a cooperative made up of 56 local households. With Wenhai Lake at its front steps and the peaks of Jade Dragon in the back garden, it's a great place for trekking. The 12-room lodge can only be reached by horse or on foot from Lijiang Valley. Moderately priced.

FOOD AND DRINK

Lijiang has nearly as many culinary choices as Dali. Plenty of canal side café restaurants offer a variety of choices on their menus, from local Naxi specialities such as *baba*, a flatbread stuffed with vegetables or meat, through Han Chinese dishes and on to Western favourites. Check prices on menu before ordering—some places cater to tour groups and are not reasonably priced. The Night Market at the north end of the old city has both kebab stalls (not just meat, but vegetables and tofu are skewered and roasted) and full restaurants, mainly offering Han Chinese fare.

Bubu's Bar
Near the Bai Sui Fang
Tel: 13708821331
Nice location along a stream and good French food. A small venue, it can get busy at night.

Le Petit Lijiang Book Café
50 Chongren Lane
Qiyi Street
Tel: (0888) 511 1255
Good Western and Chinese dishes in the courtyard or inside this old Lijiang home. A Belgian-Chinese couple offer books for sale, and travel services.

IN THE NEW TOWN

Mao's Kitchen
Mao Jia Fan Dian
Hua Ma Jie
Tel: (0888) 518 7668
Near the Black Dragon Pool, a 10-minute walk from the waterwheel at the entrance of the old town. A bit of Mao Zedong nostalgia in Lijiang. The cuisine of the Chairman's home province of Hunan is very spicy. The décor evokes the era as well with photographs and music from the 1950s and 60s . The restaurant is a newly built old-style house, three stories high, with private rooms on the upper floors. Prices are quite reasonable. English menus are available.

Southern Garden Restaurant
He Tan Xiao Zhen
Gua Dai Guo
New Lijiang
Tel: (0888) 512 8989
Located in an attractive and spacious modern building, with a nice little fish pond in the main dining area. The Southern garden specializes in the elegant cuisine of Shanghai. The prices are quite steep, by Lijiang standards. A 10 yuan taxi ride from the old city. (No English menus at the moment.)

Chao Yang Hui Guan
Shangri-La Avenue
New Lijiang
Specializes in Sichuan and Yunnan food. Again, it's beyond walking distance from the old town. The decoration is a kitsch mixture of modern and traditional styles, which is quite representative of the current trends in Chinese architecture and decoration. The dishes there are rather spicy, as Sichuan and Yunnan cooking should be. The menus have no English explanations, but with vivid pictures of each dish. Prices are reasonable. Friendly staff. Ten yuan by taxi from the old city.

OUTSIDE LIJIANG

Qing Song Lijiang
Green Pine Tree Hill restaurant, lies between Lijiang and Lashi Lake. It's called Farmers' Leisure Garden by local people. A huge traditional courtyard, with nicely decorated dining rooms on the ground and first floor. Some rooms have great views of the Jade Dragon Snow Mountain. Naxi cuisine is served exclusively here, thus it is very popular among locals. Every evening, a group of old Naxi ladies from the nearby village come to dance in the courtyard and diners are welcome to join them. Not expensive. No English menus.

TOURS AND TRAVEL

Li Jiang Qi Dian Tours
44 Xing Ren Xiang
Wu Yi Lu
Dayan Old Town
Tel: (0888) 512 3356
Email: shuiguo75@sohu.com
Adventure travel operator covering the Lijiang area, Nujiang and Tibet. Rock climbing, mountaineering and more gentle treks as well.

Lijiang Maguotou Travel
Huang Shan Park
Dayan Old Town
Tel: (0888) 512 0158
Fax: (0888) 512 3288
Email: maguotou@shangrilatour.cn
Good for local information, ticket bookings.

Lugu Lake

TRANSPORTATION

Lugu Lake is about 5-6 hours by road from Lijiang. Almost all buses go only to Ninglang, where you must change to another bus.

ACCOMMODATION

Mosuo Yuan Guesthouse
Tel: (0888) 588-1188
Moderately priced guesthouse on the lake in Luoshui.

Yasedaba Traveler's Paradise
Tel: (0888) 588 1196
Email: ligemosuo0522@126.com
A good choice in the smaller village of Lige.

Mangshi

TRANSPORTATION

Also known as Luxi, Mangshi is the site of Dehong Prefecture's only airport, with regular flights to Kunming and elsewhere in China. Mangshi is 60 km from Ruili.

ACCOMMODATION

Chang Jiang Hotel
2 Weimin Lu
Tel: (0692) 228 6055
A moderately priced, recently refurbished hotel in the centre of town.

Thai Long Hotel
Mangshi Dajia
1 Tai Long Lu
Tel: (0692) 221 0588
Considered the best hotel in Mangshi, adjacent to Shen Ya Ze, it has an excellent restaurant specializing in duck dishes.

Menghan

TRANSPORTATION

Also known as Ganlanba, this town is located 45 km southeast of Jinghong along the Mekong River. Minibuses cover the route in about an hour.

ACCOMMODATION

Dai Minorities Park
It is possible to spend the night in the homes of Dai families at this tourist site.

Yunli Binguan
Manting Lu
Tel (0691) 241 0204
Clean and basic.

Ganlanba Hotel
Near Dai Minorities Park
Tel: (0691) 241 1233
More upscale in price, but nothing special.

Mengla

TRANSPORTATION

Mengla, 150 km southeast of Jinghong, is the overland gateway to Laos, although the actual border crossing at Mohan is another 50 km farther on. Buses from Jinghong take about four hours.

ACCOMMODATION

Mengla Hotel
Mengla Nanlu
Tel: (0691) 812 2268
Located near the Southern Bus Station, it is basic, but clean and has a nice garden.

Jinqiao Hotel
Mengla Beilu
Tel: (0691) 812 4946
Another acceptable choice, located at the northern end of the town.

Nujiang Prefecture

TRANSPORTATION

The town of Liuku is the starting point for a trip to this remote but beautiful part of Yunnan. Buses from Kunming take 11 hours, or seven hours from Xiaguan. From here, regular buses travel along the river valley north to Fugong (five hours), then Gongshan (four hours) and finally Bingzhongluo (three hours). From here, you must either backtrack to Liuku, or join a trek across the mountains to Cizhong, from where you can take a bus north to Deqin or south to Weixi.

ACCOMMODATION

Only basic accommodation is found in the towns along the Nu River. They are usually located near the bus stations—reservations not required.

Ruili

TRANSPORTATION

The closest airport to Ruili is in Mangshi, a two-hour drive away, with direct flights to Kunming and Guangzhou. Buses from Ruili go as far as Kunming, about 12 hours' travel time. A sleeper bus to Jinghong takes 24 hours.

ACCOMMODATION

Jingcheng Hotel
Maohai Road
Tel: (0692) 415 9999
Fax: (0692) 415 9888
Email: jcdjd@sina.com
www.jingcheng.com.cn
Ruili's newest upmarket hotel. Indoor swimming pool, disco, bowling. 475 rooms, four stars.

New Kai Tong International Hotel
150 Biancheng Lu
Tel: (0692) 415 7777
Fax: (0692) 415 6190
Less luxurious than the Jingcheng, but still a suitable upper mid-range choice.

Bian Cheng Hotel
11 Biancheng Lu
Tel: (0692) 415 7188
Fax: (0692) 415 5199
A moderately priced, clean hotel near the city centre.

RESTAURANTS

Huafeng Market
Jiegang Lu
An outdoor food market with a good selection of dishes.

Stone Forest

TRANSPORTATION

Located 100 km southeast of Kunming, the Stone Forest is reached in about two hours, either by private car or bus. Buses leave from the bus station at the bottom of Beijing Lu. Most tours involve many stops at tourist traps such as "jade factories" and are best avoided.

ACCOMMODATION

Stone Forest Hotel
Tel: (0871) 771 1405
Fax: (0871) 771 1414
Nice gardens and restaurants in this mid-range hotel. Near the entrance to the Stone Forest.

Summer Hotel
Tel: (0871) 771 1088
A mid-range hotel with some nice views over the Stone Forest.

Stone Forest International Youth Hostel
Tel: (0871) 771 0768
Located near the bus stop, it has clean rooms and accepts youths of all ages.

Tengchong

TRANSPORTATION

Tengchong is midway between Baoshan and Ruili, a 4-5 hour ride to either destination. The closest airport is in Baoshan.

ACCOMMODATION

Tengchong Guanfang Hotel
Tel: (0875) 519 9999
Fax: (0875) 515 5555
Luxury in Tengchong—favoured by visiting delegations. New and fancy with spa, tennis courts, and Western restaurant. Five stars, 280 rooms.

Tengchong Binguan
Huancheng Nan Lu
Tel: (0875) 515 5044
Fax: (0875) 515 5566
Moderately priced government hotel.

Tong Cheng Hotel
18 Feng Shan Lu
Tel: (0875) 513 2746
A nice family-run hotel in the city centre. Moderately priced.

Tiger Leaping Gorge

A hike through this canyon on the Yangzi River 100 km north of Lijiang is one of the most spectacular excursions one can undertake in all of China. Accessible from either Qaiotou at the southwestern (upstream) end, or Daju, it is possible to walk all or part of the route, or if need be, drive through the now largely paved road and return to Lijiang as a day trip.

TRANSPORTATION

A bus from Lijiang to Qiaotou, the best starting point for a trek, takes two hours. Going north to Zhongdian is another four hours.

ACCOMMODATION

Jane's Guesthouse
Tel: (0887) 880 8579
Email: janettibetgh@ hotmail.com
Just before the trailhead at the Qiaotou end. Basic, but good information.

Yulong Hotel
Tel: (0887) 880 6196.
Standard hotel in Qiaotou town.

Woody's Guesthouse
Walnut Garden
Tel: 13988712705, 13087428371
Near the eastern end of the gorge.

Snowflake Hotel
Past the hospital in Daju.
Tel: (0887) 5326091

Tonghai

TRANSPORTATION

Located 150 km south of Kunming, it takes three hours to reach Tonghai by bus.

ACCOMMODATION

Tongprint Hotel
Huancheng Beilu
Tel: (0877) 302 1666
Mid-range hotel of no great distinction.

Li Yue Hotel
56 Huangchang Xilu
Tel: (0877) 301 1651
Basic place near the bus station.

Yuanyang

TRANSPORTATION

Located 380 km southeast of Kunming; the trip is a seven-hour bus ride. Get off the bus at the town of Xinjie.

ACCOMMODATION

Yunti Dajiudian
Xinjie District
Tel: (0873) 562 4858
Mid-range, clean and modern.

Yuanyang Chenjia Fangshe Guesthouse
Xinjie District
Tel: (0873) 562 2342
Simple but clean, with great views over the rice terraces.

Yuxi

TRANSPORTATION

Located 100 km south of Kunming, Yuxi is reached by bus in two hours.

ACCOMMODATION

Jinliang Hotel
Corner of Nanbei Dajie and Renmin Lu. Moderately priced but clean.

Traffic Hotel
Xizhan Beilu
Located near the bus station, clean rooms for a variety of prices.

Zhongdian

The town of Zhongdian, Gyeltang to the Tibetans, and Shangri-la to the Chinese tourist industry, lies 200 km north of Lijiang. Zhongdian is the largest town in the Deqin (now Shangri-la) Autonomous Tibetan Prefecture, and well and truly Tibetan it is. It lies at an altitude of 3,200 metres and the vegetation and terrain are vastly different from the lower parts of Yunnan.

TRANSPORTATION

Several daily flights connect Zhongdian and Kunming. There are also flights to and from Lhasa, Shanghai and Guangzhou. The airport, 5 km out of town, uses the name of the prefecture, not the town, so look for flights to Deqin, Diqing, or Shangri-la. There is no airport in the town of Deqin. Buses from Lijiang take six hours on a spectacular road where the verdant hills of Yunnan recede before the towering Tibetan snow-capped peaks.

ACCOMMODATION

Banyan Tree Ringha
Hong Po Village
Jian Tang Town
Tel: (0887) 533 1111
Fax: (0887) 533 2222
Email: ringha@banyantree.com
www.banyantree.com
Thirty-two Tibetan farmhouses transformed into uber-deluxe lodges and suites, with fireplaces and private spas. Located 20 km from Zhongdian near the Tibetan monastery of Da Bao Si. Masseuses from Thailand, chefs from Bali, and Tibetan trekking guides. Top of the top, including the prices.

Songtsam Hotel
Tel: (0887) 828 8889
Fex: (0887) 828 8887
Email: songtsam@yahoo.com.cn
Website: www.songtsam.com
A large Tibetan home which has been converted into an attractive 20-room hotel in the village adjacent to the Songtsam Monastery (also known as Shongzhanling Monastery) 3 km out of town. Great for exploring this famous monastery, the village and trekking in the nearby hills. Moderately, not cheaply, priced.

Dragon Cloud Guest House
94 Bei Men Jie
Tel: (0887) 688 7573
Email: dragoncloud-gh@hotmail.com
Website: www.dragoncloud.cn
Adjacent to the old town, simple but clean and good information from the young English-speaking owner. Nine double rooms with bath.

Tibet Café and Inn
Changzhen Road
Tel: (0887) 823 0019
Fax: (0887) 823 0342
Email: shangbala2005@yahoo.com.cn
A variety of rooms, travel information, internet café and good hearty Western, Tibetan and Chinese food. The main travellers' hangout.

FOOD AND DRINK

After Dali and Lijiang, the choices start thinning out in Zhongdian, but travellers fare can be found in the guesthouses, and the new steel and glass hotels catering to Chinese tourists and government officials offer sumptuous buffets. Many great cafés for watching the scene and the scenery are popping up in the Old Town. Muslim restaurants serve a fine spicy yak stew. Best food in town is found at the Puppet Café on Tuanzhe Jie.

TRAVEL INFORMATION

Both the Tibet Café and the Dragon Cloud Hotel offer good travel information. The Tibet Café can also arrange travel permits for Tibet.
Khampa Caravan is a top-flight adventure tour operator which arranges trips all over Tibet and remote locations in Yunnan.

Khampa Caravan
Beimen Jie
Tel: (887) 828 8648 or 828 8907
Fax: (887) 8288870
Email: yeshi@khampacaravan.com
www.khampacaravan.com

USEFUL WEBSITES

www.12kunming.com

www.china-travel.nl
Dali-based China Minority Travel
shows some of its interesting
itineraries.

www.chinaexpat.com
Offers a huge amount of information
on cities and regions throughout the
country, including a China's 50 Best
Websites page.

www.chinaplanner.com

www.chinatt.org
An invaluable English-language
Chinese Railway Timetable available
to buy online (pdf electronic format
US$10, A4 printed size US$20).

www.gokunming.com
Good information on hotels,
restaurants, nightlife and special
events in Kunming.

www.healthinchina.com
Medical advice and contacts for
travellers.

www.iguide.com.cn
Good accommodation and restaurant
listings, especially for more remote
areas in Yunnan.

www.khampacaravan.com
An ecologically minded adventure
tour operator based in Zhongdian.

www.mandarintools.com/
calconv_old.html
This link allows conversion of
Western calendar dates into Chinese
lunar calendar dates. Useful for
determining festival dates.

www.mychinastart.com
Offers a vast number of links to all
major regions and cities in China.

www.northwestyunnan.com
A cooperative effort between local
communities and NGOs to develop
ecotourism in the Lijiang area.
Eco-tours and home-stays are offered.

www.passplanet.com/china/sw/
yunnan_intro.htm
An independent source of travel
information mainly for backpackers.

www.pratyeka.org/yunnan/
Highly informative if somewhat
eclectic information about Yunnan,
from long-distance cycling to PDF
copies of historical texts, such as
Peter Goullart's *Forgotten Kingdom*.

www.travelchinaguide.com

www.travelchinayunnan.com

www.trax2.com
A Hong Kong-based adventure tour
operator with good background
information, new sights and maps
of Yunnan.

www.tripadvisor.com

www.virtualtourist.com/travel/Asia/
China/TravelGuide-China.html
A peer-to-peer site with subjective
but informative opinions on
accommodation, food and sights.
Online hotel bookings fund the site.

http://wikitravel.org
A constantly updated and enlarged
database of info on all aspects of
tourist travel.

www.wildchina.com
Premium tour operator for groups
and individuals.

www.yunnantourism.net
Yunnan Provincial Tourism
Information Centre.

www.yunnantravel.net

INDEX